GOA AND THE GREAT MUGHAL

GOA AND THE GREAT MUGHAL

EDITED BY

Nuno Vassallo e Silva and Jorge Flores

CALOUSTE GULBENKIAN FOUNDATION

in association with Scala Publishers, London

First published on the occasion of the exhibition *Goa and the Great Moghul* at the Calouste Gulbenkian Foundation, Exhibitions Gallery, Lisbon, 8 June to 5 September 2004
Calouste Gulbenkian Museum, Lisbon
www.museu.gulbenkian.pt
www.gulbenkian.pt

First published in 2004 in Portuguese and English editions by
Scala Publishers Ltd
Northburgh House
10 Northburgh Street
London EC1V 0AT, UK
www.scalapublishers.com

in association with the Calouste Gulbenkian Foundation, Lisbon

This edition reprinted in paperback in 2011
ISBN: 978-1-85759-693-9

Edited by João Carvalho Dias (Calouste Gulbenkian Museum, Lisbon) and Colin Grant (London)
Designed by Janet James, London
Map by TVM Designers, Lisbon
Printed in China
10 9 8 7 6 5 4 3 2

Page 1: Whistle, Goa, end of the 16th century, gold, diamonds, rubies and emeralds (see p. 125).
Frontispiece: Abu'l Hasan, *Festivities on the Occasion of the Accession of Emperor Jahangir* (detail), c.1605–15 (CAT. 97).
Opposite top: 'Portuguese' carpet (detail), Persia (?), Safavid period, 17th century (CAT. 63).
Opposite bottom: Atrributed to Payag, *Shah Shuja Hunting* Nilgae (detail), Mughal India, c.1650 (CAT. 103).

Editor's Note
The most widely used conventions (rather than a single system) have been followed for the transliteration of Persian and Arabic words. All diacritical signs except for 'ain (') and hamza (') have also been omitted. Dates in the Islamic lunar calendar are indicated by AH (*anno Hegirae*), the date in AD 622 from which the Muslim era is reckoned.

Photographs of items on display in the exhibition have been used to illustrate the essays in this volume and therefore follow the editorial rather than the exhibition order. A separate list of the exhibits, arranged in exhibition order, is given in the catalogue on pp.216–228, indicating where in the book items are illustrated if not in that section. Additional illustrations of items not in the exhibition have also been included throughout.

CONTENTS

6

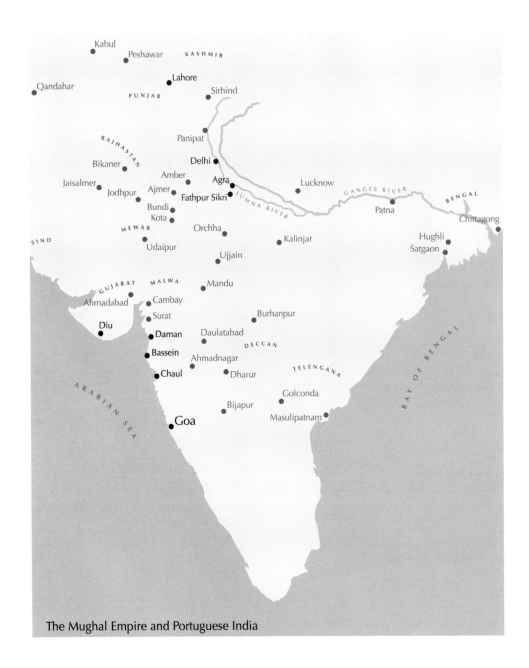

Kabul

Peshawar   KASHMIR

Qandahar   Lahore
                  Sirhind
         PUNJAB

                  Panipat
         RAJHASTAN
Bikaner   Delhi
Amber   Agra   Lucknow   GANGES RIVER   BENGAL
Jaisalmer   Ajmer   Chittagong
Jodhpur   Fathpur Sikri   JUMNA RIVER
         Bundi   Patna
         Kota
                  Orchha   Hughli
         MEWAR   Kalinjar   Satgaon
SIND   Udaipur
                  Ujjain

         GUJARAT MALWA   Mandu
Ahmadabad   Cambay
         Diu   Surat   Burhanpur
                  Daman   Daulatabad
                  Bassein Ahmadnagar   DECCAN   BAY OF BENGAL
                  Chaul   Dharur   TELENGANA
         ARABIAN SEA   Golconda
                  Goa   Bijapur   Masulipatnam

The Mughal Empire and Portuguese India

Foreword

Emílio Rui Vilar
President of the Calouste Gulbenkian Foundation

A collection as rich and varied as the one owned by the Calouste Gulbenkian Museum provides fertile ground both for research and for a wide range of exhibitions. Moreover, given the international nature of the collection, the facility to create links with Portuguese forms of cultural and artistic expression, and to contextualise and compare reciprocal influences, invariably provides interesting and often quite revealing insights. This exhibition, *Goa and the Great Mughal*, is a superb interpretation and expression of these ideas.

The Gulbenkian Museum's collection includes a small but significant section on the arts associated with the Mughal empire, while the importance of the relationship established between the empire and the Portuguese, lasting for over two hundred years, fully justifies an in-depth study of its diverse political, commercial, religious and cultural aspects.

In the years that followed the arrival of the Portuguese in India (1498), the great Muslim empires – Ottoman, Persian and Mughal – were taking shape as regional powers in Asia. This forced the newcomers into a complex web of strategic moves and political alliances that guaranteed that they could sail, trade and carry out missionary work in safety, and ensured the security of their settlements and trading posts. The relationship established with the Mughal empire, whose first contacts with the Portuguese date from the 1530s, was significantly more peaceful, not only stimulating trade, diplomatic contacts and missionary work, but also mutual associations and influences in the fields of culture and the arts.

This exhibition brings together pieces of genuine importance, while the book provides significant academic analysis. Together, they reveal a particularly rich period in the interchange between Europe and southern Asia. In addition to the intellectual and aesthetic pleasures of knowledge and discovery, the act of exploring intercultural relations of the past unquestionably contributes to the necessary strengthening of the dialogue between cultures.

José Pinhão de Matos,
View of Goa,
18th century, oil on canvas, 131 x 431 cm. Lisbon, MNAA, inv. no. 189 P

FOREWORD

João Castel-Branco Pereira
Director of the Calouste Gulbenkian Museum

The Calouste Gulbenkian Museum clearly demonstrates that the vision of the great Armenian art collector embraced the entire world, from East to West. This was, of course, attributable to the path that his life took, since he was born just outside Istanbul – the symbolic city that acts as a gateway between Europe and Asia – and later gained a profound knowledge of European culture through the fine and decorative arts.

As visitors pass through the rooms of the Museum's permanent exhibition, the Eastern and Western models of inhabiting space become obvious. The former features sumptuous carpets, glassware and luxurious ceramics, rare fabrics and sophisticated illuminations and bookbindings, revealing a world of great individual mobility. In turn, the latter is shown by the symbolic and emblematic presence of great paintings and fittings associated with European architecture, such as superb furniture and magnificent silver services. These objects were designed for places where the individual and his social power – his territory – could be publicly demonstrated.

The Eastern approach may suggest a magnificence that, paradoxically, seems to develop from an intimate lifestyle, one that demands close contact with the materials and enables more detailed examination of the sophistication and the sheer perfection of the decorations and images. This contrasts strongly with the Western approach, where the object's material quality and the individual's social power become the main focus.

This book is being published in conjunction with the exhibition *Goa and the Great Mughal*, which refers to one of the moments when these different approaches to life came into contact with each other. The pioneers in this meeting were the Portuguese, who had first reached India in 1498, and the great Mughal empire. Together, they would develop their contacts throughout the following century.

Although the fundamental interest for the Portuguese was to trade exotic products from India, this meeting gave rise to a unique cultural event. The West was keen to expand and promote the values of Christianity, while the East revealed a cosmopolitan, almost anthropological – as the exhibition curators rightly note – curiosity about such new religious values. One of the end results was the creation of surprising *objets d'art* where the two civilizations simultaneously restated their respective positions and intersected.

Powder-flask with Portuguese (?) figures, Mughal India, 17th century, ivory and brass fittings, L 26 cm. Dresden, Staatliche Kunstsammlungen, inv. no. Y 381

Several pieces from the Calouste Gulbenkian Collection have been included in the selection of works of art depicted in this volume. Pride of place goes to the fragment of a wonderful large Mughal carpet from c.1620–25 (cat. 62) and to a superb jade jar (c.1447–9; cat.1), a Timurid piece commissioned by Ulugh Beg, a cultured man and patron who was the grandson of Tamerlane. Inscriptions on the jar show that it later belonged to the Mughal emperors Jahangir and Shahjahan, two of the main characters in the history told here and in relations between the Mughal empire and other cultures.

The book and the exhibition adopt the same epistemological approach, developing universal knowledge by comparing different forms of creativity. It tells the history of the meeting between the Portuguese and the court of the Great Mughal and simultaneously reveals the interest shown by discerning collectors, which first appeared in the late eighteenth century and developed further throughout the twentieth century. In fact, this is amply demonstrated by the diverse provenance of the pieces selected, including those from the Calouste Gulbenkian Collection. Moreover, the book brings to light new knowledge and approaches in contemporary historiography, which we are delighted to present for public appreciation.

This volume both structures and acts as a record of the exhibition *Goa and the Great Mughal*, whose concept was defined by the curators and was subsequently expanded and enriched by the texts written by various specialists. From the very start the historiographical interest and outstanding quality of this project have merited my full support.

It would not have been possible to produce either the exhibition or the accompanying book without the dedicated work of staff from the Calouste Gulbenkian Museum: Manuela Fidalgo and Fátima Vasconcelos, who produced the exhibition; Mariano Piçarra, who designed the setting; Antonieta Amorim, Miguel Fumega and Rui Xavier, who installed the pieces; and João Carvalho Dias, who was responsible for the editorial production; and from outside the museum: Richard Trewinnard, who produced the translations, and António Manuel Alves Martins, who proof-read the texts and drew up the index. I would like to express my sincere thanks to all of the above, as well as to the curators, authors of the essays, public and private collectors who allowed access to their collections, and to Scala, the publishers.

INTRODUCTION

Jorge Flores and Nuno Vassallo e Silva

Between Vasco da Gama's arrival in Calicut in May 1498 and his death in Cochin at Christmas in 1524, Asia witnessed the emergence of the last great Muslim empires. In 1501 Shah Isma'il founded the Safavid dynasty in Iran, which would remain in power until the early eighteenth century. In turn, the Ottomans had conquered Cairo in 1517 and were advancing through the Red Sea with thoughts of becoming a power in the western Indian Ocean. Finally, there was the Mughal empire. Babur had pushed ahead with his conquest of Hindustan, taking the throne of Delhi and becoming the first emperor of this newly formed state in 1526.

All three empires posed new challenges for the Portuguese, who were little used to dealing with political powers in the continent. The 'Great Turk', the 'Great Sufi' and the 'Great Mughal' were large and imposing states that the European newcomers learned to respect and fear. In contrast, the Mughals saw the Portuguese as just another neighbour, one that was definitely less dangerous than the Safavids, the Uzbeks and the Turks, or even less of a threat than the sultanates in the Deccan or the Buddhist kingdom of Arrakan. Not only were they less dangerous, but also rather exotic, especially since the Portuguese were the first *firangis* to come into direct and personal contact with Emperor Akbar (1556–1605). Although this is not reflected in Mughal chronicles, the work of the court artists would record the presence of these foreigners in their kingdom, and more specifically in their various capitals.

For the Portuguese, who had established their capital in Goa (1510) and maintained a string of settlements that stretched as far as Gujarat (Chaul, Bassein, Daman and Diu) – part of the so-called *Estado da Índia* (State of India) – survival in southern Asia depended on a successful relationship with the Mughals. The words of Father Gomes Vaz in 1600 are a paradigmatic example of this great concern. Faced with Akbar's advance on the Deccan, the Jesuit priest truly believed that the Portuguese would ultimately be expelled from India and hurriedly proposed an alternative: 'We will undoubtedly be doomed, and may God prevent this, for there will be no refuge and Ceylon alone can be of service to us …, and we [can] stay there, as if Lords in their castle, governing over all this Orient.'

This was the background for a relationship that lasted over two hundred years and was expressed in a range of fields that included commerce, politics, religion, culture and the arts. The trade relationship was built up in the ports of Gujarat and Bengal, while the political and diplomatic relationship is recorded in a vast body of documents on embassies, treaties, agents and spies. In turn, the religious relationship was indelibly marked by the Jesuits' influence at the courts of Akbar and Jahangir, yet not neglecting the localized presence of the Augustinians and the Discalced Carmelites. Finally, there was the cultural and artistic relationship, which was based on multiple mutual influences that affected objects, ideas, tastes and styles.

It is this complex web of fears and fascinations, exchanges and embargoes, and real and distorted images that the five sections of the exhibition *Goa and the Great Mughal* attempt to reveal. The first section – 'Connecting the Empires' – fundamentally aims to underline for both sides the significance of the years prior to Akbar's meeting with the

Portuguese master at the imperial court, *Madonna and Child with Angels*, c.1595–1600, gouache and gold on paper, 42 x 26.5 cm.
Arthur M. Sackler Museum, Harvard University Art Museums, Gift of John Goelet: 1958. 233. A

Portuguese in 1572. On the Mughal side emphasis is placed on the importance of the Timurid legacy in creating the empire and advancing their ideology. Meanwhile, on the Portuguese side the focus is on the relationship with the sultanate of Gujarat, which was established in the early sixteenth century and would bring the Portuguese State of India face-to-face with Humayun (1530–40, 1555–6).

Once the Mughals had completed their conquest of Gujarat (1572–3) and Bengal (1574–6) – two sultanates that had enormous significance for Portuguese interests – there began a lengthy and intense process of mutual assessment based simultaneously on both myth and fact. Apart from other issues, this involved depicting the borders and the cities, describing the people and the political rituals, and learning the language of the court. This almost anthropological account was gradually built up by missionaries and crown servants.

The second section – 'The Court of the *Firangis* and the Court of the *Mogores*' – focuses on the the Mughal court as a political, cultural and artistic centre, while also emphasizing the consolidation of Goa's position as a new court in southern Asia. As the political and diplomatic capital of the State of India and the residence of the Portuguese viceroy, Goa was also where one part of India's geopolitical situation was defined. In addition to characterizing the two courts per se, this section aims to bring together fragments that provide a documentary and artistic illustration of the relations between the two states and between some of their respective leading figures.

The third section – 'Between Religions: Christianity in a Muslim Empire' – examines a central issue in relations between Timurid India and the West: the religious relations that involved the two empires. The interest that Akbar and Jahangir showed in Christianity, giving rise to Jesuit hopes that they could be converted, turned out to be nothing more than a reflection of the religious eclecticism of these two emperors, who had no hesitation in appropriating Christian imagery as a propaganda tool.

Nonetheless, the cultural and artistic repercussions of the Jesuits' misinterpretation are not to be neglected. While the missionaries worked on translating the Gospels into Persian, Mughal court painters were specializing in imagery that used Christian iconography. This section aims to highlight the images and objects whose multiple meanings and effects fuelled this religious contact, especially between 1580 and Shahjahan's ascent to the throne in 1628.

The fourth part of this exhibition – 'Exchanging Images: Visions of the West in Mughal Art' – approaches a subject that invariably arouses the interest of Western historians who study relations between modern Europe and societies from outside Europe: the perception of the Other. With this account restricted exclusively to the interchanges between the West and the Mughal empire via Goa, the challenge consists of replacing words with images, or 'probing' some of the many miniatures that record the 'infiltration' of *firangi* imagery into daily Mughal life.

The final section – 'Mughal Influence on Portuguese Art' – comprises a group of objects that reveal mutual artistic influences. The types and the decorative grammar of these pieces reflect the circulation of ideas, merchandise and craftsmen between the capitals of the two empires. The section also aims to assess the genuine scope of these influences and exchanges, leading to the conclusion that we are, in fact, dealing with a body of work that seems to be smaller than art historiography has previously suggested.

There were several different aims that lay behind this project. The first was to emphasize the importance of Goa – which Governor Afonso de Albuquerque established as the capital of the State of India – as the hub of relations between the West and Timurid India in the sixteenth and seventeenth centuries. Naturally, there were other means of access to the imperial capitals in the north, such as Surat, the key port in Gujarat and undoubtedly the most important maritime post in the Mughal empire. As such, it is no surprise that the Portuguese coveted the city. Nonetheless, it was 'Golden Goa' that combined power and religion with business and cosmopolitan life, creating a hybrid that is evident in the city's arts and architecture and impressed each and every Western traveller of that age.

Secondly, we also felt that this was an opportune moment to elevate the status of Portuguese reports on the Mughal empire, as they represent the ideas of the first Europeans to establish ongoing relations with the descendants of Timur in India. Among other factors, the language barrier has meant that Portuguese texts have generally been passed over by international specialists in favour of English and Dutch records that are now, as in the seventeenth century, far more widely known. The only exceptions to this rule are the writings of the Jesuits, many of which were translated into English during the twentieth century.

The same also applies to the objects exhibited. The nineteenth-century Portuguese colonial structure in India did not have the strength to wed knowledge of place to appropriation of its art. Yet it was unquestionably this equation that formed the starting point for many oriental collections in leading European museums. Inside Portugal collections rarely went beyond the pieces kept at the monasteries, which were suppressed in the nineteenth century, giving birth to today's leading museum collections. In the following century Portugal had no other collector or patron of the standing of Calouste Sarkis Gulbenkian to purchase objects on the international market that were frequently sold to foreign museums, especially in North America. Therefore, the pieces kept in Portuguese collections (both public and private) have been given some additional emphasis here and have thus acquired added interest.

In addition, it was felt that the Portuguese public – readers and exhibition visitors alike – needed to be made aware of the importance of the history and art of northern India. The intense Portuguese involvement in maritime southern India from the end of the fifteenth century meant that for many years historians neglected study of the continental scope of southern Asia. The superb pieces of Mughal art exhibited here, from the finest museums in the world but little known in Portugal, may lead to stimulating research proposals and help to reverse this situation.

In turn, this accompanying book brings together a wide range of studies, in terms of both subject matter and the interests and academic standing of the contributors. There was no intention to provide an exhaustive examination of the theme of the exhibition in this book, as we readily accept that two different situations and two different discourses are involved. In addition, several gaps can be observed. The one that we most regret and would like to mention is that the eighteenth century has been completely excluded. For many years the cliché of the 'Mughal decline' meant that scant attention was paid to the empire in the post-Aurangzeb period. That misconception – now mostly overcome – continues, however, to cast its shadow over the history of art. There is a similar lack of interest in eighteenth-century Portuguese India, a situation that is inversely proportional to the potential for research that the historical sources suggest is possible. Within the area covered here, the role of Dona Juliana Dias da Costa – a confidante of Bahadur Shah (r.1707–12) and central figure in relations (including artistic ones) between Goa and the Mughal empire in the early eighteenth century – certainly deserves to be reassessed.

By emphasizing the second half of the sixteenth and the early seventeenth century, we have failed to lift this 'curse' on Mughal historiography, especially as regards the diverse and rich art forms produced in the empire. However, the attention paid to these fifty years has enabled us to link this work to an important forthcoming event. The year 2005 marks the four hundredth anniversary of the death of Emperor Akbar and the accession of Emperor Jahangir, again uniting the two key figures in *Goa and the Great Mughal*.

A project of this scale is clearly not just the work of the exhibition curators, but is shared among all the colleagues and friends who have worked on this catalogue. Our particular thanks go to Milo Beach and Susan Stronge for their constant encouragement and countless suggestions from the very start. The same applies to Pedro Moura Carvalho and Gauvin Alexander Bailey, who helped us to programme the various modules and to select pieces for exhibition. Finally, we are grateful to Michael Rogers who, despite not being formally part of the group, was always there to support us.

MUGHAL EXPANSION IN THE DECCAN, 1570–1605: CONTEMPORARY PERSPECTIVES

Muzaffar Alam and Sanjay Subrahmanyam

INTRODUCTION

The present essay is presented as a contribution to the history of the complex quadrilateral relationship that existed in the late sixteenth and early seventeenth centuries between four sets of rather unequal powers: first, the expanding Mughal empire in northern India, which carried all before it in the decades after about 1560; second, the Deccan sultanates further south, and especially the kingdoms of Bijapur and Ahmadnagar; third, the Portuguese State of India, with its political heart at Goa and subsidiary centres at Daman, Diu and the *Província do Norte*; and finally, the Safavid state in Iran that from its very inception in about 1500 had maintained privileged relations with the Muslim sovereigns of the Deccan.[1] Of these four sets of political entities, three had coincidentally been founded at practically the same moment, in the very beginning of the sixteenth century. The Bijapur and Ahmadnagar sultanates had both emerged from the debris of the declining Bahmani sultanate as the fifteenth century drew to a close, being founded respectively by former Bahmani nobles called Yusuf 'Adil Khan and Burhan Nizam-ul-Mulk. The Portuguese had arrived in the western Indian Ocean in 1498, and declared the State of India to be a stable political entity (rather than deriving simply from a succession of fleets sent out from Portugal) from the time of the initial viceroyalty of Dom Francisco de Almeida (1505–9), seizing Goa from the control of the Bijapur rulers in 1510. The Safavids, a Sufi order that had long nurtured political ambitions from its base at Ardabil, erupted onto the centre of the Iranian political scene at much the same time as the first Portuguese fleets arrived off the west coast of India, and rapidly consolidated power under the charismatic figure of Shah Isma'il I, whose aura of total invincibility began to wear thin only after the defeat

Mughal Emperors and Princes Sitting with their Ancestor Amir Timur,
Mughal India, c.1658.
Paris, Collection Frits Lugt, Institut Néerlandais (CFL-IN) CAT. 3

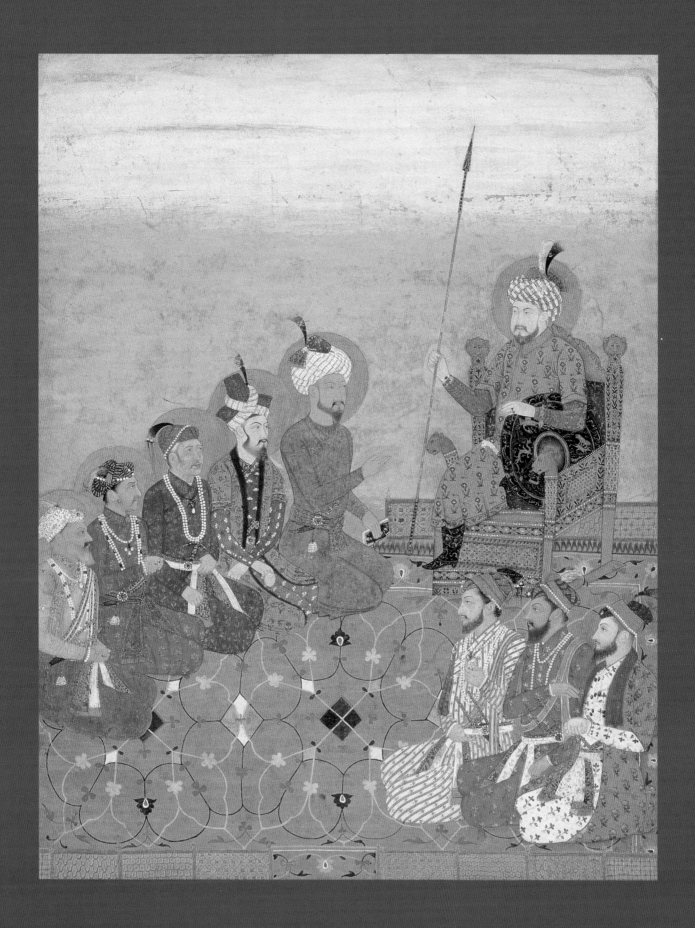

he suffered at the hands of the Ottomans in the Battle of Chaldiran in 1514.[2]

The relative latecomers among these four then were the Mughals, a dynasty that derived from the great central Asian conqueror, Amir Timur (d. 1405), and also in a more distant way from Genghis Khan. This prestigious lineage was, however, not enough to guarantee success, and the founder of the Mughal dynasty in India, Zahir-ud-Din Muhammad Babur, had to spend long years as a peripatetic prince before he eventually managed to gain control over northern India in the 1520s. His son and successor Humayun was to have a chequered career. The first of the Indian Mughals to have direct diplomatic contacts with the Portuguese, he seems in the 1530s to have nurtured ambitions in the direction of the two major maritime provinces – Gujarat to the west, and Bengal to the east. His ambitions in neither case quite came to fruition, although he did for a time make successful inroads in both directions. Eventually, in the latter half of the 1530s, Humayun's own expansionary ambitions came undone, as he himself was exiled on account of the rising power of the Afghans in northern India under Sher Shah Sur. Forced into retreat via first Sind and then Afghanistan, Humayun found refuge for a time in Iran, under the rule of Shah Tahmasp, son of the Safavid dynasty's charismatic founder. He accepted the difficult conditions that Tahmasp laid down for his support, and eventually returned to take power briefly once more in northern India, before dying in an accidental fall in 1556. This left his son, the fourteen-year-old Jalal-ud-Din Muhammad Akbar, himself born when his father was a wandering exile, to consolidate Mughal power in Hindustan. Akbar managed to achieve this in a quite remarkable fashion in the first fifteen years of his rule. Initially under the tutelage of the powerful Bairam Khan, then increasingly independent, he first defeated the autochthonous challenge of Himu Baqqal and the Afghans, and then set about systematically taming the power of the Rajputs in western India. A combined policy of carrot and stick, of marriage alliance and force, meant that in the course of the 1560s he was able to bring many of the main Rajput princely houses within the alliance structure of the Mughal dispensation. By the early 1570s the two old targets that Humayun had been unable to conquer properly – namely the maritime provinces of Gujarat and Bengal – had emerged once again as the next objects of Mughal expansion. The Mughal kingdom, at this point still a landlocked state in the plains of northern India, was about to enter the political scene of the Indian Ocean, and also transform itself from a fairly compact kingdom into a sprawling imperial state. Three major expansionary campaigns were to define this new profile, first the conquests in Gujarat and Bengal, and then, in the early 1590s, the reduction of the autonomous kingdom of Sind astride the lower valley of the river Indus.

Even if a first campaign of conquest had been completed by the mid-1570s, in fact Bengal remained a problem for decades afterwards. The local rulers and princelings in that region, whether Afghans or belonging to older local lineages, continued to resist

Miskin, Sarwan and Madhav, *Akbar Greeting Rajput Rulers and Nobles*, Lahore or Agra, from an *Akbar Nama*, 1590–95.
London, Victoria and Albert Museum (V&A) CAT. 53

Basawan, coloured by Mansur, *Hosein Qulij Khan Presents Prisoners of War from Gujarat*, from an *Akbar Nama*, 1590–95.
London, V&A CAT. 12

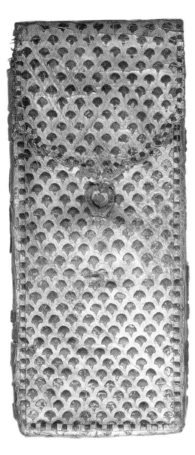  

the Mughals with a greater or lesser measure of success, so that campaign after campaign had to be mounted to 'pacify' the region in the early seventeenth century. The Portuguese presence in the region had two broad foci, to the west in Satgaon and then Hughli (Hoogly), and to the east, around Chittagong and its satellite centre of Dianga. The last lay beyond Mughal control until the 1660s, when they mounted a successful campaign there. But in Hughli, or Porto Pequeno, the Portuguese quickly succeeded in obtaining terms from the Mughals in the 1570s, and went on to maintain a prosperous trading operation both with other centres in the Bay of Bengal and with those to the west such as the Maldives, Cochin and Goa. Still, since this particular Portuguese presence was in large measure autonomous of Goa (despite the fact that a captain, an *ouvidor* and some other officials might be found there), the Mughals, too, tended to treat the residents of Hughli as somewhat distinct from their compatriots in western India.

In western India the prospect of Mughal expansion was viewed with increasing alarm in Portuguese official circles from at least the 1570s. The 'natural' limits of the expanding empire were not at all obvious to such official observers as the minor chronicler António Pinto Pereira, writing his *História da Índia* in the 1570s; rather, it was feared that the power vacuum created by the collapse of Vijayanagara power in the south-western Deccan would occasion ever further Mughal inroads into the region of Goa.[1] Much has been written on Mughal-Portuguese relations during the reign of Akbar, particularly after the Mughal conquest of Gujarat in 1573. Three clear strands are visible in the historiography, even though they often appear intertwined. First, it is pointed out that the Mughal ports of Gujarat and the Portuguese-controlled ports like Goa and

Firman (or *farman*) cases, Mughal India, 18th century, leather, stamped, painted and gilt. London, V&A CAT. 21

Hurmuz enjoyed important trade links in the last quarter of the sixteenth century, and that an accommodation of interests was necessary if the coastal *cáfilas* along the west coast or the annual fleets to the Persian Gulf were to ply. Both parties had an interest in the matter, the Mughals because Surat was thus supplied with silver *reales* and other goods, the Portuguese *Estado* because it received customs revenue and Gujarati textiles brought to Goa could be carried back to Europe. Portuguese private traders, settled at Surat, Rander, Cambay and other centres, also formed a sort of pressure group that acted on the Goa administration.[4]

A second aspect of relations stemmed from the *hajj* (pilgrimage) traffic in which the Mughal state interested itself. Here, the Portuguese, as *cartaz*-issuing authorities, and the Mughals, whose ships received the safe-conduct passes, had to enter into dealings (paralleling those between the Portuguese and the Deccan rulers for the same purpose). Such dealings were of course a source of conflict, as the Mughals evidently did not accept *cartazes* with good grace, and Portuguese officials for their part did not miss opportunities to squeeze benefits out of the arrangement. At the same time an alignment with the realities of the balance of maritime power was necessary, if the *hajj* from Surat and other ports was to be maintained.

Farman from Akbar to Aires Teles, captain of the fortress in Diu, Ahmadabad, 13 December 1572. Lisbon, Biblioteca Nacional (BNL), cod. 3776, ff. 106v–108

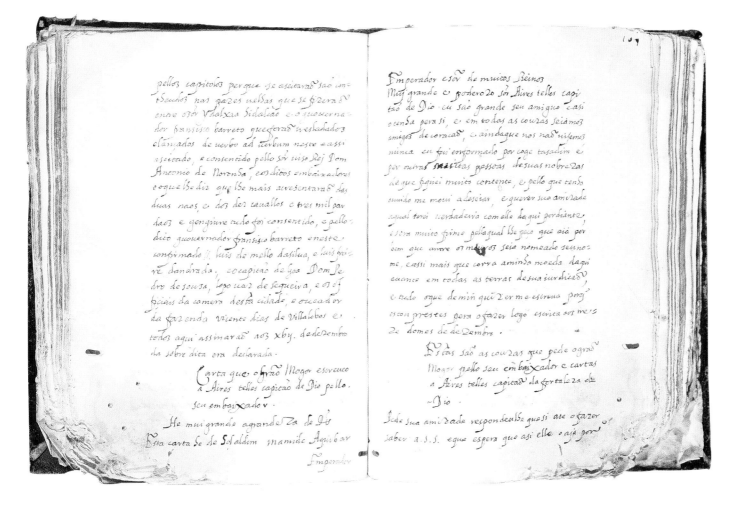

A third aspect, perhaps the best known, can be traced to the late 1570s, with the beginnings of the Jesuit presence in Akbar's court, and lent a religious dimension to the dealings. The Fathers hoped, in vain, to convert the ruler, or at least some of his prominent nobles. But they also served as a conduit between the authorities at Goa and the Mughal court, and were thus a convenient presence since the State of India and the Mughals did not maintain permanent diplomatic missions in each other's domains.

It is evident even from the bald summary presented above that relations between the Mughals and the Portuguese were potentially as much of conflict as of collaboration, since their basic interests were by no means congruent. We have to look no further than the *Mongolicae Legationis Commentarius* of the Catalan Jesuit Antonio Monserrate for a confirmation of this, for his account contains a detailed description of the difficulties between Mughals and Portuguese in Gujarat and off the Konkan coast in the years 1581–2.[5] Abu'l Fazl's official Mughal chronicle, *Akbar Nama*, is no less explicit on the question.[6]

The Mughal-Portuguese equation, then, was an ambiguous one, even if we take only Gujarat into account. Mughal expansion in other directions was not all that well received by the Portuguese either, as we see from Diogo do Couto's account of Raja Man Singh's expedition to the east in the 1590s, in *Década XII* of his huge chronicle, *Da Ásia*. It is all the more disappointing, therefore, that the surviving section of his chronicle says so little about the major Mughal expansion of the years 1597 to 1600, namely the incorporation of large parts of the Deccan, and in particular the Ahmadnagar sultanate.[7] This is in evident contrast to the detailed attention Couto pays to Nizam Shahi affairs in earlier parts of *Da Ásia*; the struggle for succession at the death of Burhan Nizam Shah (r. 1508–54), the siege of Chaul in 1570–71, earlier Mughal threats to Ahmadnagar in the 1580s, and Portuguese-Nizam Shahi relations in the viceroyalty of Matias de Albuquerque (1591–7) all receive their fair share of attention.[8]

The point to be made then is that while there is a certain retrospective inevitability about Mughal expansion, contemporaries did not wholly share this sense until the late sixteenth century. From our perspective the history of the Mughal state from its very creation in the 1520s in northern India to the early eighteenth century is one of expansion in every direction from its core at the Ganges-Jamuna *doab*, but especially southward. After the early 1590s, once Sind had been captured and the last gasp of organized resistance by Muzaffar Shah III was snuffed out in Gujarat, the west remained relatively stable; on the other hand, the expansionary campaigns to the east came to a halt only in the 1660s, with the fall of Chittagong. As for the north and north-west, they continued to harbour potential for expansion into Shahjahan's reign, as the unsuccessful campaign into Balkh shows.

But it was in the south, first the Deccan, then the Karnatak, where the Mughals fought a war of attrition, expanding step by step from the late sixteenth century to the early eighteenth century, when the furthest southern limits were defined under war-leaders like Zu'lfiqar Khan, Nusrat Jang and Da'ud Khan Panni. It was equally here that Mughal expansion seemed most uncertain, as a host of challengers, from Malik 'Ambar in the early seventeenth century to Shivaji Bhonsle later in the same century, arose to halt the advancing tide. But we should also bear in mind that the Portuguese, who had arrived in India a quarter century before Babur turned his attention to Hindustan, were uneasy observers of Mughal expansion from their coastal enclaves, and invented in this process the collective myth of the omnivorous triumvirate of giants of south and south-west Asia: the Great Turk, the Great Sufi and the Great Mughal.[9]

Portrait of Diogo do Couto, Portugal, 18th century (?).
Lisbon, Instituto dos Arquivos Nacionais/Torre do Tombo (IAN/TT)
CAT. 19

DIOGO DOCOUTO FAMOZO
ESCRITOR DA HISTORIA DA INDIA ONDE MILITOU, EFOI UNICO GOARDAMOR
DATORRE DOTOMBO NACEU EMLISBOA EM 1542. FALECEU EMGOA
EM 1616.

EXPRIMIT EFIGIES CUOD SOLUM INCÆSAPE VISUM EST

HISTORIAM CALAMO TRACTAT, ETARMA MANU.

In the first quarter of the sixteenth century, when the Portuguese initially established themselves at Cochin and Goa, the Vijayanagara state in peninsular south India had given them far less cause for anxiety, even if relations between Goa and Vijayanagara were not always amicable. From the era of Vasco da Gama and Afonso de Albuquerque, when the Portuguese king Dom Manuel I had even dreamt of a marriage alliance between the royal houses of Portugal and Vijayanagara, things began to sour in later decades. The idea of using Vijayanagara as a counterweight to keep the 'Adil Shahi rulers of Bijapur in check, and thus protect Goa's internal frontier, was the principal focus of Albuquerque's own geo-political conception of the Deccan, but other considerations were later to modify this. First, between 1520 and 1560 there was no very serious attempt by the Sultans of Bijapur to retake Goa; this limited the extent of their conflict. Second, official Portuguese policies brought them into conflict with the trading settlements of the Kanara coast, which were controlled (or at least protected) by Vijayanagara. The ports of Bhatkal, Basrur and Honawar, as also Mangalore, were seen as allied to the Mappila opponents of the Portuguese, who hence used every opportunity to harass their shipping. Third, the relative tolerance shown under Dom Manuel I for Vijayanagara – which was after all to them a 'gentile', that is, a Hindu, kingdom – did not survive into later decades, when the Counter-Reformation spirit at Dom João III's court prompted him, among other things, implicitly to permit the governor Martim Afonso de Sousa in the 1540s to essay an attack on the Tirupati temple.[10] The attack did not come off, but the fact that it was contemplated – despite the awareness that the Vijayanagara kings were major patrons of this temple – suggests that the State of India cared little about hurt feelings at the inland court.

The revival of Vijayanagara as a military power under Aravidu Rama Raya in the 1550s and early 1560s may have briefly caused the Portuguese to take pause. But they were quick to seize the opportunity, when in 1565 Rama Raya was defeated and killed by the Deccan sultans. Their 'share' of the spoils were the ports of Mangalore, Basrur and Honawar, which they took in a series of attacks in 1568–9, thus assuring Goa of a stable supply of rice and also giving them easy access to Kanara pepper.[11] It was left to the Italian Filippo Sassetti in the 1580s to point to how the decline of Vijayanagara had been detrimental to the Portuguese at Goa; there is little evidence that many other contemporary Portuguese thought so, with the arguable exception of Diogo do Couto.[12]

Sassetti's argument, like that of Couto later, was an economic one: Goa's trade had, he felt, been crucially dependent on the market for imports at Vijayanagara. Other arguments of a more political and military nature could be added. The fact that in the late 1560s and early 1570s the Portuguese settlements of the Konkan and Goa itself were attacked by the Sultans of Ahmadnagar and Bijapur was evidently no coincidence; relieved of the pressure from Vijayanagara, these rulers could now turn their attention coastward, and also use the momentum and goodwill of their earlier anti-Vijayanagara alliance against the *firangi* (European) enemy. True, when Goa was under siege from the land, its lifeline was now secure so long as the rice-fleets from Kanara came in, but on balance the geo-political shifts of the 1560s seem to have been unfavourable to the Portuguese State.

It is, however, difficult to link these events directly to Mughal expansion into the Deccan, which, while it may have been contemplated as early as 1577, in fact began only in the 1590s. Conventional accounts link Akbar's decision to expand into Ahmadnagar with the quarrels between the ruler Murtaza Nizam Shah (r. 1565–88) and his brother Burhan, which led the latter, after a brief sojourn in Bijapur, to take shelter

Powder-flask, Mughal India,
17th century, ivory.
Oporto, private collection CAT. 5

with the Mughals, who incorporated him in 1584 into their own hierarchy of notability and made him a *mansabdar-jagirdar*. It seems likely, however, that the Mughals would have turned their attention to the Deccan sooner or later, once they had secured the conquests of Bengal and Gujarat, and consolidated their northern and north-western frontier. Besides, it is useful to bear in mind that the succession struggle that ensued at Ahmadnagar on Murtaza's assassination in 1588 only set the seal on a process of fragmentation that had deeper roots; the effort by the *habashi* (or Ethiopian) element in the state to assert its autonomy, and the recourse by others – especially Deccani notables – to a form of Mahdawi millenarianism, in view of the approach of the Hijri year 1000, all point to a political situation fraught with tension.[13] The reader of the two great chronicles of the epoch, the *Burhan-i Ma'asir* of Sayyid 'Ali bin 'Azizullah Tabatabai, and the *Gulshan-i Ibrahimi* of Muhammad Qasim Hindushah Astarabadi (better known by his *nom de plume* of Firishta), is left in no doubt as to this.[14] Both writers were witness to the situation in the late 1580s, and Firishta left Ahmadnagar for Bijapur soon after Murtaza Nizam Shah's death, apparently fearing the rise of the Mahdawis and its implications for Shi'as like himself.

Burhan returned to Ahmadnagar from his Mughal exile as Burhan Nizam Shah II in 1591. He did so with Akbar's blessings, but took the aid of Raji 'Ali Khan Faruqi, ruler of Khandesh, rather than that of the Mughals themselves, in order to improve his own legitimacy once in Ahmadnagar. On his return he displaced and imprisoned his own son Isma'il, who had ruled for two years with the support of the Mahdawi leader Jamal Khan.[15] However, Mughal expectations that he would be little more than a quisling once in power were soon denied. Abu'l Fazl, in his *Akbar Nama*, expresses great disapproval of Burhan throughout his four-year reign, as the following passage demonstrates:

When Burhan al-Mulk prevailed over Ahmadnagar, he should have increased his devotion and gratitude, and been an example of obedience to other rulers in that quarter. The wine of success robbed him of his senses, and he forgot the varied favours he had received from the Shahinshah. In his evil fortune he set himself to oppress the weak, and considered that his profit consisted in the injury of others.[16]

To force him back to a more submissive posture, Abu'l Fazl's brother Abu'l Faiz 'Faizi' was sent on a mission to the Deccan in the years 1591–3, leaving a valuable account to which we shall turn presently.[17] For reasons that await detailed analysis, the Mughals still held back militarily, but did not conceal their amusement at Burhan's military failures – in respect of not only Bijapur but the Portuguese. One possible reason for Mughal reticence may have been the difficulties they faced in the early 1590s in Gujarat, where Muzaffar Shah once more led a resurgence of local chiefs, including those of Jamnagar, Junagadh, Sorath and Kacch. Akbar's foster-brother Mirza 'Aziz Koka, newly appointed *subadar* of Gujarat, set about crushing this move, in a military action that endured from 1591 until well into 1592.

In the next year, 1593, Mirza Koka began to threaten the Portuguese settlements in Gujarat, in particular Diu. Thereafter, apparently disgruntled with the lack of favour shown him by the Mughal court despite his military success, he began to display rebellious tendencies, and eventually embarked in a Mughal pilgrim ship for the *hajj*, returning only in 1594.[18] This was the very year when Burhan Nizam Shah II entered into headlong conflict with the Portuguese over a fortress he had built on a tongue of land, overlooking their settlement of Chaul in the Deccan. The Persian chronicler Muhammad Qasim Firishta, in his near-contemporary chronicle, describes matters as follows:

In the year AH 1001 [AD 1592–3], Burhan Nizam Shah marched his army against the Portuguese of Rewadanda; and despatching a large force to the sea-port of Chaul, ordered that a fort should be built to prevent the entrance of the Portuguese into the harbour of Rewadanda, and this fort he called Korla. The Portuguese sailing during the night effected their escape, but they returned with reinforcements from many other ports which had also fallen into their hands … Burhan Nizam Shah now sent a body of about four thousand men, under Farhad Khan, to reinforce Korla; and as other troops were expected from Daman and Bassein, he appointed one Bahadur Khan Gilani, at the head of all the foreign troops, governor of the fortress of Korla, to blockade Rewadanda.[19]

The chronicler goes on to describe how the Ahmadnagar forces nearly got the Portuguese to capitulate; however, the 'tyranny' of Burhan caused many of his commanders to desist from taking the enterprise to its conclusion. The Portuguese meanwhile arrived in a fleet, carried out a landing, and after a prolonged fight in which 12,000 of the Ahmadnagar forces were killed, 'reduced the fort to ashes'. This event, according to Portuguese sources, took place in early September 1594; Burhan himself died on 18 April 1595 (13 Sha'ban 1003 AH). Firishta, in keeping with his disapproval of this particular monarch, does not tell us what prompted Burhan to act in such a manner and so contravene the agreement that his brother Murtaza and the Portuguese had arrived at after the earlier siege of Chaul in the 1570s. Diogo do Couto, whose chronicle contains quite a detailed description of these events, is not much more helpful than Firishta in explaining what prompted the 'Melique' (i.e. Malik, the title by which he refers to Burhan and the Nizam Shahs in general) to build the fortress of the 'Morro' (the hill-top – referring here to Korla).[20] But whatever were the reasons for the act, there is little doubt that the episode of the 'Morro' precipitated a major crisis, leading eventually to serious Mughal inroads into the Ahmadnagar sultanate by about 1600. Although it would take them another three decades to complete the task of conquest, the years between 1593 and the death of Akbar in 1605 mark a decisive stage in the changing relations between the Mughals and the Deccan.

This takes us to the situation with regard to the other major Deccan sultanate, namely Bijapur, in these years under the rule of Ibrahim 'Adil Shah II (r. 1580–1627). Ibrahim had come to power after the controversial reign of 'Ali 'Adil Shah, who had entertained complex relations with the Portuguese. Initially, in the 1560s he seemed rather favourably inclined towards Goa and had even encouraged a mission to his own court from the Archbishop, Dom Jorge Temudo.[21] But later in the same decade relations began to sour. Eventually, 'Ali even undertook an ambitious – if unsuccessful – campaign against the Portuguese, mounting an attack on Goa that posed a serious threat to the Portuguese for a time. However, by the time of his assassination and Ibrahim's accession, it would have seemed clear to the most powerful elements in the Bijapur polity that the real threats came from the north rather than from the west. Residual Portuguese ambitions had more or less abated by then, and with the death of 'Ali bin Yusuf 'Adil Khan, the exiled son of Bijapur's founder who had sought refuge in Goa, even this element of friction no longer persisted. On the other hand, relations with the Mughals were quite another matter, for, while the Mughal claim by the 1580s was that the whole of the Deccan fell under their suzerainty, the rulers of neither Bijapur nor Golconda could countenance such a claim. In their titulature, their coinage and other claims they obviously saw themselves as rulers independent from (if threatened by) the Mughals until at least the 1630s. Besides, from the early sixteenth century there was the Safavid connection, and the fact that both Bijapur and Golconda had periodically recognized in the Safavids a form of 'ritual suzerainty', often inserting the names of the rulers of Iran for example into the Friday prayers in their capital cities. The flow of Iranian migrants into the Deccan in the last quarter of the sixteenth century, and the fact that these migrants constituted a significant part of the élite in both Bijapur and Golconda, only served to strengthen these ties. In correspondence with the ruler of Iran, the Bijapur ruler could write as late as 1613:

This letter is from the humblest slave Ibrahim to the exalted emperor Shah 'Abbas. My forefathers had always great hopes in His Majesty's ancestors' love and friendship and had banked on them. I, on my part, would do no better than to revive and strengthen those ties. The Deccan territories form as much a part of the Safavid empire as the provinces of Iraq, Fars, Khurasan, and Azarbaijan. Accordingly, the names of the Safavid monarchs have been recited in the [Friday] sermons and will continue to be recited in future. Our forefathers were appointed to rule over these territories and protect them, by His Majesty's ancestors. So our function is to rule the countries on His Majesty's behalf and defend them against foreign aggression.[22]

The manifest purpose of these letters was to complain about the 'ruler of Agra and Delhi', as the Mughal monarch is referred to. The project that is proposed, namely that the Safavids should attack the Mughals from the west (in the region of Qandahar), to divert them from attacks on the south, need not be taken too seriously. But it is clear that the Bijapur sultan, like his counterpart in Golconda, hoped in some way to counterbalance the Mughal superpower by appeals to a countervailing threat. Here, then, is a clue to how the Safavids were perceived from the viewpoint of the Deccan. No military alliance that might straddle the distance between Chaul or Dabhol and the ports of Fars was of course really possible, but other forms of real and symbolic affinity tied the predominantly Shiite sultans of the Deccan to Iran rather than to the Sunni Mughals who were gradually encroaching upon them from the north.

Young Prince Reading, Deccan, 17th century, gouache on paper, 39 x 27.8 cm.
Lisbon, Calouste Gulbenkian Museum (CGM), inv. no. M. 51

FAIZI'S MISSION TO THE DECCAN, 1591–3

A valuable account from these years showing the Mughal perspective on matters is provided by the reports of the Mughal poet-laureate, Abu'l Faiz ibn Mubarak, better known as Faizi Fayyazi. The brother of the great chronicler and ideologue Abu'l Fazl, Faizi was personally close to Akbar himself, and thus represents the viewpoint of the Mughal court with a certain faithfulness, while also bringing back crucial empirical information on matters in the Deccan for the benefit of his royal master. His despatch to the Deccan in 1591 was, however, neither in the capacity of Sunni Muslim (which he may not really have been), nor of poet (which he most certainly was), but as an intimate of Akbar charged to size up the situation in the area of Khandesh (more or less a Mughal protectorate by then), and also more particularly in Ahmadnagar, Bijapur and Golconda, regions that had a rather more ambiguous political position. It is this rather delicate situation, of contested sovereignties, that Faizi found himself embroiled in. Added to this was the fact that the ruler of Ahmadnagar, Burhan Nizam Shah, had spent some years in the Mughal court as an exile and had returned to take charge as sultan after being a mere Mughal subordinate. This, then, is how Abu'l Fazl puts it in his *Akbar Nama*: the pressing need was to bring around the 'somnolent one [Burhan] and the other rulers of that quarter. If they listened and apologised, he [Akbar] would withhold his hand from retribution. Otherwise a victorious army would be appointed, and chastisement would be inflicted.'[23]

Faizi thus left from Lahore on his travels to the Deccan on 24 August 1591 (the Hijri month of Shawwal 999), and returned to the court in May 1593, after an absence of a year and three-quarters.[24] In this time he set down a number of reports for Akbar that touch on a diversity of subjects, ranging from the situation in crucial fortresses on the route, through gossip concerning the Safavid political situation gathered from fresh migrants to the Deccan, to an appraisal of the Deccan political scene itself. He also looked into the matter of persons in the Deccan, whether poets, writers or others, who could eventually be recruited into Mughal service, thus acting as a sort of 'talent scout'. Yet, Faizi's embassy to the Deccan was not considered a success from a diplomatic perspective, a fact that even his devoted brother Abu'l Fazl implicitly admits. Writing in the *Akbar Nama*, he notes:

On the 28th [Ardibihisht] the standard of the seekers after knowledge, the *malik ush-shu'rā'* Shaikh Faizi, returned from the Deccan, and after an absence of 1 year, 8 months, 14 days, did homage. He was exalted by various favours. He had gone on an embassy. Burhan in his arrogance and self-will had not listened to his counsels. He had not sent fitting presents and had prepared the materials for his own injury. Raji 'Ali Khan had to some extent listened to his commands, and had sent his daughter with choice bridal gifts for the wooing of the Prince Royal.[25]

The unofficial Mughal chronicler, Badayuni, who is much less sympathetic to Faizi, notes that in Muharram 1002, four months after Faizi's return,

the other ambassadors arrived from the rulers of the Dakhin having succeeded in their negotiations; and paid their respects. And since Burhan-al-mulk had not sent any acceptable present, on the 21st of Muharram, the Emperor appointed the Prince Daniyal to this service, as *wakil* to the Khan-i Khanan ... and other *amirs* with 70,000 specially assigned troops.[26]

There is an implicit snide tone to this comment: the other ambassadors had 'succeeded', hence only Faizi had failed. The failure consisted above all in the fact that Faizi was unable to persuade Burhan Nizam Shah to declare unambiguously that he was a vassal or subordinate of the Mughals, and that he was willing to pay regular tribute (or *peshkash*) to his powerful northern neighbours. In other words, in comparison to the Faruqi ruler of Khandesh, who received Faizi with total self-abnegation, the Nizam Shah still showed signs that he saw himself as capable of being autonomous, partly through the privileged relations that he had with the Safavids. The final message to be derived from Faizi's reports was thus that the Mughals had no real recourse left but military conquest.

Yet, this is to reduce a rich series of materials to a rather simple one-point programme. For Faizi was able in four of his six reports to present a series of striking vignettes of various aspects of the Deccan, and also of the political situation in Iran. These range from simple descriptions of the towns through which he passed, to evaluations of the court-politics of the Deccan sultanates that are all quite valuable. We may take, by way of example, his brief but evocative description of Burhanpur, in his view no more than a small town (*baghayat tang*), but full of gardens and greenery (*bustan*). All cultivable land was made use of, Faizi notes, and figs (*injir*) of high quality were to be found there, while *firangi* melons (papayas) hung in bunches of twenty or thirty on the trunks of trees. Bananas in plenty were also to be found, while on the other hand, Indian melons were imported into the area. The wind was a little hot in the month that he visited; in the day a single layered garment was sufficient, and at night a light additional tunic was necessary. As for the water, he found it to be different from that in the neighbouring towns.[27] No doubt Akbar and his sons could have found such information of interest when planning their future military campaigns in the area, since they eventually used Burhanpur as a place of residence.

The first of Faizi's reports, written largely while he was in Mughal territory, has its share of blunt condemnations, and recommendations of officials that he encountered; we do not know to what extent these ideas were implemented at the court, and imperial servants transferred, promoted or chastised as a consequence. But the second report already moves away from such a tone and content. Instead, we get the following appreciation of the affairs of Ahmadnagar, from a time when Faizi had already taken up temporary residence in that city.

Burhan Nizam-al-mulk is one of those who has been raised from the dust by Your Excellency, and who has been reared on your munificence. It is four months that he has entered the *jagir* of 'Adil Khan in a part that is 25 *kos* from Ahmadnagar on the bank of the river Nahalwada or Bhima, a big river that separates them. And he has built two mud fortresses in the middle of the latter's territory. 'Adil Khan is still sitting in the fort of Bijapur, and has sent his army of 14,000 horsemen. There are skirmishes every day, and a large number of people are being slain on both sides.

Neither ruler of the Deccan is given the dignity of the title of 'Shah', and their territories are treated throughout as mere *jagirs*, revenue-assignments deriving from the Mughals. Further, Faizi notes that the uncle of Burhan Nizam-al-mulk (not 'Nizam Shah'), a certain Baqir, who had been living in poverty in Bijapur, had now been promoted by the 'Adil Khan (not 'Shah'), and sent against Burhan with an army. The idea was to have Baqir take over Ahmadnagar, and he had been tempted by this. Meanwhile, Raji 'Ali Khan Faruqi had sent men to both the uncle and nephew, urging them to make peace. It was hence expected that a truce would be declared, but for the moment war was still continuing. Faizi expresses great annoyance with the situation. For when Burhan had left Ahmadnagar on his Bijapur campaign, he had with great humility expressed his own sense of vulnerability, and declared that he was preparing the *peshkash* for the Mughals. However, Faizi had since tried to persuade him to expedite matters, but he kept putting things off. Four months had passed in this manner, even though Faizi had met him twice in that connection. The Mughal envoy notes how distressed he was to find himself in the city of Ahmadnagar, full of mischief and commotion (*shor wa sharr*), inhabited by sedition-mongers and ruffians (*fitnasazan wa aubashan*). He had the impression of wasting his time, even though the wretched Burhan continued to write regularly to Faizi, beseeching him to intervene to ensure that Akbar did not become angry. And each time, in his letters, he insisted he would return in a few days. Faizi adds: 'Since Burhan is your disciple (*tarbiyat karda*), and has grown under your kind eye, I hope he will always remain on the correct path, and that his conduct will be acceptable to Your Excellency, and that it will all end well for him.'[28]

A description of the city of Ahmadnagar now follows. Faizi notes that the city was built by the father of Nizam-ul-mulk Bahri, grandfather of Burhan (himself son of Husain, son of Burhan, son of Ahmad). This last Ahmad had built a stone fort at four or five bowshots' distance from the city, and the fort was the main seat of the ruler (*hakim*). Around the fort was a *maidan*, and open fields. The city was rectangular, and there were no city walls. At a distance of two *kos* was a lake, and a canal had been excavated to bring water to the city from there, so it could be distributed to households. Some houses had tanks, while others used water from a well that was not particularly good. The Mughal envoy notes that at the time that the late ruler Murtaza Nizam Shah had gone mad, a certain Salabat Khan had built a garden for him with tall cypress trees outside the town. In the middle of it was a covered pond, or *hauz*, but Faizi had not yet seen it. The air was pleasant in the area, but in certain months a quilt was necessary. Among the fruits, good melons were not to be found; rather they were sour, and lacking in taste. In fact, they were not real melons, though the local people called them that. Of all the fruits, the figs were not bad; grapes were there in abundance; other fruits were available in modest quantities. Pineapples were imported in quantities from nearby, and they were not bereft of good taste. Bananas and apples (*amritfal*) were to be had as well, and the mangoes too met with his approval. Roses were to be found, though only with difficulty, and those that he had seen lacked fragrance. On the other hand, *champa* and other Indian flowers were found in abundance. Sandal trees were to be seen there, and an abundance of white pepper (*filfil*), too.

Faizi praises the good goldsmiths of the area, and weavers, who are unparalleled, and mentions that in general very high-quality cloth was made in the Deccan. Patan is one centre and Daulatabad another that are singled out for mention. Clearly, the conquest of the area could bring major economic benefits to the Mughals. But contrasted to this rather positive situation in terms of climate and economic products is the quite disastrous political ambience. On this matter Faizi writes:

Doorway, Mughal India, end of the 17th century, wood, 278.4 x 157.2 cm. London, V&A, IS 20-1920

In the last few years, there were massacres (qatl-i 'amm) twice in this city [Ahmadnagar], in the course of which not a single person from abroad (mardum-i wilayat) was left alive. The killing spree lasted for three days. Good people like the learned men and traders, who had assembled here in this period, were all slain, and their houses were destroyed. And at another time, after the coming of Burhan Nizam-ul-mulk, a great plunder and loot was carried out with respect to the foreigners (ghariban). Whosoever had any goods was killed or wounded; the kith and kin of Shaikh Munawwar were ruined in this process, and were wounded. They are so ashamed that they do not dare come out of their houses. He expects favours from you. Lahori Afghan merchants too were plundered in large measure, and some of the servants of Salima Sultan Begam too were looted. How can the things plundered by these ruffians in this commotion be recovered? [extract]

These thugs, or aubashan, were still roaming the streets freely, a sign of how matters needed to be taken in hand in Ahmadnagar.

Having made it clear that Ahmadnagar under Nizam Shahi rule was a den of iniquity, Faizi turned his attention to Ibrahim 'Adil Khan, the hakim (governor) of Bijapur, and now some twenty-two years of age. He notes that in the early part of his reign power had been exercised by a certain Dilawar Khan Habashi, a Sunni, but that he had then fled to the camp of Burhan. In a later section of the report we learn more details to the effect that Dilawar Khan Habashi had controlled Bijapur for ten to twelve years, to the point that the 'Adil Khan did not even drink water without his approval, and rarely stirred out. However, his misbehaviour had made the people of Bijapur miserable. Hence, the previous year, a large number of people had assembled there to kill him, with the connivance of the 'Adil Khan himself. It was then that Dilawar Khan had fled to join Nizam-ul-Mulk. In the meantime 'Adil Khan invited him back, and he returned, believing he would be well treated. Instead, when he reached there, his eyes were gouged out, and his effects confiscated. His son, Muhammad Khan, was also wooed by 'Adil Khan, but when this failed, he too was blinded. Clearly, things in Bijapur were also on the decline. As for Golconda, its ruler Muhammad Quli Qutb-al-Mulk was a Shi'a, who had made a new city called Bhagnagar, named after a certain Bhagmati, a hardened whore and his old mistress (fahisha-i kuhna wa ma'shuqa-i qadim), from which fact one could draw one's own conclusions.[29] The territories of the Deccan were thus broadly divided, in Faizi's view, into the jagirs of these three men, and also some other rajas, who coexisted in a politic fashion (mubassirana). Faizi claims that he has observed them carefully, and promises a fuller report at a later date. Yet his claims for Mughal suzerainty continue to colour every part of the account. 'This territory is part of the well-protected territories (mamalik-i mahrusa)', he writes, calling on Akbar to visit it once, since the mere sound of the arrival of Akbar will have a positive effect on these recalcitrant elements.

Yet, Faizi was also keen to use his time in Ahmadnagar to look beyond the politics of the sultanates of the Deccan, and one of his primary tasks was to gather information on the situation in Iran. It turned out that in that particular year six ships had arrived from Hurmuz on the Konkan coast; a certain Khwaja Mu'ina'i, who was a merchant-prince ('umdat ut-tujjar), had made the twenty-four-day voyage with his friends, bringing with him 200 Iraqi horses in three ships. However, the Portuguese – here simply termed the firangis – had a rule that ships with horses were to be taken first to Goa, where they picked out the ones they wanted. Only then could the ships go on to the port of Chaul, which was in the jagir of Nizam-ul-Mulk.[30] Faizi now notes that some traders and some of the qizilbash (Turkoman military specialists) in Safavid service, on account of the turbulence in Iraq and Fars, had left for the Mughal domains, with the intention of 'kissing the threshold' of Akbar. The chief of them was a certain Husain Quli Afshar, a brave young man, who in the time of Shah Tahmasp had held the governorship of some districts around Isfahan. Another important man was Husain Beg, who at the time when Ya'qub Khan had been powerful in Iran had been a particular friend of his and held a high position in the province of Fars. But after the latter's death (on which more below), he had been forced to leave. These two men had come with their followers, and were temporarily staying in the port of Chaul, pondering their future. They had written to Faizi, and he had replied to both by a single letter, of which he sent a copy to Akbar.

Among the people on the ship was a certain Hamza Hasan Beg, a relative of the great Mughal general 'Abdul Rahim Khan-i-Khanan, who hence planned to go to Ihatta, where 'Abdul Rahim was. Still another migrant was Haji Ibrahim, who was a former *rikabdar* (cupbearer) of Shah Tahmasp. There was also Haji Khusrau, a former personal slave of Shah Tahmasp and well known in the Mughal court. Some of these ships' passengers had arrived eventually in Ahmadnagar, and given Faizi information concerning the current situation in Iraq, Fars and Rum. This was 'hot' gossip indeed, and he therefore hastened to retail it to his master, the emperor. Faizi writes:

Shah 'Abbas has attained twenty years of age, and is aflame with the fire of youth. His horoscope and those of his two brothers, Abu Talib Mirza and Tahmasp Mirza, are hereby enclosed for your consideration. The court-astrologers will tell you the beginning and the end of the fate of these three. Shah 'Abbas is fond of hunting, polo (*chaugan*), shooting, and javelin-throwing (*neza-bazi*). He is keen on falconry. Last year, he fell down twice from his horse while javelin-throwing, once in Shiraz and the second time in Isfahan. Both times, his knee was severely injured. He is a brave man, and proud of himself (*ghairat-mand*), and even if he is prey to the whims and passions of royal youth, he is still sober, and intelligent. He has still not taken over the reins of governance, and the fiscal and administrative affairs are so far left to the officials. Farhad Khan is his chief secretary (*wakil-i mutlaq*), and his constant companion, and Hatim Beg Urdubadi, who is very shrewd and economical, is the wazir.

The time had come, writes Faizi, when the shah would awake from his stupor and also emerge from the intoxication of youth. This was therefore a dangerous moment for his rivals and neighbours. He was now very concerned that most of the lands of Khorasan had been lost on account of his carelessness, and was making efforts for its recovery.[31] The previous year, he had wanted to attack Khorasan, but when he reached Rayy, plague broke out, and some of his troops had bubos on their side, others on their thighs, the size of a gram. Shah 'Abbas himself had fallen ill with fever at the time, and rushed back to Qazwin.[32] Thereupon, Farhad Khan with some notables had come to Khorasan, recaptured some of the towns and arrived in the vicinity of Mashhad, killing several thousand Uzbeks. The son of the Shaibani ruler, 'Abdullah Khan, had then made a flanking attack from Herat, and Farhad Khan had hence retreated to Qazwin. Faizi notes that the traders from Iran had clearly mentioned that 'Abdullah Khan's son only had 5,000–6,000 men, and if Farhad Khan had stood his ground, he would have carried the day; the implication is that Safavid military capability left much to be desired. The role of astrologers in determining Safavid policy is also noted: they had prevented the shah in the previous year from launching any expedition in Khorasan, but in the current year they had suggested that he could lead the army, and even predicted that he would emerge victorious. Faizi also makes a point of providing a detailed estimate of the armies with which the shah is planning to make the attack on Khorasan. The total force is estimated at well over a 100,000 men, and includes various commanders (who are often provincial governors) and the central forces (*lashkar-i khassa*) of about 30,000, as well as the slave-forces directly under the command of the shah, numbering about 10,000.[33]

Yet it seemed that the Safavid realm was riven with internal dissension. For example, Daulat Yar Kurd who had been sent to the area between Tabriz and Qazwin with 20,000 people had rebelled. The shah had then sent Husain Khan, the governor of Qom, with 15,000 men to quell him; Husain Khan had, however, been defeated, and it was thought that when the shah left for his campaign in Khorasan, Daulat Yar would be able to advance as far as Qazwin. In the face of this threat, the shah himself had attacked him, and persuaded some of Daulat Yar's brothers to defect. Because of this reverse, Daulat Yar had surrendered and appeared before the shah, expecting clemency. But none was forthcoming. Instead, the shah had kept him in a cage (*sanduq*), taken him to Qazwin and burnt him there. The ferocity of Shah 'Abbas is thus a recurring theme in these letters. It is claimed that he even threatened to harm some Uzbek traders in Yazd, and only relented when the Uzbeks said that if they were harmed, Iranian traders would also face similar consequences in Shaibani territories.

Besides, it was said that the previous year, Shah 'Abbas had with a hot iron blinded his brothers, Tahmasp Mirza and Mirza Abu Talib, and also Isma'il Mirza, and the son of Hamza Mirza. The last of these was so young that he died from the maltreatment. Shah 'Abbas himself had two sons, Mirza Safi and Mirza Haidar, who had been born the previous year. The shah's father Sultan Muhammad was totally blind and lived in the shah's camp in a separate tent. Arrangements had been made for his food and drink; he occupied himself with various forms of entertainment.

But most significant of all was the case of a certain Ya'qub Khan, briefly mentioned above. Faizi reports that the year before last, Yaktash Khan, the governor of Kirman and Yazd, who had a considerable force at his command, had revolted against the shah. Ya'qub Khan Zu'l-qadr, the governor of Shiraz, had been sent by the shah to chastise him; he had killed Yaktash in the fight that followed, and a huge amount of property and goods had fallen into the hands of Zu'l-qadr, which had rather turned his head. He used to claim to be a 'product of Shah Tahmasp' (*man az Shah Tahmasp hasil shuda am*), and even stated that he would one day be ruler of Iran. In pursuit of this idea he had illegally built a fort in Shiraz near the tomb of Shaikh Sa'di. The shah sent for him repeatedly from Isfahan, and asked him to deposit the goods he had gathered, but he refused to send anything. The shah therefore gathered 12,000 men and attacked Shiraz, but Zu'l-qadr went to Istakhar, where he enclosed himself inside a fort with 400 men. Shah 'Abbas besieged him there for four months, and he used to say regretfully to his companions that he had had no better servant than Ya'qub Khan, but that enemies had frightened and misled him. This news reached Ya'qub Khan, so that he at last left the fort under the influence of the seduction and soft words (*afsun wa afsana*) of the shah, and was for a time forgiven by 'Abbas. Yet rumours persisted that he was planning to kill the shah, and 'Abbas one day (while hunting) passed his hand over Ya'qub Khan's shoulder under affectionate pretext, and saw that he was wearing a coat of mail. Taking this as a sign of sedition, he at once claimed to have a headache and returned to the city, abandoning the hunt. The next day, he summoned Ya'qub Khan before the audience-hall (*diwan-khana*) with all his important servants. It so happened that in those very days a group of rope-makers had asked to show their skill at rope-play to the shah. The shah seated Ya'qub Khan by his side, jokingly took a stick in his hand and said: 'Kingship is coming to Ya'qub Khan. He shall be the king, and we his servant' (*Shahi ba Ya'qub Khan mirasad. Ishan Shah bashan wa ma naukar-i an*). He then said aloud that 'Shah Ya'qub Khan issued the order that such-and-such a servant should be killed with a rope'. The man was strangled. In this way the supporters of Ya'qub Khan were killed before his very eyes one after another, until at last it was his own turn. He was hung by a rope, his body was put to the rack (*dar shikanja kardan*), and after torture, his flesh was fed in morsels to the dogs (*luqma-i saghan sakhtand*).[34] Faizi leaves us in little doubt that he considers this to be an act of quite gratuitous cruelty, explaining why men such as Husain Beg (mentioned above) had decided to leave Iran for India.

In view of all this, it is clear that Faizi believed that the Mughal court could quite easily recruit the best talent from Iran. Thus, among the scholars (*danishmand*) of Iraq and Fars was a certain Mir Taqi-ud-Din Muhammad, famous under the name of Taqiya Nasaba. In that country he was unmatched, and he was a disciple of the great Mir Fathullah Shirazi, from whom Faizi had heard great praise of him. It was believed that Mir Taqi-ud-Din was keen to come to the Mughal court, but lacked the means for the voyage; Faizi hence suggests that Akbar should issue a *farman* with some money for him, and that this would persuade him to make the trip. Other names are also mentioned, such as the son of the *qazi* of Hamadan (a certain Ibrahim), who was a great scholar; Shaikh Baha-ud-Din Isfahani, resident in the Safavid capital; or the celebrated Chalpai Beg, who had been educated in Shiraz and Qazwin.[35] Besides, there were the Iranian savants in Ahmadnagar itself, who included two poets, Malik Qomi and Mulla Zuhuri, both of whom Faizi believed should be invited to the Mughal court.[36]

Throughout his stay in the Deccan Faizi continued to gather intelligence on the Safavids. In a later report he notes that letters from the Hurmuz traders to those in Ahmadnagar had recently arrived, and that he had managed to read some of them. These letters claimed that Shah 'Abbas had first gone to Gilan, and after quelling some rebels there, had set out for Khorasan, accompanied by 150,000 horsemen and foot-soldiers. There was a great battle (*jang-i 'azim*), and the shah had recaptured Mashhad and Herat from the Uzbeks. The letters stated that the Uzbeks had fled the battlefield; rivers of their blood were being spilt by the Qizilbash army of Iran. Besides, the great merchant (*saudagar-i buzurg*) Khwaja Baha-ud-Din had written from Chaul, stating that the captain (*nakhuda*) of a ship on its way from Hurmuz to Goa had stopped off at Chaul on some pretext, and given him the latest news from Iran, to the effect that the shah had taken Khorasan and had decided to send an envoy with sixty Iraqi horses, expensive textiles and a large quantity of goods to Akbar. The envoy (*ilchi*) was still in Hurmuz, and was about to leave for the Mughal court via Sind. Another letter (*khatt-i digar*) claims that 100 severed heads of Uzbeks and 100 live Uzbek slaves were being sent to the Mughals. Rather extravagantly, Faizi confidently asserts that in his letters Shah 'Abbas humbly states that he is a mere 'devotee' (*mukhlis*) of the Mughal emperor, who hopes for Akbar's kind attention. He even claims that the Safavids admit freely that their fortune and state (*daulat dar khandan-i safavi*) are due to the Mughals (*in dudman-i 'ali*), as is evident from the pages of history.[37] Here, Faizi's imperial rhetoric exceeds itself, but this need not detract from the significance of certain other parts of his account.

Sultan Ibrahim' Adil-Shah II, Deccan,
c.1610–15, watercolour on paper,
17 x 10.2 cm.
London, British Museum, 1937.4-10.02

Iran and the Iranian world thus feature quite prominently in Faizi's account. The Portuguese are a more discreet presence, even though we have seen them briefly mentioned above, in the context of the horse trade. One anecdote does, however, feature a Portuguese character. It emerges that Faizi had heard a story of a *firangi* physician called Bajarz (perhaps Borges), who had been invited to Ahmadnagar in the early sixteenth century by Nizam-ul-Mulk Bahri and was employed by him as a confidant. One day this *hakim* asked Khwajagi Shaikh Shirazi in the court of Nizam-ul-Mulk the following question:

If there were a fire at the end of the world, and there was nothing in between you and that place, and you were standing on a mountain, you can see the fire. Yet you people say that before the sky (falak), where the moon is, there is a layer of fire. Why is that not visible?

The shaikh replied that this was on account of the distance. The Portuguese physician then crudely mocked his reply. At that moment the celebrated Shah Tahir Husaini arrived, and asked what was happening. When he was told, he replied that the shaikh was wrong. When there is a mixture of elements, only then are things visible, as with the usual worldly fires, which had particles of earth in them. But the heavenly canopy of fire was made up of a pure element and hence invisible. This silenced the Portuguese completely.[38] From these and other minor elements in the account, we can see that Faizi set no great store by the Portuguese. At best, they were minor irritants, and at worst arrogant troublemakers.

TEN YEARS AFTER

In the ten years that followed Faizi's mission, the Mughals managed to make substantial inroads into the Deccan. Despite resistance mounted by the Ahmadnagar queen, Chand Sultana, and a certain Abhang Khan, Mughal forces had by 1599 come close to taking Ahmadnagar, and they were only temporarily halted in this enterprise by the mysterious death of Akbar's son, Shah Murad, who headed the Mughal army. Letters from the Portuguese viceroy Dom Francisco da Gama written in 1599 suggest that the State of India may in fact have been implicated in the Mughal prince's death, since the viceroy believed that this death would increase internal dissensions in the Mughal camp, and draw their attention away from projects of conquest.[39] In reality, this strategy did not bear the slightest fruit, as the Mughal armies crushed the forces of Ahmadnagar, took that city and advanced their southern frontier as far as Bijapur. Having personally supervised this campaign, Akbar then left his son Daniyal in charge of the Deccan, together with the veteran general 'Abdul Rahim Khan-i-Khanan, and returned north. The chief remaining resistance in Ahmadnagar was now provided by a group of Ethiopians, including a personage whom we shall encounter below – Malik 'Ambar.[40] The plight of Ibrahim 'Adil Shah, when faced with this situation, can only be imagined. Certain observers like the Flemish jeweller Jacques de Coutre, who was in the Bijapur court in these years, decried the sultan's cowardice, but it is clear that his only possible strategy now was a form of passive resistance through diplomacy. Coutre, who claims to have known the monarch closely (*con mucha familiaridad*) between 1604 and 1616, is nevertheless bitingly sarcastic, referring to him by turns as a coward, tyrant, arbitrary and obsessed with his harem of over 900 concubines 'who served him carnally when he wished'.[41] Indeed, Ibrahim's major virtue in Coutre's eyes was that he paid up his debts promptly (*era … puntual en lo que comprava*), besides being harsh in punishing bandits, and was regular in paying his soldiers and house-hold. Coutre noted that Ibrahim's way of dealing with the Mughals was simply to offer them 'gross gifts and tributes', and he further reported that the 'Adil Shah had justified this to his own vassals by claiming that instead of spending money and lives in making war, which always carried the risk of a loss, he would 'rather send him [the Mughal] the money in offering, and make him content, and be his friend, and remain in my house with my peace and quiet (*quedarme en mi caza con mi quietud y sossiego*)'.[42]

In fact, Ibrahim's strategy was rather more creative, but in order to understand this we need to turn to the account of a Mughal envoy to his court in 1603, a certain Asad Beg Qazwini. Asad Beg had been a loyal servant of Shaikh Abu'l Fazl, until the latter's assassination in 1601. Thereafter, his career had come briefly under a cloud, but he had managed to regain royal favour and was hence sent out to deal with Bijapur in 1603. As he himself explains in his detailed account, the *Waqa'i'-i Asad Beg*, the situation in that year was as follows.[43] When Akbar had been in Burhanpur in pursuit of his campaign against Ahmadnagar, he had decided to send a certain Iranian savant called Mir Jamal-ud-Din Husain Inju Shirazi to Bijapur as an envoy. Mir Jamal-ud-Din's principal task was to arrange a marriage between Ibrahim's daughter and Prince Daniyal, but instead of doing so expeditiously, the Sayyid from Shiraz remained at the Bijapur court for an inordinately long while, so that the emperor began to grow restive. Further, letters came in from both the Khan-i Khanan and Mir Jamal-ud-Din, in which the latter gave improbable reasons for his failure to return. The emperor at last grew angry, reports Asad Beg, and decided to set him straight. It was hence decided to send an appropriate person for this, and the royal eye fell on Asad Beg. The instructions to Asad Beg were simple: he was to bring Mir Jamal-ud-Din back without even 'giving him a chance to take a sip of water'. Further, the envoy was told to bring back goods and wealth (*zar-o-mal*) from the Deccan by way of tribute. A *farman* was also drafted for Mir Jamal-ud-Din, which stated that, if he did not return with Asad to the court, he would face dire consequences for himself and for his children. Asad Beg further asked for and was given a royal order addressed to Malik 'Ambar. And finally, Akbar instructed Asad Beg to bring back an elephant called Atish Para belonging to Ibrahim, which he had long promised but so far not given to Mir Jamal-ud-Din Husain.[44]

The envoy set out for the Deccan by way of Ujjain, where the governor was the Timurid prince, Mirza Shahrukh. From there he went on to Mandu, then to Burhanpur, where he was received by Prince Daniyal himself and the Khan-i-Khanan. The Mughal army seems to have been well settled in the Deccan by then, and the tone rather relaxed. Evenings were spent with poetry, wine and music, rather than in any extended martial reflection. The Khan-i-Khanan did, however, ask Asad Beg to try and bring around Malik 'Ambar and a certain Hasan 'Ali Beg, who, so it appears, had a disagreement. The resistance in Ahmadnagar itself seems to have been at a low ebb. On reaching Bir, Asad Beg then met with Hasan 'Ali Beg, and eventually it was decided that a reconciliation meeting between him and Malik 'Ambar would be organized. The Mughal envoy hence first met the Ethiopian warlord (whom he already knew), presented him the Mughal *farman*, and the two fell to talking about old memories. The next day, Malik 'Ambar went on to organize festivities (*jashn*), in which several nobles of Ahmadnagar and learned persons and 'turbaned scholars', as well as Sayyids, were present. It would thus seem that at this time relations between the Mughals and Malik 'Ambar were growing rather cordial. We can see this from the fact that at the time of the formal reconciliation an elephant and a fine horse were given to Malik 'Ambar by

Hasan 'Ali Beg, and also by the fact that Malik 'Ambar at this time wrote letters to the Khan-i-Khanan to be sent on to the court, in which he declared his allegiance and fervent desire to serve the emperor. Asad Beg noted that already at the time when his own master Abu'l Fazl had been in the Deccan, Malik 'Ambar had been looking around in distress for some service. He wished to join Abu'l Fazl, but certain others opposed it. So far as Asad Beg was concerned, 'Ambar was the paragon of all good qualities, a wonderful host and a devout Muslim. Indeed, were he to recount the qualities of this bravest of the men of the time, a chapter – nay, a book – would be needed. We are clearly at some distance from the malevolent image that the same Malik 'Ambar would acquire in Mughal texts of the 1610s and 1620s.[45]

The Mughal envoy now departed for the south, accompanied by 'Ambar's own young nephew as far as the frontier with Bijapur (*ta sarhad-i Bijapur*). The place at which Asad Beg entered 'Adil Shahi country was still a short distance from the town of Mangalbedha, where Mir Jamal-ud-Din and Mustafa Khan, the head of the Bijapur armies, were resident. Here, he was already given a letter from Mir Jamal-ud-Din in response to an earlier missive that Asad Beg had sent him. This letter contained rather hypocritical declarations of joy at Asad Beg's coming, and stated that the next day Mustafa Khan's son would meet him with a force. The day after that, he would be welcomed by a certain Haibat Khan, and thereafter by Mustafa Khan himself with the nobles of Bijapur and men on elephants. Orders also arrived from Sultan Ibrahim on the reception to be given to Asad Beg. The Mughal envoy was thus treated with due pomp and ceremony, as befitted the representative of a superior power.

Yet, it soon became clear that things were not as they appeared on the surface. True, Mir Jamal-ud-Din and the people with him displayed extraordinary hospitality. Several days were hence spent in Mangalbedha, until word came that festivities were to be held in honour of Ibrahim's daughter, to which both Mir Jamal-ud-Din and Asad Beg were invited. This meeting lasted all day. High quality food and drink, and all sorts of other things were made available, and when the festivities ended Asad Beg was given a fine, large elephant and two Arab horses with gilded saddles, as well as silver accoutrements. Besides, nine trays of diverse cloths, and rare chintz from the Karnatak were given him, together with a special golden tray with all sorts of jewels and rings on it. Asad Beg was also invited by the Bijapur nobles one after another in the days that followed, and each took care of him after his fashion. From each he got Arab horses, and high quality Deccani gifts, but the Mughal envoy began to chafe at the bit, and declared that he needed to see Ibrahim urgently. But the latter protested that such haste was unseemly and contrary to their custom. In keeping with Coutre's characterization, his agents even tried to tempt Asad Beg with an offer of 200,000 *huns*, if he would just stay on in Bijapur for some time. Asad Beg refused, but it soon became clear that it was by such means that Ibrahim had managed to manipulate Mir Jamal-ud-Din. This was the reason why the Sayyid from Shiraz was so reluctant to leave the Deccan. According to Asad Beg, each year Mir Jamal-ud-Din was making some 300,000 or 400,000 *huns* from Bijapur and Golconda, as if he had a *jagir* of 5,000. But the corruption went further still. Asad Beg claimed that the Khan-i-Khanan, too, was receiving like sums of money, and there was an agreement between him and Ibrahim to delay the departure of the palankeen of the latter's daughter from Mangalbedha. When asked about the delay, the Khan-i-Khanan claimed that the threat of Malik 'Ambar made the roads unsafe. What Ibrahim was unable to achieve by force, he was thus able to do by the judicious use of money.

Mughal carpet from the Santa Clara
Convent (Évora), Agra or Lahore, late
16th–early 17th century.
Lisbon, Museu Nacional de Arte Antiga
(MNAA) CAT. 48

Asad Beg's arrival on the scene was thus a nuisance to all parties. When they saw that he was impervious to bribes, Ibrahim at last invited to him to the city of Bijapur. The Mughal envoy now set out, with quite elaborate presents, including some horses, camels, Kashmiri shawls, as well as European cloth (*parchaha-i nafis-i wilayat*), worth some 20,000–25,000 rupees in all. But Ibrahim continued to procrastinate. When Asad Beg was a day short of Bijapur, he asked him to delay his arrival by two weeks, as there was an important festival to be attended to. During this further wait the lavish hospitality continued, with all sorts of food, drinks and fresh fruits, and good fodder for the animals. Besides, the custom was that the food would be brought in copper dishes (*degh*) and chinaware (*chini*), which were never taken back. Asad Beg thus accumulated a number of vessels and utensils, which became a nuisance, as it was not clear where to keep them. Ibrahim had also ordered that every day two men from among his principal courtiers (*az majlisiyan-i khassa*) would come and converse with Asad Beg to keep him entertained. They included Malik Qomi and Maulana Zuhuri (whom we have encountered above in Faizi's account), as well as Bichitr Khan, Mirak Mu'in-ud-Din and many others. Still, all of this was quite tiresome, and it was a relief when the festival of Shab-i Bar'at finally arrived. This was a rather elaborate affair, with the usual sweetmeats, fruit and dried fruits, and also a showy fireworks display, the high point of which was when two firework castles (which had been made at an expense of 2,000 *huns*) were set on fire side by side. When they were set alight, it was as if they were firing arms and cannon at each other, with an effect so frightening that the horses, camels and elephants in Asad Beg's camp became panic-stricken.

It was thus a great relief when Asad Beg was finally given permission to meet Ibrahim, and was brought to a house that had been kept ready at the edge of the tank (*tal*) of Bijapur. Here the Bijapur ruler was supposed to have a first formal meeting with him, in order ceremonially to receive the *farman* from Akbar. He agreed that he would enter alone, but when the moment came, other courtiers also barged in, which Asad Beg took to be an offensive breach of etiquette. Still, he carried on with the ceremony, which required Ibrahim to acknowledge Mughal superiority, perform the *sijda* and bow down in the direction of the absent Akbar. The *farman* was now opened and read, but at a certain moment Ibrahim began to find its contents offensive, and started to comment in Marathi (*ba zaban-i Marhata*) to his chief Brahmin adviser, Antu Pandit. Asad Beg was hence obliged to negotiate directly with Ibrahim, while sending the courtiers away, and this posed a minor problem, for while Ibrahim 'understood Persian well, … he could not answer in that language, and spoke in a broken (*shikasta*) way'. Still, the conversation was conducted, and when it ended, Ibrahim insisted once more that Asad Beg could not leave the same day as this was against their tradition (*rasm*). For his part, Asad Beg insisted that he had to leave quickly and accompanied, too, by both Mir Jamal-ud-Din and Ibrahim's daughter. And finally, there was the question of the royal elephant Atish Para. Ibrahim now replied that this particular elephant had been rendered useless (*bar taraf shuda*) two years before, and that in its place another animal called Chanchal would be sent. This arrangement was accepted, and further gifts were ceremonially exchanged.

The following day, after Asad Beg had spent several hours in festivities, a further message was brought to him, to the effect that Ibrahim was not happy to give him just one elephant. He had hence also decided to give him a rare black Arab horse, called Chini, which he had bought in Bijapur for 3,000 *huns* (equivalent to 9,000 Mughal rupees). He also invited Asad Beg to the palace, to bid him a formal farewell. Here was an occasion for Asad Beg to inspect the fort, and he noted that it consisted of triple concentric fortifications. Beyond each moat, which was wide and full of water, was a double wall. Between each level of fortification were two lines of trees and quite a large amount of greenery. When they had passed the third door, two lines of gunners, archers and swordsmen could be seen. When the Mughal party reached the interior palace (*daulat-khana*), they passed through another gate. A great display had clearly been put on to impress the Mughal envoy, for there were expensive carpets and vases spread out there. They then went into a courtyard, where they found themselves in a large open area, clean and sparkling, with decorated galleries and covered vestibules in parallel. The main gallery was 2 yards high, and some 60 hands wide, but with no visible columns. In this gallery there was a golden throne studded with jewels, near which was a seat, with a number of reclining cushions, and single and double lamps of gold and silver, some twenty in all. Small pieces of velvet and brocade were spread around, and between every two lamps and incense-burners were trellis-works of gold or silver. Asad Beg went and sat by the throne. After some time a door opened at the other side of the palace, and Ibrahim in all his splendour, accompanied by three or four persons, entered the place. Asad Beg stood up to greet him, and the Bijapur ruler advanced towards him. The three or four people with him, soaked in perfume from neck to waist, stood by. The sound of continuous music, which came from the door from where he had emerged, seemed to engage Ibrahim's attention. But since Asad Beg was his guest, he began to make conversation with him. Parallel to this gallery there were three niches, one very high and two somewhat smaller. In the largest was the elephant Chanchal. At the other two were two female elephants. All three were offered by Ibrahim to Asad Beg to take back with him. Their conversation went on until two watches of the night, and then Asad Beg took his leave. The Mughal envoy tried to drive the hardest bargain possible, extracting as much by way of tribute in jewels and precious objects as he could. By the time he reached home, it was almost dawn. However, a bone of contention remained between the two, for Ibrahim had insisted on taking Asad Beg's badge of discipleship (*shast-i muridi*), which he had received directly from Akbar, and refused to return it. It was only after elaborate negotiations that the Mughal envoy was able to have this precious symbolic object returned several days later.

Affairs were thus concluded by now from the Mughal envoy's point of view. He already had the elephant and horse, besides other significant tribute-goods, as he had been instructed. The only remaining question was how to deal with the recalcitrant Mir Jamal-ud-Din. Asad Beg put matters to him bluntly, and told him the game was up. He and the Khan-i-Khanan would now have to expedite matters with regard to the Bijapur bride. A letter was sent out to the Khan-i-Khanan, who reluctantly agreed that he would make his way to receive the princess. Still, Mir Jamal-ud-Din tried a few more desperate delaying tactics, but to no avail. The Bijapur force that was to accompany them also persisted in dragging their feet. Rumours were periodically heard that Malik 'Ambar was on his way with a force to attack them. But Asad Beg managed to keep his head in the midst of all this, and presently a Mughal party came along to accompany them as far as Ahmadnagar. Here, in the Ahmadnagar fort, the Sona Mahal was kept aside for Prince Daniyal, and everything was decorated and prepared. The newly arrived princess was also to stay in the same palace. Asad Beg's good services were brought to the prince's attention, and he was duly rewarded, with Daniyal's generosity being contrasted to the miserliness of the Khan-i-Khanan. The fact that Asad Beg had managed to persuade Mir Jamal-ud-Din to return, and brought back the daughter of the

'Adil Khan, besides the elephants and other *peshkash*, allowed him to return to the Mughal court in very good odour.[40]

In Asad Beg's account the Portuguese in Goa have an insignificant role to play. They appear on three or four different occasions: first, some European cloth emerges among the gifts; then a box of Portuguese manufacture (*sanduqcha-i firangi*) is mentioned in regard to the transport of some jewels; third, wine of Portuguese origin is listed among the return presents sent by Ibrahim for Akbar; and last, a Portuguese figure is referred to in the context of a discussion of tobacco and its qualities in the Mughal court. Where the third of these is concerned, Asad Beg informs us that Chanchal, the female elephant, was used to drinking two Akbari *man* of wine a day, and that eventually two of the casks of high quality Portuguese wine (*sharab-i nafis-i purtagali*) had to be broached to calm her down on the way to Agra. But if the Portuguese have a minor place, what is even more remarkable is the almost total absence of the Safavids – who had played such a prominent role in Faizi's account – in Asad Beg's narrative. Rather, one has the impression that the affairs of the Deccan have been reduced to a rather straightforward game between the Deccan sultanates and the Mughals, with Malik 'Ambar in the role of a minor annoyance, who can, however, be controlled by deft diplomacy. The main problem, if one is to follow Asad Beg, is that the Mughals themselves are so divided that the cunning Ibrahim can easily sow the seeds of dissension among them by the use of bribes and promises. A couple of decades of cohabitation with the Bijapur monarch has thus produced a new equilibrium, one in which he appears to hold the diplomatic high ground, conceding relatively little to the Mughals.

CONCLUSION

The remaining quarter-century of Ibrahim 'Adil Shah's reign did not see a major alteration in this relationship, and if anything, the Mughal position weakened somewhat in view of the growing power of Malik 'Ambar. It was only in the late 1620s that matters began to change, with the accession of Shahjahan corresponding broadly with the death of Ibrahim. To this extent, the reign of Jahangir (1605–27) can be seen as a hiatus where the Deccan policy of the Mughals is concerned, and in general this is a reign where few major expansionary moves are contemplated or executed. This was also a matter of some relief for the Portuguese State of India, which had its hands full already with the Dutch in South-East Asia and on the Coromandel coast, and with the English Company in Surat, to say nothing of major problems with a host of Asian polities, from the Safavids to the Tokugawas. The long reign of Ibrahim 'Adil Shah II, which lasted almost a half-century, thus marks something of a watershed in Portuguese relations with the Deccan. In the first three quarters of the sixteenth century the 'Idalcão' 'Adil Khan was a major thorn in Portuguese flesh and one of the periodic threats to Goa, as well as to other Portuguese interests on the Konkan coast. Hostilities had flared up time and again, whether in the 1530s with Ibrahim 'Adil Shah I, or the 1560s with 'Ali 'Adil Shah, to say nothing of the protracted tussle and negotiation over the status and claims of the pretender resident in Goa, Mealecão, or 'Ali bin Yusuf 'Adil Khan.[41] For the first time, from the 1580s, this equation definitely changed, and the change was principally because Bijapur and Goa finally had a common enemy in the Mughals, whose expansion into the Deccan both feared. This common fear helped define a vastly improved relationship between 1580 and 1630, when numbers of Portuguese private traders could enter Bijapur with impunity and take part in the lucrative diamond and textile trade of the Deccan, as Coutre's account amply helps us document. The reign of Ibrahim 'Adil Shah II was in a sense a 'Golden Age' for Portuguese-Bijapur relations.

But this idyll could not last. The pressure exerted by Shahjahan on his accession to the throne, culminating in the Treaty of Submission for Bijapur and Golconda of 1636, the declining economic strength of Goa itself, and a series of other minor factors meant that by the late 1630s the rulers of Bijapur were looking for other trading partners, a fact that eventually led to the opening of the Dutch East India Company factory in Vengurla. But Mughal pressure also had other unforeseen effects, forcing Bijapur into an ambitious southward campaign of its own, and leading to the conquest of lands in the Karnatak – both to the west on the Kanara coast, and in the areas from Senji to Tanjavur. The account of Asad Beg thus marks an interesting moment when diplomacy and money-power dominated over the use of armed force. But seen from the longer-term viewpoint, the period simply marked a temporary halt in the inexorable march of the Mughal war-machine into the southernmost reaches of the Indian peninsula.

Two Portuguese Visions of Jahangir's India: Jerónimo Xavier and Manuel Godinho de Erédia

Jorge Flores

INTRODUCTION

Studies of European visions of the Mughal empire during its 'golden age' – between Akbar coming to the throne (1556) and the death of Aurangzeb (1707) – have fundamentally concentrated on two diverse aspects that are supported by two series of Western texts. The first focus has been on the successive Jesuit missions from 1580 to the court of the 'Great Mughal'. Most of these studies, mainly the work of historians from within the Society itself, have published important documents and stressed the successes and failures of the respective missions, as well as examining the individual careers of the missionaries in question. This has followed a somewhat traditional approach, although the scholars have sometimes been the first to emphasize the importance of their sources for the history of the Mughal empire. It is within this context that the work of the prolific Henry Hosten, followed successively by Edward Maclagan, Henry Heras and John Correia-Afonso, deserves recognition. In conjunction, an area that has grown significantly in recent decades has focused on the impact that the Jesuit missionaries' presence at the court of the Mughal emperors had on Mughal art. Closely associated with the analysis of imperial vocabulary, the appropriation of forms and ideas and the study of mutual cultural perceptions, this line of research has developed through the important work produced by Milo Beach, Ebba Koch, Susan Stronge and Gauvin Bailey, among others.

The second line of research, examining the relationship between Europe and the 'Great Mughal' in the sixteenth to seventeenth centuries, has concentrated on the 'race' to reach the empire's treasures at a time when trading companies came to the fore. While this phenomenon was particularly focused on the ports in Gujarat, it also had

political and diplomatic ramifications at the imperial court that cannot be ignored. This issue, covering the last twenty years of Akbar's rule and above all pertinent to the reign of Jahangir, is based on the importance given to a group of seventeenth-century authors from Protestant Europe.[1] English observers unquestionably established their hegemony in this field, through such figures as the merchant Ralph Fitch (1584–6) or the adventurer Thomas Coryat (1615–17).[2] The most significant work among Dutch texts, which date from a slightly later period and were less known at that time, was the *Remonstrantie*, written by Francisco Pelsaert (1627),[3] the agent of the VOC (Dutch East India Company) in Agra. This text would be heavily used in Joannes de Laet's compilation of Western texts on the Mughal empire, written in Latin in 1631. Entitled *De Imperio Magni Mogolis*,[4] de Laet's work was an enormous success throughout Europe, including Portugal.[5]

However, there can be no denying that Sir Thomas Roe's journey and embassy to Jahangir's court in 1615–19 played the decisive role in establishing Western knowledge of the Mughal empire. Roe's diary and correspondence – alongside the report by Edward Terry, the embassy's chaplain – are a milestone in European perception of the empire founded and consolidated by the descendants of Timur.[6] Previous descriptions had failed to have such an impact, as can be seen from an intriguing text called *A true and almost incredible report of an Englishman…*, published by Robert Coverte in London in 1612. The extraordinarily long title of this pamphlet – written by an Englishman who had been shipwrecked off Surat in 1609 and had then returned to Europe overland, crossing northern India in 1610–11 – symptomatically ends: … *with a discovery of a Great Emperour called the Great Mogoll, a Prince not till knowne to our English Nation.*[7] It may be that Coverte exaggerated to make his writing and his adventure more interesting, but it is not completely unrealistic to claim that in 1612 news in London on Jahangir's empire would at best have been sparse, or at least little known.

There are also two documents that are inextricably associated with Thomas Roe's travels in Mughal India and with the resulting impact on Europe, as they provided the original imagery for Western perceptions of the Mughal empire. The first is a map by William Baffin (1619) that shows the empire according to information that must have been provided by Roe. The second is the seal of Jahangir, which became known in England from a letter that the emperor sent to King James I via the English ambassador.

This second area of study – the multiple seventeenth-century Western visions of the Mughal empire – is related to the parallel area of the cultural issues arising from observing and describing non-European societies in the modern period.[8] Donald Lach was the first to provide a framework for Asia within this field,[9] but specific studies of southern Asia have brought considerable advances over the last ten years.[10]

This is not the place to discuss the strengths and weaknesses of this analytical model, which lies at the frontier between history, literature and anthropology and is dominated by specialists in Western culture, rather than scholars working on Asian societies.[11] It is also interesting to note that there is a strong tendency to see each author as a traveller who had his own agenda and to see each text as a milestone in travel literature. This excludes anyone who fails to meet the vague definition of 'traveller': those people whose writings were not included in the main collections of travel writing in the transition from the sixteenth to the seventeenth century.

The two texts examined below were written between 1610 and 1611 and are thus contemporaries of many of the aforementioned reports. They also provide sufficient grounds to justify the need to challenge this simplistic approach and overcome the rigid classifications proposed. They were written by two very different men, the Jesuit Jerónimo (Jerome) Xavier and the cartographer Manuel Godinho de Erédia, neither of whom were truly Portuguese, despite their close associations with the Portuguese presence in Asia, and neither of the texts was published at the time. Instead, manuscript copies circulated in the Iberian Peninsula, well outside the circles that produced and read European travel literature. Within this context Xavier's text is so far removed from the canons of missionary writing that it could have been written by a lay author. Apart from its interest as a European vision of Jahangir's court, it is of equal importance for the study of the empire itself. In turn, Erédia's text should ideally be seen in conjunction with his later writings and, above all, his cartography on the 'Mogor'. His work demonstrates how a non-Jesuit Western vision of the empire had started to be constructed before Roe or de Laet, even though they achieved a level of European projection that Erédia's writings and maps would never reach.

JERÓNIMO XAVIER AND THE *TRATADO DA CORTE E CAZA DE IAMGUIR PACHÁ REY DOS MOGORES* (1610)

Jerónimo de Ezpeleta y Goñi, born in the Spanish province of Navarre, was the grandnephew of Francis Xavier, the central figure in the Jesuit mission to the Mughal court at the end of the sixteenth century and the dawn of the seventeenth. When Jerónimo joined the Society of Jesus in 1568, he adopted his great-uncle's surname and, following his time as a novice and his studies in Alcalá and Toledo, landed in Goa at the end of September 1581. Thirteen years later, in 1594, Jerónimo Xavier was chosen to lead the third mission to the court of Akbar.

Between arriving in Lahore in May 1595 as superior of the mission and returning definitively to Goa in 1615, where he was rector of the college of São Paulo until his death (June 1617), Jerónimo Xavier spent twenty years at the heart of the Mughal empire. During this time he was an eyewitness to its travails and its transformations, was in close contact with emperors Akbar and Jahangir, and was able to observe major changes in the empire.[12] He held high hopes that both emperors would be drawn towards Christianity and was delighted by the (temporary) conversion of Jahangir's nephews. He also helped solve problems between the empire and the Portuguese 'State of India' and saw many Europeans – mainly English – appear at the Mughal court.

Jerónimo Xavier wrote many texts on the empire ruled by Akbar and Jahangir, ranging from letters to his superiors in Goa and Rome through to personal messages for family and friends. He learnt to speak Persian, an essential tool in his missionary work, and translated countless works – mostly religious but also including some ethical and political texts – into that language. These works can now be found in archives and libraries around the world.[13]

The document analysed below, which is attributed to him, was written around 1610, at the end of his experience in the Mughal empire. Hereafter called *Tratado*, its full title is *Tratado da Corte, e Caza de Iamguir Pachá rey dos Mogores; Em que brevemente se trata dos Reinos que tem; e de seos Tizouros, e o grande estado e preheminencia com que se serve de suas portas para dentro; suas mulheres, filhos, e seos grandes capitais* (Treatise on the Court and Household of Iamguir Pachá, King of the Mughals; which briefly deals with the Kingdoms he has, and his Treasures, and the great majesty and pre-eminence which is used inside; his wives, children and his main noblemen) (f. 1r). The document consists of nineteen folios and includes the following chapters:

Attributed to Jerónimo (Jerome) Xavier,
Tratado da Corte e Caza de Iamguir Pachá Rey dos Mogores (Treatise on the Court and Household of Iamguir Pachá King of the Mughals), f. 81, 1610.
Lisbon, IAN/TT CAT. 26

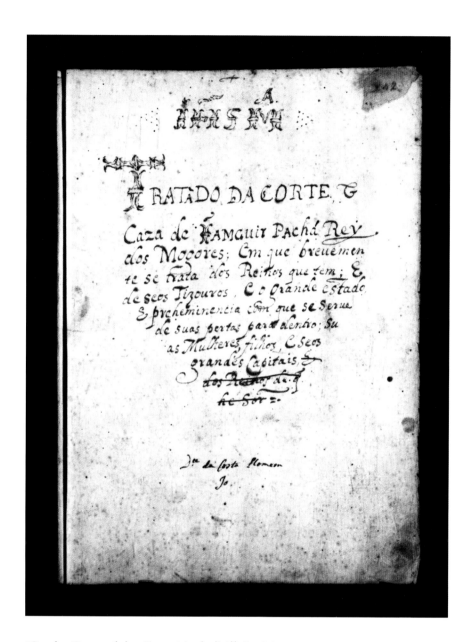

'On the Court of the Great Mughal' (ff. 2r–3r)

'On the children and generation of this King' (ff. 3r–4v)

'On when the King appears before his people, and the order of his household' (ff. 4v–6r)

'On the wives that this King has, and how service is inside, and the richness of his attire, and of his persons' (ff. 6r–7v)

'The costs of his household' (f. 7v)

'The costs of his animals and other things in the service of this King' (ff. 7v–8r)

'On the Treasures and income that this King has' (ff. 8v–9v)

'On his nobles and of their greatness' (f. 10r)

'On the Kingdoms that this King has' (f. 10v)

[Conclusion] (ff. 10v–11r)

'Incomes of the children of Iamguir Pachá King of the Mughals and of his nobles' (ff. 12r–19r)

In contrast to the annual letters sent by the Jesuit 'Mughal Mission', Xavier's *Tratado* was not concerned with the progress or setbacks affecting missionary work either in the court or indeed in the empire, which included all the narrative devices customarily found in this type of document.[14] In fact, he very rarely even mentions Christianity, and his comments on Jahangir do not concern the latter's constantly postponed supposed conversion. The only concrete reference linking the emperor to the Christian faith and the Jesuits is from the pen of the copyist rather than by the missionary (ff. 10v–11r). In this sense Xavier's text is undeniably similar to writings by other missionaries who 'restricted themselves' to describing the Mughal empire, defining the court and drawing up a profile of the emperor. Both the substance and the structure of the text mean that Xavier's *Tratado* is to Jahangir's household what Antonio Monserrate's *Relação do Equebar, rei dos mogores* (1582) was to Akbar's,[15] namely a document of ethnographic nature. To a large extent, it could have been written by any educated merchant or adventurer, provided they were curious, had a liking for writing and had spent many years at the Mughal court.

The *Tratado* was never published. However, despite only appearing in manuscript form, it appears to have circulated fairly widely in its time. In addition to the Portuguese version – the most complete – at the Torre do Tombo archive, Lisbon, there is also a very similar Castilian version in an important codex at the Biblioteca Nacional, Madrid (hereafter BNM version).[16] A third version, also in Castilian but substantially shorter, is known at the Real Academia de la Historia, Madrid (hereafter RAH version).[17] The original very probably stayed in Goa and has since been lost. Consequently, the text used here is the one at the Torre do Tombo, part of the Casa Real collection (hereafter TT version), where it was only incorporated in 1992, after coming from the Arquivo Histórico do Ministério das Finanças.[18]

There are considerable differences between the three manuscripts, although this is not the moment to analyse the details of these variations in content, date and even authorship of the text.[19] The anonymous 'digest' at the RAH, which is too brief and fragmented for comparison with the other manuscripts, is henceforth discarded and I will instead focus on the TT and BNM versions. All available evidence suggests that the *Tratado* was written at the Mughal court in 1610 or, at latest, early in 1611. Later copied in Goa by a layman (TT version), it was subsequently sent to Portugal, where other copies (presumably) and Castilian translations (RAH and BNM versions) were produced. In all probability Jerónimo Xavier wrote the text as a valuable source of information for the secular authorities, like so many other similar reports sent to Goa by missionaries working at the Mughal court, few of which have survived. One important fact is that the Society's archive in Rome contains no version of this text, in contrast to Monserrate's aforementioned *Relação*, nor yet do any passages from it appear in the reports that the Jesuits regularly published in Europe.[20]

The TT version attributes the text to Jerónimo Xavier, while the BNM version states that it is the work of Father Manuel Pinheiro. It is quite possible that the text was, in fact, a collectively written work that incorporated contributions from the other missionaries to the 'Mogor'. However, Xavier must have played the central role, not only because he was the superior on the mission, but also for the simple reason that he knew Jahangir's circles better than any. In contrast, Manuel Pinheiro is known to have been a 'grassroots' man who was closer to the common people than to the elites, a missionary who spent far more time with the Christian community in Lahore than he did at the imperial court.

The differences in content between the two main versions of the *Tratado* merit closer consideration. For a start, there are interesting differences in the proposed intention. The BNM version has a different level of involvement and contact with potential readers, and concern about public readership of the text and a relationship with that audience is present in its writing process. According to the copyist, Father Pinheiro decided not to include many other items of information on the Mughal empire, stating that 'not to make people think it was fantasy, he has omitted many things that in our homeland of Spain will seem questionable and incredible'.[21]

In contrast, the Lisbon manuscript includes a long and significant final section not found in the BNM version, an omission that seems to have been the result of an editorial decision taken by the copyist. As will be shown, the section entitled 'Incomes of the children of Iamguir Pachá King of the Mughals and of his nobles' (TT, ff. 12r–19r) totals one third of the entire text and seems very like a very dense appendix, even for the most interested reader, presenting a list of the Mughal nobility and their respective revenues. Nonetheless, it is of great significance for contemporary historians working on the reign of Jahangir. The copyist of the BNM version evidently saw it, but opted not to reproduce it, which explains the explicit reference to 'a list which is not included here to avoid prolixity' (p. 78). Instead, he gives just three general figures that can be calculated from the list, namely the number of the empire's *mansabdars* (nobles), the number of soldiers and the total income of these noblemen.

Xavier's *Tratado* includes all the ingredients found in the Western reports that would stimulate seventeenth-century European interest in the Mughal empire. He starts by describing the city of Agra – the centre of the empire, whose grandiose scale, wealth and abundance all impressed the Jesuit – before going on to the royal family, including a reference to the late Emperor Akbar. Much of Xavier's text is taken up with descriptions of Jahangir's wives and the imperial harem, coming immediately after an interesting analysis of the emperor's daily routine and the 'choreography' of his public appearances.

The second half of the text is dominated by facts and figures, as the author audits the court's expenses and calculates the value of Jahangir's treasury and revenues. This is followed by a summary of the number of nobles who served the emperor, and their respective hierarchy and incomes, which acts as a sort of prologue to the long and repetitive appendix 'Incomes of the children of Iamguir Pachá King of the Mughals and of his nobles'. Before coming to this list, Xavier's text provides an incomplete and fairly inaccurate list of the 'kingdoms' (*subas*, provinces) that formed Jahangir's empire, while the *Tratado* itself, as noted above, was actually concluded by the copyist.

It is impossible to cover each and every section of Jerónimo Xavier's text in detail here. However, some of the issues he examines are among the most important *topoi* of Western writing on the Great Mughal. Most significant among them are the fascination with the imperial treasury and the colourful description of the harem, although in the case of the Timurid rulers, this never reached the level of Europe's obsession with the Ottoman seraglio.[22] In contrast, other equally significant aspects of imperial culture under Jahangir completely escaped Jerónimo Xavier. One such area was the artistic dimension of imperial ideology, where he paid no attention to Jahangir's interest in painting or his appreciation and knowledge of art. In similar fashion, the only suggestion of a physical and psychological portrait of the emperor is a brief and negative assessment of his character.

Notwithstanding these 'failings', the *Tratado* is still an important source to gauge the perception of a Western observer – in this case, a Jesuit missionary – of both Jahangir's

Wine cup of Emperor Jahangir, Mughal
India, 1612–13, jade.
Providence, Museum of Art, Rhode
Island School of Design CAT. 59

court and of Timurid political culture at that time. John Richards's important study of imperial authority in this period is of particular interest.[23] It is known that Jahangir concentrated on court life and refining its culture rather than consolidating and expanding his empire. He acted every inch the prince, surrounding himself with courtiers rather than soldiers like a warrior leader, and opted to intensify and perfect the household gestures, rituals, symbols and practices that Akbar had established under Abu'l Fazl years before.

The almost divine aura that Jahangir ostentatiously cultivated would naturally not have gone unnoticed to an observer of Xavier's calibre:

Such is the king's majesty, for he wishes to demonstrate that his [people] serve him so truly and with such respect, that all the aristocracy and the common people are in his service as no other King in this world has. He is so respected and revered by all, and they wish so much to do whatsoever he pleases that all that is left is [for them] to worship him as God. For whenever he appears, which is three times during the day and once at night, the flattering joy with which the people wishes to receive him, some prostrating themselves on the ground should the king ask them anything, bowing down many times and touching their hands to the ground and then on their heads, praising him with a thousand words, telling him that he is the lord of the world and the King of Kings, among many other things that will exalt his position, is quite something to be seen [f. 4v].

Attributed to Manohar, *Darbar
of Jahangir*, Mughal India, c.1607.
St Petersburg Branch of the Institute
of Oriental Studies/Russian Academy
of Sciences (BIOS/RAS) CAT. 98

This also explains the reference to the ritual of the nobles offering gifts to the emperor: 'his nobles, to win over his trust, try to bring *dinários* (dinars) earrings and items to give him, of great size' (f. 3r). The act of giving *nazr* was a practice that dated back to the reign of Akbar and consisted of those nobles who held the higher *mansabs* giving the emperor gold coins (*muhrs*) that were no longer in circulation. This process of the nobility giving the emperor these *dinários* simultaneously confirmed their loyalty, a significant symbolic gesture that Xavier must have witnessed time and again.[24]

The 'pride and arrogance' (f. 3v) that Jahangir used when dealing with the local monarchs – starting with Shah 'Abbas – also merited the Jesuit's criticism. It was as if Xavier had, *avant la lettre*, been able to see the meaningful and symbolically significant embrace between the 'holder of the world' and the Safavid ruler, shown in a magnificent miniature by Abu'l Hasan from c.1618.[25] However, it is the chapter entitled 'On when the King appears before his people …' (ff. 4v–6r) that allows deeper analysis. Xavier details the emperor's ritualized daily life, from worshipping the sun 'early in the morning' and his appearance at the *Jharoka-I darshan* 'being seen by all', until his return after nightfall to his private quarters (*Khwabgah*), where he would listen to 'some good story-tellers and soothsayers' before sleeping. In between, he paid regular visits to the royal harem, led *darbar* in the *Diwan-i amn* and attended the closed meetings held at the end of the day in the *Ghusalkhana*.[26]

The following excerpt ends with a very negative image of Jahangir, where the tone is set by the emperor's apparent lack of any religious identity.

This King cannot be said to be a Moor, nor a Gentile, nor a Christian for he has no law that he definitely believes in as other people believe. He is a barbarian who lives his life according to the vagaries of fortune, taken wherever his appetites lead him, full of great pride and arrogance regarding the world, believing that he alone is the master of all, and he is most cruel and vengeful, showing no mercy [f. 6v].

Xavier's harsh image of Jahangir is based on three secular aspects rather than characterizing him as a sort of 'man of no religion'. First, a Jesuit missionary of the late sixteenth to early seventeenth century, who would be accustomed to using reason, and observing order and rules, would be ill at ease with a man who was swayed exclusively by whim. Secondly, there was the dangerous 'absolutization' of power that would, as Xavier noted in another section of the *Tratado*, 'cause the perdition of this barbarian' (f. 3v). The third aspect was the excessively iron rule that Jahangir exercised. Xavier was evidently referring to the rebellion by Prince Khusrau in 1605, which Jahangir had crushed with brutal violence. Adopting a common practice at the time, he had the sultan – his own son – blinded so that he could neither exercise power nor even dream of seizing it. Meanwhile, his supporters – especially the leading nobles among them – were executed with horrific cruelty in a public demonstration that was designed to awe the people and deter any further revolt. The same fate befell Arjun, the fifth Sikh guru who had blessed Khusrau at a meeting in Gogindwal (Punjab). The guru's approval provoked a backlash from Jahangir, who seized Arjun's property and had him killed, thereby creating the first Sikh martyr. Meanwhile, Jerónimo Xavier witnessed all these events, recording them in a letter from 1606.[27]

Another important topic in the Tratado is the author's characterization of the Mughal nobility and of their relations with Jahangir. Like so many other seventeenth-century Europeans, Xavier took the opportunity offered by the fabulous wealth of the treasury to criticize the emperor for abusively appropriating the legacies of deceased noblemen.

Moreover, they have a custom that the other Moorish Kings adopt with their vassals and noblemen and people in their service, which is that after their death, the King inherits their goods from them. Thus, he gains countless wealth and adds ill-gotten treasures from the sweat of his unfortunate vassals, and from his domains and captaincies, forcing on them one hundred thousand efforts and impositions so that they acquire this wealth which the King then takes from them. And their wives

Dagger, Mughal India,
17th century, jade and steel.
Oporto, private collection CAT. 7

and children are disinherited and [left] with little more than nothing [only what] they can hide with great secrecy to survive so that the King does not take it from them. And the children of all these [men] have to use their lances to win the favours that he grants, and little by little with their lances and good services they ultimately gain the same positions as their fathers. But it is like that in all things with the Moors, their positions as favourites are short-lived for a little gossip or complaining is enough for the King to dismiss them from their posts and captaincies. And when they fall from grace they are destroyed, and either in death or in life, he is always the heir to their goods [f. 8v].

This very harsh portrait of Jahangir – showing him preying rapaciously on the property of those who had served him faithfully throughout their lives and unmoved by the misery that he knowingly inflicted on their widows and orphans – matches the seventeenth-century Western vision of the Mughal nobility's system of inheritance. Over fifty years later François Bernier would draw up a damning indictment of the Mughal empire's political system, based precisely on the appropriation of the nobles' property and the absence of private property. This attitude was widely repeated by other Western authors, shaping European discourse on the empire and its political system for many years. In fact, this repetition has been interpreted as a warning to Europe's absolute monarchies about their excesses, and specifically against the tyrannical tendencies shown by Louis XIV and Colbert.[28]

As Xavier had done in 1610, Bernier clearly exaggerated in 1670–71, revealing their failure to understand the system.[29] In fact, the emperor only kept a very small percentage of the goods of deceased nobles. Moreover, this only applied to the highest category of *mansabdars* (5,000 zat), precisely those who, as Jerónimo Xavier himself stated 'have as much land and income as minor kings, and equal grandeur in their households and service as the Kings themselves' (f. 10r). This phenomenon presumably corresponded to an affirmation of the principle that every vassal – including the most powerful – was subordinate to the emperor. Yet, even in these cases the property was not completely confiscated. In most cases the emperor only appropriated the *mutaliba*, or the sum that the imperial treasury (*khazana*) had loaned to the deceased nobleman. In brief, it is questionable as to whether this practice had any great impact on the finances of the Mughal nobility.

The last section of the *Tratado*, a list of the empire's *mansabdars*, to some extent also returns to one of the themes that Western observers focused on most. The total number, the military might and the accounts of the nobility's wealth were an equally important *topos* in European descriptions of Mughal India. William Hawkins, who was in Jahangir's court between April 1609 and November 1611, included in his report 'A briefe discourse on the strength, wealth, and government with some customes of the

Great Mogol, which I have both seen and gathered by his chiefe officers and overseers of all his estate'.[30] It seems unlikely that he had access to reliable information on this subject, as he provides a highly inaccurate list of 41 *mansabdars* of between 3,000 and 5,000 *zat*, having mentioned the *mansabs* of the Sultans Parwiz and Khurram and – a serious error – those of the emperor and his mother, who never had them. Athar Ali uses this document in his monumental study on the Mughal nobility, but only as a curiosity and without giving it any credence whatsoever.[31]

In contrast to Hawkins, Xavier makes no mention of the names of Jahangir's nobles, merely referring to three figures apart from Sultan Khusrau – 'arrested and now subject to his [Jahangir's] grace' (f. 12r), an allusion to the violent end to the prince's revolt against his father in 1605. Thus, the Jesuit explicitly names Princes Parwiz and Khurram, while saving for last the name of the most important noble in the empire after the members of the royal family. The man in question was 'Chana Chana', the 'great favourite of the king, as was Don Álvaro de Luna, and for that reason, the king elevated him so' (f. 12r). 'Chana Chana' is clearly a corruption of 'Khan-i Khanan', or Lord of Lords, the highest of the imperial titles, which was normally attributed exclusively to one noble at a time. In this case, Xavier was referring to Mirza 'Abdur Rahim, son of the Persian Bairam Khan, who had been regent of the empire during Akbar's minority (1556–60). Mirza 'Abdur Rahim was an eminent nobleman who had distinguished himself in the service of both Akbar and Jahangir, accumulating immense power until his death in 1627.[32] This explains the intriguing comparison with Dom Álvaro de Luna who, under Juan II of Castile, was the all-powerful Constable of Castile until his execution in 1453.[33]

Jerónimo Xavier gives no further names, nor unfortunately does he consider the ethnic diversity of the Mughal nobility. Moreover, unlike Thomas Roe, he makes absolutely no reference to the existence of nobles who were the emperor's disciples (*khazanads*), a personal devotion shown by the family and hereditary imperial service. Inspired by Abu'l Fazl, Akbar had first created this form of service, while it was Jahangir who would consolidate it during his reign.[34]

There is no doubt, however, that this section of the manuscript goes beyond merely creating an image, and means far more than a simple Western exercise in representing the empire. In fact, the *Tratado* is a useful instrument for studying the Mughal nobility in Jahangir's time. Xavier had had a list of the empire's *mansabdars* in his hands, a document from the Mughal chancellery that the Jesuit perhaps copied and adapted. It was clearly not a report on the *sawar*, the level that established the cavalry contingent (*tabinan*) that depended on each *mansabdar*, but was instead a report on the *zat*, or the level that defined the personal rank of a specific nobleman and his respective salary.[35] Following the classification of the *zat*, the missionary produced an exhaustive list, on a scale of one to six, of the classes of the nobles' horses. This establishes the quality of the horses, according to a classification that the *A'in-i-Akbari* had established a decade before.[36] Nonetheless, the list of *mansabdars* at the end of the *Tratado* raises a series of questions and requires a detailed study that will obviously have to be done elsewhere.[37]

MANUEL GODINHO DE ERÉDIA, THE *DISCURSO SOBRE A PROVINÇIA DO INDOSTAN CHAMADA MOGÛL* (1611) AND THE 'TABOAS DO MOGOR'

A contemporary of Jerónimo Xavier's *Tratado*, the *Discourse on the Province of Hindustan called Mughal* is an intriguing work by Manuel Godinho de Erédia that also focuses on Mughal India. However, the similarities between the two works go little further than their date, as the texts adopt very different perspectives and their respective authors head along widely divergent paths.

Erédia was born in Malacca around 1560 and died in Goa in 1623.[38] The son of a Portuguese of Castilian and Italian ancestry (João Erédia Acquaviva) and a Malay princess from Sulawesi, he spent his life convincing himself – and trying to convince others – that he came from a noble lineage that he insisted was related to the Jesuits Claudio and Rodolfo Acquaviva. He brazenly displayed this supposed nobility in an imaginative coat of arms, and used the same openness to request honours both from the king (Order of Christ) and the pope ('Order of the Discovery of Meridional India', an order Erédia himself had founded). Equally, he had no hesitation in boasting that he had occupied posts – such as chief cosmographer of Portugal – that he never truly held.

This culturally rich figure was as well informed and multi-talented as he was an eccentric and an adventurer. Erédia lived and worked right at the border where several cultures met. His entry into the Jesuit college in Goa (1575–6), where he would later teach mathematics, evidently provided him with the learning and cultural cohesion that he often demonstrated in his writings. Nonetheless, as his Jesuit superiors soon realized, Erédia had no vocation for the spiritual life. Thus, despite being brought into the Society by Valignano in 1579, Erédia left the following year. Curiously, his earliest known writings only date from the turn of the century, when he was aged around forty. Many of the texts and maps he produced, which date from the period between *c.*1599 and *c.*1622, deal with the Malay world and relate to his lifelong obsession with discovering the 'Island of Gold' and 'Meridional India'.

As the nineteenth century dawned, Manuel Godinho de Erédia's work attracted the attention of António Lourenço de Caminha, a scholar who owned – and hurriedly published – two manuscripts by the cartographer. Subsequently, the fact that some of Erédia's most important texts and maps were kept in European libraries has brought both the man and his work a reasonably high international profile since the last third of the nineteenth century. This was further helped by the interest that much of his work has for the history of the Malay archipelago and its connections to the controversial subject of the discovery of Australia.

The vast range of Manuel Godinho de Erédia's work – covering mathematics, cartography, painting, geography and botany – fully deserved an overall study and systematic publication, a task that Jorge Faro undertook between 1950 and 1960 but unfortunately never completed.[39] Simultaneously, Armando Cortesão inventoried and assessed Erédia's cartography in *Portugaliae Monumenta Cartographica*.[40] More recently, Erédia's work has been the subject of renewed interest among historians, as shown by the projects – either completed or ongoing – to publish his writings.[41]

Considering the fundamental stages of his life and the ultimate aim of his projects – presented here in highly abbreviated form – it can easily be concluded that his relationship with Mughal India was little more than a casual one.[42] However, his contact – albeit indirect – with the descendants of Timur started at a relatively early date. While still a member of the Society of Jesus in Goa, 'Brother Manuel Godinho' painted an image of the Virgin (Nossa Senhora do Pópulo) that the Jesuits on the first mission to the

Great Mughal gave to Akbar in 1580. This altarpiece apparently made a great impression on the emperor.[43] Thirty years later, in the reign of Jahangir, Viceroy Rui Lourenço de Távora was instructed to employ Erédia 'trying him out in whatever is appropriate' but directing him away from his obsessive 'quest for [the Island of] Gold'. The first work commissioned was an atlas showing the fortresses of Portuguese Asia (1610). In the following year he was then asked to explore Gujarat and to write a chorographic description of the province. The result was the text under analysis here: *Discurso sobre a Província do Indostan chamada Mogûl e coruptamente Mogôr com declaração do Reino Guzarate e mais reinos de seu districto: ordenado por Manuel Godinho de Erédia cosmographo mor do estado de Indias orientaes, anno 1611* (Discourse on the Province of Hindustan called Mogul and in corrupted form Mogor, with a description of the Kingdom of Gujarat and other kingdoms of its area: written by Manuel Godinho de Erédia, chief cosmographer of the State of the East Indies, in the year 1611).

In both *Informação da Aurea Chersoneso* (Report on Golden Chersoneso), 1599–1600, and *Lista das principais minas auríferas* (List of the main gold mines), c.1603, Erédia had shown his competence in producing such chorographic descriptions. Hence, it is no surprise that *Discurso* should have been followed by an inventory of the minerals found in the Goa region, a work that Viceroy Dom Jerónimo de Azevedo commissioned in 1613 but has not survived. In between these two, Erédia wrote a recently discovered text – *Discurso sobre a Cathay ou Catá com as Provincias do districto da India superior* (Discourse on Cathay or Catá with the Provinces of the District of Upper India) – which, to some extent, complements his work on Hindustan. Although Erédia referred to this work in other writings, it remained unpublished and, until now, unknown.[44]

Despite never having been properly studied, Erédia's report on the Mughal empire is considered to be a minor text. However, *Discurso* would form the basis for the information on Hindustan found in his later works, such as *Declaraçam de Malaca e India Meridional com o Cathay* (Report on Malacca and Meridional India with Cathay, 1613) and *Tratado Ophirico* (Treatise on Ophir, 1616). Equally, his comments on Kashmir in the 1611 text were further developed the following year in the aforementioned description of Cathay.

Like Xavier's *Tratado*, Erédia's manuscript version of *Discurso* seems to have been fairly widely known at the time. In addition to a copy at the British Library (henceforth BL version),[45] there is another at the Biblioteca Nacional, Lisbon (henceforth BNL version), which was part of the library of the Count of Ameal, as recorded in the respective catalogue, published in 1924.[46] The differences between the two copies are negligible, although the Lisbon text is slightly more complete. Of greater significance is the fact that the BNL version (f. 51r) has a drawing by Erédia on the frontispiece, showing what the author calls the 'farman of the Mogol King', the genealogical seal of Emperor Jahangir that the author describes in the text. Having listed the Mughal rulers since the time of Timur, Erédia states:

… the 9th Noradin Mahamet Zanguir Patxagazi, who currently governs the crown of the Mogols in this year of 1611, and the seal and royal arms of his crown consists of a large circle with nine smaller circles or spheres inside it, and in each sphere is written the name of each of the aforementioned kings, inscribed in Arabic letters [p. 134].

Manuel Godinho de Erédia,
'Seal of Jahangir' [Goa], 1611.
Lisbon, BNL CAT. 27

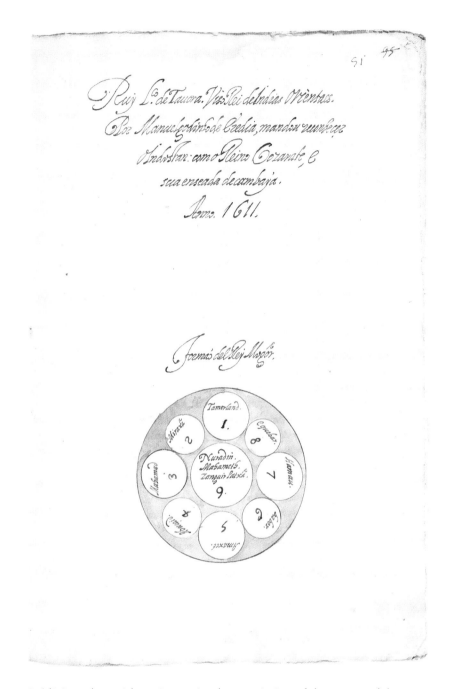

Erédia's seal provides a Romanized transcription of the names of the emperors, but has similar errors to those made by subsequent European authors. One such is numbering the circles from one to nine, starting with Timur and ending with Jahangir, when in fact, the seal should be read in the opposite order. In any case, the cartographer must have had access to Jahangir's circular seal, although he fails to disclose where or in what circumstances. It is perfectly possible that he could have seen it in the capital of the State of India, as he was a contemporary of Diogo do Couto, the chief archivist at the Goa State Archive and author of *Décadas*. Moreover, as it had been Couto who had first described Akbar's seal,[47] it is perfectly conceivable that in 1611, the Goa archive should have *farmans* from Jahangir that bore his seal.

If Erédia's *Discurso* was sent back to Portugal by Rui Lourenço de Távora for the information of Philip III, this would mean that the drawing of Jahangir's seal reached Europe – by Erédia's hand – almost a full decade before Baffin's version. Yet even before either of these two drawings, it should be noted that Father Manuel Pinheiro had sent a Portuguese translation of a *farman* from 1602 back to Rome, including a rough sketch of Akbar's circular seal. Inside the circle he placed the simple caption 'the king's seal', positioning it correctly where the imperial seal was invariably placed on documents issued by the Mughal chancellery: to the right of the name and titles of the emperor (*tughra*).[48] Immediately under the translation of the Persian document the Jesuit describes the seal itself:

this is the farman, the mark and seal of the King that appears on the above image is large: inside is the name of Tamorlão [Timurlang], from whom he descends and then those of the other descendants of Timur until his father, and his is below that of his father.[49]

Nonetheless, it was the seal that Roe introduced to Europe that gained a high public profile. Having first appeared, in a Romanized version, on William Baffin's map (1619), it was reproduced just a few years later in the original Persian and in its Latin version in the collection of travel reports assembled by Samuel Purchas. Jahangir's seal also appeared, in its Latin form, illustrating the map of the Mughal empire included in the Hondius atlas (1625), which was based on Baffin's map. Later still, Edward Terry's report (published in 1655) would use a Persian version of the seal, albeit produced by a bizarre reconstruction based on Baffin's Latin transliteration.

From then onwards, the seals of the successive Mughal emperors held an enormous fascination for European travellers. Tavernier reproduced the seal of Shahjahan, which had previously been described by Thomas Herbert, emphasizing the fact that the Mughal ancestry was inscribed inside the seal. Likewise, Manuzzi and Valentijn included reproductions of Aurangzeb's seal in their reports, further establishing a practice that was adopted by most eighteenth-century Western observers for the emperor's successors.[50] An anonymous Portuguese traveller who passed through the Mughal empire in the late seventeenth century listed the local rulers from Timur through to Aurangzeb and described the latter's seal, which he must have seen attached to a document in Ahmadabad.

There can be no mistake in what I say … for I have taken it from the sign, seal or ring with which the King signs his letters and orders; and that in the place of the coat of arms, or name of the King, are the names of all his predecessors and finally, the one who [currently] governs.[51]

In the text itself Erédia starts by dealing with the political system of government in Hindustan, going back to Timur and his direct relationship with the 'Mogores'. This is followed by a description of the empire's borders, based on physical and human geography and embellished with a list of the provinces and descriptions of the cities. As a cartographer and cosmographer, Erédia paid constant attention to his geography and never failed to include the latitudes and longitudes of the places he described.

The sequence starts with a long description of Gujarat, in which the author genuinely dissects the province. Not only does he comply with the viceroy's instructions, but also makes his writing match the importance that the former sultanate had always had in the subcontinent's economy and in the strategy adopted by the State

**'Reino de Orixa. Reino de Bengala'
(Kingdom of Orixa. Kingdom of
Bengal) in** *Livro das plantas das
fortalezas, cidades ...,* **c.1633–41.
Vila Viçosa, Fundação da Casa de
Bragança (Biblioteca do Paço Ducal)
CAT. 32**

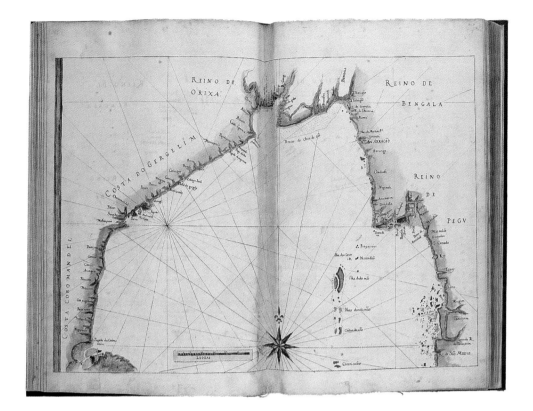

of India. Erédia initially defines the province's geographical frontiers, before adding a
brief summary of the region's political history from when the sultanate was founded until
Humayun's invasion. He then describes local society and the various religious practices,
dwelling on the Banyans (*vaniyas*) – specifically referring to the Jains – and anticipating
much of what would be written on them shortly afterwards in Europe.[52] Erédia then
assesses the cities and emphasizes the importance of the local natural resources,
particularly opium and indigo, plants that he describes in detail, being the keen botanist
he was. Finally, as a cartographer, he speaks at length on the ports along the 'Cambay
inlet' and lists the rivers of Gujarat. The remaining pages of *Discurso* provide an
introduction to a series of other kingdoms under Mughal rule. Delhi, Purab,[53] Kabul,
Kashmir, Bengal and Sinde (in this order) each merit between one and three paragraphs,
although he is somewhat briefer on Sinde and Purab and longer on Kashmir.

Erédia based *Discurso* on texts from classical antiquity that spoke of Asia, which he
mentions explicitly, as well as information from local sources that he must have
accessed indirectly. These are supplemented by oral reports, some from pilgrims, that
the author mentions sporadically and by other written sources that he does not cite but
which he certainly read. The cartographer must have had access to Diogo do Couto's
Décadas, which had been published or completed before 1611, and used information
from the Jesuit letters. For example, his description of Gujarat bears clear similarities to
the annual letter of 1595.[54]

The result is as surprising as it is unsettling. His painstaking accuracy in defining the
ports of Gujarat, which befitted a cartographer-mathematician, is in stark contrast to the
emphasis he places – in John Mandeville's style – on Western legends about the Orient.
These include 'giants twelve feet high' living along the borders of Kashmir, 'people with
one foot and others with huge ears' found in the more remote regions of Bengal. In fact,

the latter province was the place *par excellence* for the fantastic beings that Erédia mentioned, men with their 'faces on their chests', 'others with the heads of dogs', elephants and fishes, as well as black 'flesh-eating' pigmies.

Far from adding a note of realism to the text, these oral reports that he claims to have heard are invariably used to support the more wildly fantastic elements and to justify unbelievable monstrosities. Even so, they do merit further consideration. It is well known that the Muslims who settled in Bengal immediately viewed the region – especially its northern reaches – as a land of mystery and fable that was inhabited by skilled practitioners of magic and witchcraft.[55] Consequently, it seems probable that Erédia's excesses are not merely the result of his own imagination or an anachronistic reading of ancient texts, but reflected ideas and imagery that circulated throughout southern Asia. In similar fashion, his reference to the *yogi* ('iogue') that he met in the backwoods of Gujarat is also of great interest. This man 'kept 2 black dogs by him, and these dogs would take the form of tigers when he so ordered to guard and protect his person'. This description ties in perfectly with the image of a *dervish* in Persian folklore as a treacherous figure who used his supernatural powers with malice.[56]

Regardless of potential speculations as to the quality and size of Erédia's personal library, his readings at the outstanding library at the Jesuit college of São Paulo in Goa form the basis for the erudition that Erédia displays throughout *Discurso*. Yet somewhat paradoxically, this book-learning led him to follow classical authors' writings on India from 1,500 years before far too closely. He adopts their toponymy and has no hesitation whatsoever in reproducing the mythological stories and beings contained in these reports, shielding himself behind the authority of Pliny and his *Natural History* to justify what would otherwise seem to be pure invention.

Nonetheless, as noted above, not all these 'wonders' were taken from the classics. Some attention should be paid to the potential impact of Erédia's oral sources. For example, he claims to have met 'a Hindustani who saw a one-legged man in the backwoods, and I found another person who saw a large-eared man beyond the Bengal camarú'. What then was the difference between these bizarre beings described by Erédia and those of Mahmud bin Amir Wali twenty years later? The latter author, a native of Balkh, had also found a one-legged native who took giant steps and was amazed at the sight of two-legged people.[57] Bengal was indeed as strange a land for a traveller from central Asia as it was for the Portuguese-Malay cartographer living in Goa.

The occasional use of local written sources in *Discurso* also merits some comment. When speaking about the Christians of Çin and Maçin, Erédia claims to have consulted 'the Chaldean councils that are in the archives of the Archbishopric of Serra or Angamale', evidently referring to the Nestorian synods whose proceedings and decrees were brought together under the title *Synodicon Orientale*.[58] In addition, he twice claims to have read the 'itinerary of Alexander the Great, called Iskandar, written in Arabic letters in the Persian language'. It is ironic that, having been born in Malacca, Erédia had not seen a Malay version of the document that had been circulating since the sixteenth century, while he did gain access to one of the Persian copies that had been in circulation since the twelfth century. One such book had probably reached Goa via Hormuz, which is also how Dom João de Castro came to own a magnificent copy of the work – described by a contemporary as 'great to see for the work that it is' – in the middle of the sixteenth century.[59] Erédia may perhaps have had access to *Sikandar Nama* by Shaikh Nizami Ganjawi (*c.*1200) or to the version by Amir Khusrau, although it is impossible to say with absolute certainty.[60]

Sebastião Manrique, *Itinerario de las Missiones del India Oriental* (Itinerary of the Missions in East India), Rome, 1653.
Lisbon, BNL CAT. 34

Coverlet, India (Bengal), 17th century,
cotton and silk.
Lisbon, Fundação Medeiros e Almeida
CAT. 35

However, as there is no guarantee that Erédia read Persian, it would not come as any surprise if the book had been orally summarized for him in Goa. In all probability, the same procedure would also have been used to gain access to the 'histories of Hindustan on the antiquities and other Persian writings' that he mentioned when writing on Kashmir and Bengal. This could perhaps be the *Akbar Nama* or some Safavid chronicle,[61] as it is known that the viceroys and governors of Goa frequently sought out local chronicles. In the latter years of the sixteenth century, for example, Dom Francisco da Gama reported to the king that 'in the Court of the Idalcão [Bijapur] there were some books written in Persian which, they say, dealt with History from the creation of the world to the rule of this King who now governs Persia'. The viceroy sent orders for such works to be purchased and brought them with him to Portugal, but Philip III continued to request Archbishop Dom Frei Aleixo de Meneses to see if there was a copy in Goa that could be used as the basis for a translation.[62]

In brief, it appears that Manuel Godinho de Erédia's *Discurso* is of greater interest than it may at first seem to be. The text is significant for the end result, but more so for the complex web of sources and influences that underpin it: texts from classical antiquity, Indo-Persian sources (both read and reported) and oral reports that came mainly from pilgrims.

Regardless of any balance made on the potential and limitations of *Discurso* in 1611, it must be stressed that the text cannot be judged in isolation. Rather, Erédia's writings should be considered in conjunction with a vital supplement: his maps of the region produced in the 1610s. His characterization of the coastal settlements in Gujarat and of the province's hydrographic system is fully transferred onto the chart of 'Gosarate' in *Tratado Ophirico* (1616), also appearing on the 'Taboa do Reino Gozarate com a Enseada Cambaia' and the image of the 'Rio de Surrate', which appear in the so-called *Atlas-miscelânea* (*c*.1615–22).[63] In addition to portraying Gujarat as the 'bay' of Mughal India, Erédia purposefully showed the province as a rural administrative unit within the empire. The first two maps – particularly the 'Taboa' – include place-names, roads and borders, including several *parganas*.

Equally, Erédia's *Discurso* cannot be read without considering his three maps of the Mughal empire: 'Taboa do Mogor' (henceforth Mogor 1); 'Mogor' (Mogor 2); and 'Taboa de Indostan chamado Mogor' (Mogor 3).[64] This appears to be their chronological order, as Mogor 1 dates from 1616 and Mogor 2 from approximately the same period, while all evidence suggests that Mogor 3 is from a later date, probably 1622. The texts and images coincide in many aspects, yet there can be no doubt that the maps are of far higher quality than the writing. This is made all the more important since it is well known that Mughal cartography from that period is neither of high quality nor abundant.[65]

Analysis of these maps raises a series of problems regarding cartography in general and any attempt to visualize the space in question. First, did Erédia show what he knew of Mughal India or what he thought he knew? Equally, was he fully aware of the frontiers of this vast empire, or did he occasionally draw Jahangir's plans for universal sovereignty?

Like Baffin before him, Erédia focuses the two maps from *Atlas-miscelânea* on northern India, paying little attention to the south. In contrast, the 'Taboa do Mogor' from *Tratado Ophirico*, which is significantly sketchier and less accurate, offers a panoramic view of the entire subcontinent. Also like the atlas produced by Sadiq Isfahani (1647), the mountains are shown through a series of short wavy lines, far more realistic in Mogor 3, set along a long horizontal line.[66] As in Mughal cartography, Erédia concentrates on rivers and roads as the main structuring elements in space, relegating the empire's territorial borders to a secondary role.[67] Nonetheless, all the maps show a single dotted line that seems to correspond to Erédia's idea of the frontiers of the Mughal emperor's political authority. This line stretches from Sinde in the north-east over to the area near Arrakan in the east, embracing all of Bengal. To the south the Deccan is clearly a frontier, and is very clearly shown as such in Mogor 2. To the north the dividing line goes deep into central Asia while – symptomatically – the two apparently older maps (Mogor 1 and 2) show Qandahar as part of Jahangir's kingdom, while Mogor 3 clearly places both the city and its province outside the Mughal empire's borders. This intriguing detail could be pure coincidence or the result of Erédia's inaccuracy. However, if it accurately reflects the situation, it acquires greater importance in dating the map, since Qandahar, which Akbar had conquered in 1595, fell to an attack by Shah 'Abbas in 1622 and was reincorporated into the Safavid empire.

Mogor 3 is by far the most detailed and valuable of the three maps. Perhaps because it is the latest, the 'Taboa de Indostan chamado Mogor' has additional detail and accuracy in depicting the relief of the terrain and the river network. Furthermore, Erédia also provides a wealth of place-names and takes pains to show the main transport routes in a double dotted line that reveals his precise knowledge of the main arteries for communication within the Mughal empire.[68]

Sebastião Manrique, *Breve Relatione de i Regni di Pegv, Arracan, e Brama, e degl' Imperij del Calaminan, Siamom, e gran Mogor …* (Brief Report on the Kingdoms of Pegu, Arrakan and Brama, and of the Empires of Calaminan, Siam and the Great Mughal …), Rome, 1648. Lisbon, Biblioteca da Ajuda (BA) CAT. 33

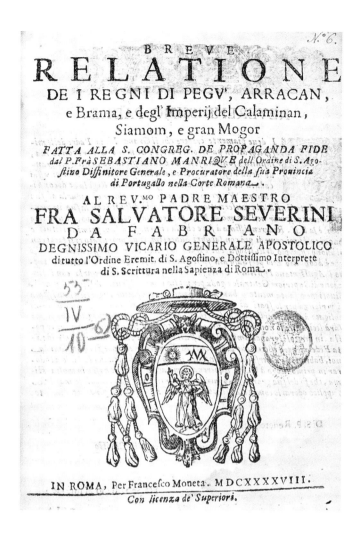

Thus, in the north-east coastal region of the subcontinent Agra is linked to the province of Gujarat via Ahmadabad, with the road ending in the port of Cambay. A longer and more winding route led from that imperial city to the province of Sind, stretching onwards to Lhahri Bhandar ('bandel lari', as the Portuguese called it). Although both these routes are also shown in Mogor 1 (Agra/Thatta and Agra/Cambay), the one linking the provinces of Sind and Gujarat via Lhari Bhandar-Cambay only appears in Mogor 3.

To the north, in the direction of central Asia, Mogor 3 shows the route from Agra to Lahore and Kabul, passing via Jalalabad, and on to Samarkand, the 'homeland of Tamerlane'. To the north-east Erédia identifies the route to Purab, passing via Allahabad, and on to the west side of the Ganges delta, making specific mention of Rajmahal. However, his image of the eastern side of the empire is far less detailed, and he falls back on fantasy, as he also did in *Discurso*. In northern Bengal, on the route to Tibet, Erédia marks the 'twelve-foot tall giants' that he speaks about in the text, almost copying the style of the ethnographic maps produced in Qing China.[69] This is all the more significant as the *Tratado Ophirico* places 'monsters where the Island of Zanzi is, inhabited by winged people' at the borders of eastern India, and even includes a picture of these strange beings.[70]

Interestingly, none of Erédia's maps goes into detail on the routes to the south of the Mughal empire. No real significance can be attached to the information on Khandesh or Ahmadnagar, regions that had been under increasing Mughal pressure since the latter days of Akbar and whose geo-strategic location was of great importance to Goa.

Although it is little known and barely studied, there was in fact European cartography showing the Mughal empire before the maps by William Baffin and his successors. An exercise in inventorying leads all the way back to the map drawn up by Monserrate during the first Jesuit mission to the Great Mughal, which has since been definitively lost but which Father Hosten saw and reproduced in the early twentieth century.[71] In addition, Erédia's three 'Taboas do Mogor' should also be joined by the drawings of Gujarat and Bengal produced by João Baptista Lavanha in 1615.[72] A systematic comparison between Portuguese and English cartography on the Mughal empire from the 1610s – merely touched on here and previously suggested by Armando Cortesão[73] – should clearly be carried out by a specialist in this field.

CONCLUSION

European portrayals of Jahangir's India are normally based on a handful of authors and texts whose authoritative knowledge is endlessly invoked by specialists on the Mughal empire. Yet these eyewitnesses were accompanied by countless others – many of them Portuguese – who have been relegated to a secondary role and whose texts are frequently anonymous (or almost so) and were rarely published at that time. In general, these texts do not have the cohesive quality required of a book, but on the other hand they were not conceived as such. For the Dutch, a recent study by James Tracy has shown how a vision of the Mughal empire as a political body, revealed by the VOC's agents based in Surat in the middle of the seventeenth century, is of far greater interest than the generalizations found in de Laet.[74]

As regards the Portuguese contribution, and taking Jerónimo Xavier and Manuel Godinho de Erédia as examples, we may speculate on the role of texts that circulated at that time – manuscripts and versions that were often in more than one Romance language – in constructing the various different European images of the Mughal world. The documentary basis – both in written and visual form – that can be used to study Western visions of the Mughal empire still holds untold secrets. Hence, the task ahead seems far more complex than simply examining the collections produced by Richard Hakluyt or Samuel Purchas.

João Baptista Lavanha, 'Descripção do Reino de Guzarate' (Description of the Kingdom of Gujarat), from João de Barros, *Ásia, Década IV,* Madrid, 1615. Lisbon, BNL CAT. 15

João Baptista Lavanha, 'Descripção do Reino de Bengala' (Description of the Kingdom of Bengal), from João de Barros, *Ásia, Década IV,* Madrid, 1615. Lisbon, BNL CAT. 31

The Palace
of the Viceroys
in Goa

Pedro Dias

'PROVIDING FOR ALL THE FURNISHINGS AND NEEDS'

In the words of Jan Huyghen van Linschoten, 'providing for all the furnishings and needs' at the Fortaleza (Fortress) Palace was one of the most pressing tasks facing any new viceroy, as when the previous incumbent left, he would take all its contents, leaving the palace like 'a ruined and robbed house'.[1] As is known from many other sources (and confirmed by Linschoten), no sooner had the new viceroy arrived in Bardez and settled into the Reis Magos College, awaiting the departure of his predecessor, than his agents started organizing the removal process. This was because it was each viceroy's own salary that had to pay for maintenance and fittings, which meant that 'not a single chair or stool [was left], nor a single payment in the treasury'. The bed, the chairs, the most humble cooking utensils and fabrics were all purchased with the viceroy's money, making him their rightful owner.

At the end of each tour of duty, the palace was transformed into a sort of Ali Baba's cave filled with precious objects that had come from all over the Orient, including the many precious items ordered by the king, his queen or the princes, which were also stored there. The viceroy would then ship all these pieces back to Lisbon. The most common objects – the items for daily use and of little value – would be sold or given to servants or institutions, as space on the ships on the 'India Route' was at a premium, used for the 'liberty-boxes' and containers holding highly priced goods. Consequently, only such goods as were really worth the trouble would be loaded, as will be shown below.

Alongside a study of the physical structure of the building, which is the fundamental aim here, this paper will also try to demonstrate how the spaces where people met in the palace were organized and what their contents were.

Cabinet, India, 17th century,
ebony, *sissó* wood, ivory and metal,
114.4 x 117 x 60 cm.
Lisbon, MNAA, inv. 1312

THE FORTALEZA PALACE IN GOA'S URBAN STRUCTURE

This palace, which acted as the viceroy's residence and the seat of government, was the most important one in the city of Goa. The group of buildings – the political and administrative heart of the Portuguese 'State of India'[2] – operated without interruption from 1554 to 1695, when Viceroy Dom Pedro António de Noronha e Albuquerque (1693–8), the Count of Vila Verde (later first Marquis of Angeja), moved the permanent residence to the Casa da Pólvora Palace in Panelim. Nonetheless, for many years after that date, official receptions were still held at the Fortaleza Palace, which explains why it survived for longer than many other buildings that soon crumbled. In fact, the last official ceremony to be held at the Fortaleza Palace took place as late as 1812.[3] It is also curious to note that there are hardly any documents that refer to construction work at the viceroys' palace, and that even the chroniclers provide very limited information.

The palace is of interest here as it was the base for the court of the State of India. In the middle of the sixteenth century, and following decades of being an itinerant structure, the court would undergo a significant evolution and settle in one location, thereby satisfying a requirement of the centralized modern state as it offered the Portuguese royal representative greater and closer control over the territory. The Fortaleza Palace became the setting for the internal and external representation of power, receiving embassies and granting privileges, alongside the far more mundane aspects such as paying the troops. Indeed, the physical form of the viceroy's palace mirrored the structure of Luso-Indian power – with all its idiosyncrasies. The growth of the palace, the increasing number of annexes and the decoration of the symbolically more important rooms were all interrelated with the vagaries of government and the varying political tensions between subjects, allies or enemies.

The earliest image of the city to show the original fortress was drawn by Dom João de Castro and included in his *Roteiro* [Itinerary] *de Goa a Diu* (1538–9).[4] At that time the viceroy's court was still in the process of settling in Goa and was based in the former Palace of the Sabaio (the local ruler).[5] Meanwhile, the city only occupied the banks of the River Mandovi, stretching from the space that would develop into Ribeira Grande to the location occupied by the customs office. Moving inland, it did not even reach the hills of Nossa Senhora do Monte and Nossa Senhora do Rosário.[6]

The fortified area was restricted to the future residence of the viceroys and an area defined by a moat that would establish the line formed by the following roads: Rua dos Ferradores and do Açougue up to Praça do Pelourinho, then going down Rua dos Chapeleiros to Terreiro dos Galos and the royal hospital. It was within this area that the most important buildings appeared, such as the cathedral, the original Monastery of São Francisco and the small Church of Santa Catarina.

Ribeira Grande, also called 'Varação dos Naus', was the natural complement to the Fortaleza Palace. Its walls stretched out into the water, perpendicular to the buildings that closed the side of the square occupied by the customs office. Two long walls running towards the river acted as the dock for the city and included a putative advanced bulwark to enable docking all along the Ribeira. Decades later, this space would be opened up, although some defensive walls were added along the waterfront.

THE VICEROY OF INDIA'S RESIDENCE AT THE FORTALEZA PALACE

Following the capture of the city, Afonso de Albuquerque established the captain's residence in the former fortress of Adil Shah. In *Lendas da Índia* Gaspar Correia records the work carried out to reinforce the palace, specifically referring to the construction of a two-storey keep that enabled large-calibre artillery to be fired. He also mentions two other square towers: one facing the city by the Mandovi gate and the other over the dock gate, both of which were built on Albuquerque's orders. There was also another gate with machicolation (or murder-holes) set between these two towers.

The Mandovi tower marked the start of a curtain wall that led to an octagonal bulwark standing actually in the river with embrasures at water level. Albuquerque also built a low wall around the fortress, a barbican with gun-ports and a broad filled moat, as well as an underground connection between the dock tower and its respective gate. The governor had an extremely strong defensive wall built on the riverside. The standard sections of the wall rose to half height, while the higher bulwarks had embrasures on the ground floor for the artillery to slaughter any approaching enemies.

Inevitably, such major building work was a lengthy procedure, but I believe that Afonso de Albuquerque's project, implemented by Tomás Fernandes, was the basis of the fortifications that appear in the various different copies of Dom João de Castro's *Roteiro*.

As mentioned above, it was only in 1554 that Dom Pedro de Mascarenhas, the seventeenth Governor and sixth Viceroy of India, moved his residence and the state departments out of the former location and into the Fortaleza Palace. Most contemporary documents record that Mascarenhas, an elderly and ill man, complained that he could no longer get up and down the stairs at the Sabaio's former residence. However, the anonymous author of *Conquista da Índia per humas e outras armas reais e evangelicas* (London, BM, Egerton Collection) also adds that the change was very beneficial for the various departments and their staff. As the new palace was closer to the river – and thus to the warehouses, customs office and docks – the staff were able to keep a closer watch on trading activities and on the movements of merchants and troops.[7] Evidently, although moving from one palace to another presupposed building work, no details of this have survived.[8]

In the second half of the sixteenth century the number of people who were permanently at the palace was considerable. For a start, there were 92 full-time court staff in 1554, a number that had risen to 115 by 1574, before dropping to 112 in 1576 and again rising to 116 by 1581. Initially, the 'senior officials' included the secretary for India, the captain of the guard (with 60 men under his command), the second-lieutenant responsible for the royal flag, the bailiff, the court accommodation officer, the senior doctor, the senior surgeon, the barber and the apothecary. In addition, there were the 'lesser officials': the clerk, 6 foot-soldiers, 7 torch-bearers and their respective officer (*mocadão*), 6 water-carriers, 1 parasol-carrier, 2 laundresses (*mainatos*), etc.

By 1581 the main differences were that the senior officials now included 2 chaplains, an interpreter, an agent for the fleet and his scribe, 10 trumpeters and 4 kettle-drum players, as well as another clerk, 7 more clerks each with an underling and a smith. However, the post of accommodation officer had disappeared, since the court had ceased to be itinerant, and even when the viceroy visited other strongholds, the state departments remained in the palace.[9]

Maintaining the building and making sure its daily operations ran smoothly required many other staff who were not mentioned, although some do appear in the list from

Chair, Goa, late 16th–early 17th century, teak.
Lisbon, Museu da Cidade CAT. 111

'Portuguese' carpet, Persia (?), Safavid
period, 17th century.
Lisbon, CGM CAT. 63

*c.*1635, drawn up by António Bocarro. This notes 34 sailors for the viceroy's ship, with the respective officer, 12 staff for the bailiff (*meirinho*), 4 porters and 4 footmen, 6 stable-boys, etc.[10] Meanwhile, the state departments that operated inside the Fortaleza Palace had also grown. In 1635 the General Records Office had 14 members of staff, the Accounts Department had around 50 and the archive a further 3.

Yet far more people were to be found at the palace. As in Lisbon and Madrid, there was the palace nobility, those who held posts in the councils and other state bodies, and the nobles and officers who were passing through *en route* to their senior positions in the various factories and fortresses in the State of India. In addition, there were permanent foreign delegations, the Indian elites – particularly Brahmans, until the governorship of Dom Constantino de Bragança (1558–61) – the leading merchants, and lay and regular priests. All of these groups or individuals had greater or lesser degrees of access to the viceroy, while he withdrew from the more public spaces and was protected by staff – starting with the secretary of state – who filtered those who craved an audience. These visitors could enter chambers and antechambers at perfect ease and might even – as a signal honour – attend (always standing) one of the viceroy's meals, taking advantage of the opportunity to request favours. This ritual had nothing to do with the banquets held in the early sixteenth century, where the viceroy's two roles as the military chief and royal representative were confused; these were even attended by people of humble origin. In fact, attending the viceroy's 'lunch' necessitated the use of the finest clothes, jewels and the most ostentatious of dress weapons, as Father Luís Fróis clearly stated in one of his letters.[11]

Public appearances outside the palace, which were described in detail by visiting travellers, were more closely linked to the ceremonies of Hindu rajahs and the Mughal emperors than those of Western monarchs. Again, the palace was a place of political and social syncretism, bringing together the two geographically distant worlds.

Between 1591 and 1597, under Viceroy Matias de Albuquerque, the palace had to be restructured. Fundamentally, this involved reorganizing the internal space to cater for several departments that were moved into the premises. The anonymous biography – *Vida e acções de Mathias de Albuquerque capitão e viso-rei da Índia* – even mentions that the viceroy rebuilt the severely damaged palace, the Appeals Office, the Accounts Department, the Records and the archive rebuilt, as he specifically wished them to be located inside the walls.[12]

One piece of construction work that is both well documented and still partially in existence is the Viceroys' Arch. The idea of paying tribute to the Count-Admiral Dom Vasco da Gama on the one hundredth anniversary of the Portuguese arrival in India was simultaneously intended to ensure that Viceroy Dom Francisco da Gama would be elevated to the nobility. Dom Francisco's highly illustrious forefather would legitimize both his presence in the post and his high-handed manner in decision making, which displeased his political opponents. It fell to Diogo do Couto, the chronicler and archivist, to make the speech supporting this project to the City Government. He won the necessary approval and handed the project over to the head engineer, Júlio Simão.[13] Evidently using Sebastiano Serlio's treaty, books III and IV, Simão designed an authentic triumphal arch that culminates in imposing statues of Saint Catherine of Alexandria, the city's patron saint, and Vasco da Gama, who was thereby elevated to a mythical figure and paired with the virgin saint. The remains of the arch now offer a different vision, as it originally led directly into the palace through a small tunnel linking the front and rear, where the side facing the Mandovi was more developed and truly emblematic. In fact,

Map of Goa, from the *Itinerario*
by J. Linschoten, 1595, gouache on
paper, 13 x 20 cm.
Lisbon, CGM, Photographic Archive

this side still has the cornerstone and dedicatory plaque, including the name of the builder. A different fate befell the statue of Vasco da Gama, which was destroyed in 1601 by Dom Francisco da Gama's enemies, although the City Council subsequently had the sculpture remade.[14]

Building work was also carried out under Viceroy Dom Miguel de Noronha, the Count of Linhares, as suggested by the 1637 report written by his successor, Dom Pedro da Silva, which criticises Dom Miguel.[15] The long original suggests that Noronha had carried out a large number of improvements that the new viceroy did not agree with. Certainly, Dom Pedro claimed that his predecessor had spent too much money on futile things that had left everything exactly as it had been before and, worse still, at a time when India was in need of that money. Certainly, Dom Miguel had built new premises for the state departments and moved the secretary of the Council of State onto the main floor of the palace, the exact same one as the viceroy himself occupied, albeit with a different entrance.

Manuel de Faria e Sousa confirms, as is well documented in other sources, that Dom Miguel de Noronha was an enthusiast of public works, expressly stating that the viceroy had the palace rebuilt as it was on the verge of collapse. There seems no reason to doubt the chronicler's word, since he at least was not directly involved in the controversies that engulfed the viceroys and their respective supporters.[16]

CONJECTURED RECONSTRUCTION OF THE FORTALEZA PALACE: IMAGERY AND DESCRIPTIONS

Several images enable a potential reconstruction of the Fortaleza Palace. The first is Jan Huyghen van Linschoten's drawing from the 1580s, printed in Amsterdam in 1596. The second source is the collection of the surveys and projects for reorganizing Goa's urban structure, produced by engineer and infantry sergeant-major José de Morais Antas Machado, part of the Military Engineering Archaeological Studies Office, Lisbon. Finally, the collection at the Sociedade de Geografia de Lisboa includes a cross-section, elevation and plans of the two main floors, produced in 1779. In 1998, under the guidance of Helder Carita, Augusto Bolotinha produced a potential model of the building, which is an invaluable aid to understanding the palace's physical structure.[17]

José de Morais Antas Machado,
'Plan of Old Goa', Goa, 1775,
47 x 146.7 cm.
Lisbon, Gabinete de Estudos
Arqueológicos de Engenharia Militar,
inv. 1237/2A-24A-III

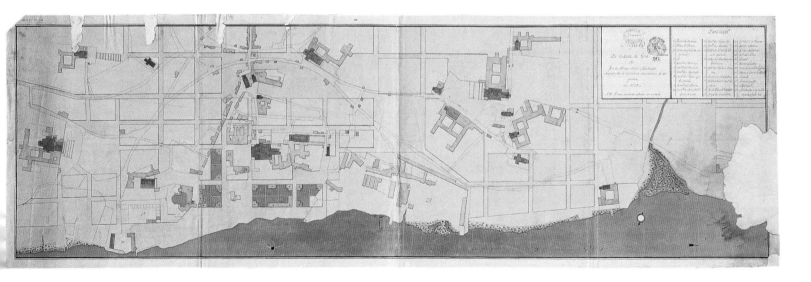

The two plans show that the building grew in size as new needs appeared, without any pre-defined or coherent project. In total, the palace had three floors covering very different areas. Only two of these are examined in the surveys, while the third appears to have been used for low-grade services and is only known from contemporary written reports. The pre-existence of a necessarily fortified building made it complex to adapt to constantly changing tastes. Even so, it appears that there were several large open spaces on the main floor and an imposing two-flight staircase in black stone, which must have been brought from Bassein, and a portico supported by four large monumental columns. This led to a long twelve-bay veranda that stretched away to the right, connecting the main residential and governmental rooms.

The main facade, facing the Mandovi, had a veranda – as Father Luís Fróis said – that overlooked the beach. This veranda was where the governor would appear and observe the Hindu Goans who had gathered below to make their petitions. He would then choose some and have them brought up into his presence.[18] This veranda was probably altered when the Viceroys' Arch was built, and replaced with bay windows. The facade, which closed off the square, was the first to be seen when coming ashore and was consequently the most imposing for those outside the building.

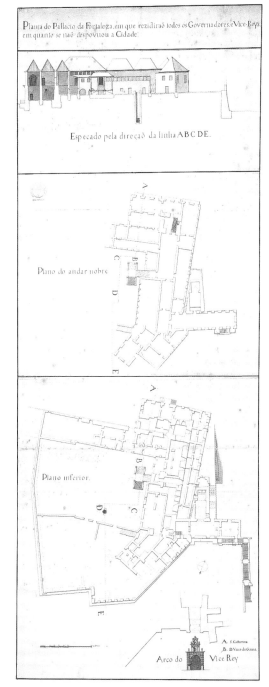

João Baptista Vieira Godinho, 'Plan of
the Fortaleza Palace, Goa', 1779.
Lisbon, Sociedade de Geografia
CAT. 43

Model of the Fortaleza Palace
of the viceroys in Goa.
Lisbon, Museu Militar   CAT. 42

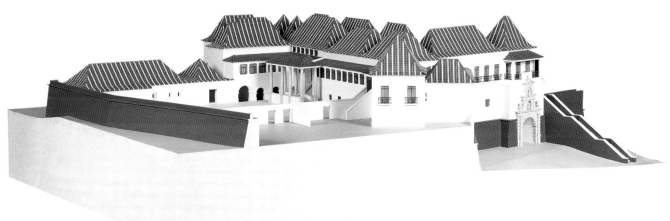

François Pyrard de Laval, a French traveller, described the palace and its surroundings as he saw them at the very start of the seventeenth century. Everything was structured around two patios that the author defined as 'very beautiful'. On entering the first one, the wide black stone staircase that led to the main floor was on the right. The room that Laval saw first was one of the state departments, a room whose balcony had a railing, which was the payments office where salaries were processed. An adjacent room was presumably the strong-room, which held the money and part of the treasure, as the latter was divided between the palace and the Monastery of São Francisco.

Following Laval's work, this was followed by a much larger room that offered views of the fleets and ships that had sailed to India. Jan Huyghen van Linschoten also described this, calling it a beautiful 'gallery', which seems to suggest that it was either open or overlooked some open space. The existing plan suggests otherwise, but the room immediately after this 'gallery' was where cornets and shawms were played when the viceroy was preparing to leave the palace.[19]

The latter room was one of the most interesting in the palace and was of evident political significance. Laval also described it as being very spacious and decorated with paintings of all the fleets that had sailed to India, including the number, date, name of captain and even the ships that had sunk, adding that it was disturbing to see the number of ships that had been lost. Fundamentally, every ship that came out from Portugal – no matter how small – was recorded in the painting and its name was noted.[20]

Jean-Baptiste Tavernier was as struck by this as Linschoten had been, although he only made a brief comment. This described the Fortaleza Palace as the best in Goa, a city whose port he also described as one of the best three in the world, alongside Constantinople and Toulon.[21]

The earliest mention of these paintings appears in Gaspar Correia's work, attributing the idea to Governor Jorge Cabral (1549–50).[22] This means that local or Portuguese artists consistently added images of the fleets that arrived, while formal portraits of the governors and viceroys were simultaneously being painted in the next room.

João dos Santos also included an interesting, albeit short, note on the paintings of the fleet in *Etiópia Oriental*, printed in Évora in 1609. He claims to have examined the paintings closely and with some amazement, which is not surprising, as they must have impressed all the people that entered the room.[23]

Some of the hardships that affected the paintings are known from information recorded in both the *Livros das monções* and a letter from Diogo do Couto in 1616. The former, sent by Philip III to Viceroy Dom Jerónimo de Azevedo, said that the king had heard that the paintings of all the fleets that sailed from Portugal were now severely damaged and that the ancient tradition of producing them was not being maintained. Therefore, the king ordered that the tradition be resumed and that paintings of the 'missing fleets' be produced, as well as restoring those that were in poor condition.[24]

Three years later, in 1616, Diogo do Couto noted that all the panels had rotted and these pictorial records had been lost. He claimed to have been pressuring Dom Francisco da Gama to have them restored for the previous three years. The viceroy had finally agreed when the last fleet arrived. As Couto recorded, in one month they had had over one hundred panels that had been produced by an artist called Godinho, using very good paints. Moreover, since the panel showing the first fleet – of Vasco da Gama, the count and admiral who had discovered the sea route to India, one of the greatest feats in the history of the world – was small, the viceroy had ordered a new one to be made. This was to be the same size as the others, and all of them were to bear the respective captions.[25] The artist named may have been Manuel Godinho de Erédia, a skilled draughtsman and jack-of-all-trades. For chronological reasons, it could not have been Father Manuel Godinho, who was active in the 1580s, producing altarpieces for Jesuit churches and chapels.[26]

These paintings are associated with the images in the *Livro das armadas*, a magnificent codex now at the Academia das Ciências de Lisboa that also shows all the fleets that sailed out to India between 1498 and 1566. Although the artist is unknown, the texts reveal that it was only taken to the Orient when Jorge Cabral became governor of India in 1549. There are obvious connections to *Livro de Lizuarte de Abreu* and the manuscript at the British Library entitled *Relação das naos e armadas da Índia*.[27]

Pyrard de Laval also records that there was another, even larger room: the audience room where the viceroy would receive senior dignitaries and embassies, as well as holding his council meetings. The same room housed portraits of all the previous viceroys,[28] some of which still exist, such as those that were taken from the government palace in Panjim to the São Francisco Museum in Old Goa. Sadly, these were ruined by an amateur artist who repainted or almost completely reworked them in the late nineteenth century. On a happier note, others are at the Museu Nacional de Arte Antiga, Lisbon, where they were painstakingly restored.

Gaspar Correia recorded the origin of this gallery in his *Lendas da Índia*, writing that Dom João de Castro, who liked to commemorate important events so that they would be remembered, decided to have portraits painted showing the governors who had served before him. He entrusted this task to Correia himself, as he was both a skilled draughtsman and had served under all the governors of the State of India, ordering him to produce as true a likeness of them as possible. Correia later added that he had summoned a skilled local artist who painted their faces according to the information that Correia provided so that whoever saw them would immediately recognize them. Dom João de Castro also had a portrait of himself painted, showing him entering Goa in triumph. All the full-size portraits were individually painted on separate panels, showing the governors wearing corselets, some bearing their own arms, over their black silk attire with gold stitching and trimmings, and carrying ceremonial swords. Their respective coats of arms were depicted above their heads, while each had his name and the dates when he governed written in gold at his feet. Finally, Dom João ordered them to be placed in the main room of the palace and covered with vestments.[29]

It therefore seems clear that the portraits of the following governors and viceroys were the work of the author of *Lendas da Índia* and his Goan assistant: Dom Francisco de Almeida, Afonso de Albuquerque, Lopo Soares de Albergaria, Diogo Lopes de Sequeira, Dom Duarte de Meneses, Dom Vasco da Gama, Dom Henrique de Meneses, Lopo Vaz de Sampaio, Nuno da Cunha, Dom Garcia de Noronha, Dom Estêvão da Gama, Martim Afonso de Sousa and Dom João de Castro himself. Jan Huyghen van Linschoten also saw this series when he visited the palace,[30] which means that it was added to on a systematic basis.

I believe that these original paintings have not survived, and the earliest portraits to show the governors date from the early seventeenth century. These would have been produced when the iconographic programme was totally reformulated, including the images of the fleets. This conclusion is based on the portraits of Dom Francisco de Almeida, Afonso de Albuquerque and Dom Francisco de Mascarenhas, now at the Museu Nacional de Arte Antiga, Lisbon, and those of Dom João de Castro and Dom Vasco da Gama, at the São Francisco Museum, Old Goa. Nonetheless, given the

Portrait of Afonso de Albuquerque, Goa, 16th century, mixed technique on wood, 182 x 108 cm.
Lisbon, MNAA, inv. no. 2144 P

Dom João de Castro, 4th Viceroy of India (1545–8), Flanders, 16th century.
Oporto, private collection CAT. 37

O GOVERNADOR AFFONÇO D ALBOQVERQVE SVÇEDEO NA JNDIA
A DOM FRANÇISCO D ALMEĨDA EM NOVEMBRO DE
609 TOMOV DIAS VEZES A ÇIDADE D GOA E A SĨ DE MALA
TE ORVZ E FEZ A FORTALEZA E CALECVTE FOI A PERÇIA E AO
ESTRETO DE ORMVZ E MAR ROXO

GOVERNOV   ESTE   ESTADO ATE
ANNO D 1515 FEZ A FOR TALEZA DA CIDADE
COA E FA   LCEO NA   BARRA DELLA

drawings contained in Gaspar Correia's *Lendas da Índia*, which were the basis for the paintings by this converted painter, and those in *Livro de Lizuarte de Abreu*, from c.1560, it seems that the re-paintings attempted to stay true to the original images.

These paintings used a mixed technique of tempera and oil on wood panels that were roughly the same size, measuring approximately 110 cm high and between 98 and 108 cm in width. Stylistically, they are far removed from European models. The figures are invariably full-length and show no signs of modelling, perspective or any suggestion of the surroundings. Instead, they stand out against a single-colour background or an imitation of damask that is always painted in a dark colour. The governors and viceroys face either right or left, holding their staffs of office in their right hands, while their left hands rest on sword handles or, in the case of Vasco da Gama, a display helm standing on a small table. The coats of arms are always clearly visible and there are two areas bearing captions: one at the top, behind their heads; the other at their feet. In total, these areas cover around one quarter of the surface of the paintings.

This was the most magnificent room in the palace, the one where the viceroy would sit on his official chair under a rich red velvet canopy and receive oriental princes and ambassadors, and grant audiences to Goans and Portuguese. The ceremonial etiquette of the viceroys' court developed, becoming ever more complex and keeping the royal representative at greater distance from his subjects. Dom Luís de Ataíde brought orders from King Sebastião that this should be so, since the goal was to construct a symbolic image of the viceroys' superiority. Consequently, court gentlemen started to be issued with stools, whereas they had previously had chairs with backs, and they were also forced to remove their hats when meeting the governor of the State of India in this room and on other occasions. Sitting in a chair with a back became a privilege of the viceroy inside the palace, precisely as it was for the monarch and his throne.[31] According to Jan Huyghen van Linschoten, the guardroom for the halberdiers was located right next to this room.

Descriptions by foreign travellers also mention the viceroy's meals, which seem to have taken place in a smaller room adjacent to the main hall. Alongside was another room where food was placed so that guests who were 'attending' could serve themselves, always out of sight of the governor.

From the very start the palace had a private chapel, which Father Saldanha says was built in 1512–13 and where the governor or viceroy would attend mass celebrated by a chaplain. By the end of the seventeenth century it had become a relatively large space located on the ground floor of the residential wing near the Viceroys' Arch. Yet the chapel was high enough for the ceiling to be practically at the same level as the roof over the main floor, its axis running parallel to that of the arch and creating a rectangular room that acted as an entrance hall. The body of the chapel consisted of a single, long, rectangular nave that ended in a single chapel, apparently with crossed ribs. The plan at the Sociedade de Geografia de Lisboa shows that there was an upper choir opposite the apse that was connected to the main hall or royal hall on the first floor. This in turn overlooked the Mandovi, and allowed the viceroy direct and discreet access to the chapel. Friar João dos Santos makes a brief reference to this chapel, describing it as beautiful,[32] which means – in his well-known language – that it was richly decorated, as befitted the elevated status of the man who used it.

As Father Luís Fróis noted in 1559, the ground floor also housed the stables and departments of lesser importance.[33] This floor was substantially larger than the first, as a very large, single-storey structure closed the patio off to the south side, while leading to the square that housed the *tronco* (prison). This block may have consisted of warehouses, since there do not appear to be any large openings for lighting, comprising a very large space at one end and a group of four others leading to the exterior. Two of these four were nothing more than minuscule spaces.

This corner, facing approximately north-east, holds the base of a mighty tower that may have been built by Afonso de Albuquerque or could be from an earlier period. This is the culmination of two equally wide and solid walls that form a right angle: one establishing the north facade; the other running almost perpendicular to the dock. These walls were probably three times as thick as the others, running from one end to the other and ending in the block before the private chapel. At this point the palace falls back at an angle of 120º, creating a major new square opposite the main facade, the one that could be seen directly from the viceroys' room on the upper floor and from the arch that commemorated Vasco da Gama and St Catherine.

New, paired sets of rooms, almost all of which are rectangular and interconnecting, were built along the old western wall. At least six of them had no exterior lighting. As a whole, this block created a very elongated and irregular rectangle. The existing tower defined the form of another group of rooms that had the same width and followed the line of the defensive curtain wall that connected the two old towers. These interior rooms had no direct light unless interior yards were created where the structures met, though this is difficult to establish from the existing information. There were also at least two large areas to the left and the right of the main entrance, since the monumental staircase with portico seems to have had transversal arcades that would clearly have supported the upper floor. The area to the north-east of the old tower also had a web-like structure of nine or ten rooms that continued up to the exit to the northern open space. At the other end the southern block had an important means of access outside the perimeter and the walls of the main patio, while there were approximately another ten rooms inside. The last three of these, which had a more regular form – one larger rectangular room in the centre flanked by two square ones – were located before the entrance to the chapel.

The plans seem to show that there were two internal staircases linking the floors: one inside the old tower; the other in the room adjacent to the entrance hall to the chapel. Exterior access was easier, since there was a long staircase running perpendicular to the end with the Viceroys' Arch and on the main facade overlooking the Mandovi, Terreiro da Alfândega and the Ribeira. This staircase had three flights that then formed a right angle and continued over the void space. Another large staircase that was reached from the viceroys' square led to the southern block. It had just one flight and stood against one of the walls that closed off the central patio. In addition, there was at least one other staircase on the north side, located on the other main facade that overlooked the *tronco* square.

The main floor was far more coherent, with larger and more regular rooms, and communication systems that are more readily understood. The total area of this floor was smaller, as it did not extend as far as the block that closed off the internal square to the north. The viceroys' room was on the southern side, with bay windows all along and a direct connection to the upper choir. Meanwhile, the plans showing the irregular advance structure define five relatively large rooms, one of which has a direct connection to the *sala das armadas* ('fleet room'). Running north to south, there are two sets of parallel spaces defined by the old wall, as on the ground floor. These house around twelve rooms that form the basis for governor's residence. There were no corridors, just direct connections between rooms, especially at the ends. It seems that people basically moved along the veranda that ran all along the section overlooking the inner patio, which had the aforementioned staircase with portico.

The palace also had a well in the square, as can be seen in the plan used so far, and an ingenious system for collecting rainwater, which was then distributed to the areas where it was needed, as the travellers also reported.

Despite all this data and the descriptions, hardly anything is known about the palace. Neither the residential area nor the area reserved for the state departments can be accurately identified, as at least some of the latter had to have been on the main floor. Access for courtiers must have been restricted to the veranda, fleet room, viceroys' room and their respective antechambers. Otherwise, the contemporary descriptions would have provided more information. Nor yet is it known precisely where the viceroy slept or ate, although, given the location of the passage to the upper choir and the fact that he normally appears to have worked in the main hall, it was probably in the southern section. More specifically, it may have been in the rectangular block that protruded at an angle into the square. This building also had direct access to the outside, an essential feature of any palace as this enabled individuals or groups to move in and out without the court noticing. If this is true, then the state departments and public offices would have been on the north side that faced the city and even had direct access from the viceroys' square.

The third floor mentioned in contemporary texts must only have covered a small area and been used for storage and as quarters for the slaves and servants. The relative lack of importance is confirmed by the fact that there is no image depicting this floor.

Despite the eulogies found in the travellers' reports, the Fortaleza Palace was of modest size in comparison to its contemporaries in the subcontinent, particularly those that the Mughal emperors had already built or were in the process of building. While not small, it was not even as large as the palace in Sintra, and fell far behind the Ribeira Palace in Lisbon. Moreover, although the Baroque period now dominated in stylistic terms, it still maintained a mediaeval structure, the arrangement of the rooms lacking any prior plan or rationale. Rather, it was the end result of consecutive adaptations introduced according to the needs of every specific moment. A visit to the small archbishops' palace that was attached to the cathedral gives some idea of how people must have moved around the palace. The praise that Laval and Linschoten lavished on the palace would surely have been more restrained if the new cathedral had been built when they wrote, or such buildings as the Casa Professa do Bom Jesus, Santo Agostinho, or Divina Providência, which were of comparable size to the finest churches and monasteries in Europe. Since Goa in 1600 had only small and modest buildings as terms of comparison, it was no surprise that the Fortaleza Palace should stand out, especially as the daily luxury of the court contrasted so starkly with the respective surroundings.

I do not believe, as some have suggested, that the building reveals any influence from Hindu palaces and mansions, other than possibly in the structure of the roofs, whose eaves may have included means to help air circulate and cool the building. It is quite possible that the windows – as in the archbishops' palace – had slats instead of glass, but these were minor elements that were adopted from local architecture, as were the jalousies that appear in the picture of houses in Rua Direita, included in Linschoten's *Itinerário*.

Bed, Goa (?), late 16th–early
17th century, teak and lacquer.
Azeitão, Quinta da Bacalhoa CAT. 44

THE CONTENTS OF THE FORTALEZA PALACE

During each governorship treasures from all over India and beyond – in fact, from wherever Portuguese traders, missionaries and diplomats travelled in Portugal's service or wherever embassies came from – were brought together inside the Fortaleza Palace. Not only did the viceroy need furniture, fabrics, utensils and a whole range of objects for his daily needs (and those of his staff), but he also collected such items that Asian potentates sent him either for his service or for that of his king. Diplomatic gifts – called *sagoates* – were initially donated to the Jesuits, as a result of either a genuine or a hypothetical royal order. While the priests originally kept a close control over such gifts, this changed with the arrival of Viceroy Dom Luís de Ataíde, the Count of Atouguia, who in our opinion correctly argued that such things belonged by right to the viceroys and not to the kings of Portugal. As such, he added, the gifts should be handed over to him, which was precisely what happened from that moment on, despite the Jesuits' protests.[34]

As noted above, whenever a new viceroy arrived in Goa, he would find the Fortaleza Palace stripped bare, and he would have to furnish it, fit it out and decorate it with the money he received for holding his senior post. Thus, every three years – occasionally six, when the viceroy's mandate was renewed, and in one case a nine-year period of service – a ship would be loaded up with oriental household goods and set sail for

Writing box, Mughal India,
16th century, ebony, exotic wood, teak,
ivory and iron.
Oporto, private collection CAT. 107

Cabinet, Mughal India, first half
of the 17th century, ebony, *sissó* wood,
ivory and horn, iron and brass.
Funchal, Museu da Quinta das Cruzes
CAT. 108

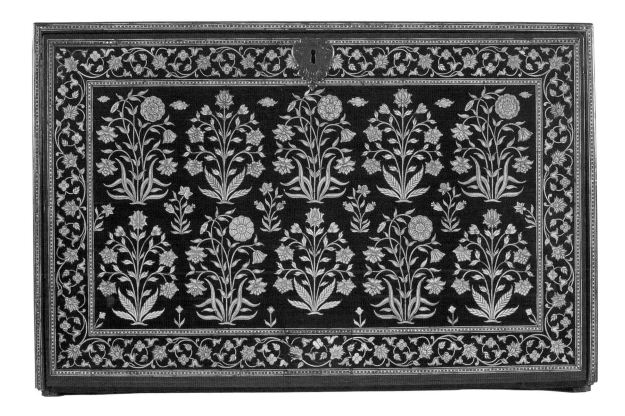

Lisbon. The incoming viceroy would then contact local traders and craftsmen and suppliers from Taná, Chaul, Bassein, Cochin, Gujarat, Cambay and even China to replace the essentials. The optional extras would be gradually added later, especially during visits to the strongholds in northern India. It is consequently no surprise that there is so much Indo-Portuguese or typically oriental art in Portugal, much of which came via Goa, as the Portuguese who served in the Orient brought back the property they had purchased or been given.

This raises the question of what goods the viceroy's servants could purchase when he arrived and had to fit out the bare palace. The answer can be found in official documents and travellers' reports. The first and most obvious need was for furniture, which would necessarily have to be of the type that is now called 'Indo-Portuguese', as Indian furniture was incompatible with the lifestyle of Europeans – particularly those from the upper classes.[35] Naturally, some pieces of furniture were adapted or even adopted, but this was the exception rather than the rule. The English would later experience the same difficulties in trying to find appropriate furniture, especially beds. Indian craftsmen soon started to imitate the furniture that came over on the fleets, and within a short space of time there was a flourishing industry in several cities that catered for the new clientele's needs. All this is thoroughly documented, as was the option of purchasing furniture from the strongholds in northern India, the Mughal Empire and further flung zones such as China and Japan.

François Pyrard de Laval mentioned that two or three times each year, convoys of three or four hundred ships would bring travelling beds and painted and lacquered bed-frames, chairs, footstools and stools from Cambay and Surat. The same cities also produced superbly crafted German-style desks with mother-of-pearl and ivory marquetry set with gold, silver and stones. In addition, they also made smaller cabinets, caskets and tortoiseshell boxes, using a technique to make the shell turn very pale and highly polished.[36] João de Barros, the head chronicler, reported back on what was said in Lisbon, claiming that Patan could be compared to Florence or Milan, exporting all manner of beds, chairs, vessels, weapons and so forth there. In similar fashion, Jan Huyghen van Linschoten was delighted by Sind, a region that produced desks, cabinets, caskets, boxes and many other pieces inlaid and decorated with mother-of-pearl. These items were shipped all over India and sold in Goa and Cochin before being taken on to Portugal.

Alongside Bassein, Thana and Bombay, Chaul was also an important production centre for the furniture that supplied Goa. Pyrard de Laval said that the city produced many richly decorated and high quality caskets, boxes – then called *bocetas* (purses) – cases and Chinese-style desks, as well as beds and bed-frames that had many differently coloured lacquers.[37] Friar João dos Santos repeats this in *Etiópia Oriental*, more accurately adding that about half a league up river, away from the Portuguese city, there was a 'Moorish' settlement called Upper Chaul where many 'gentiles' (Hindus) lived. These people were almost all traders or various sorts of craftsmen that produced all kinds of coverlets, marquetry desks, travelling beds and other items. They also made highly detailed pieces on a lathe called *brincos* or gewgaws (trinkets).

These texts confirm the importance of work from Gujarat and other regions of the Mughal empire or neighbouring areas that were heavily influenced by the empire, as well as proving that these items were in plentiful supply at the height of the sixteenth century. Therefore, there are no documented grounds for maintaining the attribution of all the surviving items of furniture to the seventeenth century.

Coverlet, India (Gujarat or Sind),
mid-17th century, cotton and silk,
260 x 209 cm.
Lisbon, MNAA, inv. 2164 Tec.

The travellers also speak about the professions exercised in the different streets in Goa: lapidaries, goldsmiths and producers of precious objects, each of which had a specific street, as well as furniture makers. Although the city was mainly inhabited by administrative staff, men of the cloth, soldiers and their respective servants, there were also many specialist craftsmen who depended directly on the administration. These included smelters, minters, caulkers and such like, alongside others whose work was of high economic value and therefore had to be supervised, such as the lapidaries.

As Linschoten noted, most of these artists and traders were Indian. Many of the gentile Indians living in Goa were rich – leading merchants who did great trade. In one street the shops were all owned by Indian gentiles who sold not only all the silks, satins, damasks and porcelain curiosities from China and other parts, but also products made of velvet and silk, satin and similar materials from Portugal. Their agents would buy such goods wholesale, before selling them retail, apparently a natural ability that they had. Others on the opposite side of the street had a vast variety of fabrics, shirts and made-to-measure clothes for sale, both to slaves and to the Portuguese. In brief, there were all the gewgaws that one could imagine. Linschoten later added that there was another street where the Banyans from Cambay lived, selling all the products and merchandise from their homeland, including a vast range of precious stones, such as coral and pearls, which they knew how to pierce with great skill. Other streets that only housed gentiles produced all sorts of goods using lathes, including beds, chairs and similar pieces of furniture, which they then covered with artistic multi-coloured lacquer decorations, also preparing lacquer to suit their clients' tastes. In turn, another of the main streets was occupied by gentile jewellers who produced both gold and silverware.[38]

One previously unnoticed report was written by Francesco Carletti, a merchant and adventurer who was born in Florence in 1573 or 1574 and left Italy in 1594 to trade in slaves. He travelled throughout the Spanish empire in South America and the Orient until he reached Portuguese-ruled territory, staying in Goa for almost two years and returning to Europe in 1606.[39] The comparison he made between the State of India and the Mughal empire is of particular interest here, as their merchants and diplomats crossed paths in the respective capitals, confirming the close links between the two powers in the early seventeenth century. He also mentioned the quantity of goods that Gujaratis brought from the lands of the Great Mughal, and marvelled at some gems of truly exceptional size, adding that it was all sent on to Portugal. More important still are his comments on the contents of the houses. This clearly refers to the most important ones, which can be extrapolated to include the Fortaleza Palace, where the luxury would necessarily have been even greater. In Carletti's own words, in Goa the houses were solidly built and had rich decorations. Everything that one could desire in terms of the quality and beauty of furniture came from China: from luxurious printed cloths and silk embroidered with gold to beds, caskets, travelling beds, desks and chairs. All these pieces of furniture were gilded and covered with black lacquer that came from the bark of a Chinese tree. This varnish stuck like pitch but immediately became waterproof and as shiny as a mirror; all these pieces of furniture were of exceptional quality. The Portuguese used to decorate their houses with these objects and others that were brought from other parts of India, and they stayed inside these houses most of the time, for the great heat prevented them from going outside.

Evidently, the preferred pottery was Chinese porcelain, which was sold in several shops, as noted above. When the Italian Jesuit Father Francesco Pasio arrived in Goa in

Shaving basin with the coat of arms of
Dom Rodrigo da Costa, Viceroy of
India (1686–90), China, c.1690–1710,
white porcelain with cobalt blue
underglaze decoration.
Lisbon, Fundação Oriente CAT. 52

1578, he was most impressed by the quantity of such pieces and their low price, adding
that it was not even worth making copies. Pyrard de Laval's comment on the use of fine
porcelain, even at the local hospital, is well known, but Pasio's less famous statement
merits wider knowledge.

There is so much porcelain and at such an attractive price that I saw nobody there making plates,
cangirões, bowls or similar things in clay, for porcelain is sold so cheaply that they could not sell
clay pots for any price without wasting their time and losing money. And they even have porcelain
under the bed to be used during the night …[40]

Carletti made similar comments, also linking porcelain's beauty to the excellence of the
food that was served in the plates and dishes.

I firmly believe that Goa was where the bulk of the trade in Asian works of art and
craft took place. Again, Pyrard de Laval significantly noted, referring to Cambay and
Surat: 'When the fleet arrived, the joy of the merchants and all the people was great,
although they rarely let the Malabar corsairs take anything.' He went on to add: 'Yet the
main wealth that it brought was in silk and principally cotton clothes, which everybody
wore, from the Cape of Good Hope to China, men and women, from their heads to their
toes.' He also mentioned coverlets (embroidered, painted and padded or not), heavily
lacquered travelling and other beds, German-style desks with mother-of-pearl, ivory
and gold marquetry, small cabinets, caskets and boxes, etc.[41] Although he was referring
specifically to Cambay, the same was true of the fleets that arrived from Malacca, China
or Japan.

THE FORTALEZA PALACE AS AN ENTREPÔT FOR ORIENTAL TREASURE
EN ROUTE TO PORTUGAL

Many works of art – particularly pieces of jewellery, silverware and what may be classed as examples of *exotica* and *naturalia* – passed through the Fortaleza Palace before being sent on to the court in Lisbon. Such items were often specifically commissioned by members of the royal family, while others were purchased by the governors and viceroys as presents for their monarchs, very frequently as diplomatic gifts, although some were kept by the royal representative. Nonetheless, those that had been specifically given by Asian potentates as gifts for the king of Portugal were forwarded to Lisbon at the earliest opportunity.[42]

Great use must have been made of textiles in decorating the palace. In the early days of the Portuguese presence in India throne-rooms with Flemish tapestries were temporarily set up on poop-decks or inside ships and galleons to formally receive rulers and ambassadors.[43] However, some decades later, oriental goods had taken the upper hand. An extrapolation of the importance of such materials can also be made from the decorations in churches and the buildings run by the religious institutions, which had countless curtains, door-hangings, carpets, bench-covers and other 'mountable' fabrics. Carpets from the Middle East – Turkey, Persia and the Caucasus – and from the area that is now Afghanistan, as well as from northern India, were very common in Portugal. Logically, the same would be true of the viceroy's palace in Goa, as the floors of the main rooms and of campaign tents would be covered in such carpets. The main hall in the palace also featured a large velvet canopy and a dais that must have been covered with carpets. Indeed, the portrait (now at the Museu Nacional de Arte Antiga, Lisbon) of Viceroy Dom Francisco de Mascarenhas, which was unquestionably painted in Goa, shows a table covered with a red velvet cloth.

Portrait of Dom Francisco de Mascarenhas, 13th Viceroy of India (1581–4), Goa, 16th century. Lisbon, MNAA CAT. 38

Portuguese and foreign collections also include embroidered coverlets and quilts whose exact origin is as yet unknown, but which are unquestionably Indian. The iconography on some of these pieces proves that they were specifically commissioned, while others were evidently influenced by individual engravings or illustrations in European books. Door-hangings – some with European coats of arms – are also known,[44] and there are frequent references to curtains exported to Portugal following the first voyage in 1498.[45] Equally, liturgical vestments in fine Indian fabrics can still be found in Portuguese churches, having evidently been brought back as bolts of cloth and then tailored, although it is perfectly natural that others should have been produced in the Orient. Examples include three albs in Braga Cathedral and another at the Museu Nacional do Traje (National Costume Museum), Lisbon.[46] There would also naturally have been a large number of parasols at the palace, as shown in the engravings that illustrate Linschoten's *Itinerário*, the same principle applying to the pillows and cushions used when travelling in litters.

It is possible to draw up a list of the many types of fabrics that were most probably found in the Fortaleza Palace, either for use there or to be sent to Portugal. To start with, there was the coverlet in white cotton now at the Museu Nacional do Traje, measuring 2.61m long by 2.16m wide.[47] This piece is embroidered with chain stitch using white cotton thread and has traces of the tow filling between the two layers of cloth, while the lining and fringe are in white linen. The central medallion surrounds the arms of Dom Vasco de Mascarenhas, first Count of Óbidos, who was the forty-ninth Governor and twenty-seventh Viceroy of India. Although his term of office, between 1652 and 1653, ended badly, he was later appointed to other senior posts, such as Viceroy of Brazil.

The Museu Nacional de Arte Antiga collection includes a door-hanging measuring 3.34 m by 2.62 m and showing the arms of the Cunha family, as studied by Maria José Mendonça when the piece was first purchased. Almost certainly commissioned by João Nunes da Cunha, the first Count of São Vicente and thirtieth Viceroy of India,[48] the form shows the branch that corresponds to the lords of Tábua. Another coverlet, this one with the arms of the Mascarenhas family, specifically of Dom Filipe de Mascarenhas, the twenty-sixth Viceroy, is now in a private collection.[49]

Dom Francisco da Gama also brought a range of fabrics back with him when he finally returned to Portugal in 1628.[50] As is known, he was delayed at the Reis Magos College in Bardez, where an inventory of all the goods he was carrying was drawn up. The resulting document is exceptionally important, since it reveals the items that viceroys would normally bring when they completed their tours of duty. Clearly, not all of them would have been interested in the same products, but there is no other such document from that period, although similar ones do exist for the eighteenth century.

The inventory mentions several velvet and taffeta bags holding all manner of objects inside. The list includes two cloths to cover *bufetes* (sideboards), three silk carpets, two satin coverlets, four silk coverlets and two other very fine coverlets, whose material is not identified but may have been cotton and also embroidered, as well as one piece of camlet (type of velvet made of silk, wool and camel's hair). Many clothes for everyday use were also listed, but it is impossible to tell if they were made in India or Portugal. For example, the Museu Nacional do Traje has a luxurious cotton cloak with silk chain stitch, garland stitch and knot stitch embroidery that the leading specialist Maria Helena Mendes Pinto has dated to this period.[51] Although its origin is not known, it can give some clue as to the style of the cloaks that Dom Francisco must have worn.

Sixteenth-century Portuguese furniture, which has been superbly studied by Bernardo Ferrão, still showed little differentiation, a situation that would only change during the seventeenth century, leading to the establishment of new types in the eighteenth century. The pieces produced were fundamentally beds and travelling beds, chairs and stools (sometimes footstools used for ceremonial occasions), chests and trunks, cabinets, desks, writing-desks and drawers, in addition to the less commonly mentioned screens. The chests were of fundamental importance, as they were used to store everything, including books, clothes and kitchen utensils. The shape of the lid differentiated these chests from trunks, as the latter had dome-shaped lids – a clearly Western form that was designed for maritime voyages, since water would run off the surface.

As shown above, the Fortaleza Palace had state chairs and footstools, but the chroniclers made no note of anything else. However, the aforementioned inventory of the goods that Dom Francisco da Gama brought back to Lisbon in 1628 can be used to supplement the sparse data, as it was to good effect by Maria Helena Mendes Pinto.[52]

Coverlet with the coat of arms of
Dom Vasco de Mascarenhas,
27th Viceroy of India (1652–3), Goa,
cotton and linen.
Lisbon, Museu Nacional do Traje
CAT. 45

The number of desks or chest-writing desks that Dom Francisco brought back to Lisbon was exceptional: no fewer than fourteen. One was lined with partially gilded silver on a teak structure; at least five were made of black-wood and two had their respective supporting tables or sideboards, as well as silver fittings. One is said to have been for a dais and another for a shelf, while two were *namban* chests 'from Japan', decorated with gold and mother-of-pearl. As can be seen, these desks varied in size, material and the number of drawers. The cargo also included three small writing desks or chests of drawers and a silver-lined cabinet.

It is strange that there were so few pieces of furniture, especially cabinets – which were already common by then – state chairs or tables, although there were many small boxes. In fact, while there are many cabinets that may date from the seventeenth and eighteenth centuries, few definitively belonged to any of the viceroys. Two known examples bear the arms of Dom Filipe de Mascarenhas, a nobleman who had a lengthy career on the coasts of the Indian Ocean and who was in Goa in 1633, before going on to govern the east coast of Africa. His career included being Viceroy of the State of India, a post to which he was appointed in 1645, staying in the capital of the oriental empire until 1651. One of his cabinets is now at the Museu Nacional de Arte Antiga;[53] the other – its pendant – is in a private collection.[54] There is also a small writing box, measuring little over one hand-span in width, which may have belonged to a governor of India and certainly bears the arms of the Costa family on the central drawer. If it is a late work, then it could have belonged to Dom Rodrigo da Costa, who did not actually hold the title of viceroy. However, he was resident in Goa when the first Count of Alvor died and, as the first in line of succession, governed from 1686 to 1690.

During the period under examination, much of the furniture at the Fortaleza Palace would have been adapted to immediate needs, specifically for ceremonies. As the foreign travellers reported, servants even took chairs to the church for religious events or placed them in the viceroys' room for receptions, depending on who was visiting. The same also applied to the tables, which could often be dismantled and had trestles, whereas the many famous chests where everything was stored enjoyed a more fixed position. However, while some were plain, solid and utilitarian, others – such as the valuable desks and cabinets that had more sophisticated decoration – presumably belonged in the rooms reserved for ceremonies and socializing.

Countless items of gold and silverware, jewellery and precious materials passed through the palace treasury. Many of them later formed part of the sixteenth- and seventeenth-century *Wunderkammer* belonging to European royal and noble families, as proved by the abundant documentation and the many objects in foreign collections that were based on these royal treasures.[55] The leading collector of Indian gold and silverware and jewellery in sixteenth-century Portugal was Catherine of Austria, the wife of King João III. However, most of her collection dated from an earlier period than the one under examination, with viceroys such as Dom João de Castro purchasing several items for her, while others were acquired by Portuguese factors or her own emissaries.[56]

In similar fashion, the Fortaleza Palace had also temporarily stored a dagger measuring 2.5 spans and decorated with gold and precious stones, which the ambassador of the Sultan of Bijapur gave to King Sebastião.[57] Likewise, a set comprising a ceremonial saddle and related trappings for the king's horses was produced in 1568

Sacristy armoire, Goa, c.1660–70, teak, ebony and gilded copper. Oporto, private collection CAT. 46

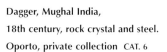

Dagger, Mughal India, 18th century, rock crystal and steel. Oporto, private collection CAT. 6

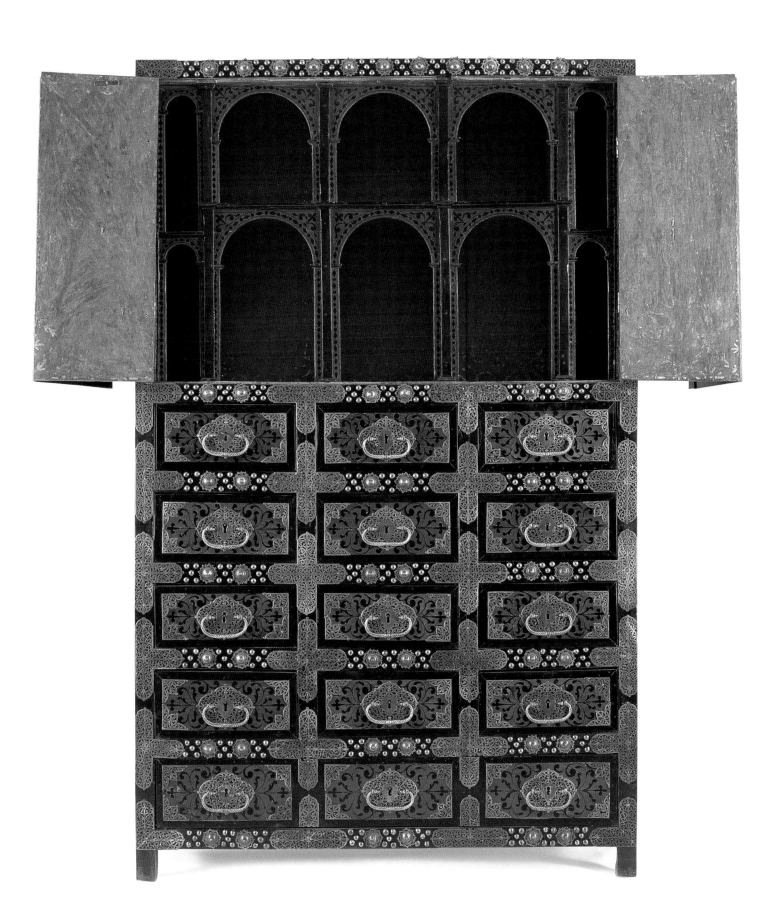

by order of Viceroy Dom António de Noronha.[58] However, it was kept for too long at the palace and ended up in poor condition, leading to major and costly restoration work. Not only does this demonstrate that the conditions for conservation inside the treasury or strong-rooms were not ideal, but also that the required care was not always taken, even with outstanding pieces that were for the king himself. The weight of the gold alone on the saddle, which was apparently made up of ten separate parts, was approximately 4 kg. In addition to the quality of the work, it was also decorated with precious stones, including some rare ones of exceptional size.

One outstanding piece that was purchased or expressly commissioned in Goa by Viceroy Dom Matias de Albuquerque is the gold filigree casket that belonged to the Graça Monastery in Lisbon. This was a gift from the viceroy's widow, D. Filipa de Vilhena, who donated it for use in the main chapel of the private section of the church, which she patronized.[59] Dated approximately 1597, it is now at the Museu Nacional de Arte Antiga.[60]

The cross that Dom Frei Aleixo de Meneses, Archbishop and Primate of the Indies and Governor, gave to the Nossa Senhora da Graça monastery in Lisbon is another extremely valuable object that was undoubtedly stored in the palace treasury. The archbishop himself said that it had cost between sixty and seventy thousand *cruzados*, and was brought back to Lisbon in 1612[61] on the *Nossa Senhora da Penha de França*.[62]

Casket of Matias de Albuquerque, 15th Viceroy of India (1591–7), Portuguese India (Goa?), third quarter of the 16th century, gold filigree with enamels.
Lisbon, MNAA CAT. 49

A rock crystal casket, recorded as being from Venice, also probably followed the same route. This magnificent casket, a gift from the king of Hormuz, was later adapted for use as a box to hold the sacrament.[63]

Bezoar stones were also highly desirable items in Europe, especially when decorated with filigree and precious stones. Amongst other properties, they were reputed to be able to dispel melancholy, as noted by Garcia de Orta.[64] Dom Francisco da Gama, a lover of exotic items, also purchased several bezoar stones that were first kept at the palace before being sent on to Lisbon. His *Livro de lembranças*, analysed when he was under arrest, records hundreds of gems and jewels that he sent back to his family, friends and even merchants in Lisbon during his time as governor.[65] Suffice it to say that, when arrested, the viceroy was taking many jewels with him. The origins of these jewels, already in their settings, included northern India, the Mughal empire and Ceylon, but he was also carrying loose gems, most notably diamonds. During his time in government, the treasury at the Fortaleza Palace was evidently an authentic Ali Baba's cave. It is also known that a goldsmith named Domingos Nunes set several stones for the viceroy, who made one single order for a box with twelve jewels that had been purchased in Malacca. Likewise, in 1625 and 1626 he had others made for family and friends, keeping one whistle-shaped piece decorated with gold for himself.[66]

Few of the many pieces of porcelain that the governors and viceroys must have used at the Fortaleza Palace, or that they ordered to be sent back to Portugal, can definitively be included here. In fact, only those bearing heraldic devices can be positively identified. The Museu Nacional de Arte Antiga has a plate with the arms of Matias de Albuquerque, the thirty-second Governor and fifteenth Viceroy of India. However, this may have been a previous commission, as Albuquerque had served as the captain of Malacca and Hormuz, and excavations carried out in 1977 in the latter city revealed part of an identical – or at least very similar – plate.[67] Whether purchased in one or the other location, it is highly likely to have been one of many at the palace in Goa.

Venetian casket, a gift to the Convent of Graça, Lisbon, from the Archbishop of Goa, Governor Dom Fr. Aleixo de Meneses (1607–9), rock crystal, 66.5 x 96 x 68 cm. Lisbon, MNAA, inv. no. 576

Left: Plate with the coat of arms of Matias de Albuquerque, 15th Viceroy of India (1591–7) China, Qing dynasty, Wanli period, last quarter of the 16th century, blue-and-white porcelain. Lisbon, MNAA CAT. 50

Below left: Plate with the coat of arms of Dom Francisco da Gama, 16th Viceroy of India (1597–1600), Portugal, c.1600, gilded silver. Lisbon, Santa Casa da Misericórdia de Lisboa/Museu de S. Roque, inv. no. 613 CAT. 51

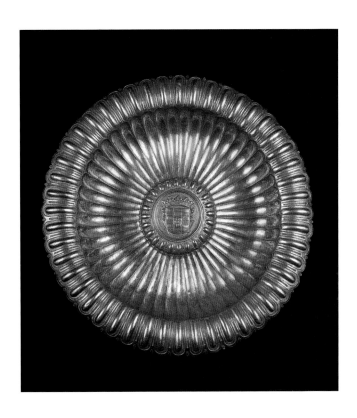

There are also several other pieces with the heraldic devices of viceroys and governors from later periods than the one studied here.

The aforementioned inventory of Dom Francisco da Gama's goods refers to many other types of works of art and craft objects for daily use. Such pieces were both commonplace and normally found inside the palace. However, the *namban* items are of particular note: small *urushi* (lacquer painting) and *maqui-e* (sprinkled picture) boxes; a gilded bronze cross with relics; two other small boxes, one containing powder; a round box that may well be a wafer-box; four enamelled tobacco-holders; eight crosses and more. The list also includes several devotional sculptures in ivory: a large figure of Christ crucified; three more measuring about 60cm tall; two more measuring 40cm and two figures of the Christ Child. In addition, there was a Good Shepherd sitting on a heart, a black-wood sacrarium with a figure of Christ inside and several other images of less worth inside a box. The list goes to record an almost endless number of rock crystal pieces, including six forks, six spoons and five knives whose handles were made of crystal and had gold inlay, which was clearly Mughal work. There was also a rock crystal whistle set with gold and precious stones, and a reliquary decorated with stones, bells, etc. In contrast, there was little silverware – some reliquaries, a complete inkstand and a basin – although there were also several pieces associated with clothing and weaponry, such as swords and decorated daggers.

Pompeu J. Batoni, *Portrait of Dom Luís de Meneses* (5th Count of Ericeira), Viceroy of India (1717–20), 1781. Cascais, Câmara Municipal de Cascais/Museu Condes de Castro Guimarães CAT. 41

Portrait of António Pais de Sande, Governor of India (Council of 1678–81), Goa (?), 17th century. Lisbon, collection of José Lico CAT. 40

CONCLUSION

It seems valid to conclude that the Fortaleza Palace never gained the dimension it deserved because the governors and viceroys spent relatively little time in the post and consequently avoided making large-scale investments, which had to come from their own pockets. The structure was no better than adequate, as was also true of the decoration and furnishings, which were only used during each mandate. Consequently, and in contrast to the royal courts in Europe and the Orient, there was no accumulation of treasures. Even so, foreign and Portuguese visitors were impressed by what they saw, and the ante-chambers, chambers, inner chambers, strong-rooms and warehouses held many of the objects that can still be seen today in major European museums and collections. Not only was the palace the centre of political power, but it was also an entrepôt where precious goods, works of art and crafts waited to be shipped back to Europe.

'RARITIES FROM GOA' AT THE COURTS OF HUMAYUN, AKBAR AND JAHANGIR (1530–1627)

Pedro Moura Carvalho

The arrival of the Portuguese in India had several consequences, some of which are well known and easily identifiable. One example is the introduction of animals and plants from America that became common in the subcontinent. It is therefore no surprise that the names for these species in Hindi are often the same as in Portuguese. Other consequences are less direct, since the Portuguese, as the first Westerners to arrive there in considerable numbers, acted primarily as a point of contact between Europe and India. Again, one case in point is the absorption of Renaissance artistic notions by Mughal painters.

However, the absence of records makes other areas of study, as for example music, difficult to evaluate. The arrival at the Mughal court of musicians who played European instruments and the fact that Western music could be heard in the successive Mughal capitals for several decades does arouse speculation as to whether they had an influence on the development of local music.

The scarcity of documented sources has made it difficult to assess the impact of the Portuguese presence in the subcontinent and, more specifically, in Mughal India. Nevertheless, there are sufficient extant works of art to allow us to establish the unique role that Goa, the capital of the Portuguese State of India, played in bringing the two cultures together.

A Turkey, Mughal India, c.1678–98.
Cambridge, Fitzwilliam Museum
CAT. 60

Phoenix Attacking a Gaja-Simha
[elephant-lion], album leaf, Mughal
school, first half of the 17th century,
gouache on paper.
London, British Museum,
1920.9-17.0126

INTRODUCTION OF NEW PLANTS AND ANIMALS TO INDIA

By linking Europe permanently to India, America, Africa and other regions of Asia, the Portuguese laid the foundations for trade on a worldwide scale. However, they were more than mere traders. On numerous occasions they perceived the potential for certain plant species in the subcontinent. It is difficult for those who at present visit India to conceive that fruits such as the pineapple arrived there from South America during the sixteenth century. Contrary to what might be thought, the enormous success of this fruit and the Indians' great love for it do not date from modern times. As early as the end of the sixteenth century it was already appreciated at the Mughal court. In c.1590 Abu'l Fazl, the chronicler of Emperor Akbar, described both the plant and its fruit, noting that it adapted and developed well during long journeys.[1] By the early seventeenth century pineapples were being grown in large quantities in one of the capitals of the Mughal empire. Akbar's son Jahangir (r. 1605–27) explains its arrival and describes it in his *Memoirs*:

In the reign of my father many fruits of other countries, which till then were not to be had in India, were obtained there [in Agra] … Among fruits, one which they call ananás (pineapple), which is grown in the Frank [i.e. Portuguese] ports, is of excessive fragrance and fine flavour. Many thousands are produced every year now in the Gul-afshan garden at Agra.[2]

It is thus no surprise that the word for pineapple in India is the same as in Portuguese.

What is presumably the earliest depiction of a pineapple plant in India is to be found on an Indo-Portuguese writing chest probably made on the Coromandel Coast in the late sixteenth century.[3] This and other plants and animals are painted in gold against a background of lustrous red lacquer on the inner side of the lid. This in itself is unusual, since evidence of the earliest contacts between Europeans and Indians is normally found in the Mughal arts.

Mughal miniatures showing either pineapples or the respective plant are unknown, but it is highly likely that they were produced, since the Mughal emperors displayed a special interest in botany from an early stage. Babur (r. 1526–30), the founder of the dynasty, describes many plant varieties, while his descendants took this interest still further,[4] commissioning celebrated artists to depict them.

Yet this interest was not restricted to flora, as fauna also warranted due attention from the emperors and Mughal painters. The most famous example is perhaps a depiction of a dodo, an animal that must have arrived in India not long before 1615 when the miniature was painted.[5] Unlike that unfortunate bird, which was ignored by contemporary chronicles, a turkey and an exotic monkey were described enthusiastically and in some detail by Jahangir. In fact, the emperor even ordered that the animals be portrayed 'so that the amazement that arose from hearing of them might be increased'.[6] The animals had reached the court via Goa, having been acquired to satisfy the wishes of the emperor, who sent one of his officials there in 1612 to obtain 'certain rarities'. At least two miniatures of a turkey have survived, the one at the Victoria and Albert Museum perfectly demonstrating the skill of such artists as Mansur, one of Jahangir's favourite painters, responsible for some of the finest animal portraits ever produced.[7]

The introduction of the pineapple and the turkey into the subcontinent was thus a direct consequence of the Portuguese presence in India. However, not all the plant and animal species brought on board sixteenth-century vessels are nowadays so attractive.

The tobacco plant, introduced into Portugal in 1558, was one such case. Although the precise date when tobacco reached the subcontinent is unknown, the imperial chroniclers once again provide exact information on its appearance at the Mughal court. This occurred in 1604 when Akbar became the first Mughal emperor to inhale tobacco smoke, having received it as a gift from one of his officials, Asad Beg, who had acquired it previously in Bijapur.[8] Given the proximity of this sultanate to Goa, it seems valid to conclude that the growing of tobacco first expanded in the Deccan,[9] the central Indian plateau where Bijapur is located. Asad Beg also mentions that the plant was totally unknown to him. To consume it, he had a jewelled pipe that the emperor used until stopped by his doctor, who forbade him to smoke. Even then, tobacco gave rise to contradictory reactions: Europeans believed it had beneficial pharmacological properties, while locals chose to reject it because it was something new. Jahangir might have been the first ruler in history to forbid tobacco. Although the emperor was a self-confessed consumer of narcotics and alcoholic drinks, he prohibited the use of tobacco in 1617.[10] This measure proved nevertheless to be of very little consequence. The large number of extant *huqqas*, the name given to the water pipes used for smoking on the subcontinent, many of which were made of precious materials, demonstrates the failure of these first 'anti-smoking' edicts. Tobacco continued to be greatly appreciated at the court in later periods; in the first decade of the eighteenth century tobacco – possibly from South America – was still included in the list of presents to be taken by the embassies sent by the Portuguese viceroy in Goa to the Mughal court.[11]

WESTERN MUSIC AT THE MUGHAL COURT

The interest that the Mughals showed in European inventions reached one of its peaks in 1575 when Akbar sent a mission to Goa to acquire all kinds of European 'novelties'. As I have shown elsewhere,[12] the results of this mission and its impact on local arts are not well known. The arrival at the court of at least one organ, however, is well documented.[11] As well as referring to this instrument, Abu'l Fazl also records that when the mission returned in 1577, the musicians from Goa played other musical instruments.[14] It is interesting to imagine the impact that the sounds produced by these instruments must have had on the imperial audience. Abu'l Fazl described this moment as fascinating, 'ear and eye were delighted, and so was the mind'.[15] The fact that musicians were included on this cultural mission is not surprising since music was essential in both religious and secular ceremonies. When Dom João de Castro was given a triumphal reception in Goa in 1547 to celebrate his victory in Diu, chroniclers Gaspar Correia and Diogo do Couto detailed the many *charamelas*,[16] trumpets, *atabales*,[17] drums, flutes, timbrels, pipes and other 'lively instruments' that were played.[18] In all likelihood the instruments that were taken to the Mughal court would have been similar.[19]

It is also relevant that Renaissance music was heard for at least several decades in some of the most important Mughal urban centres. Music is of course an integral part of Christian liturgical rituals; the fact that the Jesuits founded several chapels and churches in different parts of the empire, notably in the capitals of Agra and Lahore, meant that the local residents were in permanent and relatively prolonged contact with European music. For example, in 1599 the Jesuits celebrated the Pentecost in Lahore with the baptism of a group of recent converts. The ceremony, 'performed publicly, and with great magnificence', was preceded by a procession that was accompanied on the way to the church by 'musicians [who] marched in front of them with drums, trumpets, clarions, flutes, and other musical instruments'.[20] Likewise, in 1607, as part of the celebrations surrounding the Passion in that same city, 'another grand procession' was 'accompanied by musicians with hautboys, which they had learnt to play in Goa, having been sent there for that purpose; and as these instruments had never been heard or seen in the country before they attracted many people and caused much astonishment'.[21] Before the Christmas midnight mass in the same year, and in addition to the hymns, once again flutes, *charamelas* and drums were played.[22]

The possible consequences of the introduction of Western instruments into the Mughal court are difficult to establish. Abu'l Fazl states in his *A'in-i-Akbari* that among the instruments that made up the *nakkara-khana* – a term used to describe the military band that normally accompanied Muslim rulers – were '*nafir*(es)[23] of Persian, European and Indian origin'.[24] It could therefore well be that the European instruments, described by the chronicler as being part of the imperial insignia, also came from Goa. More recently it has been suggested that the organ was incorporated into the Indian *instrumentarium* in the form of a particular type of harmonium,[25] known in India as *peti* or *baja*.

EUROPEAN INFLUENCE ON MUGHAL PAINTING AND MANUSCRIPTS

The arts of the book, specifically bookbinding, illumination, painting and calligraphy, are generally considered to be the most important arts in any Muslim culture, and Mughal India was certainly no exception. The study of Mughal miniatures has been the subject of increasing interest in recent decades and has made correspondingly great progress. Nevertheless, many issues are still to be clarified, in particular those related to the assimilation of Western artistic concepts and iconography. From the 1560s onwards the artists working in the Mughal scriptorium demonstrated a profound knowledge of Renaissance European painting. This is particularly evident in the application of notions of perspective. A large number of Mughal miniatures also reveal other traditional concepts of European painting from this period, such as *sfumato*, as a way of conveying a distant horizon, and modelling, both of figures and clothing. Miniatures from the last quarter of the sixteenth century not only confirm that these influences had been assimilated, but that they became an intrinsic part of the Mughal school of painting.

As the means of this transmission has been the subject of a number of analyses, another summary of the existing ideas is superfluous. In general terms, the introduction of these influences is attributed to the circulation of European engravings and illustrated works within the Mughal court.[26] Within this context Plantyn's Polyglot Bible, printed between 1568 and 1572 in Antwerp and offered to Akbar in 1580, is considered of particular relevance in the development of Mughal painting.[27] Yet, it is unknown how European engravings reached the Mughal court before the arrival of the first Jesuit mission in that same year.

It was only in 1572 that Portuguese and Mughals met officially for the first time, following the Mughal conquest of Gujarat, where the Portuguese had already established themselves, specifically in Diu, from 1535. However, all evidence suggests that some Portuguese resided at the court long before that first meeting. At least one miniature from the *Hamza Nama*[28] – a manuscript recounting the adventures of Hamza, the uncle of the Prophet, illustrated between c.1562 and 1577 – includes reproductions of buildings clearly based on traditional Portuguese architecture.[29] The facade of the building in the lower left corner also appears to be 'decorated' with a cross, suggesting

European Lady Writing a Book,
Mughal India, 1610.
London, British Museum CAT. 112

*The Spy Zambur Takes Mahiya
to Tawariq, where they Meet Ustad
Khatun*, from a *Hamza Nama*,
Mughal school, c.1570, painting on
cloth, 68 x 51.6 cm.
New York, Metropolitan Museum of
Art, Rogers Fund, 1923 (23.264.1)

that the residents were Catholics.[30] The fact that an Indian woman is at the door has no bearing on this, since it is known that the Portuguese in India were encouraged to enter into unions with local women.

The materials used in the construction of the building also reinforce the view that it was based on Portuguese models. The detail with which the Mughal artists painted this miniature leaves little doubt that they intended to show a roof made of clay tiles, which are identical to those used in the Indian territories where Portuguese influence was stronger, and up to this day in Portugal. Likewise, the shape of the roof was that traditionally found in territories under Portuguese rule. Not surprisingly, these and other structures in the upper right corner of the miniature have whitewashed and undecorated walls – again following a Portuguese/European fashion – in stark contrast to the highly ornate and coloured walls of the many other buildings reproduced on this and other pages of the *Hamza Nama*. The authors of this miniature, painted c.1570, evidently resided at the court, since the manuscript was commissioned by Emperor Akbar himself. This suggests that artists actually saw similar houses and incorporated them into their work to heighten the realism of the scene. The miniature also displays European influence both in terms of the composition – the two figures depicted at the top clearly suggest Mary and Joseph on the road to Bethlehem – and in the way the principal figures are portrayed, where the volume of the figures' clothing shows a strong European influence.

A second imperial Mughal manuscript connects this type of building with the Portuguese. One of the miniatures in the *Padshah Nama* – the manuscript that recounts the life of the Emperor Shahjahan – depicts the capture of the port of Hughli (Hoogly) in 1632 by the Mughal army and includes a number of Western-type buildings.[31] This city, located north of Calcutta, was one of the main Portuguese trading posts in Bengal, which justifies the prominence given to the subject. Equally, it is not surprising that the illustrations show a number of houses very similar to those depicted in the *Hamza Nama*, with the same type of roof and undecorated walls.

The Capture of Port Hoogly, from
a *Padshah Nama*, f. 117a, c.1634.
Windsor, Royal Library/The Royal
Collection © 2004, Her Majesty
Queen Elizabeth II

The possibility that Portuguese traders resided at the court around 1570 suggests that it was they who were responsible for the transmission of European artistic concepts to the Mughal ateliers. Besides they were in constant contact with Europe, having regular access to different types of goods, including those of an artistic nature. The lack of references supporting the view that Portuguese traders were present in the Mughal court during the first half of the sixteenth century is probably more connected to the crisis of the Mughal empire in 1540 than to the merchants' non-existence. It is important to bear in mind that during the years between 1540 and 1555 the second Mughal emperor, Humayun, was forced to seek refuge in the Persian court, only returning to reclaim the throne in 1555.

During this interregnum Portuguese traders had established themselves in several courts in northern India, as shown by the words of Leonardo Nunes, author of the little-known *Crónica de D. João de Castro*, written c.1546. He clearly refers to the 'many Portuguese who were in Cambay [i.e. Gujarat] looking after their businesses,'[32] adding that 'there were many Portuguese in Cambay and they resided at the king's court, which is in the city of Amadaba [i.e. Ahmadabad, the capital of Gujarat], a very populated and large city'.[33] It is thus likely that many other Portuguese resided and/or traded in earlier periods and at other courts. Indeed, documentary sources show that products from Europe and more precisely from Portugal were to be found at the Mughal court as early as 1530.[34]

According to Gulbadan Begam – Humayun's sister and author of the manuscript *The History of Humayun* – her brother's victory in Chunar was duly celebrated in Agra in 1530. On that occasion the large tent for audiences was decorated inside with European brocade and outside with Portuguese cloth.[35] The fact that the princess specifically mentions Portuguese textiles implies that these and probably the European brocades had reached the Mughal capital via the Portuguese rather than by some other means.

Dove pendant, Mughal India (?),
17th century, gold, rubies, diamonds,
emeralds and rock crystal, 10 x 6 cm.
Paris, Museé national des Arts asiatiques
– Guimet (MNAAG), MA 6768

MUGHAL ABSORPTION OF CHRISTIAN ICONOGRAPHY

As mentioned above, European iconography was assimilated by Mughal painters. Western prints are thought to be the origin of these, but another factor in this transmission may well be the engravings with prayers and images of saints that were being produced in Goa before the introduction of the press in that city. Letters from members of religious orders in Goa show that from at least 1539 wood blocks were used to make engravings.[36] This was a naturally economical technique for producing copies in large numbers and ideal for the diffusion of missionaries' ideas. The introduction of printing in 1556 fuelled a larger-scale and faster spread of Western models, since locally printed works were inexpensive when compared to manuscripts or even imported works; they also became available in greater numbers. Since it was the Jesuits who were responsible for this innovation, the programme for publications naturally focused, albeit not exclusively, on religious works.[37] Many of these were certainly taken to the court to facilitate their missionary work.

It is therefore no surprise that the Mughals absorbed Christian iconography. Apart from imagery portraying the Mughal emperors with haloes – which may or may not have been inspired by Western models – other iconographic motifs clearly exhibit this influence. For example, several portraits show the emperors accompanied by chubby, winged angels (*putti*) clearly copied or derived from European models.[38] In similar fashion, representations of the Holy Spirit – traditionally depicted in Western art as a

'The Conquest of Diu', from Jerónimo Corte-Real, *Sucesso do Segundo Cerco de Diu* (The Success of the Second Siege of Diu), Part XII, Lisbon, 1574. Lisbon, IAN/TT CAT. 18

CERCO DE DIV. CANTO. XII.

dove portrayed frontally with open wings – inspired Indian artists or, in this case, jewellers, for a number of dove-shaped jewels have survived.[39] Representations of the Holy Spirit can still be seen adorning some facades[40] and interiors[41] of Goan chapels and churches – suggesting that the same was previously true in other regions under Portuguese rule[42] – yet the inspiration for such jewels lies in a different Christian tradition. When Christianity was introduced into sixteenth-century India, 'the dove was the symbol with which Christian women replaced the jewel known as *murtnunim* or *mangala-sutra*[43] which the Hindu husband usually places around his wife's neck during the wedding ceremony'; this tradition did not disappear until the end of the nineteenth century when the dove symbolizing the Holy Spirit was replaced by the cross.[44] The existence of Catholic communities throughout the subcontinent explains therefore the existence of a variety of jewels that have the form of a dove. While this does not mean that such pieces were made exclusively for Catholics nor that they exclusively represented the Holy Spirit, there seems to be little doubt that they were inspired by a Christian tradition. Significantly, Akbar and his successors, as well as Mughal artists of different periods, had access to this same iconographic motif from a very early stage (1580) since the opening illustration of the first volume of the *Polyglot Bible – Pietatis Concordiae*, by Pieter van der Borcht – is surmounted by an image of the dove symbolizing the Holy Spirit.[45] Curiously, the same dove surrounded by solar rays is also seen in a few Mughal portraits, including one in a canopy above Shahjahan's throne in Agra, illustrated in the *Padsha Nama*.[46]

Of interest is the fact that Jahangir had himself portrayed with a sun and a crescent moon.[47] While the use of such powerful symbols by a ruler may now seem excessive, that was not then the case. Suffice it to mention that when he came to the throne, Jahangir did not hesitate to change his name to 'World Seizer' (Jahangir), also giving himself the honorary title of 'Light of the Faith' (Nur-ud-din). The justification that the emperor himself provided for the latter title – that sunrise had coincided with the first time he sat on the throne – has been used to explain the appearance of haloes in his imagery, but no reason has been put forward for the use of the crescent moon. However, both this moon and the sun are known attributes of the Virgin,[48] which were reproduced by Renaissance artists and, at later periods, in both European and Portuguese Indian painting. Seventeenth- and eighteenth-century Indian artisans also produced large numbers of ivory images of the Virgin standing on a crescent moon.[49] It is therefore possible that some of these had reached the court or that he had admired them in a Jesuit chapel.

European engravings are regarded as fundamental in this transmission process, but they cannot explain the relatively rapid and highly successful adoption of artistic concepts that were foreign to Hindu and Muslim artists. Besides the fact that they were not coloured, prints were far from ideal in expressing such Renaissance concepts as *sfumato* or the chromatic changes in a distant horizon. On the other hand, the existence of oil paintings and of European painters working at the court does explain, at least partially, the rapid assimilation of these concepts. Documentary sources confirm that oil paintings did indeed reach the court a few years after the first meeting between Portuguese and Mughals. In 1580 the missionaries on the first Jesuit mission from Goa to the imperial court gave Akbar two paintings: a portrait of Jesus Christ and a second of the Virgin. Pierre du Jarric, who reports that occasion, also notes that the second work was a copy of a painting that was then in the Church of Santa Maria Maggiore, Rome.[50] This provides direct evidence that at least one Italian-style work had been seen both by the emperor and presumably by his most renowned artists. Subsequently, the Jesuit added that the two paintings were among the best that had been sent from Portugal,[51] a practice that had begun as early as 1511, when painted altarpieces arrived in Cochin from Lisbon.[52]

More important, 1595 saw the arrival at the Mughal court of a European painter – an anonymous Portuguese layman who accompanied a group of Jesuits. Although Portuguese-European painters were recorded in Goa from at least 1552,[53] it is not known whether any of them reached the Mughal court. However, it is known that Prince Salim, Akbar's eldest son and future Emperor Jahangir, commissioned this artist to copy a painting of the Virgin that the missionaries had taken to Lahore.[54] Du Jarric also states that the 'Portuguese, or other Christians' resident at the court offered Salim other works 'from India or Portugal', i.e. Goa. However, the imperial family was not only given works from Europe. The Jesuits also offered Akbar paintings of Christ and St Ignatius of Loyola produced in Japan,[55] and an *Our Lady of Loreto*, apparently from China, since it was painted on a copper alloy commonly used in that country.[56] Among other more unusual gifts are the life-size portraits of Afonso de Albuquerque and the then Viceroy Aires de Saldanha, given to Akbar in 1602.[57] These works may have increased the emperor's interest in physical and psychological portraits, as may be seen in the numerous portraits from that period and is confirmed by contemporary chronicles.[58]

Follower of Juan Pantoja de la Cruz,
Portrait of Aires de Saldanha,
17th Viceroy of India (1600–1605),
Spain, c.1590.
Lisbon, Museu Nacional do Traje
CAT. 39

The arrival of religious works based on Italian models can easily be explained by the prestige enjoyed by the Italian school, but also by the fact that many missionaries had trained there or were from there. This also explains how Mughal painters absorbed Italian mannerisms, particularly evident in the depiction of clothing and the use of perspective. It is, however, more difficult to understand the successful absorption of artistic concepts that are normally related to northern European schools. This includes the way in which distant landscapes are painted, using subtle variations in colour to create atmospheric effects of varying intensity. On various occasions it has been suggested that this transmission of styles was initially achieved through Flemish tapestries,[59] as some miniatures – such as the ones that illustrate one version of *Khamsa* of Nizami (c.1595) – are 'so clearly vastly reduced versions of much larger compositions'.[60]

A FLEMISH TAPESTRY-MAKER IN INDIA

Besides Humayun, his successors also received European textiles.[61] Jahangir, for example, was given a 'European curtain', probably a tapestry, of remarkable beauty in 1608, sent from Cambay by one of his officials.[62] Although this tapestry may have had some impact on the paintings produced at the time in the Mughal workshops, the relatively late date of its arrival at the court cannot explain earlier uses of these technical devices. More significantly, the fact that Herman Vermeiren, a Flemish tapestry-maker, was in India during the 1580s may make a decisive contribution to clarifying this issue. Little is known of Vermeiren's life other than that he was born in 1544, and at some point moved to Lisbon, where he set up a tapestry factory. Before 1584 he was due to return from India to Lisbon, where he married the daughter of Gaspar Condertorf, then one of the most important Flemish traders living in the capital. This undoubtedly contributed to his thriving business, since he owned at least one ship involved in the Antwerp–Lisbon trade.[63] In 1596 he accompanied Cardinal-Archduke Albert (1559–1621) as his head tapestry-maker back to Brussels,[64] which was the most famous production centre of European tapestries at the time. The fact that Herman Vermeiren held such an important position not only meant that he was well versed in the technical aspects of this demanding industry, but also that he was fully aware of the most recent artistic trends. After all, Cardinal Albert was no less than the brother of Emperor Rudolf II and, more importantly, had been Viceroy of Portugal.

The factors that led a tapestry-maker to embark on such a long and dangerous voyage to Goa in the late sixteenth century remain unknown. It would be no exaggeration to claim that Herman Vermeiren, an entrepreneur by nature, set off in search of new opportunities for trade. The fact that he lived in Lisbon guaranteed direct access to sophisticated Indian textiles that arrived regularly, perhaps leading him to believe that there was a market for tapestries or that he would be able to set up a tapestry factory in India. He would naturally have taken samples of his work with him, but soon must have realized that Mughal palaces wanted ventilation and had no great walls in contrast to their European counterparts, for whom tapestries became popular for, among other things, keeping out draughts. Furthermore, their conservation in the difficult monsoon climate was to prove problematic. Nonetheless, this may not have prevented some of them reaching the Mughal court, where they would certainly have been seen at the highest level.

The study of jewellery is a second area where substantial progress has been made in recent years. Techniques used to produce filigree and enamels, for example, may have been transmitted to Mughal artisans – described as 'many clever craftsmen'[65] – during the mission in 1575. On their return to the court they were made to show how much they had learnt during their stay in the capital of the Portuguese State of India, and received great praise from the emperor for their work.[66]

Furthermore, the participants in this and other missions had access to the best that Goa had to offer. At that time Goa was one of the most cosmopolitan territories of its age. Besides the trade with Europe and indirectly with the Americas, ships from every territory where the Portuguese had settled, ranging from the Far East to the most diverse points on the African coast, all reached Goa. Only after 1600 did other Europeans, the English and the Dutch, begin to travel to India in large numbers, as a result of the formation of their various Indies trading companies. The report written by the Fleming merchant Jacques de Coutre in c.1595 is enlightening on this trade. A vast range of goods came from Ceylon and other parts of the subcontinent, including Sind, Gujarat, Chaul, Bengal and Meliapor. The local markets had 'large pieces of amber … curiosities from Germany'; ivory and slaves from Mozambique; pearls from Bahrain ('the best in the world'), which came via Hormuz and Muscat; horses from Persia; dried fruits and so on. Silver came in from Manila, and many kinds of silk, gilded furniture and porcelain from China. Other regions of South-East Asia, known at present as Indonesia, Malaysia, Thailand and Myanmar, supplied many different kinds of textiles and spices, in addition to precious stones.[67]

Gemstones such as emeralds, which are particularly closely associated with the Mughals, were imported from South America, especially Colombia and Peru. Vast quantities of normally small, cabochon emeralds were used in jewels, but also to decorate all manner of objects, ranging from flasks and dishes to such items of furniture as tables and thrones.[68] The Mughals also had access to large emeralds, but unlike their Ottoman counterparts – who preserved them in their original crystalline form, that of a hexagonal prism[69] – the local lapidaries cut them in transverse sections. The purpose of this was to create larger surfaces, since the uniform structure of emeralds allows them to be carved, as seen in an example in the Khalili Collection.[70] Its decoration suggests a dating between 1650 and 1675, while its deep green colour and unusual size (164.33 carats) indicate that it is from Colombia. According to Tavernier, South American emeralds were by this time reaching India on Spanish ships sailing via the Philippines,[71] but in earlier periods their port of entry was Goa. Little attention has been paid to Garcia de Orta's reference in his *Colóquios*, published in Goa in 1563, that the emeralds in India had originally come from Peru.[72] These were acquired by Portuguese merchants in Seville, then the European capital for trade with the New World.[73] This route must have been used to transport to the Mughal court a famous emerald with relief decoration, now in the al-Sabah Collection, dated 1580–1600.[74]

Carved emerald, Colombia/Mughal India, 3rd quarter of the 17th century, 164.33 carats.
London, Nasser D. Khalili Collection of Islamic Art, inv. JLY 1856

MUGHAL INFLUENCE ON THE INDO-PORTUGUESE ARTS

The arts of painting, music and jewellery are areas where the influence of European cultures was at its strongest. Encouraged by the Mughal emperors, court artists were prompted to discover and absorb foreign artistic ideas and concepts. As in other periods of the history of the subcontinent, they managed this with great success, assimilating these concepts and transforming them into something intrinsically Indian. However, this was not the case in the Portuguese-ruled territories: with one exception – a particular type of furniture decorated with ivory inlays and normally described as being of Mughal influence – the Mughal arts had virtually no impact on their Indo-Portuguese counterparts.

It is noteworthy that this exception to the rule occurs precisely in an area where the Mughals had no great tradition: the use of furniture. Several explanations for this can be put forward. First, this type of furniture was not produced in Goa, but in Gujarat and Sind, territories that were located far from the capital of the State of India and were, consequently, less influenced by European traditions. Miniatures and documentary sources show that emperors such as Akbar, Jahangir and Shahjahan, as well as their ruling classes, used European-style furniture, including chairs/thrones and cabinets.[75] Among the miniatures showing this type of furniture is the *Portrait of Rustam Khan*, from the mid-seventeenth century, in the Chester Beatty Library.[76] The upper border of the miniature shows two figures, presumably servants, placing different jewels in the drawers of an undecorated writing-cabinet. It can therefore be concluded that many of these pieces were produced not for the Portuguese market, but for the local one. The same conclusion applies to pieces decorated with inlays.

Cabinet, Goa, 17th century,
wood and ivory.
Lisbon, MNAA CAT. 117

Left: *Portrait of Rustam Khan,*
Mughal India, c.1650–58.
Dublin, The Chester Beatty Library
(CBL) CAT. 113

17th century, teak, ebony, ivory and brass.
Lisbon, Fundação Ricardo do Espírito Santo
Silva (FRESS) CAT. 105

Left: Cabinet and table, Gujarat or Sind, late
16th–early 17th century, ebony and ivory.
London, V&A CAT. 116

The main decorative themes used in the latter pieces include hunting, courtly scenes and animal fights, normally based on Mughal models. This is certainly the case with the decorative motifs on the cabinet in the Fundação Ricardo do Espírito Santo Silva[77] and of those on the cabinet and table in the Victoria and Albert Museum.[78] Very similar motifs also appear, for example, on the tile mosaic panels on the outer walls of the Fort of Lahore. These date from the reign of Jahangir and may have been the source of inspiration for the craftsmen who produced the inlaid work.[79] Only very occasionally do figures dressed in Portuguese fashion or other European motifs appear, such as those on the table top at the Victoria and Albert Museum.[80]

The origin of the form of the so-called *contadores de capela* or pyramidal cabinets is more enigmatic. Only a few such pieces are known, including one in London and another in the Távora Sequeira Pinto collection,[81] both of which date from the seventeenth century. The form does not appear to be European, and it is unlikely to have been based on Mughal prototypes. It is therefore possibly a local innovation. Given that most of the known examples are in Portugal – where they began to arrive at the end of the sixteenth century – the pieces were probably made specifically for this market.

With the exception of this type of furniture, it may be stated that the Portuguese and the artisans who worked for them systematically ignored Mughal aesthetics. There are various reasons for this, including geographical issues and cultural elitism. Questions relating to the aesthetic criteria of the age must also be considered, as well as the fact that the Portuguese and other Europeans in India had very limited access to the products made by the imperial workshops. Indeed, Sir Thomas Roe highlighted this fact while visiting Agra in 1615. Despite being an ambassador and thus presumably having easier access to goods of higher artistic quality, the Englishman complained that carpets were the only merchandise available.[82] This confirms that the imperial workshops worked – as might be expected – exclusively for the imperial family and the ruling classes; such goods therefore had a limited circulation.

In geographical terms, Goa was far removed from the various imperial capitals. This applied equally to the period when Mughal art had reached a certain maturity – i.e. c.1570–80, which to some extent matches the golden age of Goa as the capital of the State of India – and to later periods. The capitals successively established at Agra, Fathpur Sikri, Lahore and, once again, Agra were not just the residences of the sovereign and his court, but also the places where many hundreds of artists and craftsmen from the karkhanas, or imperial workshops, plied their trade. Even when the Mughal armies conquered the sultanates of the Deccan in the mid-seventeenth century, and the territory of Goa became much closer to the frontiers of the Mughal empire, it always remained on its periphery.

Issues of taste are also relevant. The governing classes of Goa were culturally elitist and Eurocentric in attitude. While undoubtedly admiring the boundless wealth of the Mughal court, they viewed its attraction as lying more in its splendour and ostentation than in the artistic quality of the imperial workshops. The absence of documentary sources does not permit definitive conclusions, but the comments of contemporary European travellers place more emphasis on the prodigious richness of the court than the quality of the art produced for the Mughal sovereigns. When, for example, William Hawkins gained access to the treasures of Jahangir in 1609, he described them by enumerating the different types of precious stones and other gems, as well as miscellaneous objects such as German swords, saddles and drinking vessels. While his fairly exhaustive listing is practical for precious stones, the same is not true for objets d'art. The English captain stated that of the 500 vessels 'fifty are very rich', since each one was made from a single spinel ruby, emerald, turquoise, piece of jade or other type of precious stone,[83] but he makes no mention whatsoever of the quality of

Pyramidal cabinet, Mughal India (?), 17th century, ebony, teak, ivory and gilded copper.
Oporto, collection of Távora Sequeira Pinto CAT. 106

**Altar front preserved as a table top,
Gujarat or Sind, 1600–10, lignum vitae
and ivory.
London, V&A** CAT. 84

the lapidaries' work. Even travellers, who were supposed to possess greater artistic sensitivity, are notorious for their lack of this type of reference. Around 1660 a professional jeweller like Tavernier produced a highly detailed description of the thrones and jewels of the Mughals. However, once again he is most struck by the richness of the materials, the uncommon size of the gems, and their great abundance,[84] not by the artistic quality of the works in question. This may seem strange when we observe extant pieces, since many of them are of very high technical and aesthetic quality and are comparable to the best work produced at contemporary European courts; this applies equally to *pietra dura*, textiles and jewelled objects. Therefore, it may be that the high quality displayed both in technical terms and in the design of a particular object did not arouse the same enthusiasm among sixteenth and seventeenth-century travellers as it did in later periods.

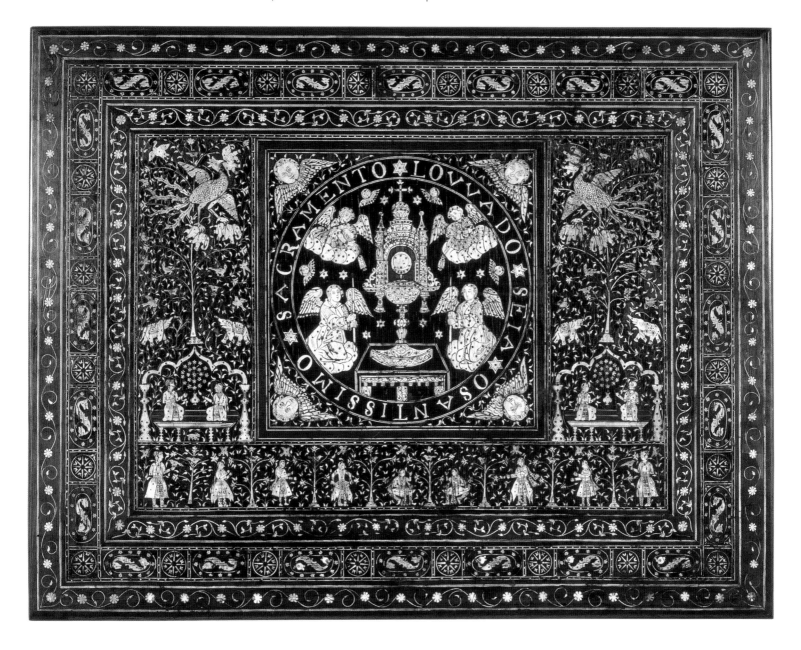

Precious Stones, Jewels and Cameos: Jacques de Coutre's Journey to Goa and Agra

Nuno Vassallo e Silva[1]

The name of Jacques de Coutre (1577–1640), a merchant of precious stones, is no longer unknown. The importance of his memoirs, a record of the forty years spent in the Portuguese Orient, has been emphasized over recent years, specifically in terms of the trade in precious stones in Goa during the seventeenth century.[2] This article will focus on his visit to Agra in 1619, setting it within the framework of the Portuguese oriental trade in precious objects and relations between the Portuguese State of India and the Mughal empire.

INTRODUCTION

From 1575, the date of the first Mughal embassy to Goa, the number of missions, the volume of trade and the exchange of highly skilled craftsmen between the State of India and the empire all multiplied. Within this framework the first Mughal embassy, led by Haji Habibullah, has (especially since the 1980s) aroused great interest among art historians, although study of his mission has come nowhere near saturation point.[3]

Like those that came after it, this first embassy combined a variety of different purposes, ranging from diplomacy to trade, from exchanging merchandise to hiring craftsmen, and even embraced the purchase of rarities for the emperor. To a large extent, this explains the interest in the mission, as it acted as the genesis for subsequent cultural and artistic exchanges. In turn, these were chronologically defined cultural catalysts that art history has managed to reconstruct within a minimally credible – albeit necessarily truncated – framework.

Beaker and cover, Mughal India, second half of the 17th century, silver. London, V&A CAT. 118

As part of the Mughal embassy to Goa in 1575, Emperor Akbar sent Governor António Moniz Barreto a gift of two exceptionally fine brocade robes of honour and a velvet cap decorated with gold. One of the men who saw these items was Diogo do Couto, who described them and added that the gold decoration on the hat was embroidered in the Portuguese style. This itself is a very significant fact, given that the Mughal emperor 'had a great liking for Portuguese dress',[4] an attachment that mainly developed after the emperor's first meeting with a group of Portuguese merchants in Cambay in 1572. Akbar demonstrated his curiosity about the 'Portuguese-style' clothes that the merchants were wearing and was consequently given countless such items of clothing. His interest was renewed at his next contact with the Portuguese (March 1573), but in a more official manner when he met António Cabral, the ambassador of Viceroy Dom António de Noronha, in Surat.[5]

When he sent his first mission to Goa, Akbar instructed Haji Habibullah to bring back many clothes, swords, sword-belts and all the other accessories required for attire. Mughal interest in the Portuguese style of dress would later be demonstrated by its appearance in many surviving Mughal portraits and paintings, and would in fact go still further. In 1620 Viceroy Dom Francisco da Gama decided to give Emperor Jahangir's nephew, who was then visiting Goa and had expressed some interest in embracing Catholicism, some 'Spanish-style' clothes, namely black hats with coloured feathers and a sword.[6]

Returning to the 1575 embassy, it is very interesting to note that Couto spoke to Haji Habibullah several times during the latter's stay in Goa, and left a written portrait of 'a very serious man and widely read in their history'. Although Portuguese sources emphasize the political aspects of the embassy, this was clearly not the only issue. Couto's *Década IX* includes a transcription of the letter that Akbar sent to the governor but ignores the lengthy period of time spent in Goa by the craftsmen who were part of the embassy. Even so, he does emphasize that the Mughal emperor had ordered that some curiosities and silks from Portugal should be taken back.[7]

The Jesuit Duarte de Sande provided a fine commentary on this embassy in a description that he sent to Rome in 1579, relegating the political questions to second place and highlighting the pragmatic issues. 'In the time of António Moniz, he sent here an ambassador with many Mughals who stayed for one year and learnt almost all our crafts, so they – with some Portuguese that they took with them – introduced our dress and other Portuguese customs there.'[8]

Shortly afterwards, in 1596, several goldsmiths from Goa were working in Lahore, 'continuously' producing Portuguese-style gold jewellery for Akbar. Some of the pieces were shaped like reliquaries – even though this is a rather vague term – which the Jesuit Jerónimo (Jerome) Xavier much admired.[9] As early as 1601 the emperor sent another embassy to Goa, when Aires de Saldanha was viceroy, requesting that

if there are any skilled craftsmen who desire to visit our royal court, which is like the mansions of the blest, he shall give them all that they need in food and apparel, and ... having been in our service, they shall freely be given leave to return to their country whenever they so wish.[10]

The taste for Western craftsmen and for European-style pieces was obvious at the court in Lahore.

Casket, India, late 16th century,
silver and tortoiseshell,
11.3 x 22.5 x 12.2 cm.
Diocese de Lisboa

Casket, India, c.1570–80,
tortoiseshell and silver.
Lisbon, private collection CAT. 114

Casket, India, c.1570–80,
tortoiseshell and silver.
Montijo parish church CAT. 115

Many years later, Portuguese craftsmen could still be found working for the Mughal emperors. One such case was Lourenço Mendes, who designed jewels for Shahjahan, as Susan Stronge demonstrates below. As new nations came into contact with the empire, the Mughal idea of Europe expanded far beyond the Portuguese world, and more foreign craftsmen would enter the service of the Mughal court.

From the start the embassies promoted at the Mughal court many of the precious items that had been unloaded in Goa, not all of which were of European origin. In 1598 Francesco Carletti noted that much of the Chinese porcelain traded in the Portuguese-governed city of Macao was to be shipped to Goa, before being sent on to the Mughal empire. It was known that the emperor had a particular liking for this yellow and green porcelain.[11]

From a very early stage one of the main aims of the Mughal embassies to Goa was to acquire precious stones, as the city was then unquestionably a major centre in this trade – perhaps the most important in India. In the 1601 mission Akbar wrote to ask Viceroy Aires de Saldanha to help the ambassador with these purchases, specifically by extending credit for items, stones and 'other similar items worthy of the treasury'.[12] The movement of stones in the opposite direction was also well established. In the early seventeenth century a large diamond weighing around 200 carats was to be found in Goa, brought by an ambassador of the Great Mughal.[13] Thus, embassies to Goa became the most efficient means of supplying luxury goods to the Mughal empire, moving in parallel with the economic and commercial development that the business brought.

The presence of Mughal craftsmen and works of art in Goa inevitably had an influence on local work, especially precious objects, although on a relatively limited scale. One small group of silver objects that reveals a significant stylistic unity, albeit with some minor variations, appeared at the same time as the first Mughal ambassadors reached Goa. The items, produced between 1575 and 1600, stand out among pieces from Goa's workshops as they introduced naturalistic motifs that were foreign to local work and very probably due to the influence of Haji Habibullah's embassy in 1575 and the presence of Mughal craftsmen in Goa. This group consists of the so-called 'Vidigueira treasure', whose silver mounts for a set of tortoiseshell caskets are stylistically very coherent. The gold pieces also include a whistle from the Deutscher Orden, now in Vienna (see below).

Unfortunately, it cannot be claimed that the latter years of Akbar's reign saw a trend or even a fad in Goa that was influenced by this Mughal art, as these pieces may suggest. Even the means of introducing Mughal art raises countless questions that have yet to be answered, although it probably became known mainly through the many textiles that the embassies took to the capital of the State of India. However, there can be no doubt that the workshops of the silversmiths and jewellers produced items that had an exotic feel that was not only Mughal. This is demonstrated by the lidded tankard at the Museu Nacional de Arte Antiga, Lisbon, and the rhinoceros-horn cup with a silver mount at Ambras castle, pieces that never again appear in Goan work. The most creative period in terms of precious objects was, beyond doubt, the last quarter of the sixteenth century, when a range of motifs from a vast array of origins all came together.

The 'Vidigueira treasure' consists of a lectern for a mass-book, an oratory-reliquary and a pax, all made by the same workshop. The name derives from the Carmelite Convent of Nossa Senhora das Relíquias in Vidigueira, the Alentejo region. They originally belonged to a larger group of silverware bequeathed to the convent in 1597 by Father André Coutinho, who had taken vows towards the end of his time in the

Manuel Furtado, *View of Goa*, Goa, 1716.
Lisbon, private collection
CAT. 36

Left: Oratory-reliquary, Goa,
c.1570–80, silver and enamels,
60 x 40 cm (open).
Lisbon, MNAA, inv. 99

Orient, having previously amassed a huge fortune as a merchant during his thirty years in China and Goa. Prior to his return to Lisbon (c.1575–80) he commissioned a large set of silver liturgical items in Goa, of which only the above-mentioned pieces are now known. In general terms they are skilfully constructed in Late Renaissance style, but also possess certain decorative elements that make them unique.

The reverse of the pax is decorated with engraved floral designs and small birds, a motif that is repeated on all three works that make up the Vidigueira set, also appearing on the rear of the lectern and the base of the oratory-reliquary. Branches rise from the ground, flanked by rabbits and gazelles, and end in bunches of grapes, vine (?) leaves and flowers, as well as the small birds. The origin of this design has yet to be established. The stylized treatment of the branches is similar to that of some paintings of the 1590s, specifically those on certain pages of the *Babur Nama* that Akbar commissioned.[14] The vine leaves and bunches of grapes are comparable to images in one of the miniatures in *Tilasm and the Zodiac*, painted around 1565–70 and now at the Raza Library, Rampur.[15] While the rabbits and gazelles in the margins of the paintings, *A Chained Elephant* and *A Mogol Chieftain and Attendants*, on two loose pages from an album commissioned by Jahangir (now at the Freer Gallery, Washington),[16] are more accomplished, they are very similar to the animal motifs engraved on the silver.

Right: Pax (front and back), c.1570–80,
silver, H 20 cm, L 13 cm.
Lisbon, MNAA, inv. 98

Another element that characterizes the set is the use of decorated bands with highly individual motifs. The circular base of the reliquary has one such band with scrolling foliage and occasional flowers, birds and gazelles. These motifs are in low relief so that they stand proud of the flat stippled backgrounds. The same motif is repeated on the lectern, crowning the front where the mass-book stood and forming a double frame on the back. In artistic and iconographic terms this is the most important motif, as it highlights the spectacular 'IHS' encircled by a halo and surrounded by the figures of the four evangelists. These bands also recall the silver ones applied to the small but decoratively uniform set of tortoiseshell baskets.[17]

A most important piece, evidently produced at the same time as the Vidigueira set, is the casket at the Barbadinhos church in the Graça area of Lisbon.[18] In addition to the solid silver bands, which have chased and engraved motifs, the plaques of tortoiseshell that form the casket are painted inside with aquatic, floral and animal motifs that are of unparalleled sophistication in comparison to work that is known to have been produced in Portuguese India.

In addition, a small group of caskets produced in the 1590s shares the same decorative motifs, with spiralling vegetation and animals, although the work is more stylized and has none of the technical skill of the above pieces. In comparison to the first group of works mentioned, the motifs on the bands are smaller yet simultaneously more complex and elaborated, while maintaining the same decorative theme.

The provenance and date of two caskets now at the Chapel-Reliquary of the Basilica of San Lorenzo de El Escorial make them of particular importance. Significantly, they were incorporated into the chapel in 1597, which helps to establish their date,[19] and one of them is known to have been purchased in Lisbon by Empress Maria, the sister of Philip II of Spain.[20]

Three similar works are known in Portugal. The first was originally at the Convent of Santa Clara, Coimbra, and was incorporated into Coimbra Cathedral Treasury in the nineteenth century, following the dissolution of the religious orders. The second – whose size and type are identical to the Coimbra casket – was part of the Hipólito Raposo Collection in Lisbon.[21] Finally, mainly owing to its size, pride of place goes to the casket at the mother church of Montijo. The similarities between the silver mounts on these caskets are such that it is tempting to attribute them all to the same workshop or to workshops that were very closely linked. However, great care must be taken with attributions of workshop origins when referring to pieces produced in Portuguese India or, in general terms, outside Europe.

It is very significant that the decoration on these bands, particularly those on the first group of works from Vidigueira, can also be found on the silver bottle at the Museum of Indian Art in Hyderabad.[22] Although this was recently dated to the middle of the seventeenth century, I believe it may be from an earlier period.[23] The bands that spiral around the body are strikingly similar to the ones described above, which have scrolling branches dotted with small animals on the stippled surfaces. Until other works appear, this suggests that the motif was well known and widespread across northern India and that the silversmiths of Goa had, in all probability, incorporated it after direct contact with art from that area, which reached Portuguese India through Akbar's first embassies.

The treasury of the Deutscher Orden, Vienna, owns an item of jewellery that is of great importance and was recently published as having been produced in Goa. The item in question is a gold whistle with applied rubies and diamonds, called the 'Portuguese whistle'.[24] This jewel, known through documents since 1619, was very probably produced in the last quarter of the sixteenth century and is somewhat hybrid in nature, combining Mughal and Portuguese features.

This is evident in the delicate engraved floral motifs, which are similar to some pieces produced in the Mughal empire, while the ring setting for the precious stones is typically European. Thus, the engraved decoration can be associated with such works as the gold spoon with precious stones at the Victoria and Albert Museum, produced late in the reign of Akbar,[25] and the gold surface of the rose-water sprinkler (*gulabpash*) taken when the Delhi treasury was sacked.[26] In contrast, the setting for the stones has nothing in common with the process used on these pieces, which suggests it may have been produced in Goa – though not necessarily by a European craftsman – using a type that was well known in Europe.

Significantly, after the early seventeenth century, this type of Mughal-style decoration seems to disappear almost completely. The floral silver filigree motifs – typical of the Shahjahan period – that flank the rhinoceros-horn cup at the Kunsthistorisches Museum, Vienna, are exceptions to the rule in the known body of such work.[27]

Another interesting work from the period after Akbar's reign is a silver filigree and translucent green enamel frame at the treasury of the Basilica of Bom Jesus, Old Goa, made using the champlevé technique. In the frame is an outstanding Mughal miniature, which I believe has never been studied, depicting Our Lady and Child. In all likelihood, this was a gift from the members of the Jesuit mission in the empire to the basilica that held the body of St Francis Xavier. The use of the champlevé technique is particularly noteworthy, as it was highly developed within the Mughal empire but had fallen into disuse in contemporary Portuguese work.

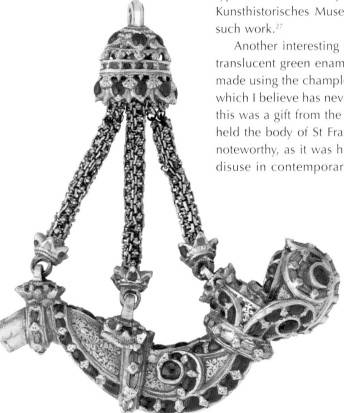

Below: Whistle, Goa, end of the 16th century, gold, diamonds, rubies and emeralds; H 9 cm, L 8 cm. Vienna, Deutscher Orden,

Right: *Our Lady and Child* in a frame of silver filigree and green enamel, Goa/Mughal India, first half of the 17th century, 27 x 23 cm. Old Goa, Museu de Arte Sacra

JACQUES DE COUTRE

In 1592, like so many other European fortune-seekers, Jacques de Coutre and his brother Joseph set out from Lisbon for Goa. Both were natives of Bruges, and Jacques (the younger brother) was just sixteen when he arrived in Lisbon to meet his brother, who had reached the city previously and then summoned his sibling in the light of good business opportunities.

Coutre did not start his career in India as a merchant, but instead as a soldier, serving the Portuguese crown until 1603. This was one of the most effective ways of entering the colonial empire. Following eleven years of military service, he reached Goa on 2 May 1603 and married D. Catarina do Couto, a Portuguese lady and sister-in-law of his brother, just six days later, immediately settling in the city. He joined forces with his brother in Goa and began a staggeringly successful twenty-year career as a merchant of precious stones. He only left in 1623, when there was a wave of xenophobia that also saw the expulsion of many other foreign merchants who were accused of dealing with the Dutch. The latter, who were then Portugal's enemies, coveted Portugal's overseas possessions and flourishing trade.

Yet the brothers had come into contact with oriental precious objects long before arriving in Goa. While still a soldier in Malacca, Coutre was already trading fabrics for jewels for a Venetian merchant called 'Sequin Martinela'.[28] In 1594, before his eighteenth birthday, he was even sent on an embassy to the Kingdom of Pahang (*Pão*) to buy diamonds and bezoar stones since, so he claimed, he understood such things, a fact that must have attracted the Portuguese authorities' attention. In his career as a gem-merchant Coutre twice came to Europe overland, disobeying the Portuguese crown's prerogatives, which correctly saw the revival of this route as a serious threat to its monopoly over oriental precious stones. Coutre's clients were not just the residents and merchants in Goa. Rather, his memoirs show that he was involved in a range of activities all over the Indian continent, from Cochin to Agra. However, he did concentrate on Goa's neighbouring kingdoms, such as Bijapur and Vijayanagara, whose rulers were among his regular customers for jewels and precious stones.

In 1623, when both he and his brother were expelled from Goa, they were sent to Lisbon as prisoners, where they were kept at the Aljube jail.[29] However, they were released and later worked as lapidaries for Kings Philip III and IV of Spain in Madrid.[30] It was there that Coutre wrote his memoirs, which were unfortunately only printed 350 years after his death. The original version of the text, now lost, was written in Portuguese and then translated into Castilian by his son, Dom Estêvão de Coutre, in 1640, perhaps in the frustrated hope that it would be published.

FROM GOA TO AGRA

In the early seventeenth century the main trade in diamonds and precious stones in Goa was dominated by a small group of merchants from a range of different geographical origins. They included Europeans – mainly Portuguese, Flemish and German nationals – as well as Indians, mostly from Gujarat and Goa. Among the most important were the Portuguese Domingos Nunes and João Roiz de Lisboa,[31] as well as the German Ferdinand Cron and, of course, the Flemish brothers Jacques and Joseph de Coutre.

It was from the last three that 'Mir Musa Moluco', Jahangir's ambassador, purchased a large amount of jewels and pearls when he travelled to Goa in 1619. Since he was a known and trusted client who paid punctually, the merchants advanced goods worth 12,000 *xerafims*, of which 9,000 were for purchases from Cron and 3,000 from the

Coutre brothers. Little is known about 'Mir Musa Moluco' (Mir Musa [Mu'izzul Mulk]), although it is likely that he was a 'merchant-prince' of Iranian origin who served as *Mutasaddi* of Surat in 1629–35, 1639–41 and 1646–9.[32]

Since the ambassador left Goa without paying any of his debts or providing guarantees to his creditors, which certainly went against his normal procedure, Coutre set off for Agra in 1619, having been granted special licence by the Viceroy Count of Redondo. His aim was to catch up with the ambassador's caravan and ensure that the debt was paid, while also making a complaint to the emperor of his mistreatment at the hands of Mir Musa during the latter's time in Goa, a part that the memoirs pass over.[33]

Coutre travelled the route from Goa to Agra, which passed through several major centres that were habitually frequented by merchants. The first was Bijapur, a city that the Portuguese knew well. The sultan, one of Coutre's clients, sent a message to the Mughal ambassador, instructing him to pay his debts, but Mir Musa ignored this request from one of the emperor's vassals and continued on his way. However, while in Bijapur, Coutre fortuitously encountered a Mughal ambassador named 'Sagramolo', who took the jeweller into his entourage, which was then returning to Agra, and guaranteed that both the prince and the emperor would immediately pay their debts. Both 'Mir Musa Moluco' and 'Sagramolo' were part of the household of Prince Khurram, the future Emperor Shahjahan, a relationship that presumably led Mir Musa to promise Coutre that he would pay him during the next stage of the journey, in the city of Burhanpur. However, the ambassador's caravan did not stop there, heading straight on to Cambay and abandoning the route to Agra.

Coutre continued to travel with 'Sagramolo' and reached the capital of the empire, where he was received by five of the emperor's servants; they were all Europeans who had lived in Agra for many years. Coutre made particular mention of two of them: Augustin de Hiriart, a French merchant from Bordeaux who received from the emperor the title 'Honarmand' (meaning 'engineer', according to the merchant), and Francesco Corsi, an Italian Jesuit who accompanied him and acted as his interpreter during his time in the city and at his meetings. Coutre was clearly impressed by the fact that all the Europeans who came to meet him were riding either on horseback or on elephants, which he interpreted as indicating high social status. In Goa it was quite exceptional for merchants to travel on horseback, requiring a royal licence. As late as 1617 two Goan merchants named 'Poinda' and 'Goinda' requested that Philip III should grant them the post of 'broker of [gem] stones' and that they be allowed to travel in litters or on horseback with parasols.[34]

During his time in Agra Coutre gave the royal family several minor gifts that he had brought from Goa for that specific purpose. It is perhaps the nature of these pieces that makes his story of such interest for the history of art. His first audience was with Prince Khurram, which is no surprise as Mir Musa was a member of the latter's family. Coutre, as a merchant of precious stones, was particularly interested in meeting the man who was then famed as a true connoisseur of gems and precious objects.[35] In fact, Mir Musa had evidently acquired the precious stones in Goa for the prince. Khurram, who was indeed a connoisseur of stones, was even more knowledgeable about the trade in gems. In one of his meetings with the prince, to whom he sold several jewels, Coutre noticed that Khurram haggled over the prices as if he were a 'poor merchant', when he actually had a vast fortune.

At this first audience, while explaining the difficulty he faced in collecting the payment due from Mir Musa, Coutre gave the prince a large cameo whose motif he unfortunately did not describe. This gift so pleased the prince that he took the merchant in as his personal guest, providing accommodation in one of his palaces near that of his father, the emperor. Coutre was delighted, as the view from his window allowed him to observe the comings and goings of the lords and grandees of the empire as they had audiences with Jahangir.

On the day after his audience with the prince, Coutre was received by the emperor's brother-in-law – the *wazir* Asaf Khan – whom he described as the second most important figure in the empire, as he had evidently been referred to by Father Corsi. He gave Asaf Khan two cameos that were described as 'very good', as well as a square stone of white jasper decorated with brick-shaped motifs in inlaid lapis lazuli, a truly extraordinary piece of work.[16]

The most important reception was obviously with Jahangir himself, which took place on the same day at nine in the evening. Coutre's vivid description of the magnificence surrounding the emperor is exceptionally revealing.

He was seated in a most majestic corridor, with all the gentlemen standing and he sitting on a most rich throne made like a bed, on a cushion, and he had hanging around his neck many precious stones and large spinel rubies, emeralds and all manner of large pearls on his arms, and many large diamonds hanging from his turban. In sum, he had so many jewels that he seemed like an idol.[17]

The emperor was flanked by two of his sons, Khurram sitting at the foot of the throne on the right and Parwiz on the left. Coutre had kept his most important gifts for the emperor. One was a silver ship that used a clock's action to move across the floor. Another was a square stone plaque with differently coloured inlays, made in Florence and showing the Archangel Michael, with hell and demons at the base of the composition. The demons were particularly to the liking of the emperor and those around him, which led to exchanges that Coutre recorded with delicate irony, especially noting the courtiers' concern to flatter the emperor, even if they contradicted what they had stated moments before. Coutre, who seized every opportunity to encourage sales, also gave the emperor a pair of daggers with sheaths and gold chains, weighing five carats and described as 'most curious and subtle'.

Coutre's gifts are of great interest as samples of the trade in European luxury objects in India, especially those that had been shipped via Goa to the Mughal empire. The mechanical ship was most probably the work of a silversmith from Augsburg or Nuremberg, which then produced mechanical table decorations, although they were not the only production centres.[38] Their appearance in Goa may be related to the contacts that Ferdinand Cron had with Augsburg, his hometown, enabling him to import the most flamboyant pieces for sale both in Goa and throughout India.

Significantly, another mechanical item appears in the miniature *Jahangir Entertains Shah 'Abbas*, painted shortly after Coutre had visited the court in Agra. This picture shows Khan Alam, the Mughal ambassador to the Iranian court, holding a figure of Diana mounted on a deer, a Mannerist work presumably in the gilded silver commonly found in Augsburg's workshops. The miniature – an authentic display-case of precious objects that the Mughal court would have considered 'exotic'[39] – almost seems to illustrate the following annual letter from the Jesuits in Agra (1618–19). 'The rich and curious pieces from the world are all in the hands of this king [Jahangir], and it seems that all Europe is involved in making pieces for him.'[40] In addition to the figure of Diana,

Jahangir Entertains Shah 'Abbas, Mughal India, c.1618, gouache and gold on paper, 25 x 18.3 cm. Washington, Freer Gallery of Art/Smithsonian Institution, inv. 42.16

the same miniature also depicts a table that was probably made in Venice, a ewer that is very similar to one of the 'Medici porcelains' produced in Florence between 1575 and 1587, a glass bottle shaped like a pilgrim flask that may be Venetian, and a small Chinese porcelain bowl.

It is not known whether these automata and silver table figures had any influence on Mughal work using precious metals. The lidded jar at the Victoria & Albert Museum, London, is perhaps the only Mughal work where there is unanimous agreement on the European origin of its type.[41] Even if this type cannot be directly attributed to Portuguese silversmiths, it was certainly not unknown in the Iberian Peninsula.

The Florentine picture showing St Michael in inlaid stone that Coutre gave the emperor was part of the work specially exported at that time from Tuscany to the court in Madrid. This type of work reached its highest level of sophistication in the early seventeenth century with the production of plaques for the altar at the Princes' Chapel at the Basilica of San Lorenzo, Florence. These marble pieces with inlays were not only used as decorations on buildings – a style that developed enormously in Portugal during later years – but also as pieces of furniture. Examples include the large tabletops such as the one in the Burnay Collection at the Museu Nacional de Arte Antiga, Lisbon.[42] Pieces like this feature delicate compositions, small commessos, some of which are decorated with flowers and birds, while others show religious themes, such as the one that Coutre gave.[43]

The arrival of a commesso de pietra dura in Agra is all the more interesting when we consider the development that the art of hardstone inlays would attain under Shahjahan, culminating in his tomb in Agra, completed in 1643. Thus, this is a rare documentary record of the way in which this type of work penetrated the empire, predating the taste for Florentine plaques and the subsequent copies and adaptations in Mughal architecture. One example of this is the plaque depicting Orpheus, found at the top of the rear wall in the jharoka of the Red Fort in Delhi. The building was completed in 1648, shortly after the Taj Mahal, and the plaque appears alongside local decorative motifs.[44]

The reference to the piece of jasper with lapis-lazuli inlays that Coutre gave to Asaf Khan is most unusual. It may have been either an Indian or a European piece, as Coutre makes no reference to its origin, and the description of the piece and its inlays does not clarify the situation. The best-known pieces of jade in the Mughal empire were inlaid with fine gold, such as the kundam, with precious stones and sometimes with more jade. However, it is not known if lapis-lazuli decoration – widely found in luxury Florentine goods using hardstones[45] – was used there.

The cameos that Coutre took to Agra were, as he himself notes, greatly appreciated. It is significant that this appreciation can be associated with the development of glyptics (carving on precious or semi-precious stones) under the patronage of Jahangir and Shahjahan, even if only in isolated cases and with few surviving examples.[46] There is no doubt that foreign lapidaries who settled in the court contributed to this, specifically the French and Italians, who had a long-standing tradition in this field of work.[47] Naturally, this should also include the different examples of foreign – and not just European – production that may have reached the imperial court. In the absence of mounts that link them to the empire, there are now no signs that can relate them to Mughal collections. The exception to this is the cameo that can be dated to the first to second century BC, mounted on a jade lotus flower that is clearly Mughal work.[48] The pieces that Coutre took with him illustrate once again the empire's interest in foreign cameos, which were clearly seen as both exotic and beautiful. Unfortunately, there are no known examples of Coutre's pieces that can be positively identified as having come from any of the imperial collections. Identified Mughal pieces suggest that the art did not survive after the end of Shahjahan's reign, or at least that it lost its dominant position. The fact that Mughal production of cameos seems to have ceased may be due to the fact that there were fewer foreign lapidaries in the court during the following reigns. If this is proved, it reinforces the theory that most of these pieces were the work of foreigners.

Besides the three cameos with portraits of Emperor Shahjahan, other examples of Mughal work – decorated with various different animals – are also known.[49] Perhaps the most famous shows Prince Khurram's victorious fight against an enraged lion, illustrating an event that took place in December 1610 and was made famous by a miniature. This is the only cameo that combines a royal portrait with the depiction of an animal. It is also of particular note as it is the only work to be signed. The signature reads Khan Attam, or 'Supreme Engraver', very probably a European craftsman who had been awarded this imperial title, just as Jahangir attributed the title 'Honarmand' to Augustin of Bordeaux.[50] Among other cameos showing animals is a sleeping lion at the Bibliothèque Nationale de France and a leopard head engraved onto agate in the collections of the British Museum. Both these large cats are, with some acknowledged artistic licence, associated with Shahjahan's liking for such animals, a love that Jacques de Coutre would experience first-hand in a dramatic event that hastened his return to Goa.

During his second meeting with the emperor's son Coutre was sent to a patio into which four lions were then released, while Khurram watched. As the merchant showed no fear, the animals did him no harm, although one even held his leg in its jaws – without actually biting. Another Portuguese merchant had previously been less fortunate and died as he tried to escape. This humiliation was probably caused by Coutre's complaint to the emperor about Mir Musa, Khurram's servant, and by the fact that the merchant had not given the prince a jewel that he had brought from Goa – probably to sell – and that Khurram coveted.[51] Following this incident, Coutre was paid for the jewels that Khurram had purchased, and the prince himself informed the merchant that Mir Musa was returning to Goa and that he had already paid him in full, questioning the merchant's word. Coutre noted in his memoirs that the prince was lying, manifesting the arrogance and cruelty that he considered to be typical of the future Emperor Shahjahan.[52]

The glyptic technique used on cameos with imperial portraits recalls the small alabaster plaque showing the man who built the Taj Mahal. The plaque, probably produced around 1630–40 by a European craftsman, is a genuine 'enlargement' of a cameo created by one of the many artists whom the emperors summoned to their courts, as Akbar had written in his letter to the Portuguese viceroy in 1601.

One major reservation must be made regarding Coutre's gifts of *objets d'art*. Tempting though it may be, given the date of his journey, to claim that he introduced such work into the Mughal court or workshops, this is not accurate. It is true that the pieces were greatly appreciated in Agra, which seems to suggest that they were not as common or well known as may be thought. However, it must be recalled that the written work in question is an autobiography whose narrator is naturally interested in inflating his achievements. The fact that it was around this time that the copying and adaptation of foreign art forms were strongly encouraged is a very significant point that will be developed in the future. Yet this was still part of the interest in new techniques that had flourished since Akbar first sent his craftsmen to Goa for the first time, rather than the influence of a single agent.

It is far more significant that the collection of precious objects that Coutre took to Agra – produced by some of Europe's most flourishing art industries – can be linked to the forms that would later become the most developed at the Mughal court. This explains why study of his visit to Agra is so important and relevant for understanding the production of luxury goods in the empire and their relationship with the market in Goa.

THE IMPERIAL TREASURY AND THE RETURN TO GOA

Thirty-five days after arriving in Agra and with his situation still unresolved, Coutre was fortunate enough to be able to observe one of the most famous items in the imperial treasury: the Throne of Jahangir. His description is all the more important as it was by a man who knew about jewellery and who also had the opportunity to compare notes with the man who had actually made the throne – Augustin 'Honarmand', or Augustin of Bordeaux, called 'the talented'.[53]

The throne was made in gold and covered with several precious stones. According to Coutre, the work and beauty were so perfect that they brooked no criticism, making it similar to the biblical throne of Solomon. Only the feet were not fashioned in gold, consisting instead of four gilded silver lions that each weighed four *quintães* (four hundredweight). The throne was also set high up, halfway along a corridor or veranda overlooking a patio. A silver staircase with around twenty steps led up from the patio to the base of the throne, and each step was flanked by a silver figure of a soldier dressed in German style, like the king of France's bodyguard. All these figures were life-sized. The throne had a gold canopy with very rich brocade, supported by two columns in enamelled gold that had been produced by Honarmand's own workshop.[54] This reference to the production of the enamels helps support the most recent theories of the European introduction of enamelling techniques to the art of Mughal jewellery.[55]

Despite being a connoisseur of precious objects, Coutre was unable to visit the imperial treasury, which must have been one of the empire's main sources of pride and a mirror of its magnificence. Nonetheless, he did leave a description drawn up by his Jesuit companion Francesco Corsi, who had seen it. The 'Mogor' had, it seems, more precious stones, pearls, gold and silver than all the kings of Europe put together.[56] Corsi had seen, among other items, eight to ten gold trays covered with pearls the size of hazelnuts and other smaller ones that were quite perfect. In fact, there were so many of them that one man alone could not manage to lift more than a single tray. He also noted that there was an equal quantity of precious stones and jewels.

Coutre corroborated the Jesuit's description from first-hand experience: 'It was very true that from all parts of the World, they send pearls, emeralds, rubies and jewels of great value to Eastern India, and we all know full well that they came to the Mughal.'[57] During his thirty-two-year career in India he and his brother had dealt in precious stones and jewels, and he claims that they were well aware that they had all ended up in the Agra treasury. This is evidently a wild exaggeration, but one that is perhaps justified by Coutre's concern to leave for posterity signs of the importance of his business as a merchant of precious stones and jewels in Goa. In the early seventeenth century Francesco Carletti in Goa stated that the Great Mughal purchased all the spinel rubies from all over the world, as these gems brought high profits when sent on for sale

**Sheath for a dagger, Goa (?),
late 16th–early 17th century, gold.
London, Nasser D. Khalili Collection
of Islamic Art** CAT. 119

in India.[58] Yet spinel rubies, emeralds, pearls, rubies and other gems and stones were not the only variety to be sent: large diamonds also appeared.

Coutre himself admired the three large gems that hung from Jahangir's turban during his audience, confirming the Jesuit's description of the riches kept in the imperial treasury. One of these stones weighed some 250 carats, the second 180 and the third, while smaller, still weighed around 140 carats. All of them were perfect and clear. In addition, the emperor's turban was intensely decorated with countless small diamonds. Coutre also recorded, with considerable interest, the important practice of the great lords – and more specifically of their heirs – to offer the emperor jewels that they had secretly acquired over many years. This practice was presumably an excellent means of pleasing the emperor and thus confirming that the privileges and lands that had belonged to their fathers would be passed on to them, or – better still – to increase these royally granted privileges.[59] Such gifts were simultaneously one of the main ways of increasing the size of the imperial treasury.

Coutre's description of the imperial treasury matches other known reports from slightly later dates, which suggests that his record is trustworthy. One of the most famous descriptions was written by Sebastião Manrique, an Augustinian who travelled round India from his base in Goa and left a detailed description of the treasury in Agra, which he visited in the early 1640s, over twenty years after Coutre. Manrique wrote that it consisted of several precious metals that had been or were to be fashioned, such as gold, silver and copper, as well as several liturgical items, jewels and precious stones, which he grouped into fifteen different categories.[60] In addition to the precious metals, which he valued at 198,342,666 rupees, the collection included embroidered tunics and decorations covered with gold, silver and precious stones that were to be worn by horses. The missionary valued the diamonds, rubies, emeralds, sapphires and other gems alone at 70,520,521 rupees. Interestingly, Manrique's fifth category included silver that had not only been moulded into vases and 'other utensils' but also into columns, beds and sideboards. This reference is to Mughal silver furniture, which is now unknown, while Manrique's scholarly interests possibly explain the addition of the contents of the imperial library – comprising 24,000 volumes – to his description of the treasury.

CONCLUSION

Jacques de Coutre's autobiography, especially the section covering his time in India and his visit to Agra in 1619, reveals the trade in precious items and the Mughal court's fascination with the 'exotic goods' that came from Europe, mainly via Goa. These memoirs – written largely as a result of his conflict with the Portuguese authorities – are both a record of the many years he spent in the Orient and of trading practices that had a considerable artistic influence. His specific case reflects a broader experience felt mainly by anonymous European and Indian merchants who took their wares to the Mughal court. The image of foreign ambassadors bearing royal gifts or Christian missionaries with religious offerings as the driving force behind transformations in and influences on art in the empire is simplistic, albeit appealing. The consumption and aesthetic demands of the Mughal empire required a constant flow of goods, jewels and countless rarities that only a port such as Goa could properly supply.

THE LAND OF 'MOGOR'

Susan Stronge

In 1498, as Vasco da Gama sailed towards the Indian subcontinent, the future founder of the Mughal empire was failing in his attempt to regain the central Asian city of Samarkand. The fifteen-year-old prince Babur was a great-great-grandson of the infamous Timur whose empire had stretched across eastern Iran and central Asia. After Timur's death in 1405 the dynasty fragmented and Babur inherited the throne of the small kingdom of Ferghana (now in Uzbekistan) in 1494.[1] However, he saw the great sovereign city of Samarkand as his rightful inheritance, and briefly took it after a seven-month siege in 1497. Other Timurid descendants unfortunately saw the city in the same way and soon ousted the young man during an ill-judged absence. By the time of Vasco da Gama's second eastward voyage in 1502 Babur had briefly reoccupied and lost Samarkand yet again and was wandering, throneless, seeking refuge with various members of his extended family.

By 1504 he had established himself in Kabul, and there formulated plans to invade the northern lands of the Indian subcontinent known as Hindustan throughout the Persian-speaking world to which he belonged. The region was regarded as another legitimate goal on the basis that Timur had made a short-lived occupation of it in 1398, but Babur had to make five separate attempts on Delhi before finally succeeding in 1526. At his death in 1530, the rule of a dynasty that would become one of the greatest Hindustan had ever known covered only a sliver of land stretching from Kabul to Delhi and Agra, and another from Kabul to Qandahar. Goa, by then the capital of the Portuguese State of India, must have been almost entirely unknown, and it could not have been guessed that the subsequent meeting of these two distant worlds would so profoundly influence the development of Mughal art.

Farrokh Beg, *Akbar's Triumphal Entry into Surat in 1573*, Lahore or Agra, from an *Akbar Nama*, 1590–95. London, V&A CAT. 11

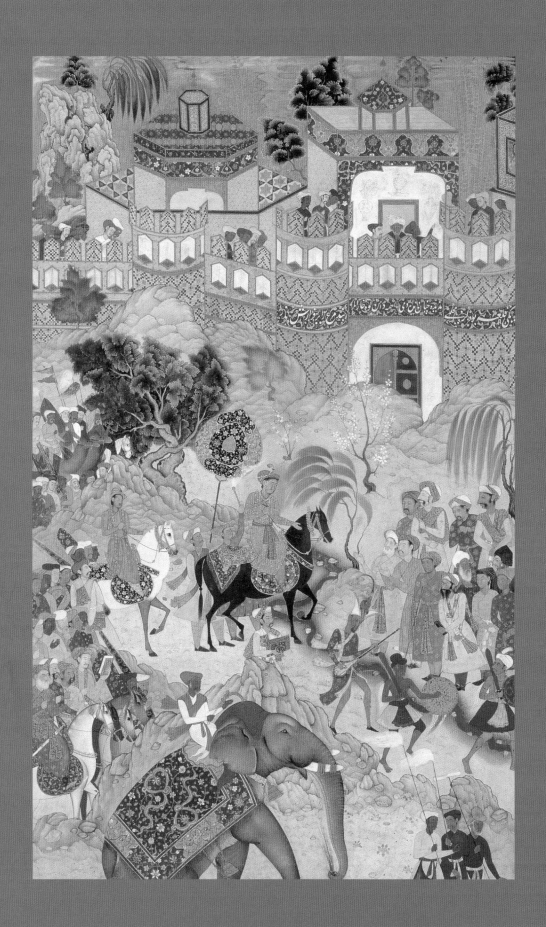

Mughal rule, meanwhile, was threatened on all sides by enemy factions. Babur's son Humayun lost the throne by 1540 and was forced to seek refuge in Iran at the court of Shah Tahmasp, whose support eventually allowed him to retake Delhi in 1555. His triumph was short-lived: the following year he died after an accidental fall and he was succeeded by his thirteen-year old son Akbar. Although the boy would reign for forty-nine years, firmly establishing the dynasty that would become known by the Persian word for 'Mongol', Akbar's inheritance was precarious, and swift territorial expansion was essential. Under the guidance of Humayun's friend and leading general Bayram Khan, the young emperor waged long and difficult campaigns against the courageous Rajput kings until most of them were defeated or formed peaceful alliances and became valued members of the court. The Mughal army then moved further west. The Gujarat campaign of 1572–3 allowed the Mughal empire to stretch to the coast, and to capture the rich trading ports of Cambay and Surat. It also gave Akbar his first encounter with exotic Europeans.

As the imperial army besieged Surat, 'a large number of Christians came from the port of Goa' and sought an interview, presenting gifts.[2] Akbar's triumphal entry into the city is recorded in the illustrations to the official Mughal history of his reign, the *Akbar Nama*, or 'Book of Akbar'. The famous meeting between the emperor and the *firangis*, which would lead to an exchange of embassies and the first Jesuit mission to the Mughal court,[3] is perhaps alluded to by the presence of a man in the crowd dressed in midnight blue robes, his foreign features and clear blue eyes distinguishing him from the others who press forward.

Farman of Akbar to the empire's officials, 18 March 1573, from Diogo do Couto, *Ásia, Década IX*, ch. 13, pp. 82–4. Lisbon, BNL CAT. 20

Tulsi and Bhawani, *The Construction of Fathpur Sikri*, Lahore or Agra, from an *Akbar Nama*, 1590–95. London, V&A CAT. 10

The members of the mission arrived at Akbar's newly built city of Fathpur on 18 February 1580. By now Akbar was a powerful monarch, sufficiently secure in his kingdom to concentrate on vast new architectural projects. In the early days of the reign the court had resided in Humayun's citadel in Delhi, the ancient royal capital of northern Hindustan, but in 1565 Akbar ordered the construction of a massive fort at Agra, followed by other forts in strategically important locations, notably Lahore which controlled the trade (and invasion) route from the north.[4] Agra Fort was completed by 1571, and by the late sixteenth century the city was of considerable size, with large mansions on each side of the river Jumna which flowed through it, and a place where people 'from all countries' came to trade.[5]

Akbar's most remarkable commission of 1571 was a new city at Sikri, a village 38 kilometres east of Agra, to commemorate the birth in 1569 of his long-awaited male heir who was named Salim after the Sufi shaikh who had predicted the event and lived there.[6] The palace, mosque, dwellings for leading members of the court, mint, schools, workshops, baths, a bazaar and gardens were all substantially completed by 1580. The city was a major trade centre, with shops and markets lining the road from the outer walls to the palace. Artists and artisans worked there, and some at least lived within the walls – Abdu's Samad, for instance, the Iranian head of the royal scriptorium who was later given charge of the mint, had a house there as early as 1575 or 1576.[7]

Visitors arriving at the southern entrance would climb steep steps to walk through a massive gateway almost certainly built to mark the successful conclusion of the Gujarat campaign when the city was named Fathabad, 'City of Victory', evolving into the more Indianized 'Fathpur' and later anglicized to 'Fatehpur Sikri'. Beyond the gateway was the Jami' Masjid, then the largest mosque in the empire. In its courtyard the Fathers would have seen the white marble-domed tomb of Shaikh Salim Chishti, who died in 1572, nearing completion.[8] To the north-east lay the palace complex where the emperor first greeted the Fathers.[9] Most of the city's buildings were constructed from the local red sandstone that Father Monserrate noted had been prepared a short distance away before being assembled on site, thus sparing the palace the constant hammering of the stonemasons.[10] The general tumult of the busy city must nevertheless have been considerable, as suggested by the Fathers' removal to a quiet house when Akbar heard they were disturbed by noise at their first lodgings.[11]

Many of the principal monuments still stand, but give only a partial impression of what they must have looked like when the court lived in them. Some walls are intricately carved with vegetal decoration or have inset pierced screens known as *jalis*,

or fragments of glazed tiles, but others are now unadorned. Here and there, traces of painted decoration reveal that these plain walls originally had pictorial panels, beautifully calligraphed poetic inscriptions framed within long cartouches, and floral or geometric decoration, all in polychrome and gold. Occasionally, the subjects of the paintings are faintly discernible – figures in boats sail on water in scenes strongly reminiscent of the contemporary *Hamza Nama* paintings, while other scenes contain figures closer to the Iranian tradition, though in a style unlike anything that has survived in the Mughal art of the book.[12] As Gauvin Bailey has pointed out, Father Monserrate also saw 'hanging pictures' on the walls of Akbar's dining hall depicting Mary, Jesus and Moses.[13] Seemingly unaware of the pre-eminence they are given in Islam, the Fathers took this as a hopeful sign that the emperor might convert to Christianity. Although this was never a remote possibility, Akbar's keen interest in the principles of the Christian faith (as in those of Hinduism, Zoroastrianism or Jainism) is not in doubt, neither is his enthusiasm for the paintings and prints brought by this and subsequent missions.[14]

The monuments the Fathers saw in Fathpur would also have been decorated with rich hangings and carpets woven in the city or at the specialist centres of different provinces in the empire. Fathpur had its own carpet weavers, as did Lahore and Agra, and Fathpur and Agra both produced fine cloth.[15] Gujarat supplied velvets, embroideries and brocades, while Kashmir, then as now, produced exquisitely soft woollen shawls.[16] Silk was woven in Hindustan, but beautiful figured silks from Safavid Iran or China were also prized. Delicately painted cotton cloth may have come from the city of Burhanpur, or the Deccani kingdom of Golconda, whose manufactures were known from the beginning of the seventeenth century and may have been made earlier. Sheer white muslin came from Bengal,[17] and 'cloth of the best texture' was woven in the province of Malwa, notably at Saronj (also famous for its muslin) and Hasilpur.[18] Gujarat

was a major source of de luxe fabrics, including velvet, brocades and 'imitations of stuffs from Turkey, Europe and Iran'.[19] Genuine European cloth was also to be found in the royal stores, as indicated by a list of what was destroyed during a catastrophic fire at Fathpur in 1579.[20]

The gold and silver vessels used within these richly ornamented settings would have been made in the royal workshops at Fathpur or Agra, but goldsmiths' work from Augsburg or Nuremberg may also have begun to arrive in the late sixteenth century and was definitely in the royal treasury by the early seventeenth century.[21] Bronze artefacts and weapons of watered steel inlaid with gold could have been made either in Hindustan or Iran, both of which had extremely long-established and sophisticated metalworking traditions. Hindu and Muslim bronze-makers from Hindustan, and Iranians based at the court, all worked either in their own indigenous styles or borrowed forms and motifs from each other.[22]

While living in Fathpur, the Fathers must soon have become aware of the emperor's daily routine. Akbar rose at sunrise to say the prayers that provided the framework to the day and then formally showed himself from an upper balcony in a ritual known as *darshan* before attending to affairs of state. Drums announced his arrival in the Hall of Public Audience where he sat enthroned, his sons and grandsons in attendance. Reports were presented

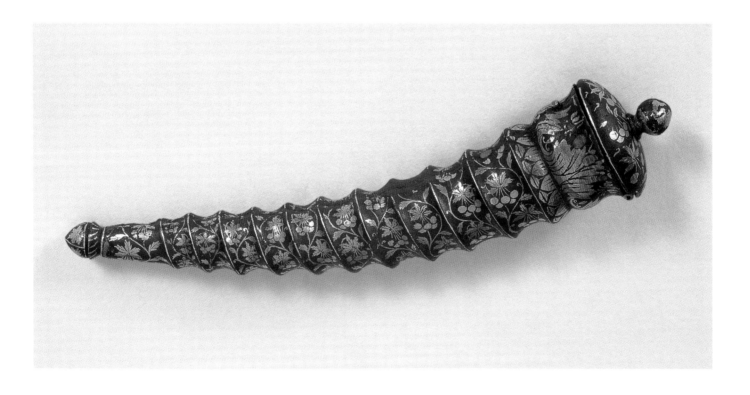

from all over the empire and visiting dignitaries were officially received; learned or skilled men of all kinds would pay their respects; the holders of new appointments in the administration or in the royal workshops were presented; and every detail would be carefully recorded by the court writers.[23] Wrestlers, singers, jugglers and acrobats were on hand to provide entertainment, which might also be in the form of elephant or camel fights. Other pastimes included hunting, of which Akbar was extremely fond; polo; hawking; pigeon flying; and playing cards or board games such as chess.[24]

In private gatherings the assembly was allowed to sit in the imperial presence. They might listen to religious debates in the 'Ibadat Khana, to the music of Iran and Hindustan performed by individuals such as the great Tansen of Gwalior,[25] to poetry contests between the many practitioners at court, to the stories of professional storytellers or to readings from volumes in the vast royal library. Although Akbar never learned to read or write, he built up an extensive collection of books that were read to him daily. His keen intelligence, exceptional memory and lively curiosity thus allowed him to develop a highly cultivated knowledge of literature, history and philosophy.[26] Fathpur was both the repository of his library and one of the places where new books were written or copied, and illustrated.[27]

The Mughal year was punctuated by a number of public ceremonies and festivals. Akbar was weighed on his solar and lunar birthdays against materials including metals,

Above left: *Commentarios do Grande Afonso d'Albuquerque* (Commentaries of the Great Afonso de Albuquerque), published by João de Barreira, Lisbon, 1576 (2nd edn).
Lisbon, BNL CAT. 24

Above: *Ordenações Manuelinas* (Manueline Laws), published by Valentim Fernandes, Lisbon, 1512.
Lisbon, BNL CAT. 22

silk, expensive perfumes and grain, which were distributed to the needy according to a formula determined by his weight and the number of years he had lived.[28] The princes were weighed only on their solar birthdays and against a smaller range of items. The ceremony adopted from Hindu tradition continued under subsequent rulers, becoming more lavish under Shahjahan who had himself weighed against gold on his solar birthday and silver on his lunar birthday, until the practice was stopped by the austere Aurangzeb, Akbar's great-grandson, in 1668.[29]

After 1584, following the introduction of the 'Divine Era', the major festival was Nowruz ('New Year'). Akbar had decreed that the Islamic lunar calendar should be replaced by the Iranian solar calendar, and adopted Persian names for the months.[30] The year now began at the spring equinox and Nowruz was celebrated by the exchange of lavish presents between the emperor and his wives, and between his sons and daughters, that might include precious manuscripts, spectacular jewels, exotic rarities or the greatest works of the court's leading artists and craftsmen. Another opportunity to see fine workmanship came at the monthly bazaar instigated by Akbar.[31] Open to all the men and women of the court, it allowed them to buy the luxury products of Hindustan and foreign goods brought by merchants. The imperial craftsmen also showed their wares, and everything would be closely inspected by the emperor who inevitably had first choice in his purchases.

The success of Akbar's administration depended on a tightly regulated administrative system, some of which was inherited from Sher Shah Suri, the Afghan ruler who had forced Humayun out of Hindustan, and maintained with little structural change by Akbar's successors throughout the seventeenth century.[32] If the royal household and the empire's administrative departments, including the mint, were properly ordered, and the army run effectively, revenues could be collected efficiently and disbursed fairly. Crucial to the system was the office of the treasury, which included nine separate departments for cash forwarded from each province, and three more holding precious stones, gold and inlaid artefacts. The hierarchical listing of the gemstones suggests that spinel was the most highly regarded, followed by diamonds, emeralds, rubies, sapphires and pearls.[33] These were acquired through trade (predominantly with the Portuguese), as tribute or seized from the treasuries of defeated rulers. The items of gold and silver would have included thrones and the vessels in every day use; the jewelled artefacts included vessels, utensils and jewellery. European visitors provide detailed lists of the contents of these, as they had done for the Western books in the royal library in 1595.[34] The imperial workshops, of which there were nearly a hundred by the 1590s, each had their own treasurer.[35] The enormous wealth of the court combined with the energetic interest of the emperor attracted artists and craftsmen from all over Hindustan as well as foreign artists who came mainly from Iran but also, in a very few cases, from Europe. They entered royal service or that of leading court personages, and it must be assumed that their work would have been of a quantity and quality rarely seen before, though with the exception of book painting, little has survived from the sixteenth century.

In 1581 Akbar left Fathpur to deal with a threatened rebellion by his step-brother, Mirza Muhammad Hakim, in Kabul. The mere presence of the Mughal army eliminated the problem, but Akbar stayed in his northern capital of Lahore and annexed the province of Kabul when the Mirza died in 1585. The army was subsequently despatched to take Kashmir, Sind, Baluchistan and Qandahar, all achieved with relative ease and without the need for Akbar's personal participation. Now free to travel through his empire, he seldom returned to Fathpur, though the city continued to be significant up to the reign of Shahjahan who held his first birthday weighing ceremony as emperor there.[36]

Even while travelling, the main features of courtly life continued. The encampment was the size of a small city, identically laid out at each halting place and with the emperor's royal red tents at the centre, near the women's quarters and the accommodation of their servants. When the army moved with the court, the encampment expanded to include offices, workshops and a bazaar, all again laid out to a standard plan to allow ease of orientation.[37] Whether the emperor appeared in public in the large encampment or before his entourage in a forest clearing where a small expedition might pause during hunting to be entertained by the official storyteller, the formality of the court was always maintained: Akbar would be enthroned and surrounded by the usual insignia of royalty. Distinguished visitors were recorded as coming to 'the court', which was wherever the royal person was to be found rather than a single place.

When not travelling, Akbar returned to Lahore, where his sons married and had children and where his mother also stayed, or to Agra. The large northern capital, full of splendid buildings and beautiful gardens, was a convenient base from which to make expeditions to Kabul, thus enabling the Hindustani members of his entourage to see snow for the first time, or to the newly acquired 'paradise-like' Kashmir, equally enjoyed by Akbar's son and grandson during their own reigns. Artists in the city worked for the emperor or his son Salim, who shared Akbar's keen interest in painting and his fascination for the exotic works brought to court by the Jesuits or foreign merchants. Competition between father and son seems to have been intense, as the members of the third Jesuit mission from Goa mention Salim commandeering their Portuguese artist to copy works in Akbar's collection that the emperor was clearly unwilling to give to his son.[38] As at Fathpur and elsewhere, wall painting was an integral part of the decoration of monuments, Salim adding new structures with painted decoration in his renovations to Lahore Fort in about 1612. In one small pavilion the impact of European imagery is strikingly apparent: male and female saintly figures, including a pope who may be Gregory the Great, look down on the visitor.[39]

The rapidity with which foreign images were absorbed into Mughal art may be gauged by the example of Hieronymus Nadal's *Evangelicae Historicae Imagines*, published in Rome in 1593.[40] This book of prints by leading north European artists arrived in Lahore with the third Jesuit mission in May 1595 and, as Frederike Weis has recently pointed out, directly influenced the composition of three illustrations towards the end of the partial *Akbar Nama* in the Victoria and Albert Museum, London, that must have been completed by the same year.[41]

When Akbar died in 1605, the main institutions of the empire and the rhythms of courtly life were well established. The major battles had been won or deferred, and Salim, who took the title 'Jahangir', had time to indulge his artistic tastes fully, even during his almost ceaseless travels through the empire. He had a passion for collecting foreign rarities, sending agents to Cambay and Surat, the great trading ports where the merchandise of Europe, the Levant, Iran and Africa could be found. European merchants also came to court to sell the specialities of their own lands speculatively, or because experience showed that they would find a ready market there, and Jahangir's memoirs contain frequent references to the acquisition of foreign curiosities, ranging from crystal boxes and gold and silver vessels to strange beasts. A consignment of animals and birds bought by Jahangir's trusted noble Muqarrab Khan in Goa in 1612 was particularly successful, the emperor finding the turkey cock so bizarre that he described it at length in his journal and ordered it to be painted as an illustration when the book the *Jahangir Nama*, or 'Book of Jahangir', was copied and distributed to favoured individuals. Several versions of the painting have survived, including one signed by the great Mansur and bearing Jahangir's own written comments.[42]

Foreign curiosities also included people who now arrived at court from Europe in increasing numbers. Their presence, and their gifts of European pictures and prints, account for the inclusion of a range of Western figures appearing in Mughal painting from the 1570s onwards.[43] The Portuguese were the most familiar, having sold precious stones to the immensely knowledgeable jewellers of the court for decades, and their European garb adapted to the Indian climate must have been seen by a Mughal artist. The flat black hat, lace ruff, short doublet and baggy trousers are all found in the illustrations to the account of the Dutch traveller van Linschoten, based on drawings he made during his three-year residence in Goa.[44] Portuguese observers inevitably singled out familiar features in the foreign landscape in their accounts: thus, the Portuguese Jesuit, Father António Botelho, likened the river Jumna that flowed through Agra to the Tagus, and noted roses and medicinal herbs of Portuguese origin in the royal gardens of the city.[45]

A number of highly distinctive styles were now apparent in the works produced for the court in Hindustan, developed from the complex intermingling of very different traditions. The dominant cultural influence from Iran was the legacy of the Timurids, constantly renewed by the arrival at court of artists, poets, philosophers and craftsmen. Jahangir's immensely powerful wife was Iranian, and her father was Jahangir's highest-ranking minister. Persian was the language of the elite, and of the administration, as it was until the British replaced it with English in the nineteenth century. Iran thus provided models for art and literature, and Mughal artists and calligraphers, whether Muslim or Hindu, copied the work of the finest Iranian masters preserved in the royal library.[46] The studio itself had originally been established under the supervision of Abdu's Samad and Mir Sayyid 'Ali, the two Iranian masters who were brought to Hindustan by Humayun and taught Akbar painting when he was a boy. Craftsmen working in widely different media, from hardstone carving to gunsmithing, also came from Iran.[47]

Staff handle, Mughal India, 17th century, jade, emeralds, rubies and gold.

Oporto, private collection CAT. 65

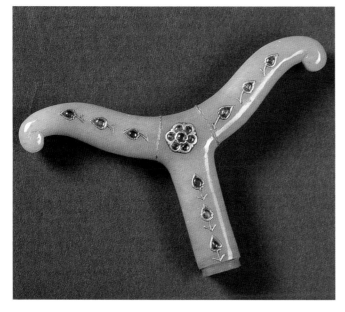

The subcontinent, however, had its own equally distinctive and extremely diverse styles, with a broad range of artistic production of the highest order. Localized industries that depended on proximity to certain raw materials or on particular combinations of environmental conditions supplied a wide market that included both the Mughal court and the court of Goa, while luxury goods might be imported from faraway lands. Thus Gujarat sent canopies inlaid with tiny fragments of mother-of-pearl for the tombs of Muslim holy men held in specially high regard at the Mughal court, and its craftsmen made small boxes and cabinets that were bought by European travellers and residents of Goa.[48] The court used the fine Chinese porcelain, as well as wares of lower value, which were brought in quantity by sea and used widely in the subcontinent, including Goa.[49] A small amount of glass was produced in Hindustan, for example Alwar, and Bihar which produced gilded glass,[50] but most of the glass used at court probably came from Italy or Iran, which almost certainly supplied the flasks with long slender necks in vivid blues and greens seen in paintings done for Akbar.[51]

Little is known about the artists and craftsmen of the imperial workshops. Although many names of painters are known, biographical details are scant; where craftsmen are concerned, even the names are missing as few artefacts are signed. Beyond the sphere of court patronage, their lives must have been extremely difficult. The French physician François Bernier remarked on the hardship they endured if not attached to a household or wealthy patron, and the consequent effects their lack of resources had on the quality of the work.[52] Disasters such as the severe famines of 1630 in the Deccan and Gujarat, and 1642 in Kashmir, would inevitably have interrupted all artistic life in these regions.

Within the court, however, artists and craftsmen were protected from such suffering and could occupy extremely privileged positions. The scant details that survive of the lives of particular individuals show that at least some of them were highly cultivated, and participated fully in the intellectual and artistic life of the nobility. Notable among them was the head of the goldsmiths' department under Jahangir and Shahjahan, the Iranian Sa'ida-ye Gilani who is mentioned in contemporary texts as a poet, calligrapher and lapidary as well as a goldsmith. He accompanied the emperor on his travels and was praised in Jahangir's memoirs for a poem composed during an expedition to Kashmir. His royal goldsmithing commissions imply mastery of the art of enamelling, which may have been introduced to Mughal India through contact with European goldsmiths in Goa.[53] Sa'ida was entrusted with inscribing royal titles on the most precious hereditary gemstones, notably spinels, and because he is known beyond doubt to have inscribed one that still survives, A.S. Melikian-Chirvani has convincingly identified his hand in the inscriptions on a small number of inscribed jades from the royal treasury. Given his skills as a lapidary, it would seem logical to conclude that he also made the jades he inscribed.[54] Most intriguingly, the same scholar has suggested that Sa'ida added a handle to the jade wine jug formerly owned by Ulugh Beg. The inscription on the rim recording Jahangir's acquisition of the precious heirloom in 1621–2 is almost certainly in Sa'ida's hand, and the handle is placed with such mastery that the opening words in praise of God seem to come from the mouth of the dragon terminating it.[55]

A second exception to the general anonymity of craftsmen at court is provided by the example of a French jeweller who reached India in 1612 or 1613. Augustin of Bordeaux travelled to Agra and then made his way to Lahore with the German traveller Heinrich von Poser in 1620–21.[56] He had made a golden throne with lion supports and enamelled decoration for Jahangir's father-in-law I'timad ad-Daula to present to the emperor at Nowruz in 1619, which was mentioned briefly by Jahangir in his memoirs and in Augustin's own letters. A little-known description of this throne in use survives in an account of Jacques de Coutre, the jeweller who visited the court and saw it in 1619. He specifies that it was 'all of gold and precious stones' and had four feet of gilt silver in the form of lions. The throne was positioned at an upper level with silver steps, perhaps as many as twenty, leading from the throne to a courtyard below. On each side was a life-size statue of a man 'all in silver dressed in the German way as the French king's guards', corresponding to Augustin's 'Swiss guards' like those at the Louvre. The canopy Coutre saw over the throne was of rich brocade supported by two columns of enamelled gold, whereas Augustin stated that his canopy design was for a dome set with precious stones. Jacques de Coutre saw Jahangir in the Hall of Public Audience, where Jahangir appeared before an assembly whose senior members were separated from the others by a railing.[57]

Archer ring, Mughal India, c.1630–40,
white jade, gold, rubies and emeralds.
London, V&A CAT. 61

Augustin went on to work for Shahjahan in 1632, and died in Cochin on his way to Goa some time later. Both he and Sa'ida were goldsmiths at a time when the court outshone even its own glittering past. The pages of the contemporary histories of Shahjahan's reign are filled with descriptions of gorgeous textiles and lavish furniture made of gold, enamelled and sparkling with diamonds, rubies and emeralds. The celebrations for the Nowruz surpassed any that had been held before, and were the occasion for the unveiling of Shahjahan's most extravagant commissions.

His coronation in 1628 had been conducted against the tense background of a threat to his succession posed by his half-brother, supported by Jahangir's powerful and ambitious wife Nur Mahal. The swiftly arranged ceremony preceded the first Nowruz of the reign, traditionally regarded as the coronation day,[58] and although splendid jewelled weapons and precious stones were bestowed on leading personages of the court, the event must have seemed inadequate because a second, more lavish coronation took place subsequently. That same year Shahjahan gave Sa'ida-ye Gilani a new commission that would transform later court celebrations: a new golden throne, studded with the most precious stones in his collection. Seven years later, at Nowruz, the fabulous Jewelled Throne that would be recorded in orientalist literature as 'The Peacock Throne' made its first appearance.[59]

Shahjahan's passion for and knowledge of precious stones are well attested. The famous gemstones presented to him by his father included the spectacular rose pink spinel inscribed with the names of Ulugh Beg and Shah Abbas after his successful campaign against the Deccan sultanates. This was given the most prominent position in the decoration of the throne, surrounded by the most significant emeralds, rubies, diamonds, spinels and pearls from the vast treasury. The throne henceforth held centre stage at major court festivities, notably the inauguration of Shahjahan's new city of Shahjahanabad in Delhi. On an auspicious day in April 1648 the emperor arrived to inspect the new buildings, making his way to the Hall of Public Audience where he mounted the Jewelled Throne in the triumphant climax of the event. Honours were bestowed on the princes and nobles, offerings were made by the court to the emperor, and those who had directed the building were rewarded. The poets whose verses and chronograms (phrases where the numerical value of each letter added up to the number of the year being celebrated) marked the occasion were given robes of honour and large sums of money; and more money was distributed among the craftsmen who had built and adorned the new structures. The festivities continued for nine days, during which the emperor's fifty-eighth lunar birthday was marked by the usual weighing ceremony.

European involvement in the production of jewellery provides another link with Portugal. In 1648 Father Botelho travelled to Delhi, and thence to Agra, where he recorded the splendour of Shahjahan's ceremonial departure to inaugurate his new city in Delhi. The emperor's subsequent visit to Lahore allowed Father Botelho to visit the new palace fort in Delhi, guided by Lourenço Mendes, whom he fascinatingly described as 'a Portuguese, a native of Damão, who was many years in the King's service, drawing the models of the jewels which he (the King) ordered to be made, the goldsmiths then applying the enamel and the precious stones'.[60] The presence of individuals such as Augustin of Bordeaux and Mendes, and the continued collecting of European artefacts, led to the continued absorption of Western motifs in the artistic expression of the court, which now attained a stylistic coherence hitherto unknown.

This is seen most strikingly in Shahjahan's most significant legacy, architecture. Long before he became emperor, he had commissioned new monuments and laid out

146

Relief portrait bust of Shahjahan,
Mughal India, second quarter of the
17th century.
Amsterdam, Rijksmuseum CAT. 54

gardens, including the renowned Shalamar Gardens in Kashmir.[61] The ornamentation of his monuments demonstrates that the most important imperial decorative identity consisted of a floral style partly influenced by European herbals, providing a grammar of ornament that could be applied with equal success to the borders of albums and manuscripts, to jewellery and vessels, or to textiles. The ubiquity of the style is vividly evoked by contemporary paintings of court scenes and would endure far beyond the reign of Shahjahan.

By the end of Shahjahan's reign, however, the relationship between the Mughals and Goa had become more distant. The Jesuit mission was still resident at court, but suffered persecution in the wake of the siege and capture of the Portuguese settlement at Hughli by the Mughal forces in 1632; the earlier loss of Hormuz in 1622 had affected Goa's trade, and it suffered still further due to the onerous presence of the Dutch and their frequent blockades of Goa in the 1640s. Goa's significance in the subcontinent was diminishing; over the next fifty years the Mughal empire itself began to change radically.

In 1657 Shahjahan had fallen seriously ill. His son, Aurangzeb, imprisoned him, usurped the crown and took the title 'Alamgir in 1658, ruthlessly eliminating any threat from his brothers. His coronation, when he appeared in the Hall of Public Audience at Agra seated on the Jewelled Throne, did not suggest the austerities that were to come. As the reign progressed, the emperor became increasingly pious and issued decrees that reduced the splendour of the court. In January 1669, during the celebrations of his son's marriage, the ground on which Aurangzeb walked towards a gold throne was covered with gold cloth, but ten days later he issued an edict that 'men should not use in their garments cloth of gold, as the wearing of it was opposed to the Holy Law'.[62] In 1677 the coronation ceremony was abolished; the court clerks were ordered to use inkpots made of Chinese porcelain or hardstone rather than precious metal; robes of honour were to be embroidered rather than made of gold or silver brocade, and the manufacture at Chanderi of fine cloth for the court was to cease.[63] Although Aurangzeb had enjoyed listening to music early in his reign, he stopped 'out of extreme abstinence'; he was an accomplished poet with a wide-ranging knowledge of literature, but listened only to poems full of moral advice; his calligraphy was admired, but his greatest effort was expended on copying the Koran, twice, rather than writing poetry.[64]

While other members of the royal family such as Aurangzeb's daughter Zeb un-Nisa Begam patronized poets and calligraphers,[65] and the demands of courtly life meant that luxury production also carried on in the royal workshops now scattered across the empire in major centres,[66] the inexorable decline of Mughal rule had begun. As Aurangzeb waged interminable battles against the sultans of the Deccan, his northern lands were neglected, and he personally took little interest in the *firangis* in his domains. Leading figures in his empire continued to take account of the Portuguese authorities in Goa: the great shipowning merchants of the Mughal port of Surat, for example, made sure they obtained the usual *cartazes* from Goa, and the governor of Surat corresponded with its viceroys.[67] The Jesuit missions that remained until the Society was expelled from the subcontinent still included remarkable men who travelled to other Indian courts.[68] But the close personal relations that had existed between Akbar, Jahangir and Shahjahan and their foreign visitors from Goa, which had such intriguing consequences for the arts of the Mughal court, were never to be repeated.

Mughal carpet (fragment), Kashmir or Lahore, c.1620–25. Lisbon, CGM CAT. 62

BETWEEN RELIGIONS: CHRISTIANITY IN A MUSLIM EMPIRE

Gauvin Alexander Bailey

Christians and Muslims have been traditional enemies ever since Pope Urban II called the First Crusade in 1095, and an animosity between the two groups helped shape many of the political events of the late Middle Ages and Early Modern Period. During these centuries a mutual ignorance also coloured each group's perception of the other's world. Where diplomacy existed, it was provisional and focused on individual tasks and short-term goals, not deeper knowledge or respective understanding. Western European envoys and missionaries occasionally visited Muslim cities to free Christian captives or forge temporary economic or military alliances, and from at least the fifteenth century Muslim diplomats and merchants sojourned in cities like Florence and Paris to gather technological information or make their own expedient diplomatic deals. There was little opportunity or willingness on either side for more long-term contacts, where an exchange of ideas and culture could allow Christians and Muslims to recognize their substantial commonalities – a situation that did exist, ironically, in the Latin kingdoms of the Levant during the Crusades themselves. This attitude of indifference lasted even into the eighteenth century, as the two sides grew ever closer to each other, European powers expanding their influence in Asia through conquest and trade and Ottoman armies pushing far into Europe. The new proximity seemed only to harden peoples' resolve.

One brilliant exception was an exchange that took place in northern India, in the realm of the Muslim Mughal Emperors Akbar (1556–1605) and Jahangir (1605–27).[1] In an atmosphere comparable to Lorenzo de' Medici's Platonic Academy in Florence a century earlier, these enlightened rulers invited scholars and priests from around the world to their court, hosting them in their palaces and fielding weekly interfaith debates

into the small hours of the morning. Operating in a spirit of experimentation, creativity and receptiveness, the emperors and their distinguished guests engaged in cultural dialogues of the highest intellectual calibre, expounding on the texts and traditions of faiths as varied as Judaism, Hinduism and Zoroastrianism, and occasionally finding similarities and connections between them. Some of the most vocal and influential participants in these debates were Jesuit priests, representatives of Catholic Christianity, who had been invited by Akbar from Portuguese Goa in 1580 and who would remain at court with a few short interruptions until 1773. Members of a religious order with an unusual willingness to learn from foreign cultures, the Jesuit fathers proved to be an ideal addition to the debates and to the imperial court. Although it should be stressed that the Jesuits and the Muslim mullahs rarely agreed on the key tenets of their faiths, the emperors themselves openly tried to bridge the gap between the two religions and bring their teachings into harmony. In the history of Muslim–Christian relations, few encounters were as tolerant or culturally rewarding.

The most visual manifestation of this Christian–Muslim encounter can be found in Mughal painting and sculpture. Sacred pictures played a role in the interfaith debates from at least 1580, and one of the reasons Akbar invited the Jesuits in the first place was to serve as a conduit for artworks from Europe. Akbar had been interested in Western art since at least the 1560s, especially in pictorial realism and visual drama, as well as the aura of devotion that he recognized in Catholic imagery. The Jesuits served their new host well, bringing a considerable collection of engravings, printed books and oil paintings with them to northern India. The third Jesuit mission, which began in 1595, even brought a Portuguese painter with them, who tirelessly executed oil paintings on paper for Akbar and his son.[2] The emperor demonstrated an immediate fascination with the ritual properties of Christian altarpieces, and the Jesuits reported that he observed and imitated the behaviour of a worshipper, prostrating before an image in the Jesuit chapel and making obeisance to it. Akbar and his court were also impressed by the theatrical way in which the Jesuits used curtains, incense and candles to enhance the spiritual power of their images.[3] In fact, in 1581 a member of the royal family displayed one of the Jesuits' altarpieces, draped with rich textiles, in Akbar's audience hall to celebrate his return from a military campaign in Kabul, and Akbar exhibited the same picture on other state occasions, as well as the Christian feast of the Assumption (15 August), when he made his courtiers bow before it.[4]

Encouraged by the emperor himself, court artists quickly mastered the Late Renaissance style in their book illustrations and album pages – especially Western conventions of modelling and perspective, which they adapted to mainstream Mughal painting. Although the mixture of East and West remained eclectic throughout Akbar's reign, under Jahangir it matured into a new manner characterized by an extremely refined naturalism, an enthusiasm for psychological portraiture, and a taste for dramatic gesture. Some paintings depicted overtly religious themes. Mughal artists such as Kesu Das (act. c.1570–90s) and Manohar (act. c.1582–1620) created images of Jesus and Christian saints that not only adopted Western style but clearly demonstrated a sympathy for the devotional value and identity of the subjects. This new style and Christian subject matter soon extended to monumental wall painting. European visitors to Mughal palaces and tombs in the late sixteenth and early seventeenth centuries were astonished to find them prominently adorned with mural paintings depicting Christ, the Virgin Mary and Christian saints executed in the style of Late Renaissance Italy. Their wonderment led to false reports of the imminent

After Jost Amman (1539–91),
Salome Receives the Head of St John the Baptist, Mughal India, c.1590,
stone relief, 6.6 x 5.4 x 4.3 cm.
Arthur M. Sackler Gallery,
Harvard University Art Museums,
private collection: TL29329

conversion of the Muslim emperors, and hopeful Portuguese governors, English merchants and Catholic clerics scrambled to forge alliances with this new 'Prester John' (a semi-mythical Asian Christian prince).

Yet, despite their mutual cordiality and interest in fine art, the Mughals and the Jesuits were engaged in a subtle subversion of each other. As I have discussed elsewhere, the Mughal emperors appropriated Euro-Christian imagery as a form of royal propaganda, capitalizing upon links between Catholic iconography and Indian and Islamic symbols to communicate their message of divinely sanctioned kingship.[5] Akbar's early interest in Christian traditions of image veneration already shows an acknowledgement of the power of sacred iconography and of the ways in which it could be manipulated. On the other hand, the Jesuits capitalized upon Catholic imagery's affinities with Islam, Hinduism and Sufism to promote their own goals of Christian salvation. This approach came through especially clearly in the series of Persian-language catechisms written in high prose style by the Jesuit missionary Jerome Xavier. Full of complex Indo-Islamic cultural allusions, these treatises were lavishly illustrated by the emperor's own artists in a style usually reserved for panegyric royal biographies.[6]

THE INTERFAITH DEBATES AT THE 'IBADAT KHANA

The interfaith debates are the key to understanding the Christian–Muslim cultural exchange at the Mughal court. The Mughals inherited their religious tolerance and interest in debate from their central Asian Mongol ancestors more than three hundred years earlier. The shamanist Mongol religion was open to borrowings from other faiths, and early Mongol rulers such as Ghengis Khan (d. 1227) made it official policy to respect all religions and to honour all priests and holy men.[7] In 1245 the widow of Ghengis's son Ögedei (1229–41) welcomed a Franciscan mission from Italy, led by the sixty-five-year-old Franciscan John de Piano Carpini, to her court at Karakorum.[8] Enthused by the legend of Prester John, the Franciscans had travelled to Mongolia in a desperate last-ditch attempt to save the Crusades through an alliance with the Mongols. Although ultimately a failure, Carpini's mission and later expeditions by the Dominican Andrew of Longjumeau (1248) and the Franciscan William of Rubrock (1253) brought Europe face-to-face with China decades before Marco Polo and even introduced Western art to the East, including an illuminated Bible and breviary.[9] In a foreshadowing of the events of Akbar's court William of Rubrock's mission was invited to participate in a theological debate between Nestorian Christians, Muslims and Buddhists.[10]

It was in the same spirit of tolerance that Akbar began sponsoring interfaith debates in 1575 (the last recorded debate was under Jahangir in 1608). For this purpose he converted a shaikh's cell into a special hall called the 'Ibadat Khana (house of worship) at his grand sandstone palace-city of Fathpur Sikri, where he would meet every Thursday night and again on Fridays with scholars from different branches of Islam and non-Islamic faiths. At first the groups only included Sunni and Sufi Muslims, but they soon welcomed Shiites, and by 1578 they were joined by Jains, Hindus and Parsis.[11] Shaikh Nur al-Haqq left one of the most detailed descriptions of these sessions:

One of the strange things that happened that year [1578] ... was that learned men from Khorasan and Iraq and Transoxania and India, both doctors [hukuat] and theologians [fuqaha], Shi'ah and Sunnis, Christians [nasara], philosophers [falasafah] and Brahmins – indeed lords of all nations ... assembled together at the sublime court of this world-seizing Monarch ... and they discussed the rational and traditional methods of discourse [ma'qalat o manqalut], travels and histories, dialectic subjects [masa'il-i kalamiya] concerning the community, and each other's prophecies [nabawat]. They widened the circle of debate, and each attempted to prove his own claim and desired the propagation of his school [madhhab], as is the way with the ... opinion of theologians and the habit and disposition of all people. Outstanding thinkers appeared ... And since knowledge of the events of the ancients and the methods of their school reached the exalted ears for the first time ... he was spurred on to inquire into the goals and lofty topics, with the purpose of reflection, careful consideration and measurement of the opinions of each group. The aim of the lofty Lord, in reflection and holding the debates about different opinions, was to find the truth and to acquire merit ... [The Emperor Akbar] declared out loud before the people: 'Oh learned Mullas! Our purpose is to seek the truth!'[12]

It was in a similar vein that one of Akbar's court historians was asked in 1603 to write a history of the philosophers of the West, including the ancients. `Abd al-Sattar Ibn Qasim Lahori wrote in the introduction to that work: '[Akbar] desired that the secrets be reported of the religions and lives of the monarchs of every nation and the insights of the celebrated wise men of the auspicious assembly ... until an analysis of every culture could be made.'[13]

The Deposition from the Cross,
Mughal India, c.1610,
gouache on paper, 20 x 13 cm.
Paris, CFL-IN, inv. no. 988-T.12

The Nativity, Mughal India, c.1605–10.
London, V&A CAT. 83

The first Jesuits to join Akbar's interfaith debates were the Italian aristocrat Rodolfo Acquaviva and the Catalan Antonio Monserrate. In his fascinating chronicle, finished in prison in Yemen in 1590, Monserrate fondly recalls the Thursday night debates: 'an opportunity was given for a discussion, which was held at night … in which the priests met the religious teachers and doctors and debated keenly with them the question of the accuracy and authority of the Holy Scriptures …'[14] Although much of the discussion revolved around theological and religious issues, such as the relative legitimacy of Muslim and Christian texts and the concept of the Trinity, other conversations dealt with the history and customs of Portugal and Western Europe, and several focused specifically on imagery and the visual arts. In one such conversation Father Monserrate used an art metaphor when explaining to Akbar that while Christians imitate Christ they do not presume to equal him: 'No painter or sculptor, however accurately and carefully he may paint his picture or carve his statue, endeavours actually to imitate nature: he would say rather that he desired to appropriate for himself the strength and virtue of nature.'[15] On several occasions Akbar had the priests explain the meaning of Christian images, many of which were by then in his personal collection. Such was a painting of the *Ark of the Covenant*, which inspired a long discussion on idolatry and the Muslim disinclination towards imagery, and a picture of Christ, which Akbar kissed publicly to show his devotion for this figure who is also revered in Islam.[16]

The most detailed records of debate discussions date from the reign of Jahangir, and many of them included similar references to imagery. In Lahore in 1607, during the first series of interfaith debates after Akbar's death, Jahangir invited the Jesuits to his palace and ordered his librarian to bring out his personal albums of engravings and Christian paintings so that he could learn their stories and the significance of their symbols and allegories. Jahangir's many pointed questions demonstrated a keen interest in the role of images and the function of allegory in Christian art. For example, he found it difficult to separate honour from beauty. Referring to a Crucifixion, the emperor asked: 'Why, if [you] adored Christ Our Lord so much, did [you] paint him in such a dishonourable state?'[17] One of his nobles added, 'When we depict Christ we always paint him very beautifully and not on the Cross.'[18] When the missionaries explained that it was a great honour because it showed that Christ had died for our sins, they also indicated the mnemonic value of the wounds as reminders of his sacrifice. Jahangir approved of the explanation and equated it with a courtier whom he had blinded because he was involved in an assassination plot, yet whom he kept around to discourage others. In another discussion one of the nobles brought up the perennial question of images as idols, asking them whether they pay homage 'Before an image of the Virgin, or before the Virgin herself?' The fathers explained it in Mughal terms:

Sire, we do not venerate the images for what they are, because we are well aware that they are merely paper or canvas with pigments; it is because of those whom they represent. Just as with your *farmans*: you do not touch them to your foreheads because they are papers covered in ink, but because you know that they contain your order and will.[19]

Jahangir was also curious about the function of symbols. When he was shown a picture of God the Father surrounded by angels, he wanted to know why the angels were put there, and the priest replied that the 'angels depicted as boys with wings' refer to a vision of God experienced by several prophets.[20] This must have struck the emperor as an appropriate symbol of reverence and honour, since he subsequently co-opted precisely that kind of angel for many of his own portraits. Jahangir was also interested in the ability of a symbol to represent an abstract idea, for example when he asked the fathers to explain the significance of a boar's head in an illustration of the *Death of Sardanapalus*: '"What is the significance of this boar's head which is shown here?" [The priest] answered, "It is a symbol of the effect which dishonesty has, that the unchaste are unclean, etc."' Jahangir frequently demonstrated his mastery of Christian stories and tenets by preaching at these debates with the assistance of devotional images.[21]

Many of the discussions at the interfaith debates are echoed in a Persian catechism written by the Jesuit missionary Jerome Xavier in 1609 entitled *Mirat al-Quds* ('The truth-showing mirror'), which includes an entire chapter on the use of images and their veneration. The book is set up as a mock debate between a 'Philosopher' (a thinly veiled reference to the emperor), a 'Padre', or Jesuit father, and a Muslim mullah. Most likely based on actual discussions in the '*Ibadat Khana*, the text includes detailed explanations of the Catholic veneration of images and of the use of images as didactic and mnemonic devices, both crucial concerns for Catholic churchmen in the years after the Council of Trent (1545–63). At one point the Father remarks: 'We revere and honour images of the saints … because these likenesses [*shaklha*] remind us of their stories and episodes, so that they revive us like a doctor,' stressing the curative properties of holy pictures in a way which reflected Jesuit teachings in Rome.[22] Elsewhere the text proclaims the affective power of imagery, which is 'more captivating' than writing mere words: 'What an astonishing invention, that enables one to bring things that are remote and long past close up into view!'[23]

Allegorical figure in Polyglot Bible (*Biblia sacra Hebraice, Chaldaice, Graece & Latine*, vol. I), published by Christopher Plantyn, Antwerp, 1569. Lisbon, BNL CAT. 85

St Luke, Mughal India, *c*.1600–4.
London, V&A CAT. 78

MUGHAL PAINTINGS WITH CHRISTIAN SUBJECTS

The principal painters of the Mughal court responded enthusiastically to the Western art works brought by the first two Jesuit missions (1580–91), and four of them came to specialize in Renaissance-style pictures. Kesu Das and Manohar favoured overtly Christian images, while Basawan (act. *c*.1560–*c*.1600) and Kesu Khurd (act. *c*.1580–*c*.1605) preferred more generically allegorical scenes based on biblical figures. Other painters, including La'l (act. before 1590), Miskin (act. *c*.1580–1604) and Husain (act. *c*.1584–98), created genre scenes that combined Christian and profane European figures.[24] Instead of copying directly from a print, they tended to make pastiches from a variety of sources, a tradition common in earlier Indo-Islamic miniatures. Especially typical are complex architectural settings, based loosely on Greco-Roman models, which often recall stage scenery. Some motifs are inspired by the actual Portuguese costumes, objects and men brought to court by Akbar's embassies.[25]

Kesu Das was probably Akbar's first specialist in the occidentalist mode, and Prince Salim (the future Jahangir) may have hired him later on to reproduce European images in his father's collection, since he copied many of his own works again in the 1590s.[26] Kesu's Christian pictures often show an appreciation of the devotional nature of their subjects, and sometimes his figures are expressive of pathos. A careful draughtsman, Kesu limited his models to a small number of engravings, and he painstakingly mastered the style of each before moving onto the next. Sometimes he would produce a version of the whole engraving, at other times he would combine figures from different sources, but he always gave the image his own personality, whether by altering the angle of the head, the pose of the arm, or the fall of the drapery.

Typical of Kesu's work is a signed copy of an engraving of Michelangelo's *Noah* from the Sistine Chapel, taken from an adaptation in reverse entitled *St Jerome* (1564) by the Italian printmaker Mario Cartaro.[27] The nearly nude figure gives Kesu a rare opportunity to practice muscular modelling, a feature entirely alien to Indo-Islamic tradition, and one at which he excelled. The trees, horizon and birds are characteristic of much of the artist's subsequent work, and had been incorporated into standard Mughal repertory from Flemish prints. Kesu's *Meditation on the Eucharist* is a collage of figures adapted from different prints and from the artist's own imagination. The picture looks like it was inspired by one of the Jesuits' catechism lessons. The theme is the Eucharist, a major preoccupation of the Catholic Church after Trent, with the Last Supper on the left side and the Virgin and Child holding the holy wafer with attendants on the right. This painting includes several elements typical of Kesu's painting, including the fantasy pavilion that looks like a chapel; the billowing, Venetian-style red curtains; and the lavish, Flemish-inspired landscape with its use of atmospheric perspective.

Kesu's only dated European-style work is his *St Matthew the Evangelist* of 1587–8. Here, the artist has followed the smallest details of the original, a 1565 engraving by Philip Galle after Maarten van Heemskerk, even going so far as to copy the inscription 'M.emskerc' on the bookend, although he has altered the poses and facial types of the figures to give them a more animated sense of interaction. Kesu leaves no doubt about the subject's identity when he adds 'Sanctus Matheus Evangelista' in Latin letters (taken from the caption) to the pages of the book held by the angel. The painting is full of European-style objects, including the vase bearing his signature, and the candlestick, books and other objects – perhaps gifts brought on embassies from Goa. Inside the pavilion is what looks like a Christian altar, covered with a rich brocade altarcloth. The curtains in the chapel-like pavilion add to the sense of mystery, and show a knowledge

Right: Kesu Das after Michelangelo, *St Jerome*, Mughal India, *c*.1580–85. Paris, MNAAG CAT. 76

Far right: Attributed to Kesu Das, *The Last Supper*, Mughal India, *c*.1580–85. Paris, MNAAG CAT. 77

Mario Cartaro, *St Jerome in a Landscape*, print, 1564, 81 x 61 cm. Vienna, Graphische Sammlung Albertina

of Christian ritual practice. The picture may be Kesu's finest work, and demonstrates the highly finished, polished treatment of drapery and fine brushstrokes that are typical of his later period.

Manohar began his career in the 1580s, when he worked under his father Basawan's shadow.[28] Born an intimate of the court, or *khanazad*, Manohar collaborated with his father on manuscript illustrations, and also imitated his works in the Euro-Christian mode. Manohar came to appreciate European paintings and engravings much more than his father, and by the advent of the third Jesuit mission in 1595 he appears to have succeeded Kesu Das as Akbar's chief specialist in Christian art. He later used his skills in pictorial realism to serve Jahangir as one of his principal portraitists. Distinct from his father's style is a tendency toward crisp, hard outlines and a more linear treatment of modelling, with less interest in spatial depth. His drawings have a very finished, burnished appearance, as can be seen in his several studies of the Madonna. In a drawing of the *Borghese Madonna*, a pseudo-Byzantine image copied by the Jesuits for its miraculous properties, Manohar alters his model by tilting the head slightly forward and enclosing the child completely in her arms, giving his Mary a more human aura than the stiff, iconic original. The folds of her veil are treated here with the utmost delicacy, and the draughtsmanship is expert.

Manohar's role as Akbar's chief Western-style painter earned him the position of project director of the *Mirat al-Quds* illustrations. Xavier's catechism and other Christian texts were probably first illustrated around 1600, in a venture that probably involved a whole workshop of artists. Unlike the other European-style paintings of the Akbar school, the *Mirat al-Quds* pictures do not derive primarily from engravings, but are executed in a more mainstream Mughal style, reminiscent of late Akbar-period illustrations of historical or literary works. Their theatricality is enhanced by stage-like architectural settings, vibrant gestures, and a variety of *mise-en-scène* figures such as priests or choirboys, all of which demonstrate the influence of preaching and Christian mystery plays performed by the Jesuits at court, as I discuss elsewhere.[29] In the brilliantly coloured scene of *Christ and the Woman of Samaria* Manohar has even cast a catechumen, or altarboy, as Christ's attendant. The boy holds a book and appears to be explaining the scene to the viewer. Meanwhile, down below, an audience of nobles stands and watches the biblical scene being enacted above.

Amina Okada assigns a nativity from a *Mirat al-Quds* manuscript to Manohar, and the figure types, angels and drapery confirm her attribution.[30] Like many of the *Mirat al-Quds* pictures, this painting does not derive from an engraving, and it includes such un-European features as a high horizon, a pavilion used to accent the figure of the Madonna, some Persian-style embracing trees in the background, and a very Indian-looking cow, reminiscent of the work of Basawan. The figure of the angel, with its feathered body-suit, looks like a performer in a stage play. Manohar has given considerable tenderness to the scene through the expressions of Mary and Joseph, and even the sympathetic treatment of the cow's face. Nevertheless, the painting still has the feeling of a pastiche (in fact, the figure of Christ was literally pasted on afterwards).

One of the most delightful painters of Akbar's studio was the enigmatic Kesu Khurd, about whom next to nothing is known.[31] Like Manohar, Kesu Khurd was from a younger generation of painters who worked in the shadow of Basawan and Kesu Das. Kesu Khurd specialized in crowded and animated scenes set against a backdrop of fantasy architecture, and his figures' drapery is remarkably expressive. In his *Virgin and Child* Kesu Khurd brilliantly juxtaposes the iconic (an image of the Holy Family) with the

Attributed to Manohar, *Christ and the Woman of Samaria*, Mughal India, c.1602.
Paris, CFL-IN CAT. 74

narrative (the genre detail of the attendant figures). Here we find the artist's most lively and expressive use of drapery, in which he contrasts the staid, calm folds of the Virgin's gown with the nervous flutter of her supplicants' garments. The robe of the man (Joseph?) at lower right is so agitated that it almost sweeps him off his feet. The man's sense of astonishment is enhanced by the alarmed gestures of the men on his right and left, the terrified snarl of the dog and the apoplectic stare of the figure's own face.

Akbar's court artists did not limit themselves to painting Euro-Christian artworks. From the earliest days of the mission Akbar sent his artists into the Jesuit chapel to carve ivory and marble copies of their crucifixions and other statuary, some of them large in scale.[32] Their artists also produced small pieces of jewellery and stone plaques with Christian scenes for the emperor's personal collection. One of the latter is a miniature bas-relief carving in sandstone after an engraving of *The Feast of Herod* by Jost Amman (1539–91), which reproduces its model in reverse and in three dimensions – quite a feat for artists who had only just begun to explore the new style.[33]

In the 1590s Prince Salim began to emerge as a fully fledged patron of the arts, and he quickly dominated the production of European-style paintings, taking Mughal painting in a new direction (see Asok Kumar Das's essay in this volume).[34] Salim demonstrated a passion for exact, direct copies of engravings, both because of his connoisseurly insistence on stylistic accuracy and his obsession with the identities of Jesus and Christian saints. Whereas Akbar had been content to allow Christian figures to populate his eclectic artistic landscape, at times in a religious context and at times a more secular setting, Salim demanded more consistently that their devotional meaning and stylistic integrity be kept intact. Salim trained his artists to be exacting and consistent. Abu'l-Hasan (1584–c.1628), who became Jahangir's greatest painter and earned the name *Nadir al-Zaman* ('Wonder of the Age'), as well as legions of lesser artists, apprenticed in the European style by painting over actual engravings in colour.[35] At least three of the painters in this school were women (Nini, Nadira Banu and Raqiya Banu), reminding us that the artistic enterprises of the Mughal court were equally directed towards a female audience, and that art instruction existed within the harem.[36] Nearly all the paintings are explicitly Christian subjects.

The technique of making pastiches, employed by many of Akbar's artists, found its ultimate expression in the margins (*hashiyas*) of Prince Salim's royal albums.[37] In two phases, the first c.1598–1604 and the second c.1608–9, the prince's (and later emperor's) artists painted figural borders to adorn poetical texts, mostly inscribed by the great Safavid calligrapher, Mir `Ali. The earlier group, directed by Aqa Reza and apparently including work by Basawan,[38] combine Christian and other European images with Islamic and Hindu figures, probably to represent world religions. One page is made up almost entirely of drawings after Albrecht Dürer, such as *St John the Baptist* from the *Small Passion*, the *Crucifixion*, the 1513 *Madonna and Child*, and the St Peter from *St Peter and St John Healing a Cripple*. Some of the prints that served as models for this border may have been in Mughal collections even before the arrival of the

Attributed to Manohar,
The Nativity, Mughal India, c.1600–2.
Paris, CFL-IN CAT. 75

Kesu Khurd, *The Virgin and Child*,
Mughal India, c.1590–95.
Dublin, CBL CAT. 79

Jesuits. The unity in subject matter in the *hashiya* is complemented by a consistent interest in northern European drapery. The relationship of these border paintings to the mystical love poems that they frame is negligible. Only rarely can a connection be drawn between the meaning of the verses and perhaps one or two of the figures in the margins, suggesting that the figures relate more to each other than to the text.[39]

The Mughal emperors' artists gave visual expression to one of the most intriguing and sophisticated cultural exchanges in the history of Christian–Muslim relations. Drawing on ideas and attitudes expressed at a remarkable series of interfaith debates, these miniature paintings, murals, sculptures and pieces of jewellery illustrate the high level of interest and curiosity that enlivened the dialogue between the Mughals and their Jesuit guests at the turn of the seventeenth century. Nevertheless, the door of opportunity would soon be closed, and this active dialogue between Christians and Muslims ended with Jahangir's death in 1627.[40] With the return to more orthodox policies under Shahjahan and the increasing influence of Protestant nations with little interest in missionary work such as England and Holland, the Mughals and European powers went back to a more traditional arms-length diplomacy until northern India was slowly swallowed up by the British empire in the later eighteenth and nineteenth centuries. By then, any hope of an equal exchange had passed forever.

PRINCE SALIM AND CHRISTIAN ART

Asok Kumar Das

In his letter of 20 August 1595 addressed to the General of the Society in Goa Father Jerome Xavier noted:

I say the same with respect to the Prince for he was seriously angry with Mohammedan guide for bringing with him no image of the Mother of God, and when bidding another to make extensive purchases, he particularly ordered him not to fail to bring with him a fine picture of our Lord, and as a Portuguese painter had come with us, he at once desired a copy to be painted of a picture of the Blessed Virgin which we had with us. So also when he came with his Royal Father to our Chapel, and saw there the child Jesus and a crucifix, he immediately wished to have similar images made of ivory by his own workmen.[1]

From this first-hand account by one of the most learned Westerners visiting the Mughal court we learn of the deep and abiding interest taken in European paintings and works of art by Salim, the prince regent. It reveals that he wanted to have an 'image of the Mother of God' brought from Goa, and when the Muslim guide to the mission failed to bring it, instructed another to procure a 'fine picture of our Lord'. We are also told that an unnamed Portuguese painter came with this mission, who was employed by him to paint a picture of the Blessed Virgin that was with the Jesuits. Xavier further informs us that Prince Salim had his own ivory carver who was instructed to make images of the Child Jesus and a Crucifix that he had noticed in the Father's chapel.

Salim was interested in the arts from an early age. From the reports of the first Jesuit mission arriving at Fathpur Sikri in 1580 we come to know that he visited the Father's

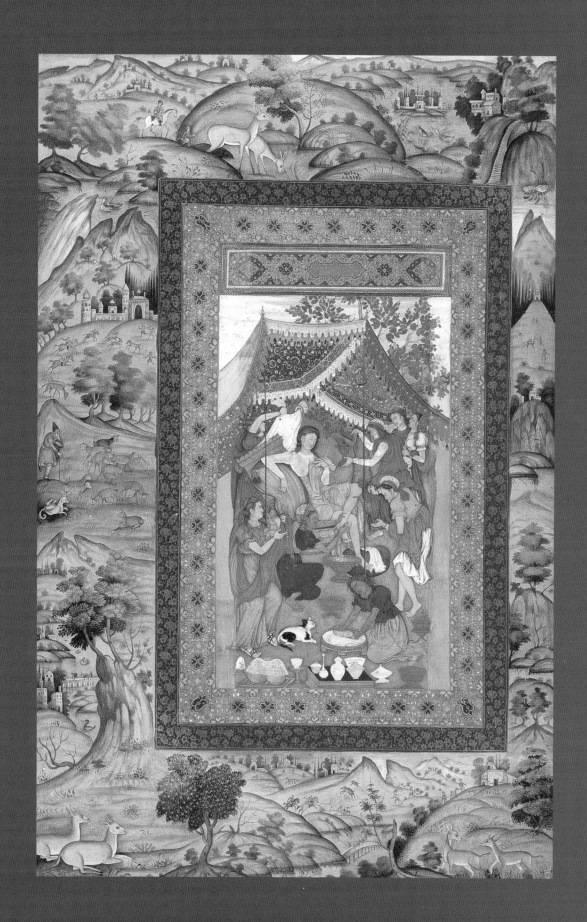

chapel there with his father Emperor Akbar and his brothers to look at the two paintings of the Madonna and Child exhibited there.[2] At that time he was only eleven.

He grew up in an atmosphere where Christian paintings were much respected, collected and copied, as well as used as wall decoration in palaces where he lived along with paintings of every other kind and style. He must have started his own *taswirkhana* while he was still in his late teens, when a middle-ranking émigré Persian painter, Aqa Reza, was appointed. Reza's son Abu'l Hasan was born while in Salim's service in 1587–8. This information comes from a note written by Abu'l Hasan on a remarkable study of the young St John the Evangelist that he made in March 1600, where he specifically mentions himself as a *khanazad*, 'one who was born in the royal household', and gives his age as twelve.[3]

We are not fully aware of Salim's art activities during these intervening years, but from a close inspection of the albums bearing Salim's name it appears that he was busy making a collection of Persian drawings and paintings, early Mughal works and copies of European paintings and engravings arriving at the Mughal court. Akbar himself sent his painters to the Jesuit chapel to study technique and subject matter and also

Manohar, *The Madonna,* **Mughal India,
c.1600.
Paris, CFL-IN** CAT. 73

to prepare copies of important paintings brought by the Jesuits. He had large-size paintings of the Virgin and Christ in his private chambers. He even embellished the inner walls of some palaces and chambers in Fathpur Sikri with elaborate pictures of Christian scenes. This continued in Lahore, where Akbar established the capital until 1598 after leaving Fathpur Sikri in 1585.

Salim's holding of European art objects was still not very elaborate, as he showed the Fathers of the third Jesuit mission only one carved image of Christ on the cross with two thieves hanging on either side, and two large pictures of the Madonna and Jesus kept in his sleeping chamber, which one day he exhibited at his 'window'. They had a chance to look at his collection of European engravings and paintings sometime later when they found him busy directing his painters to mount them in bound albums (registers).[4]

We know what these albums looked like and the richness and variety of their contents. Started during the closing years of the sixteenth century, they were given their final shape later when he inherited the Mughal throne and took the title Jahangir. At least two were assembled: *Muraqqa'-i-Gulshan* and *Muraqqa'-i-Gulistan*. The bulk of the folios of these albums are preserved in the Gulistan Palace Library, Tehran, while nearly fifty folios were removed from them and are now to be found in different public and private collections in Europe and the US, including twenty-five folios in the Staatsbibliothek, Berlin. Following the general pattern of album-making in Timurid, Ottoman and Safavid courts, Jahangir arranged his collection of calligraphic specimens – Mughal and Persian drawings, paintings and portraits, and European engravings and their coloured versions and copies framed with lines and narrow borders – leaving wide margins on three sides and the last side near the spine narrow. In positioning the images the major consideration was their size and subject. In some examples, where the central image is smaller than the available space within the frame, strips of engravings or calligraphic bands or paintings were added to fill the space. On the reverse side calligraphic panels coming from the pens of eminent calligraphers like Mir 'Ali were mounted in the same manner. The folios were put together in such a manner that in each opening one would see either images or writings on facing pages.

The most remarkable feature of these albums is the decoration of the folio margins. Those containing calligraphic panels have borders of landscape or vegetal design in two tones of gold interspersed with minutely drawn figural details. While the folios with images have borders of arabesque or floral illuminations in gold, sometimes with tiny birds of colourful plumage, the figural drawings on the margins of calligraphic panels open up a new vista and demonstrate the superlative efforts of his carefully selected group of painters.

These albums, along with the remnants of another rather commonplace album, contain a very large variety of European engravings, paintings and their coloured versions and copies, along with a wide repertoire of figures and motifs chosen from these engravings. The arrangement is often bizarre as it does not follow any meaningful order but is purely aesthetic in intention.

In his youth Salim was interested in these paintings and engravings for their technical quality and their naturalistic renderings. He wanted to know from the resident Jesuits their true meaning and symbolism. When he was presented with monochrome engravings he often sent his painters to the Jesuits for their guidance in ascertaining the colour scheme of the original paintings. He was, it appears, more concerned with their outward look than their true import.

While leading masters of Akbar's *taswirkhana* carefully studied the European paintings and engravings arriving at the Mughal court and absorbed the stylistic and technical details to moderate their own style, this was not so with the painters of Prince Salim. As Akbar took his 'chief painter and other painters' to look at the large oil paintings of the Madonna and Child,[5] and painters like Kesu Das produced a series of images of breathtaking beauty, Salim wanted his painters to prepare good replicas. When they failed to deliver he employed the unnamed Portuguese painter who came with Father Xavier's mission to make a copy of the painting of the Madonna brought by them for their own chapel. He permitted him 'to work for no one but himself, ordering him to paint the devotional images in the Jesuit chapel and in Akbar's collection'.[6] Gauvin Bailey has recently identified two of his works, *Suzanna at her Bath Surprised by the Elders* in the Freer Gallery of Art (no. F1996.9) and *Madonna and Child with Angels* in the Arthur M. Sackler Museum, Harvard University Art Museums (no. 1958.233). Both are copies of engravings by Antoine Wierix and Hieronymus Wierix of the Antwerp Guild, and as discovered by Bailey, 'painted in warm oil on paper with a much thicker brush and more limited palette than Mughal artists traditionally used'.[7]

He must have utilized the services of Kesu Das as well – the pages of his grand albums contain several signed and attributable works by him. The superb painting *Joseph Telling his Dream to his Father* signed by Kesu Das and now in the Chester Beatty Library, Dublin, has a replica attributable to Kesu Das mounted on a detached page of the Jahangir album, now in the St Louis Art Museum.[8] The painter of this version made several changes that differ from the earlier copy, which followed the 1544 engraving by the German engraver Georg Pencz. Further additions were made while fitting it into the picture frame at the time of making the album. However, Salim's painters did not stop there, as the three principal figures, Joseph's father Israel, Joseph, and his brother leaning on a club, are used as marginalia in folio 36 of the Gulshan Album.[9] A minute inscription in the lower corner of the folio reads *Padshah Salim murid wa ikhlas reqm-e Aqa Reza* (work of Aqa Reza, desciple of Padshah Salim) dating the work to the period between 1600 and 1604 when Salim styled himself as 'Padshah Salim' at Allahabad. (Aqa Reza used another detail in the lower part of this folio culled from an engraving, *Adonis*, by Etienne Delaune after Luca Penni, while the source of the bearded figure with a long staff seated on the rock on which the inscription is written remains unidentified.)

The figure of Joseph's brother is used yet again in the painting of a lady writing under a canopy in folio 99 of the same album, where he is shown reversed and now leaning upon a long sword instead of the club.[10] Joseph's father is also to be found in folio 51, where he appears reversed and fully painted.[11] Instead of listening to his son's story, Joseph's father is participating here in a conversation with a woman with a letter in her hand, based on a European source. The composition with its arches, pillared veranda and a minutely drawn distant landscape looks very similar to the St Louis Art Museum picture. These examples amply demonstrate how Salim's painters not only prepared replicas or coloured versions of monochrome prints but also used details from them in a completely different context, devoid of their true import and meaning.

It should also be noted that the detached page from the Jahangir album in the St Louis Art Museum contains a coloured version of an engraving of St Anthony Abbot by Martin Sadeler after Martin de Vos, bearing the signature of 'Nadira Banu, daughter of Mir Taqi, disciple of Aqa Reza'.[12] It is a very competent piece of work where she expertly translates the hatchings into washes and applies warm colour tones in selected

Kesu Das, *Joseph Telling his Dream to his Father*, Mughal India, c.1590. Dublin, CBL CAT. 80

areas like the cloak, cape, cap and beards. There is another signed painting by Nadira Banu in folio 127 of the Gulshan Album.[13] This is a coloured version of Jan Sadeler's engraving of St Jerome after Petrus Candido. Her name is written on the open pages of the book held by the saint, 'work of Nadira Banu, daughter of Mir Taqi, disciple of Reza, slave of Padishah Salim'. The folio contains four more coloured studies, all derived from European sources (clockwise from upper left): bust of the Madonna, a rather inept study of the upper part of Jacob Goltzius's engraving; *An Old Man Offering Money to a Young Woman* after Hendrik Goltzius; Jan Sadeler's engravings of St Peter; and an Apostle. Though these are not signed they appear to be the work of Nadira Banu.

There are several works signed by three other female painters, Ruqaya Banu, Sahifa Banu and Nini – mostly copies of European engravings or Persian paintings by masters like Bihzad – found in the Gulshan Album or other detached album pages. They reveal an interesting aspect of Salim's interest in paintings, which he shared with members of the purdah-bound zenana, encouraging the womenfolk to study and prepare copies of important art objects including European engravings. He considered their quality consistent with other members of the circle of Aqa Reza and included them for mounting in his grand albums. Even a cursory glance at the marginal details of these albums would show how women from different strata of society as well as various aspects of harem life are also depicted there in a realistic manner.

Apart from *Joseph Telling his Dream to his Father*, there are several other subjects that the painters of Salim's *taswirkhana* favoured. Crucifixion fascinated Prince Salim and a considerable number of Crucifixion pictures were prepared for inclusion in his albums both as a principal subject and as a marginal detail. But perhaps the best-known image or subject was *St John the Evangelist* taken from Albrecht Dürer's print *Christ on the Cross* (1511) in the *Engraved Passion* series and painted by Abu'l Hasan, son of Aqa

Above left: Nini, after an engraving by Hieronymus Wierix, *The Martyrdom of St Cecilia*, Mughal India, c.1600. London, V&A CAT. 82

Above: *The Deposition from the Cross*, Mughal India, Lahore, c.1598. London, V&A CAT. 69

Reza, in March 1600, when Salim was still waiting at Agra before moving to Allahabad to start his rebel court.[14] Abu'l Hasan, who became the favourite and most versatile painter at Jahangir's court, reveals his future promise in this early work, where he reinterprets the great German engraver's figure with naturalism and psychological insight. The expression of conventional grief in the engraving has been transformed into an expression of anguish. The same figure is used again taken out of context as a marginal illustration in folio 5b of the Jahangir Album in the Staatsbibliothek, Berlin.[15] Surprisingly, it also shows three other figures drawn from three different Dürer engravings: *Virgin under the Tree* of 1513, the Moorish king from the *Adoration of Magi* in the *Life of the Virgin* woodcut series, and Peter from *St Peter and St John Healing a Cripple*. The painter has suitably altered the expression of Mother and Child but successfully reproduced the folds of her drapery. This is also true of the tall and impressive figure of Peter. Only the youthful St John appears turning in the opposite direction. Though there is no corroborating textual evidence, it is certain that Salim was able to procure at this time a number of prints by the great German painter and engraver. A fully coloured copy of his *Virgin under the Tree* of 1513 is preserved in Windsor Castle Library.[16]

On a closer examination of the contents of these grand albums many such examples can be found. As there is some hope of getting all the album folios in Tehran and Berlin and stray folios in other collections published in the near future, it should be possible to shed more light on Salim's collection of European art objects and the manner in which these were studied, copied, coloured and reused as decorative elements by his painters.

To close this brief survey, another interesting subject favoured by Salim and his painters should be noted: scholars and teachers with a book. Numerous studies of scholars, teachers, Sufis, Jesuit fathers, Jain savants, Hindu religious men, sadhus and fakirs crowd the marginalia of his albums. The figure of St Luke (or St Lucas) with a book in his hand or tucked under his arm became a very popular subject. On the right-hand side of the picture in folio 94 of the Gulshan Album, showing a pensive lady with an open book on a table before her, are four original engravings by Hans Sebald Beham, which include a print of St Lucas from the series *The Four Evangelists* (1541).[17] There is a tiny replica of the same figure among the marginalia of folio 113 of this album. As Milo Beach noted, 'Beham's Saint has become an Oriental scholar, and the covers of the book he carries are now decorated, in Indian fashion, with figures and painted designs'.[18] His wings have been removed and he has been shown within an aureole of winged rabbits. A minute inscription on the book held by the Virgin among the decorations in the centre of the left-hand side of the margin reads 'Shah Salim, work of Padarat', which with the title 'Shah' dates the illustration to the time before he moved to Allahabad in early 1600.

A further example of St Lucas completely transformed as an Indian saint holding books is found on the marginalia of another detached leaf of the Jahangir Album now in the Arthur M. Sackler Museum, Harvard Art Museums (no. 1958.187).[19] There is a larger and freer rendering of the tiny Beham print of St Lucas mounted on the folio of a different and smaller album generally known as the Salim Album, now in the Victoria and Albert Museum, London.[20] This album originally contained pictures of officials, nobles, scholars, Jesuits and men of religion, as well as copies of European prints, some containing signatures of artists including two by 'Ghulam, servant of Shah Salim'. Yet another picture of St Lucas mounted on a different album page is in the collection of the Fondation Custodia, Paris. Here the saint has his wings intact![21]

Calvary, northern India (?),
17th century, wood and ivory.
Oporto, private collection CAT. 86

VISIONS OF THE WEST IN MUGHAL ART

Milo C. Beach

Well before Mughal historical chronicles make any reference to Europe or the Europeans increasingly seen in the port cities and bazaars of India, common people were developing awareness of these foreigners. The *Journal of the First Voyage of Vasco da Gama, 1497–1499*, for example, records: 'When we disembarked … the road was crowded with a countless multitude anxious to see us. Even the women came out of their houses with children in their arms and followed us.'[1] And, as any human being would, Indians near the coast must have quickly begun to discuss these voyagers, speculating about the world from which they came and spreading word to others about the new arrivals.

It was not only conjecture and rumour that moved from the ports to the interior of the subcontinent, however. The second voyage led by Pedro Álvares Cabral in 1500 had been supplied with things appropriate for official presentation. The *feitor* Aires Correia described the outfitting of the ships:

The King also ordered all sorts of merchandise of what was in the kingdom and from outside of it … cloths of gold, silk, and wool, of all kinds and colours … so as to be fit for presentation to the Kings and rulers of the countries where they might put into port.[2]

Cloth, an easily transportable material and highly desirable in India, would have been central to the image of Europe that was being developed there. The opulence of textiles brought for official presentation would have been immediately welcomed by the wealthy, while the clothing of the foreigners, and the goods they might have brought for

private trade, would have aroused interest among people in the bazaars – although relatively few people would actually have had a chance to see such novelties themselves.

Following their arrival off the Indian coast, the Portuguese quickly developed extensive contacts with the kings of Ceylon, and the exchange of gifts at their various diplomatic encounters during the second quarter of the sixteenth century especially has been well studied.[3] These years also correspond with the establishment of a new dynastic power in north India, where lands were being claimed by a Mongol-Turkic group known as the Mughals. The long-established network of merchants at work throughout the subcontinent responded immediately to such a potentially strong new market and were a prime source for the first European goods to reach the court. The historian Khwandamir, for example, wrote in his contemporary history of the Mughal Emperor Humayun's reign: 'He [Humayun] loved and respected merchants, who came from overseas and various countries … he granted them much protection.'[4] Contemporary chronicles confirm that European textiles became especially popular, for they conformed to existing patterns of interest and usage. Gulbadan Begam, Humayun's sister, describes in her memoirs a celebration to welcome the triumphant return to court of her brother after a victory at Chunar early in his reign: 'The covering of the pavilions and of the large audience tent was, inside, European brocade, and outside, Portuguese cloth.'[5] Such references abound. Khwandamir, for example, says of an unusual and innovative movable palace constructed for Humayun:

Manohar, *King David Playing the Harp*, Mughal India, c.1610–20. Copenhagen, David Collection CAT. 92

this marvelously decorated palace was adorned in various colours by the most skilful painters … The chamberlains of the throne, the nest of religion, had covered it with curtains of seven colours, made of cloths from Khotan, Turkey, and Europe; and raised its adornment to the height of beauty and delicacy.[6]

Given the eagerness with which later painters responded to new visual stimuli, it may be safe to presume that the painted decorations in this palace were influenced by the European textiles that were hung on its walls. Perhaps most significantly, Humayun designed for himself a new kind of turban or crown to distinguish his rule. It consisted of a tall pointed cap wrapped loosely with sashes of richly woven and designed cloths. Khwandamir describes this innovative headgear, which appears in Humayun's many portraits and states that 'the crown [cap] of honour … was adorned with various rarities, such as the European velvet, embroidered satin [etc.]'.[7]

Yet while merchants were important, they were only one source for these novelties. In 1534 Humayun was in Gujarat at war with Bahadur Shah, a local sultan resisting the spread of Mughal power. This ruler had 'sent, in 940 [= AD 1533–4], experienced ambassadors bearing valuable presents to him [Humayun] and set in motion the process of friendship'.[8] The relationship quickly degenerated, however, and Bahadur Shah rejected Humayun's authority. The opposing troops of the two armies moved through the ports of Cambay and Diu (where the Portuguese were to build a fort in 1535), and other territories along the coast controlled by the foreigners. The treasure that fell into Humayun's hands as he conquered these territories, as well as the earlier presents from the Gujarati sultan, may certainly have contained some of the gifts given to Bahadur Shah by the Portuguese, from whom he had sought aid. Eventually he proved untrustworthy for them also. In an attempt to exert control, 'the [Portuguese] Viceroy intercepted him and requested him to stay till some present should be brought before him'.[9] Finally he drowned off Diu in February 1537, an episode illustrated in a later manuscript in which the Portuguese were the prime suspects.[10]

'Tavoa de Dio' (Map of Diu) from
Dom João de Castro, *Roteiro de Goa
a Diu*, 1538–9.
Coimbra, Biblioteca Geral da
Universidade CAT. 16

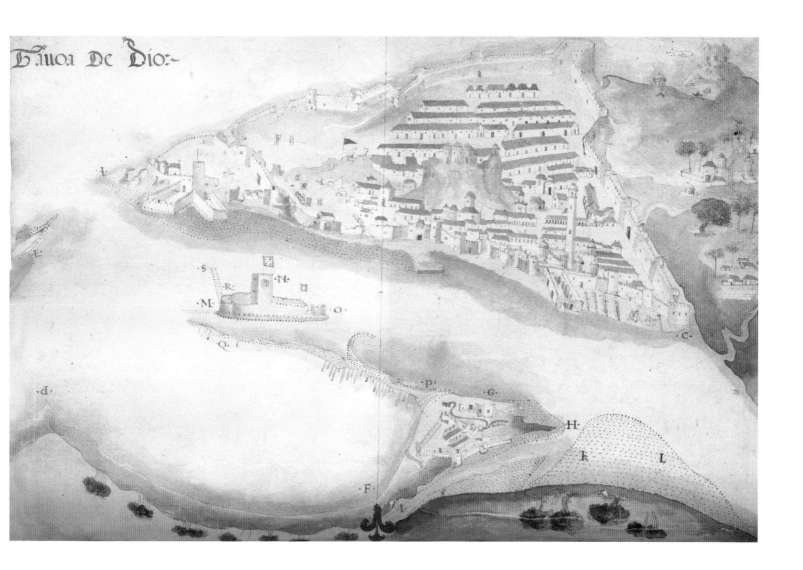

The taking of booty and the exchange of gifts thus also provided goods that arrived at the Mughal court. European images and objects – things considered curious as well as precious, which could easily have included religious images and perhaps even the portraits that would have belonged to many Europeans in India, alongside the textiles often referred to – were therefore known before Europeans themselves appeared in a court context. If there were further goods for which interest at court could not be expected, they would have entered the marketplace for anyone to acquire and many would have been of particular interest to artists and craftsmen.

Some of the European textiles coveted in the highest circles must have been decorated with human, animal and floral forms, and these would have helped to introduce European figural imagery to India. With the establishment of the Portuguese at Goa in 1510 and the commencement of missionary activity, European prints and religious images became an even richer and more constant stimulus for the imagination within limited circles. Thus, while we have no visual depictions of Europeans by Mughal artists until the reign of Akbar, Humayun's son, these later portrayals were built on several decades of observation and imaginative speculation about Europe, fuelled by reports of people encountered, their costumes, their behaviour and the occasional access to the things they had brought with them.

At the Mughal court the earliest illustrative painting now known began in Humayun's reign. He established a workshop of painters dominated by two masters whom he brought from Persia: Mir Sayyid 'Ali and 'Abd as-Samad, and the styles they practised only slowly moved away from long-established traditions of Persian imagery. The workshops (and their output) grew substantially after Akbar's accession in 1556, however, and Indian painters from many different regions, like merchants earlier, came to this newly powerful court attracted to a patron known to be interested and wealthy. The earliest work by these Indian artists is datable to years before Europeans first penetrated court circles in the 1570s, but that some painters were already aware of Europeans is shown in two of the earliest Akbari manuscripts: the *Tuti Nama* (c.1560–65) and the *Dastan-i Amir Hamza* (or *Hamza Nama*; c.1558–72).[11] Both include figures who are recognizably European (which at this date means Portuguese) in dress and appearance. There is no reason to think that painters introduced these figures from sources other than their own visual experience or reports they had themselves heard. The sailors and soldiers depicted were exactly the men they would have seen.

Khorshid's Travels to Mecca, from the *Tuti Nama* ('Tales of a Parrot'), may provide the earliest visual reference to Europeans in Mughal art.[12] The narrative relates that the heroine 'Khorshid boarded a vessel for pilgrims',[13] and there is nothing in the story to justify so exotic an inclusion as Portuguese sailors – men recognizable by their hats or by bare (and often bald) heads.[14] It is hardly surprising that such generalized references to the Portuguese first placed Europeans into Mughal paintings. The unique characteristics of individual humans had been of interest to the Mughal emperors from the time of Babur, who wrote the first real autobiography in the Islamic world and filled it with precise depictions of the people, the flora and the fauna that he encountered.[15] We know of no paintings made for Babur, however.

While many of the figures in *Khorshid's Travels to Mecca* seem to be based on people seen by the painter, the style shows that the artist had somehow also seen European works of art. The illustration includes a dramatic modelling of cloth, stressing its weight and mass, and the play of light in its folds, rather than its surface decoration

Gul Mohammad (copy of an engraving
by F. Bolognus, after Velázquez),
Isabel of Bourbon, Queen of Spain,
from the St Petersburg *Muraqqa,*
Mughal India, mid-18th century.
St Petersburg BIOS/RAS CAT. 99

(the interest of Persian and pre-Mughal Indian painters). This could only have been learned by looking at European images, although it does also correspond to one of the manners in which cloth was actually used by Europeans. Whereas Indian and Persian traditions suspended cloth in ways that reinforced the planar character of architecture, European cloth was often gathered and draped, and the light on its folds stressed its bulk, not its flat pattern.[16] It was by the incorporation of such interesting and unusual new elements into their paintings that artists often captured and held their patron's attention and support. So, whereas imperial historical chronicles, which tended to be highly sycophantic in tone, have attributed the interest in Europe to the emperor's first meeting with the Portuguese in 1572, the Mughal court actually did not lead in this regard; it seems to have followed the discoveries its painters had earlier made on their own.

Of this first meeting, Akbar's historian Abu'l Fazl wrote that Akbar 'encamped at the port of Cambay ... the merchants of Rum [Europe], Syria, Persia, and Turan regarded the advent of the Shahinshah as a great boon and paid their respects'.[17] It is inconceivable, of course, that they did not make the emperor aware of the most unusual and valuable objects available to them. A few weeks later,

a large number of Christians came from the port of Goa and its neighbourhood and were rewarded with the bliss of an interview ... They produced many of the rarities of their country ... [Akbar] made inquiries about the wonders of Portugal and the manners and customs of Europe ... he did this from a desire for knowledge ... [and] wished these inquiries might be the means of civilising this savage race.[18]

Three years later, Akbar sent an expedition to Goa 'to bring for H.M.'s delectation the wonderful things of that country',[19] and they returned with, among other things, an organ. The historian al-Badaoni wrote in 1582:

An organ, which was one of the wonders of creation, and which Haji Habib-ullah had brought from Europe [Goa], was exhibited to mankind. It was like a great box the size of a man. A European sits inside it and plays the strings thereof, and two others outside keep putting their fingers on five peacock-wings, and all sorts of sounds come forth. And because the Emperor was so pleased, the Europeans kept coming at every moment in red and yellow colours, and went from one extravagance to another. The people at the meeting were astounded at this wonder ...[20]

One senses that the Mughals were as enthralled by the instrumentalists as the instrument. Eventually, seeking to learn more substantially about the religion they represented, Akbar invited a group of missionaries to court to discuss Christianity. They arrived in 1580 with paintings, prints and illustrated books. From this decade onwards, European contacts were overt, acknowledged and highly influential.

The introduction of prints following the arrival of the Jesuits in 1580 vastly increased the stimuli for painters: their knowledge of Europe was no longer limited primarily to observation of Europeans in India; it came now from illustrated scenes of events, many of which would be only partially, if at all, understood. Nonetheless, the repertoire of forms and subjects that prints and other works of art brought to the attention of painters and patrons allowed a systematic exploration of European techniques and subjects that had earlier been learned through occasional and haphazard contacts.

La'l, *The Drowning of Bahadur Shah*,
Agra, c.1603–4.
London, British Library CAT. 13

Dharm Das, *Akbar Receives
Congratulations on the Birth of his
Son Murad*, from an *Akbar Nama*,
c.1603–5.
Dublin, CBL CAT. 94

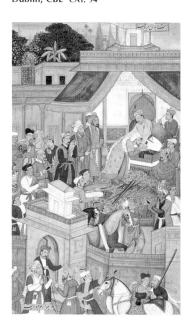

Men with this first official mission presented Akbar with the *Royal Polyglot Bible*, an illustrated volume printed in Antwerp by Christopher Plantyn between 1568 and 1572. Many of the greatest Mughal artists were involved with the study and assimilation of these and other European illustrations subsequently brought to court by Portuguese and other missionaries and traders. And because of Akbar's interest in Christianity, they began to copy the subjects as well as the styles. One of the finest of the early copies is the *St Matthew*, dated 1588, by Kesu Das (Bodleian Or.a.1/41v). The artistic interest in cloth – and its dramatic impact – are far more sophisticated here than in the earlier *Tuti Nama* scene, as is the use of modelling to give a seemingly individual, innovatively thoughtful character to St Matthew's face. These achievements were recognized and appreciated by Akbar, for Abu'l Fazl wrote 'the wonderful works of the European painters who have attained world-wide fame ... the minuteness in detail, the general finish, the boldness of execution, etc., now observed in pictures, are incomparable; even inanimate objects look as if they had life.'[21] Mughal painters took from their study the tools to develop further the interest in physical reality first articulated by Babur. In none of these early illustrations is the exoticism of the European presence noticed; nor do Europeans embody some fantasy invention – as do the orientalist figures and otherworldly landscapes of European chinoiserie decoration, for example, or the curious creatures described in early European travel accounts. That this visual realism is not accompanied by substantial textual documentation, however, is puzzling. While foreign curiosities are mentioned in official chronicles and Europeans are acknowledged as a category, individuals from Europe who actually came into contact with the emperor are barely noticed in the *Akbar Nama* and other contemporary Mughal histories.

Paintings therefore become an important Indian source for information on early European visitors and the curiosa that accompanied them. Dating from the end of Akbar's reign, there are several illustrated manuscripts of historical texts that depict Europeans involved in important court events. *The Drowning of Bahadur Shah*, from the *Akbar Nama*, a history of Akbar's reign, shows the death in 1537 of that Gujarati sultan, whom we discussed above. Before European art introduced new attitudes towards humanity and the techniques to allow portraits or portrait-like depictions, painters used general character types. The artist here makes no physiognomic distinction between Indians and Europeans. Only the clothing and headgear identify the Portuguese sailors.

Akbar Receives Congratulations on the Birth of his Son Murad, from the same early seventeenth-century manuscript but depicting an event dated 1570, portrays a European amid the crowds congratulating Akbar on his second son's birth. Unlike *The Drowning of Bahadur Shah*, no Portuguese was present at this ceremony, although as a youth Murad was sent to study Christianity and Portuguese language with the Jesuit Fathers. The figure may therefore have been included either because of this association or because Europeans were of interest to the court at the time the illustration was painted and it made the presentation fashionably up-to-date.

In the most famous of these scenes, *Akbar Presiding over Discussions in the* 'Ibadat Khana, by Nar Singh, two priests are shown debating with the emperor. This depicts one of a series of meetings that Akbar held with the Jesuits once they had arrived at court in 1580, and here finally we have a specific person. An inscription names the priest closest to the emperor as Father Rodolfo Acquaviva, who led the first Jesuit mission.[22] While there is little sense of personal individuality in the face, or any indication of the thought process that must have been at work, the inscription indicates at least an intention to

show a specific man. These figures again all conform to a personal formula invented by the painter, although Nar Singh paints features less full-bodied and expressive than those of Dharm Das. Nonetheless, these illustrations make it clear that the Mughals wanted to record historically important scenes, and that painters were slowly becoming more skilled in the specificity of what they could depict. As always, however, intentions precede ability.

Akbar himself was highly interested in realism and portraiture. As Abu'l Fazl wrote: 'His Majesty himself sat for his likeness, and also ordered to have the likenesses taken of all the grandees of the realm. An immense album was thus formed: those who have passed away have received a new life, and those who are still alive have immortality promised them.'[23]

Several individual portraits of Europeans are also known from the late sixteenth and early seventeenth centuries.[24] Among the most elegantly executed is *A Portuguese Man*, although the facial characteristics are not yet convincingly those of a specific, recognizable person. On the other hand, a well-known depiction of *A European*, probably Portuguese (and certainly not Indian), may have been copied early in the seventeenth century from a work brought to India some decades earlier.[25] Whether or not the small head of *A Portuguese Man* is a copy or made from life, it builds on such

Portrait of a Portuguese Gentleman,
Mughal India, c.1600.
Boston, Museum of Fine Arts CAT. 95

achievements as Kesu Das's *St Matthew* and shows a depth of understanding of human character not seen in Mughal art before the seventeenth century.

From the end of the sixteenth century through the reign of Jahangir, portraiture in Mughal India became increasingly perceptive and individualized, no matter who was the subject. More extensive contact with Europeans over longer periods of time, and Jahangir's insistence on specific details of appearance, led to keener perceptions of physiognomies and personality traits. The emperor also maintained an interest in curiosities, for which Goa remained the source. Like his father, the emperor sent a mission to the city and it returned in 1612 with such novelties as a turkey. A scene from the illustrated memoirs of Jahangir and the accompanying text record its arrival in Agra,[26] where it was carefully studied by the artist Mansur, the Mughal master of flora and fauna.[27] A far less well-known depiction by an unidentified artist further attests to the interest provoked by this arrival – and to Jahangir's interest in having his artists make precise observations of whatever they encountered.

Courtiers portrayed in *Darbar of Jahangir*, painted about 1620, for example, are highly individualized. These are true portraits: many of the men are recognizable in other contexts, while the Jesuit priest who stands at the bottom left, thin of face and countenance, may be Father Corsi, who was resident at court at the time this event took

Europeans Bringing Gifts to Shahjahan, from a *Padshah Nama*, f. 117a, c.1634.
Royal Library, Windsor/The Royal Collection © 2004, Her Majesty Queen Elizabeth II

Attributed to Manohar, *Darbar of Jahangir*, c.1620.
Boston, Museum of Fine Arts CAT. 25

place.[28] Given the opulence of dress and the full features of the men around him, the artist seems to have understood the severe and ascetic character of the priesthood, just as he has now isolated the characteristics of a European facial type. The most amusingly observed European, an image in which the perceptive observation of the priest in *Darbar of Jahangir* evolves into social comment, is the man attending *Festivities on the Occasion of the Accession of Jahangir*. Placed by the artist Abu'l Hasan amid the throngs shown in the left half of this double-page composition, he disdainfully turns his back on the scattering of gold coins and the resulting hubbub. His evident sense of personal superiority, shown by gesture and stance as well as facial expression, is quite a new observation of the European presence. Another thin-faced Jesuit priest is also in evidence, as is a bare-headed European – behind the red rail in the right background.

Such historical manuscripts continued under Jahangir's son, Shahjahan. *The Capture of Port Hoogly*, from the *Padshah Nama*, the illustrated memoirs of Shahjahan, is dateable to about 1634. This, too, depicts an actual event when Portuguese merchants in the city of Hughli (Hoogly) were attacked by Mughal troops, from whom they fled by boat: the scene shows their goods being loaded, although one vessel sinks and its passengers drown.[29] In comparison to *The Drowning of Bahadur Shah*, both the Mughal troops and the Europeans are convincingly individualized, although they are certainly invented personalities. Some of the Portuguese men, behatted and moustached, are presented as dandies – more social comment, but one equally often made of the imperial circle – while several of the women are opulently bejewelled. The townscape in the background, unusually prominent and including a Gothic church, carefully details the density, solidity and order found in European towns.

Women actively involved in daily events, rather than shown simply as mothers, consorts or entertainers, illustrate a Mughal observation of European behaviour, one that may be an especially provocative aspect of the European presence. Akbar himself showed awareness of the differences of attitude towards women in Europe and India. At one meeting with Europeans Akbar is quoted in the *Akbar Nama* as he refutes a Christian claim that monogamy and equality of the sexes produces greater reverence and love than the harems of the Mughals. 'There are numerous concubines,' he admits, 'and many of them are neglected and unappreciated and spend their days unfructuously in the privy chamber of chastity, yet in spite of such bitterness of life they are flaming torches of love and fellowship.'[30] But, once again, there is no attempt to make European behaviour conform to Mughal social expectations. On occasions, however, reality is altered. Another *Padshah Nama* scene depicts the Portuguese prisoners taken at Hughli and brought to Agra. While they were actually imprisoned and tortured, suffering 'unbearable hardships',[31] they are shown here as an embassy offering homage to Shahjahan.

Until the beginning of the seventeenth century no European is illustrated in a way significantly different from his Mughal counterparts – with the exception of dress. The often fictional presence of Europeans at events, however, suggests that their actual presence was desirable. This is not unexpected at a court where so many people came from other regions, whether from central or west Asia, Iran or elsewhere in India. The emperor would appear most powerful, after all, when his court was thronged with attendants representing the great kingdoms of the world.

While it was the Emperor Akbar who invited Europeans into the imperial circle, and first asked his painters to incorporate foreign subjects and styles into their work, his son Jahangir showed far more profound understanding of European imagery. He had been interested in Europeans, and in the images brought by missionaries and traders, from his youth. We learn this from Jesuit chronicles, however, not from his own memoirs. A letter written in 1595 by Father Jerome Xavier stated that Prince Salim (as Jahangir was known before his accession) 'was very angry with those who had conducted the Fathers, because they had not brought him any picture of Our Lady from Goa'.[32]

When he reached his thirtieth birthday in 1599 and his father showed no signs of diminishing his authority or sharing his power, Prince Salim rebelled and established his own court to the east at Allahabad, taking his father's title *padshah* and claiming imperial authority for himself. During these years he launched one of the greatest of all Mughal book projects, a bound album of single illustrations and calligraphies that he had collected.[33] The images included contemporary as well as earlier Mughal paintings, Persian works and illustrations from other Islamic courts (such as those of the Indian Deccan), and European prints and paintings – as well as copies and adaptations of these images. This is the greatest single source for the study of Mughal contact with European art. The illustrations and calligraphies were glued onto book pages and surrounded by elaborately intricate borders, in which figures of European source were often placed decoratively within the marginal designs exemplifying the visual richness and figural inventiveness of these pages.

European imagery was not confined between the covers of books, however. Shown suspended above the imperial throne in the St Petersburg *Darbar of Jahangir* (p.53) are two European paintings: one illustrating the story of Tobias, the other portraying a European couple. Images were displayed in this way, both at court and for Christian religious ceremonies, and would have been seen by anyone attending those events. European subjects were also found in wall-paintings.[34] In the architecture above the throne in the Boston *Darbar of Jahangir* the head of the Virgin Mary has been painted.[35] Jesuit accounts describe extensive and elaborate wall-paintings in the palaces based on Christian subjects and European portraits, but they also note that such imagery was unacceptable to many:

The King's way of decorating his palace was very offensive to the Moors, who regard pictures of all kinds with such disfavour that they will not tolerate portraits of their own saints ... On a wall of one of the halls he had painted figures of the Pope, the Emperor, King Philip, and the Duke of Savoy, whose portraits he possessed.[36]

The uses of such images therefore reflected a purely personal imperial enthusiasm, but the pervasiveness of the imagery must have reinforced Jahangir's sense that he presided over a realm that extended to the farthest reaches of the globe. The name *Jahangir* means 'he who seizes the world'.

Of the artists working for Prince Salim before his accession, no one was more brilliantly inventive that Abu'l Hasan, who had begun to copy European works by at least the age of twelve.[37] His *Timiditas* and *Dialectics* were both painted over actual engravings by the Antwerp printmaker Jan Sadeler; this was one way in which European techniques and subjects were absorbed. In this case Abu'l Hasan would have been reproducing and absorbing the means to show a freedom of movement and gesture – in other words, a behaviour – unknown to Islamic or Indian painting of the time. Such studies explain the skill with gesture seen in his *Festivities on the Occasion of the Accession of Jahangir*.[38]

Above (lower part): Attributed to
Abu'l Hasan, *Timiditas*, from the
St Petersburg *Muraqqa*, Mughal India,
c.1602.
St Petersburg BIOS/RAS CAT. 100

Above right (lower part): Attributed
to Abu'l Hasan, *Dialectics*, from the
St Petersburg *Muraqqa*, Mughal India,
c.1615.
St Petersburg BIOS/RAS CAT. 101

Attributed to Payag, *Shah Shuja*
Hunting **Nilgae, Mughal India,** *c.*1650.
Providence, Museum of Art, Rhode
Island School of Design CAT. 103

As artists copied in varied ways, they learned to make changes, and for some artists these alterations grew into new, often fantastic compositions. While Akbar had asked his artists to explore the realistic and rational, Jahangir became increasingly interested in the symbolic and allegorical. During his rule a new allegorical portraiture developed in which the emperor is shown attended by the spiritual and temporal rulers of the world, or standing above a lion and a lamb.[39] One of the great heroes of Persian literature is Majnun, whose love for Laila turns into madness when their families keep them apart. Majnun retreats to the wilderness, where he physically wastes away. A drawing of the emaciated hero with an opulently clad European woman, a creature bearing no relation to the traditional beauty of Laila, became so popular that several copies are known.[40] Yet, however imaginary the scene, the face of Majnun – which in each case is subtly different – is drawn with a sensitivity to inner emotion and a seeming individuality that indicate close study of European portraiture and graphic techniques. The realism of his expression reinforces the poetic allegory of unattainable desire represented here by the European woman (and in more traditional illustrations by Laila).

Manohar, *Majnun with a European Lady*, Mughal India, c.1600. Dublin, CBL CAT. 93

Above: *European Scene with Portuguese Figures*, Agra or Lahore, c.1595.
London, British Library/India Office Library CAT. 89

Left: *Angel Receiving a Group of Europeans*, Mughal India, c.1600.
Copenhagen, David Collection CAT. 91

Sanwlah, *A European Scene*, Mughal
India, c.1590–95.
Dublin, CBL CAT. 90

Angel Receiving a Group of Nobles in European Dress is a more complex, if less sensitive, example.[41] Rich clothing, free association of the sexes, drapery wrapped around figures and hanging in doorways, imaginary architecture, and figures moving freely over a deep landscape – these are the most usual elements of these fantasy scenes. *A European Scene* provides a more earthbound variant of this composition. By the artist Sanwlah, it is associated with the young prince Salim by his seal, placed at the upper right.[42] Similar scenes are found in abundance in Jahangir's album and reflect his taste and patronage.

Each of these illustrations shows a distant landscape with the bluish hazing of European atmospheric perspective. Landscape became an important element in Mughal art, but was almost never a separate subject unless – as in *A Distant Landscape* – it was a study taken from European sources. Almost certainly these views were understood as further emphasizing the vast extent, and the peacefulness, of Mughal control.

Left: *A Distant Landscape*, Mughal
India, c.1585–90.
Providence, Museum of Art,
Rhode Island School of Design
CAT. 102

Right: Ruknuddin, School of Bikaner,
*The Private Pleasures of the
Portuguese Commander-in-Chief*,
Mughal India, Rajasthan, c.1678–98.
Cambridge, Fitzwilliam Museum
CAT. 104

At the courts of Jahangir and Shahjahan the advent of the British and the new works of art that they brought with them eventually displaced the earlier enthusiasm for religious imagery. Shahjahan was not interested in Christianity, in any case, and artists had exhausted the visual innovations inspired by the religious prints and paintings introduced by the Jesuits. References to Europeans in Mughal art continued unabated, but the heyday of the Portuguese presence in painting was over. Such images as *The Private Pleasures of the Portuguese Commander-in-Chief*, painted in the Hindu princely state of Bikaner at the end of the seventeenth century, is a witty bit of social comment, but it retains nothing of the profound effect on Mughal painting of the Portuguese and the works of art they introduced into India. Mughal art would have been an utterly different tradition had European contact not been available during the early years of the Portuguese presence. But it was only because Babur and his descendants had developed an ability to learn from the world around them, and a receptivity to new ideas from whatever source, that this meeting of cultures proved so astonishingly fruitful.

THE REPRESENTATION OF JESUIT MISSIONARIES IN MUGHAL PAINTING

Amina Okada

Mughal painters, especially during the reign of the Emperor Akbar (1556–1605), were quick to copy or adapt European engravings of religious or edifying subjects that the Jesuits brought to the court, yet they rarely portrayed the missionaries themselves. The imperial painters had plenty of opportunity to meet the Jesuit Fathers and, on occasions, even to talk to them and ask questions about the subject of the engravings they had to study and reproduce.

Documents also show that about a month after the arrival of the first Jesuit mission to the Mughal Court, in 1580, Akbar summoned the painters to the imperial studio and went with them to the chapel where the missionaries were installed. The chapel contained two altarpieces with the Virgin and Child, one copied in Goa by Brother Manuel Godinho, after the *Virgin and Child* in the Borghese chapel of the church of Santa Maria Maggiore in Rome, the other brought from Rome by Father Martim da Silva. In a letter describing the emperor's visit Father Henriques wrote, 'The painters were astonished and declared that there could not possibly be better paintings nor better artists than those who had produced these pictures.'[1] A letter from Father Jerome Xavier, dated 1608, also stated that the Emperor Jahangir, who had a passion for European engravings, sent his painters to the house of the Jesuits to ask about the strange people (Europeans) they had been commissioned to paint; they had been told that 'the colour of the costumes should be retained' and that they should strictly abide by the missionaries' recommendations.[2]

Despite these regular, though infrequent contacts Mughal painters seldom painted the missionaries themselves in spite of their unusual robes and their undoubtedly exotic appearance that naturally attracted the artists' attention. Father Monserrate could not

Nar Singh, *Akbar Presiding over Discussions in the 'Ibadat Khana*, from an *Akbar Nama*, c.1604.
Dublin, CBL CAT. 67

help but note the amazement tinged with incredulity that the arrival of the first Jesuit missionaries caused in Fathpur Sikri, in 1580, and the astonishment of the people at their strange appearance.

When they entered, their outlandish appearance created a stir. All eyes were turned on them. People stopped, agape in wonderment, rooted to the ground, forgetting to get out of the way betimes, for who were those men coming along, unarmed, dressed in long black robes with their faces shaven, and their close-cropped heads stuck in hats?[3]

Few portraits are known today of the 'black robes' (siyaahposh), as the Jesuits were called at the Mughal court in a reference to their dark soutanes; their enemies even went so far as to call them the 'black devils'.[4] In some cases it is not clear whether they are really portraits or imaginary, idealized evocations of some of the missionaries who circulated and worked in the Mughal court, whose names and identities, if not their faces, are well known.

Although the isolated studies and portraits of the missionaries by Mughal painters are material for conjecture as regards the identity of the person portrayed, the rare scenes of the court and royal audiences (durbars) where the Jesuit fathers appear provide more reliable identification, due to the historical context and records of them in imperial chronicles and memoirs. This is the case for the famous page from *Akbar Nama* (c.1603–5) showing the Emperor Akbar presiding over a religious debate in the House of Worship (*'Ibadat Khana*) at Fathpur Sikri, a debate that took place between the *ulemas* (scholars) and members of the first Jesuit mission. The monarch in the company of two of his sons – no doubt the young princes Murad and Daniyal – and his minister and counsellor Abu'l Fazl, acting as translator, were present at the vehement discussion about the nature of the True Faith between supporters of orthodox Islam and the Jesuit fathers.[5] Nar Singh, who painted the illustration,[6] depicts two of the three missionaries, Fathers Rodolfo Acquaviva, Antonio Monserrate and Francisco Henriques, who made up the first Jesuit mission of 1580.

A number of interpretations have been put forward regarding the identity of the two missionaries represented by Nar Singh. The younger of the two, who is beardless, with an open book (the Bible?) on his knees and a second book in front of him, and making an explicit gesture with his left hand to stress his meaning, is apparently Rodolfo Acquaviva, who, as head of the Jesuit mission, led the debate. Moreover, his name 'Padre Rodolfo' appears in the Persian text that accompanies the illustration. Abu'l Fazl describes Father Acquaviva in *Akbar Nama*, praising him for his calmness and self-control in the face of the virulent attacks of the *ulemas*:

One night, the Ibadat-Khana was brightened by the presence of Padre Rudolf, who for intelligence and wisdom was unrivalled among Christian doctors. Several carping and bigoted men attacked him, and this afforded an opportunity for a display of the calm judgement and justice of the assembly! These men put forward the old accepted assertions, and did not attempt to arrive at the truth by reasoning. Their statements were torn to pieces and they were nearly put to shame … With perfect calmness and earnest conviction of the truth, the Padre replied to their arguments …[7]

The identity of the bearded missionary next to Acquaviva is debatable and has been given as either Antonio Monserrate[8] or Francisco Henriques.[9] The presence of Father Henriques, a Persian convert, who acted as interpreter, would appear to be fully

Manohar, *Jesuit Missionary*, Mughal
India, c.1590.
Paris, MNAAG CAT. 71

justified in such an important debate, but it is also very likely that Father Monserrate, a historian and chronicler of the mission,[10] would take part in religious discussions and debates held in the *'Ibadat Khana*. Fathers Acquaviva and Monserrate, the latter particularly, were able to speak some rudimentary Persian, though, according to L. York Leach,[11] the presence of Abu'l Fazl next to the Emperor Akbar may explain the absence of Father Henriques, for the historian and biographer of Akbar, who spoke some Portuguese,[12] may have acted as translator. According to Father Monserrate's testimony, Abu'l Fazl used to listen to the Jesuits' points of view in private and make them known publicly afterwards in a more polished fashion than they themselves could.[13] L. York Leach also noted that the features of the person depicted by Nar Singh appear to be more western than oriental. Father Monserrate, a Catalan by birth, who was forty-three years of age when he arrived at the Mughal court in 1580, could well have been the missionary next to Father Acquaviva on this memorable occasion.

As regards actual 'portraits' of Fathers Acquaviva and Monserrate, the undeniably stereotyped and only slightly personalized character of the people in the manuscript illustrations at the time of Akbar, between 1580–1600, were generally the work of two, sometimes three artists, each with his own speciality. The first truly expressive, individual portraits of Mughal dignitaries and nobles, with which Akbar hoped to make an album,[14] were done more as separate miniatures and not as the illustrations for the imperial manuscripts full of people with conventional or stereotyped features. The painter Nar Singh made a clear distinction between the two missionaries, one young and clean-shaven (Acquaviva) and the other somewhat older and bearded (Monserrate).

The possibility that these are two actual portraits is confirmed by another portrait of a Jesuit missionary in the Musée Guimet: in this single image, not part of a group, the general appearance and features particularly resemble those of one of the two Jesuit priests depicted by Nar Singh, in this case Father Antonio Monserrate. The missionary, standing, facing left, is again bearded and bears a strong resemblance to the supposed Monserrate in an illustration in *Akbar Nama*. Wearing a soutane, a long, dark cape and a high, blocked cap, the priest has a book in his left hand and a pair of spectacles in his right. While the book, probably a Bible or the Gospels, is a conventional and almost obligatory accessory for a missionary and also underlines the importance of the texts in Jesuit teaching and converting,[15] the spectacles are more rarely seen in the hands of Jesuit missionaries and may be an indication that this is a true portrait and not one of the more or less stereotyped figures of missionaries that sometimes appeared in the repertoire of Mughal painters in the early years of Akbar's reign. Although neither Monserrate nor Acquaviva is represented wearing or holding spectacles on the page by Nar Singh, we do on the other hand know that Father Acquaviva wore glasses, thanks to the remarks of Monserrate himself in his celebrated *Commentarius*:

Always abstracted in God he forgot what he was about. Very often he could not remember where he had left his hat, his spectacles, his books, etc. His face reflected his virginal modesty: Whenever he spoke to the King his modesty betrayed itself in a blush. His patience was admirable and his humility most sincere.[16]

This subtle portrait of the missionary is attributed in the lower left-hand corner of the page to the painter Manohar, son and disciple of the renowned Basawan. Manohar, who began his career early in 1580,[17] worked in close collaboration with Basawan from whom he adopted a number of preferred subjects, such as the copying and adaptation of European engraving, producing in this way attractive and often original works. Besides the European engravings, Manohar, in portraying Father Monserrate, seems to be interested in making the Jesuits known in the Mughal court.

As well as the portrait in the Musée Guimet, the faint silhouette of another missionary dressed and coiffed in black appears in the centre of a durbar scene dating from the reign of the Emperor Jahangir (1605–27), which is also attributed to Manohar.[18] The Jesuit priest, identified by *Padri* written on the collar of his soutane, is almost certainly Francesco Corsi (1573–1635), who arrived at the court in Agra in 1620, the year in which Manohar painted the imperial durbar.[19] Father Corsi, clean shaven, with a high forehead, delicate sharp features and a slightly pointed nose, also seems to be present on the left-hand side of the double-page composition of the crowning of the Emperor Jahangir in 1605 by the painter Abu'l Hasan, now in the Academy of Sciences (Institute for Asian Peoples), St Petersburg, though some authors are of the opinion that the clean-shaven, emaciated features are those of Father Jerome Xavier.[20] It seems that Father Corsi appears again in a miniature with the Emperor Jahangir, celebrating the anniversary (*urs*) of the patron saint of the Mughals, Khwaja Mu'in-ud-din Chisti, at Ajmer in 1615. This miniature, conserved at the Victoria Memorial in Calcutta,[21] has also been attributed to Abu'l Hasan. G.A. Bailey has, moreover, identified a fourth portrait of Father Corsi in one of the illustrations in *Mirat al-Quds* (or *Dastan-i-Masih*), a text narrating the life of Christ, which was translated into Persian by Father Jerome Xavier of Navarre and in which the oldest illustration, completed in 1602, is said to have been supervised by Manohar himself.[22] In one of the illustrations, the presentation of the Virgin in the Temple, two Jesuits, rather curiously included in the disparate assembly of people, appear at the lower right-hand side, and one of them seems to be Father Corsi, whose profile is easily recognizable.[23] He remains to this day one of the rare Jesuit missionaries whose features, clearly individualized, have become known to us with some plausibility. Mughal painters, particularly Manohar, seem to have executed a true portrait of him, together with, but to a lesser extent, the more stereotyped and less characterized portraits of Acquaviva and the supposed Monserrate. There is a portrait of a Jesuit priest that has often been identified as Father Monserrate in the National Museum collection in New Delhi.[24] The missionary stands against a rolling landscape with a book in his left hand and a rosary in his right, wearing a strange, wide-brimmed hat, not the high blocked cap ordinarily worn by Jesuit priests. His expressive, heavily wrinkled face, with a beard that is less well trimmed than in the portraits by Nar Singh and Manohar, bears a vague resemblance to the Catalan missionary. It is naturally tempting to see this as a third portrait of Antonio Monserrate, though there is nothing at all to confirm this.

The representation of priests and missionaries, such as Father Corsi, in illustrations in the *Mirat al-Quds*, the manuscript narrating the life and passion of Christ, may seem

Abu'l Hasan, *Festivities on the Occasion of the Accession of Emperor Jahangir*, Mughal India, c.1605–15. St Petersburg BIOS/RAS CAT. 97

Arms of the Society of Jesus in *Dastan-i-Masih* (Life of Christ), Mughal India, c.1604, coloured pigments and gold on paper, 25.3 x 16.6 cm. Lisbon, BA, 52-XIII-32

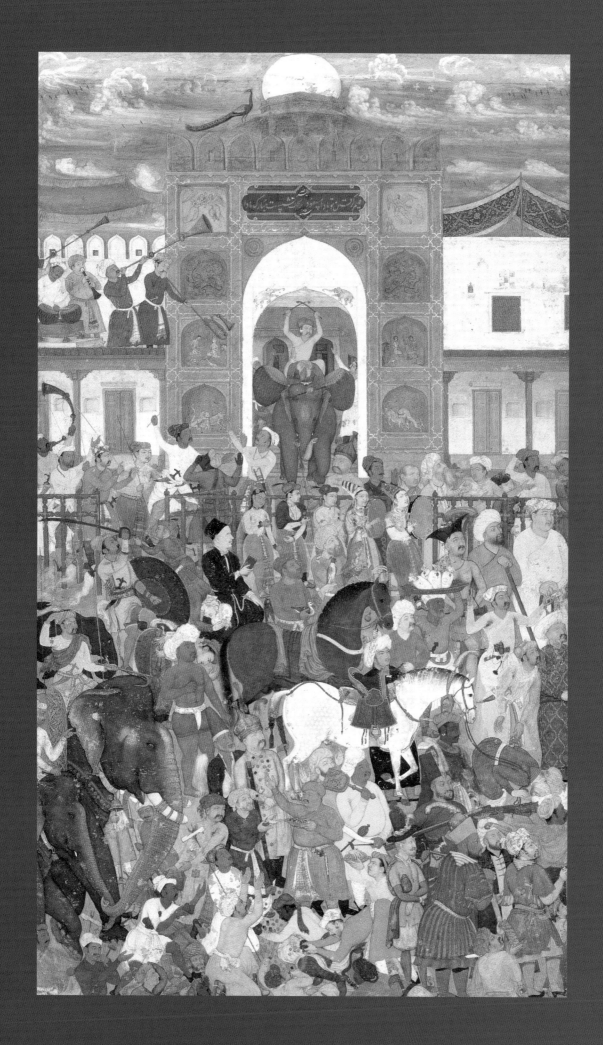

surprising, even incongruous. G.A. Bailey, however, has put forward the hypothesis that the illustrations in this important manuscript are both representations of scenes and iconographic subjects from the Bible that have been stylistically inspired by copies and adaptations of European engravings available to the painters, and also reflect religious customs and rituals introduced to the court by the Jesuits. Thus not only the influence of the liturgy and the celebration of religious festivals, but also the role of religious processions, pantomimes and other mysteries – Jesuit theatre – can be detected in the composition and production of the illustrations and could explain the kind of 'theatricality' of the characters, often caught in ostensibly dramatic attitudes.[25]

This also explains, in these illustrations strongly influenced by Jesuit liturgy and theatre, the presence of priests or choirboys strangely mixed in with biblical figures – and even, in some illustrations, lay figures dressed in European costume.[26] Among the most astonishing of the *Mirat al-Quds* illustrations combining episodes from the New Testament with evocations of Jesuit theatre is, without doubt, the page to be found in the San Diego Museum of Art, *The Ascension of Jesus into Heaven, Dressed as a Jesuit*.[27]

In the 1590s – 1590, 1591 and 1595 respectively – three Jesuit missions were received at the court of the Emperor Akbar, and Mughal painters produced numerous representations of Jesuit priests. The 'black robes' appear in a number of scenes of royal or princely audiences, but their features remain conventional and stereotyped, their identity undetermined and the emphasis essentially on their long black or dark grey robes, their black or dark blue capes and their high blocked caps. One miniature preserved in the India Office Library in London depicts a princely figure in somewhat provincial style, perhaps Prince Daniyal, third son of Akbar, seated on a throne giving an audience.[28] In the midst of the courtiers who surround the prince are two Jesuit priests dressed in black, one of them holding a book, the other a pair of spectacles, like Father Monserrate in the drawing by Manohar. Unlike the plate by Nar Singh in *Akbar Nama* illustrating a specific, historically witnessed event, at which Fathers Acquaviva and Monserrate were present, the two Jesuits depicted here are conventional figures, lacking historical reality and placed in the throng of nobles and courtiers to highlight the diversity and testify to the international nature of Akbar's court. The art of the period clearly reflects the subtle shift in iconographic meaning that led from the representation of missionaries as real subjects and models to their representation as simple pictorial motifs, who were unusual and 'exotic'. The curious portrait of a Jesuit in the Chester Beatty Library in Dublin, attributed to Kesu Das, a renowned painter of copies and adaptations of European engravings,[29] emphasizes this. Standing against rolling, European countryside, the Jesuit is wearing the usual high blocked black cap and is holding in his hand an open book with imaginary, indecipherable characters. Although his costume consists of a long robe like a soutane and is worn with a sort of cape or ample coat, it differs from the traditional costume adopted by the Jesuits, notably because of the yellow colour of the soutane.

As L. York Leach has justly pointed out, the rather artificial character of this person suggests that this portrait is based more on an adaptation of a European engraving than on a live model.[30] Using the customary eclecticism of Mughal artists, the painter of this singular work subtly blends two distinct sources of inspiration, creating a new iconic motif in the Mughal thematic repertoire, a sort of variant or variation on the theme of Western figures and motifs, and in the same vein as representations of soldiers or Portuguese gentlemen, or even biblical characters and angels, discovered through European engravings.

Attributed to Kesu Das, *A Jesuit Priest*,
Mughal India, *c.*1595–1600.
Dublin, CBL CAT. 81

Fernão Guerreiro, *Relacam annval das cousas que fizeram os Padres da Companhia de Iesus na India & Iapão nos annos de 600 & 601* (Annual report of the things that the Fathers of the Society of Jesus did in India and Japan in the years 1600 and 1601), Évora, 1603.
Lisbon, BNL CAT. 23

A number of miniatures, most of them dating back to the end of Akbar's reign and the first decade of Jahangir's reign, confirm this new trend towards turning representations of Jesuit priests into simple, pictorial motifs among other ones, an almost anecdotal element in imaginary compositions, though ostensibly mixed together. A miniature in the British Museum in London shows a woman with a child in her arms in a country scene, clearly inspired by some Virgin and Child; standing before them is a Jesuit, recognizable by his dark soutane and holding the inevitable book.[31] The Jesuit is wearing a hat with a wide brim instead of the usual high blocked cap,[32] once again showing the composite nature of the miniature that quite arbitrarily mixes, in an amusing transposition, two 'European' subjects unrelated to each other. Even more eloquent, because it is more elaborate and complex in concept and composition, is a *Crucifixion* in the British Museum that might also be the work of Kesu Das.[33] The miniature is clearly inspired by various European engravings or paintings. Two groups of anomalous characters are shown prostrate at the foot of the Cross bearing Christ in agony, among them a number of biblical figures (the Virgin, Mary Magdalene and St John), most of whom are Portuguese or, at least, easily recognizable as Europeans, or *firangis*, because of their clothes and hats. Among the latter, the painter has taken particular care to depict two Jesuits, recognizable by their high caps. In this astonishing miniature, which illustrates in an almost exemplary way the contribution and transference of European themes and motifs to Mughal painting, the presence of anomalous persons – biblical figures, European visitors to the Mughal Court, Jesuit missionaries, figures copied from various engravings – attests to the emergence of and gradual craze for the theme, still new, of the *firangi*, a subject that, though of lesser importance, nevertheless creates a separate genre in the repertoire of Mughal painters up to the nineteenth century. In the same way a miniature from the *Akbar Nama* (c.1603–5), which, like many separate pages from this second manuscript of the chronicle of the reign of Akbar, has been remounted in the borders of the pages of *Farhang-i-Jahangiri* – written in Persian by Jamal ud-din Husain Inju, dated 1608 and commissioned by Jahangir – is decorated with scenes in the margins dealing with various aspects of the *firangi*. Four Europeans in the midst of foliage and golden bushes, wearing baggy pantaloons, tunics and quilted doublets, as well as large, plumed hats, are depicted performing various activities, while the fifth *firangi* next to them is a Jesuit wearing a cassock and blocked cap, holding a book in one hand and a baton (or cross) in the other.[34] No less surprising and incongruous is the appearance of a Jesuit in an illustration of an episode of the well-known tale of Yussuf and Zuleika by Jami. In the miniature showing the scene where Yussuf (Joseph) is sold in the slave market, in the midst of a multitude of caravaneers and traders all wanting to buy the handsome Jewish slave, there is a Jesuit priest, easily recognizable by his vestments and black headgear.[35] There is no doubt that his surprising, anachronistic presence in this huge crowd gathered in an oriental market, with Persians and Abyssinians (Habshi), was designed to highlight its ostensibly heterogeneous, international nature.

Like Edward Maclagan in his magisterial work *The Jesuits and the Great Mogul* (pp. 257–8) dated 1932, one must conclude that, with the exception of a very small number of Mughal miniatures dating primarily from the first two decades of Akbar's reign and the beginning of Jahangir's, few have survived up to the present day, so it can reasonably be assumed that representations and portraits of Jesuit missionaries and priests were never produced in great quantity. What is more, in the absence of works duly identified by reliable descriptions, the true identity of these Jesuits continues to be in doubt, with the exception of the portraits presumed to be of Fathers Acquaviva, Monserrate and, above all, Corsi. In the same way the absence of engraved, realistic, contemporary portraits in the European style of these missionaries makes it impossible to make a positive identification based on the comparison of European engravings or paintings with Mughal miniatures in which a particular Jesuit priest appears. It is quite astonishing how few portraits of Jesuit missionaries and priests appear in the abundant Mughal works. It is surprising not to find a confirmed portrait of Father Jerome Xavier, author of, among other works, *Mirat al-Quds*, who lived almost twenty years at the Mughal court, where he was close to the Emperor Akbar and his son and successor Jahangir,[36] nor one of Father Busi with Prince Dara Shikoh (1615–59), who was frequently represented discussing philosophy and theology in the company of saintly and religious men of all creeds. While their clothing and singular bearing may not have greatly inspired imperial painters, the Jesuit missionaries, nevertheless, played an important role in widely diffusing European paintings and, above all, the engravings that were to radically renew, in both style and iconography, Mughal artistic perception and pictorial production, and were lavish in their advice to painters who consulted them at the behest of the Great Mogul.

NOTES

MUGHAL EXPANSION IN THE DECCAN, 1570–1605: CONTEMPORARY PERSPECTIVES (PP. 14–43)

1. For an earlier essay on similar themes, see Muzaffar Alam & Sanjay Subrahmanyam, 'Uma sociedade de fronteira do século XVI: Perspectivas indo-persas no Decão Ocidental', in *Oceanos*, no. 34 (1998), pp. 88–101.

2. For an overview of political circumstances in about 1500, see Sanjay Subrahmanyam, *The Portuguese Empire in Asia, 1500–1700: A Political and Economic History*, London, 1993, ch. 1.

3. António Pinto Pereira, *História da Índia no tempo em que a governou o visorey D. Luís de Ataíde*, introduction by Manuel Marques Duarte, Lisbon, 1987.

4. For an earlier analysis, see Sanjay Subrahmanyam, 'A matter of alignment: Mughal Gujarat and the Iberian world in the transition of 1580–81', in *Mare Liberum*, no. 9 (1995), pp. 461–79.

5. 'Mongolicae Legationis Commentarius', in *Memoirs of the Asiatic Society of Bengal*, ed. H. Hosten, 1914, vol. III, pp. 513–704; *The Commentary of Father Monserrate S. J. on his Journey to the Court of Akbar*, trans. S.N. Banerjee & John S. Hoyland, London, 1922.

6. Abu'l Fazl, *Akbar Nama*, trans. H. Beveridge, reprint, Delhi, 1989, vol. III, pp. 409–10 (personal names have been modernized). Akbar's anti-Portuguese posture at this time is also echoed in his letter to 'Abdullah Khan Uzbek, for details of which see Mansura Haider, 'Relations of Abdullah Khan Uzbeg with Akbar', in *Cahiers du Monde Russe et Soviétique*, vol. XXII, no. 3–4 (1982), pp. 313–31. A later letter to 'Abdullah Khan, from 1586, again stressing the desire to expel the Portuguese, may be found in Abu'l Fazl 1989, vol. III, pp. 754–60. For another view, see M.N. Pearson, 'The Estado da Índia and the Hajj', in *Indica*, vol. XXVI, no. 1–2 (1989), pp. 103–18, especially pp. 117–18.

7. Diogo do Couto, *Da Ásia, Décadas IV–XII*, reprint, Lisbon, 1974. Couto's *Década XII* is divided into five books and a total of sixty-three chapters, all dealing with the viceroyalty of the Count of Vidigueira (1597–1600). Of these, Malabar affairs dominate by far, but four chapters are Mughal-related. Two of these (pp. 24–39) are devoted to the affairs of Man Singh ('Manacinga'), and another two to the conversion of a prince of Badakhshan ('Abadaxam'), son of Mirza Shahrukh, to Christianity by the Augustinians at Hurmuz (pp. 483–505).

8. But also see such contemporary letters as those in British Library (henceforth BL), Addn. 28, 432, ff. 13r–16v; Biblioteca Nacional, Lisbon (henceforth BNL), cód. 1976, ff. 117r–121v. The latter volume contains several other letters of interest for Mughal-Portuguese relations.

9. Elements of this portrayal, in respect of the Ottomans and the Safavids, may already be found in João de Barros, *Da Asia, Décadas I–IV*, reprint, Lisbon, 1973–4, and the legend of the 'Grand Turk' itself, of course, goes back at least to the fifteenth century; see Lucette Valensi, *Venise et la Sublime Porte: La naissance du despote*, Paris, 1987. For one of Couto's earliest uses of the term 'Grão-mogor', see Maria Augusta Lima Cruz, *Diogo do Couto e a Década Oitava da Ásia*, Lisbon, 1993, vol. I, p. 39, the context being a Mughal attack on Daman.

10. For the most detailed account, see Gaspar Correia, *Lendas da Índia*, ed. M. Lopes de Almeida, reprint, Oporto, 1975, vol. IV, pp. 299–305 and 324–5; also the anonymous 'Verdadeira enfformaçam das coisas da Índia (1544)' in *As Gavetas da Torre do Tombo*, ed. A. da Silva Rego, Lisbon, 1963, vol. III, pp. 199–234. The Tirupati affair is also referred to, oddly enough, by Henrique de Sousa Godinho in 1603, while discussing

nominations for the viceroyalty; see BL, Addn. 28, 432, f. 72r.

11. Portuguese relations with the Kanara coast have been extensively discussed in Sanjay Subrahmanyam, *The Political Economy of Commerce: Southern India, 1500–1650*, Cambridge, 1990, especially pp. 120–35 and 260–65.

12. Couto 1974 (n. 7), *Década Oitava*, pp. 93–4; *Lettere da Vari Paesi, 1570–1588, di Filippo Sassetti*, ed. Vanni Bramanti, Milan, 1970. For general Portuguese official indifference to the fate of Vijayanagara, see José Wicki, 'Duas relações sobre a situação da Índia Portuguesa nos anos 1568 e 1569', in *Studia*, no. 8 (1961), pp. 133–220; also the earlier letter from the Viceroy Dom Antão de Noronha to the king, 17 December 1566, in *Documentação para a história das missões do Padroado Português do Oriente*, ed. A. da Silva Rego, Lisbon, 1953, vol. X, esp. p. 161.

13. Mahdawi movements in the region are conventionally traced to Sayyid Muhammad Jaunpuri (1443–1505), who was born in the Sharqi sultanate of Jaunpur, and after performing the *hajj* in 1495–6, settled down in western India, where he attracted numerous followers and sympathizers in Gujarat, and Ahmadnagar, including – it is claimed – Sultan Mahmud Begarha of Gujarat and Ahmad Nizam Shah. He was, however, expelled from the area by Sultan Mahmud and died (or was killed) in Afghanistan. For details, see S.A.A. Rizvi, 'The Mahdavi movement in India', in *Medieval India Quarterly*, vol. I, no. 1 (1950), pp. 10–25; M. M. Saeed, *The Sharqi Sultanate of Jaunpur: A Political and Cultural History*, Karachi, 1972, pp. 284–92.

14. See *The History of the Nizâm Shâhî Kings of Ahmadnagar*, translation by T. Wolseley Haig, Bombay, 1923, pp. 201–3, an abridged translation of the third *tabaqa* of Sayyid 'Ali bin 'Azizullah Tabatabai of Samnan's chronicle, *Burhan-i Ma'asir* (the Persian edition is from Hyderabad, 1936–7). Tabataba was first in Qutb Shahi and then in Nizam Shahi service; his work goes on to the negotiations between Chand Sultana and the Mughals, ending 27 Rajab 1004 (14 March 1596), when the author was probably present. For the *Gulshan-i Ibrahimi* or *Tarikh-i Firishta*, by Muhammad Qasim Hindu Shah, see *History of the Rise of Mahomedan Power in India*, ed. John Briggs, 4 vols, reprint, New Delhi, 1989; earlier editions London, 1829, and Calcutta, 1908–10, in which vol. III deals with the five post-Bahmani Deccan sultanates. A third, as yet unpublished, chronicle is the *Tazkirat al-mulûk* of Rafi' al-Din Ibrahim Shirazi (1540/41–c.1620), written between 1608 and 1612; for a discussion of this see Iqtidar Alam Khan, 'The Tazkirat ul-Muluk by Rafi'uddin Ibrahim Shirazi: As a source on the History of Akbar's Reign', in *Studies in History* (N.S.), vol. II, no. 1 (1980), pp. 41–55.

15. Firishta, in Briggs 1989 (n. 14), vol. III, pp. 168–71.

16. Abu'l Fazl 1989 (n. 6), vol. III, p. 909.

17. H.K. Sherwani, *History of the Qutb Shahi Dynasty*, New Delhi, 1974, pp. 352–3. See also *Insha'-i Faizi*, ed. A.D. Arshad, Lahore, 1973, pp. 95 and 101–3, *passim*. An extensive discussion of this text may be found in Muzaffar Alam & Sanjay Subrahmanyam, 'A place in the sun: Travels with Faizi in the Deccan, 1591–93', in *Les sources et le temps / Sources and Time: A colloquium*, ed. François Grimal, Pondicherry, 2001, pp. 265–307.

18. Abu'l Fazl 1989 (n. 6), vol. III, pp. 979–82, 1006; 'Abd al-Qadir Badayuni, *Muntakhab al-Tawârîkh*, trans. George S.A. Ranking, W.H. Lowe & T.W. Haig, 3 vols, Calcutta, 1884–1925, reprint, New Delhi, 1990, vol. II, pp. 400–01 and 412.

19. Firishta, in Briggs 1989 (n. 14), vol. III, pp. 172–3 (proper names have been modernized). For Mughal responses to Burhan's defeat, see Abu'l Fazl 1989 (n. 6), vol. III, pp. 1023–5.

20. Couto 1974 (n. 7), *Década XI*, pp. 164–73; also see Sanjay

Subrahmanyam, '"The Life and Actions of Mathias de Albuquerque" (1547–1609): A Portuguese Source for Deccan History', in *Portuguese Studies*, vol. XI (1995), pp. 62–77.

21. On this mission, see Sanjay Subrahmanyam, 'Palavras do Idalcão: Um encontro curioso em Bijapur no ano de 1561', in *Cadernos do Noroeste*, vol. 15, nos 1–2 (2001), pp. 513–24.

22. Translated in Nazir Ahmad, 'Adil Shahi Diplomatic Missions to the Court of Shah Abbas', in *Islamic Culture*, vol. 43, no. 2 (1969), pp. 143–61; text in Nazir Ahmad, 'Letters of the Rulers of the Deccan to Shah 'Abbas of Iran', in *Medieval India: A Miscellany*, Aligarh, 1969, vol. I, pp. 280–300. For a general discussion, see also M.A. Nayeem, *External Relations of the Bijapur Kingdom (1489–1686 AD.): A Study in Diplomatic History*, Hyderabad, 1974.

23. Abu'l Fazl 1989 (n. 6), vol. III, p. 909.

24. Badayuni 1990 (n. 18), vol. II, pp. 389–90, mentions that four envoys were sent out: Faizi to Asir and Burhanpur, Amin-ud-din to Ahmadnagar, Mir Muhammad Amin to Bijapur, and Mir Munir to Golkonda.

25. Abu'l Fazl 1989 (n. 6), vol. III, p. 982.

26. Badayuni 1990 (n. 18), vol. II, pp. 402–3.

27. Arshad 1973 (n. 17), p. 97.

28. *Ibid.*, p. 103.

29. For comments on this legend, and Faizi's recounting of it, see Sherwani 1974 (n. 17), pp. 339–48.

30. Goa is misread in the edited text as 'Kuda', and 'Chaul' as 'Jival'.

31. On the siege and capture of Herat by Shaibani or Uzbek forces in 1587–8, see R.D. McChesney, 'The Conquest of Herat 995–6/1587–8: Sources for the study of Safavid/Qizilbash-Shibanid/Uzbak relations', in *Études Safavides*, ed. Jean Calmard, Paris/Teheran, 1993, pp. 69–107.

32. On the peripatetic life of Shah 'Abbas in this epoch and later, see Charles Melville, 'From Qars to Qandahar: The itineraries of Shah 'Abbas I (995–1038/1587–1629)', in Calmard 1993 (n. 31), pp. 195–224.

33. On this subject, also see Masashi Haneda, *Le Chah et les Qizilbas: Le système militaire safavide*, Berlin, 1987.

34. Compare this description with the slightly later suppression of the Nuqtawis by Shah 'Abbas, described in Kathryn Babayan, 'The waning of the Qizilbash: The spiritual and the temporal in seventeenth century Iran', Ph.D. dissertation, Princeton University, 1993, pp. 57–62.

35. On the issue of the migration of Iranian savants to Mughal India, see the details in Ahmad Golchin-i Ma'ani, *Karwan-i Hind (The Caravan of India: On Life and Works of the poets of Safavid era emigrated to India)*, 2 vols, Mashhad, 1990.

36. Both poets are later to be found in Bijapur, as we see from Asad Beg's account. For their work, see M.A. Ghani, *A History of Persian Language and Literature at the Mughal Court*, reprint, Westmead, 1972, vol. II, pp. 181–219.

37. This was, of course, the exact opposite of the real relationship between Babur and Humayun and the Safavid dynasty.

38. On Shah Tahir, see the brief comment in Richard M. Eaton, *Sufis of Bijapur, 1300–1700: Social Roles of Sufis in Medieval India*, Princeton, 1978, pp. 68–9.

39. See Sanjay Subrahmanyam, 'The Viceroy as Assassin: The Mughals, the Portuguese and Deccan Politics, c.1600', in *Santa Barbara Portuguese Studies*, special number (1995), pp. 162–203.

40. On this person, see B. G. Tamaskar, *Life and Work of Malik Ambar*, Delhi, 1978; also Radhey Shyam, *Life and Times of Malik Ambar*, Delhi, 1968.

41. Jacques de Coutre, *Andanzas asiáticas*, ed. Eddy Stols, B. Teensma &

J. Verberckmoes, Madrid, 1991, pp. 174–98 and 287–98; the quotation is from p. 297.

42. *Ibid.*, pp. 296–7; for Ibrahim's relations with the Mughals in the early 1610s, see Khursheed Nurul Hasan and Mansura Haidar, 'Letters of Aziz Koka to Ibrahim Adil Shah II', in *Proceedings of the Indian History Congress*, 27th session, 1965, pp. 161–7, containing a calendar of some diplomatic documents in 'Abdul Wahhab bin Muhammad Ma'muri al-Husaini, *Gulshan-i Balaghat*, for a manuscript of which see Asiatic Society of Bengal, Calcutta, Curzon Collection, II, 312 (IvC 131).

43. For an earlier discussion (with manuscript references) of this important text, see Muzaffar Alam and Sanjay Subrahmanyam, 'Witnessing transition: Views on the end of the Akbari dispensation', in *The Making of History: Essays Presented to Irfan Habib*, ed. K.N. Panikkar *et al.*, 2000, pp. 104–40.

44. See also the earlier account by P.M. Joshi, 'Asad Beg's mission to Bijapur, 1603–1604', in *Mahamahopadhyaya Prof. D.V. Potdar Sixty-First Birthday Commemoration Volume*, ed. S.N. Sen, Poona, 1950, pp. 184–96.

45. See, in this context, B.P. Saksena, 'A few unnoticed facts about the early life of Malik Amber', in *Proceedings (Transactions) of the Indian History Congress*, 5th session, 1941, pp. 601–3.

46. See P.M. Joshi, 'Asad Beg's return from Bijapur and his second mission to the Deccan, 1604–1606', in *Studies in Indian History: Dr. A.G. Pawar Felicitation Volume*, ed. V.D. Rao, Bombay, 1968, pp. 136–55.

47. See the extended discussion in Sanjay Subrahmanyam, 'Notas sobre um rei congelado: O caso de Ali bin Yusuf Adil Khan, chamado Mealecão', in *Passar as fronteiras: II Colóquio Internacional sobre Mediadores Culturais, séculos XV a XVIII*, ed. Rui Manuel Loureiro & Serge Gruzinski, Lagos, 1999, pp. 265–90.

TWO PORTUGEUSE VISIONS OF JAHANGIR'S INDIA: JERÓNIMO XAVIER AND MANUEL GODINHO DE ERÉDIA (PP. 44–67)

1. I have restricted this study exclusively to texts from this period, as the political situation in the following years – the latter days of Emperor Shahjahan, the war of succession and the reign of Aurangzeb – already aroused the interest of many Europeans. The works of François Bernier and Niccolò Manuzzi are perhaps the two most important and well known from among an impressive group of texts that has captured the attention of historians and other scholars.

2. The collection by William Foster, *Early Travels in India, 1583–1619* (reprint, New Delhi, 1985), brings together some of the most important of these texts.

3. See the English translation by W.H. Moreland & P. Geyl, *Jahangir's India: The Remonstrantie of Francisco Pelsaert*, reprint, New Delhi, 2001.

4. English translation by J.S. Hoyland, with notes by S.N. Banerjee, *The Empire of the Great Mogol: De Laet's Description of India and Fragment of India History*, reprint, New Delhi, 1974.

5. At least one copy is known from Livraria Duarte de Sousa (*Catálogo da Livraria Duarte de Sousa*, 2 vols, Lisbon, 1972–4, I, no. 153, p. 82), now owned by the BNL (DS-XVII-49). Another was at the library of the convent of Nossa Senhora de Jesus, Lisbon, and now belongs to the Biblioteca da Academia das Ciências de Lisboa (11-47-17). I would like to thank Susana Vassallo e Silva, part of the team producing a computerized catalogue for the Academia's library, for informing me about this copy. There is also a third copy at the BNL, with contemporary manuscript notes in Latin (Elz. 41).

6. *The embassy of Thomas Roe to India, 1615–19, as narrated in his journal and correspondence*, ed. William Foster, reprint (1st edn 1926),

New Delhi, 1990. See also the recent studies by Colin Paul Mitchell, *Sir Thomas Roe and the Mughal Empire*, Karachi, 2000, and Sanjay Subrahmanyam, 'Frank submissions: The Company and the Mughals between Sir Thomas Roe and Sir William Norris', in *The Worlds of the East India Company*, ed. H.V. Bowen, *et al.*, Suffolk, 2002, pp. 69–96.

7. Facsimile edition, Amsterdam/New York, 1971.

8. *Inter alia* see the important collection of studies co-ordinated by Stuart B. Schwartz, *Implicit Understandings: Observing, Reporting and Reflecting on the Encounters between Europeans and other Peoples in the Early Modern Era*, reprint, Cambridge, 1996.

9. This is the monumental *Asia in the Making of Europe*, which is more descriptive than analytical, produced in conjunction with Edwin J. Van Kley. *A Century of Advance*, vol. III, book 2 (*South Asia*), reprint, Chicago/London, 1998, is of particular relevance here.

10. Cf. Joan-Pau Rubiés, *Travel and Ethnology in the Renaissance: South India through European Eyes, 1250–1625*, Cambridge, 2000; and Kate Teltscher, *India Inscribed: European and British Writing on India, 1600–1800*, New Delhi, 1995.

11. See Subrahmanyam's criticism of this trend, both in the article mentioned above (n. 6) and in 'Profiles in transition: Of adventurers and Administrators in South India, 1750–1810', in *The Indian Economic and Social History Review*, vol. 39, no. 2–3 (2002), pp. 197–231.

12. The importance of his observations on this was stressed by Muzaffar Alam & Sanjay Subrahmanyam in 'Witnessing transition: Views on the end of the Akbari dispensation', in *The Making of History: Essays Presented to Irfan Habib*, ed. K.N. Panikkar *et al.*, Delhi, 2002, pp. 104–40.

13. Hosten was the first to focus on Jerónimo Xavier, writing a large number of articles about him that were published in the early twentieth century in various journals in what was then British India. He was followed by Edward Maclagan's seminal *The Jesuits and the Great Mogul* (London, 1932). Angel Santos Hernandez S.J. wrote a rather traditional biography of Xavier entitled *Jeronimo Javier S.J. apostol del Gran Mogol y arzobispo electo de Cranganor, en la India, 1549–1617*, Pamplona, 1958). The best global work on Jerónimo Xavier, which emphasises the theological issues, is by Arnulf Camps, O.F.M., *Jerome Xavier S.J. and the Muslims of the Mogul Empire: Controversial Works and Missionary Activity*, Schöneck-Beckenried, 1957.

14. For instance, see the exemplary study by Ines G. Zupanov on the Madurai mission, *Disputed mission. Jesuit experiments and Brahmanical knowledge in seventeenth-century India*, New Delhi, 1999.

15. Several copies of the latter text exist in Portuguese, Latin and Italian at the Archivum Romanum Societatis Iesu (Rome), and it was published in *Documenta indica*, ed. J. Wicki, S.J., 18 vols, Rome, 1948–88, vol. XII, doc. 114, pp. 645–62. In addition, there is another Portuguese copy at the Torre do Tombo (published in *Documentação para a história das missões do Padroado Português do Oriente, Índia*, ed. António da Silva Rego, reprinted, Lisbon, 1996, vol. XII, doc. 62, pp. 665–78) and yet another in Latin at the Jesuit archive in Alcalá de Henares (E-2: 104,11). The *Relação* was published in English by H. Hosten, 'Fr. A. Monserrate's Account of Akbar', in *Journal of the Asiatic Society of Bengal*, new series, vol. VIII, no. 5 (May 1912), pp. 190–221.

16. 'De la Corte del Gran Mogor y sus Grandezas', Madrid, BN, Mss. 3015, ff. 63r–69v. This manuscript was published in complete form in *Documentação ultramarina portuguesa* (Lisbon, 1962, vol. II,), where this text appeared on pp. 69–78. I have used the printed version, except where the potential readings raise doubts and imply direct consultation of the manuscript.

17. 'Breue relaciõ de las tierras, Poder y Casa del Grã Mogor', Madrid, RAH, 9/3716, doc. 8, no folio number.

18. It is recorded as such in *Guia de fontes portuguesas para a história da Ásia*, Lisbon, 1998, vol. I, p. 46. I would like to thank António Vasconcelos de Saldanha for drawing my attention to this reference, which led us to 'recover' the document at the Torre do Tombo. The precise reference is: Lisbon, IAN/TT, *Cartório da Casa Real*, bundle 49B, box 7420.

19. A detailed study will be done in a critical and annotated edition of the *Tratado*, to be published in a bilingual Portuguese and English version, currently in progress.

20. *Raguagli d'alcune missioni fatte dalli padri della Compagnia di Giesu nell' Indie Orientali ...*, Rome, 1615.

21. *Documentação ultramarina portuguesa* 1962 (n. 16), p. 77.

22. See K.S. Lal, *The Mughal Harem* (New Delhi, 1988), whose first chapter presents the Mughal and European sources on the subject. For European ideas on the Ottoman sultans' harems, see Alain Grosrichard, *The Sultan's Court: European Fantasies of the East*, London, 1998.

23. 'The formulation of imperial authority under Akbar and Jahangir', in *Kingship and Authority in South Asia*, ed. J.F. Richards (Madison, 1978), reprinted in *The Mughal State, 1526–1750*, ed. Muzaffar Alam & Sanjay Subrahmanyam, New Delhi, 1998, pp. 126–67.

24. See Douglas E. Streusand, *The Formation of the Mughal Empire*, Delhi, 1989, pp. 138 *et seq.*

25. Page in the St. Petersburg album; Washington, D.C., Smithsonian Institution, Freer Gallery of Art, inv. no. 42.16A.

26. The imperial routine, which underwent some alterations according to the individual emperor's tastes, is broadly explained in the political and administrative histories of the empire; cf. *inter alia*, I.H. Qureshi, *The Administration of the Mughal Empire*, New Delhi, n.d., chapter III, pp. 45 *et seq.*; Ibn Hasan, *The Central Structure of the Mughal Empire, and its Practical Working up to the Year 1657*, reprint, New Delhi, 1980, pp. 68 *et seq.*

27. Hasan 1980 (n. 26), pp. 70–74; John A. D'Silva, 'The rebellion of Prince Khushru according to Jesuit sources', in *Journal of Indian History*, V (1927) pp. 267–81.

28. Sylvia Murr, 'La politique "au Mogol" selon Bernier: Appareil conceptuel, rhétorique stratégique, philosophie morale', in *De la royauté à l'état. Anthropologie et histoire du politique dans le monde indien*, ed. J. Pouchepadass & H. Stern, Paris, 1991, pp. 239–311; Teltscher 1995 (n. 10), pp. 28–34; Peter Burke, 'The philosopher as traveller: Bernier's Orient', in *Voyages and Visions: Towards a Cultural History of Travel*, ed. J. Elsner & Joan-Pau Rubiés, London, 1999, pp. 124–37.

29. On the following, see M. Athar Ali's seminal study, *The Mughal Nobility under Aurangzeb*, reprinted, Bombay, 1970, especially pp. 63–8. More recently, Firdos Anwar, *Nobility under the Mughals (1628–1658)*, New Delhi, 2001, pp. 45–8.

30. In Foster 1985 (n. 2), pp. 98–9. De Laet offers a brief numerical report on the empire's *mansabdars* (Hoyland & Banerjee 1974 [n. 4], pp. 113–14). Manrique would return to this list with few modifications, although he claims to have had access to original documents from the Mughal chancellery (*Itinerário de Sebastião Manrique*, ed. Luís Silveira, Lisbon, 1946, vol. II, chapter LXXV, pp. 313 *et seq.*).

31. 'The ranks assigned in Hawkin's lists [...] are little more than curiosities'; M. Athar Ali, *The Apparatus of Empire: Awards of Ranks, Offices and Titles to the Mughal Nobility (1574–1658)*, New Delhi, 1985, pp. xii, 90–1.

32. He lived from 1556 to 1627. For an overall vision of his career under Akbar and Jahangir, see Shahnawaz Khan, *Ma'asir-ul Umara, Being Biographies of the Muhammadan and Hindu Officers of the Timurid Sovereigns of India from 1500 to 1780 A.D.*, trans. H. Beveridge, 2 vols, reprinted, New Delhi, 1999, vol. II, pp. 50–65. His cultural impact was studied by C.R. Naik, '*Abdu'r Rahim Khan-i Khanan and his Literary Circle*, Ahmadabad, 1966; and Anne Marie Schimmel, 'A dervish in the guise of a prince: Khan-i Khanan 'Abdur Rahim as patron', in *The Powers of Art: Patronage in Indian Culture*, ed. Barbara Stoler Miller, Delhi, 1992, pp. 202–23.

33. On the question of who wrote the *Tratado*, this interesting comparison is more appropriate to the work of Jerónimo Xavier, a native of Navarre, than to that of the Azorean Manuel Pinheiro, even though Luna was evidently far from unknown in Portugal.

34. J. Richards, 'Norms of comportment among Imperial Mughal officers', in *Moral Conduct and Authority: The Place of 'Adab' in South Asian Islam*, ed. Barbara Daly Metcalf, Berkeley, 1984, pp. 255–89.

35. It is known that these two lists were drawn up separately (cf. William Irvine, *The Army of the Indian Moghuls: Its Organization and Administration*, reprinted, New Delhi, 1994, pp. 9–11).

36. Abu'l Fazl, *A'in-i-Akbari*, ed. H. Blochmann, Calcutta, 1927, pp. 243–45.

37. See Jorge Flores, 'A Jesuit *Tratado* as a source for the study of the Mughal nobility under Jahangir' (unpublished).

38. The most recent and complete biography of Erédia, which includes an inventory of his work, is by J.G. Everaert (see *infra*, n. 41, pp. 23–87).

39. Jorge Faro, 'Manuel Godinho de Erédia, cosmógrafo', in *Panorama*, II série, nos 13–14 (1955), n.p.

40. 'O cartógrafo Manuel Godinho de Erédia e a sua obra', in A. Cortesão & A. Teixeira da Mota, *Portugaliae monumenta cartographica* (henceforth *PMC*), Lisbon, 1960, vol. IV, pp. 39–60.

41. *Lyvro de plantaforma das fortalezas da India* (c.1620), ed. Rui Carita, Lisbon, 1999; *Suma de árvores e plantas da Índia Intra Ganges* (1612), ed. J.G. Everaert, J.E. Mendes Ferrão & M. Cândida Liberato (with a significant preface by Luís Filipe Thomaz, pp. 7–22), Lisbon, 2001.

42. This issue is further developed in Jorge Flores, 'The Mughal Expertise of a Luso-Malay Cartographer: Manuel Godinho de Erédia and the *Mogor*' (unpublished).

43. Excerpt from a letter from Fathers R. Acquaviva, A. Monserrate & F. Henriques to the captain of Daman, Fathpur Sikri, March–April 1580, published in Wicki 1948–88 (n. 15), vol. XII, doc. 3, p. 16; the same to Father Rui Vicente, Agra, 13 July 1580 (*ibid.*, doc. 5, p. 40).

44. Rome, ARSI, *Goa*, vol. 33 II, ff. 399r–401r.

45. London, BL, *Add.* 9854, ff. 77r–81r. This entire codex was published in vol. III of *Documentação ultramarina portuguesa* (Lisbon, 1963), with Erédia's text on pp. 134–42. Everaert (quoted *supra*, n. 41), p. 84 mentions an annotated English translation of the text, published by Henry Hosten in the *Journal of the Asiatic Society of Bengal*, 3rd series, vol. IV (1938), pp. 533–66. However, this reference is inaccurate (for a start, Hosten died in 1931 and, as far as is known, no further works of his were published subsequently) and I have not been able to read the translation. In 1949 Charles Boxer considered the document to be unpublished and made no reference to any potential edition by Hosten ('More about the Marsden Manuscripts in the British Museum', in *Journal of the Royal Asiatic Society* (1949), pp. 63–86, reprint in *Opera minora*, ed. Diogo Ramada Curto, Lisbon, 2002, vol. I, pp. 199–221 [204].

46. José dos Santos, *Catálogo da notavel e preciosa livraria que foi do ilustre bibliófilo conimbricense Conde do Ameal*, Oporto, 1924. The document is part of a codex that was then catalogued as no. 2795 (now cod. 11410 of the *Reservados* section at the Biblioteca Nacional), which was one of an important group of documents from the dawn of the seventeenth century on the province of Gujarat and Portuguese involvement in that region. This document appears between ff. 51r and 56r, and has a slightly different title from the BL version: 'Discursso sobre a Provincia do Indostan chamada Mogûl ou Mogôr com declaração do Reino gozarate, e mais Reinos de seu destricto, ordenado por Emmanuel Godinho de Eredia mathematico, cosmographo mor. Anno 1611'. The first folio bears the following note: 'Ruy Lourenço de Tauora, Viso Rei de India Orientais. Por Manuel Godinho de Eredia, mandou reconhecer o Indostan com o Reino Gozarate, e sua enseada de cambaya. Anno 1611'.

47. In his history of the first contact between the Portuguese and Akbar, which began in Gujarat, and after publishing the Portuguese version of the imperial *farman* from 1573, Couto added that he had seen 'the same with the hanging seal of Hecobar [Akbar] made on a large sheet of paper' (*Da Ásia. Dos feitos que os portuguezes fizeram na conquista e descubrimento das terras e mares do Oriente*, Lisbon, 1974 [facsimile of the 1786 edition], Década IX, chapter XIII, p. 84).

48. Cf. Momin Mohiuddin, *The Chancellery and Persian Epistolography under the Mughals*, Calcutta, 1971; Father Felix, O.C., 'Mughal Farmans, Parwanahs and Sanads issued in favour of the Jesuit Missionaries', in *Journal of the Punjab Historical Society*, vol. V, no. 1 (1916), pp. 1–53.

49. Rome, ARSI, *Goa*, vol. 46 I, f. 51r (also f. 46r). Another *farman* dated 1598, whose Persian original has survived but which has no Portuguese translation, also bears Akbar's seal; cf. Father Felix 1916 (n. 48), pp. 7–8 and 10–11), which has the respective English translation.

50. See the excellent work of Annabel Teh Galop, 'The genealogical Seal of the Mughal emperors of India', in *Journal of the Royal Asiatic Society*, 3rd series, vol. 9, no. 1 (April 1999), pp. 77–140; see also the earlier study by Father Felix, 'The Mughal Seals', in *Journal of the Punjab Historical Society*, vol. V, no. 2 (1916), pp. 100–25.

51. Lisbon, BN, *Reservados*, codex 846, f. 43v.

52. Henry Lord, *A display of two forraigne sects in the East Indies, viz: the sect of the Banians, the ancient natives of India … together with the religion and maners of each*, London, 1630.

53. *Pûrab* means 'the Orient'. This vague term was used by most European authors to define eastern Hindustan, specifically the Allahabad and Bihar regions.

54. Father Manuel Pinheiro, Goa, 29 November 1595, in Wicki 1972 (n. 15), vol. XVII, doc. 46, pp. 374–6.

55. See Richard M. Eaton, *The Rise of Islam and the Bengal Frontier, 1204–1760*, Delhi, 1997, pp. 77 et seq.

56. See Simon Digby, 'The *Sufi Shaikh* as a source of authority in Mediaeval India', in Marc Gaborieau, *Islam et societé dans l'Asie du Sud*, Paris, 1986, pp. 57–73 (60), which refers to the study by L. Elwell-Sutton, 'The *Darvish* in Persian folklore', in *Proceedings of the Twenty-Sixth International Congress of Orientalists*, Delhi, 1968, pp. 200–3.

57. See Richard Foltz, *Mughal India and Central Asia*, Karachi, 1998, chapter 6 ('Travelogues'), pp. 118–19; Iqbal Husain, 'Hindu shrines and practices as described by a central Asian traveller in the first half of the seventeenth century', in *Medieval India 1. Researches in the History of India 1200–1750*, ed. Irfan Habib, Delhi, 1999, pp. 141–53; Muzaffar Alam & Sanjay Subrahmanyam, 'From an ocean of wonders. Mahmud bin Amir Wali Balkhi and his Indian Travels, 1625–1631', in *Récits de voyage des Asiatiques. Genres, mentalités, conception de l'espace*, ed. Claudine

Salmon, Paris, 1996, pp. 161–89.

58. *Synodicon Orientale ou recueil des synodes nestoriens*, ed. J. B. Chabot, Paris, 1902. On the meaning of the expression Çin and Maçin, see the excellent study by Luís Filipe Thomaz, 'A *Carta que mandaram os Padres da India, da China e da Magna China* – Um relato siríaco da chegada dos Portugueses ao Malabar e seu primeiro encontro com a hierarquia cristã local', in *Revista da Universidade de Coimbra*, vol. XXXVI (1991), pp. 119–81 (note 15, pp. 144–47).

59. Bastião Lopes Lobato to Dom João de Castro – Hormuz, 3 February 1546 – published by Armando Cortesão & Luís de Albuquerque, *Obras completas de D. João de Castro*, Coimbra, 1981, vol. IV, pp. 22–6 (25); Garcia de la Penha to the same – Hormuz, 5 February 1546 – *ibid*. 1976, vol. III, p. 124.

60. See Denys Lombard, 'La conquête du monde par Alexandre: un mythe aux dimensions euroasiatiques', in *Asia Maritima. Images et realité. Bilder und wirklichkeit, 1200–1800*, ed. Denys Lombard & Roderich Ptak, Wiesbaden, 1994, pp. 165–76; S. Subrahmanyam, '"Persianization" and "Mercantilism": Two themes in Bay of Bengal History, 1400–1700', in *Commerce and Culture in the Bay of Bengal, 1500–1800*, ed. Om Prakash & Denys Lombard, New Delhi, 1999, pp. 47–85 (79–80).

61. For the Persian sources that Diogo do Couto may have used in *Década IV* (Lisbon, 1602), Sanjay Subrahmanyam provides a complete record of chronicles that, with some probability, may have circulated in Goa in the early seventeenth century (see Diogo do Couto, *Década Quarta da Ásia*, ed. M. Augusta Lima Cruz, Lisbon, 1999, vol. II, note 114, pp. 111–14). Subrahmanyam's approach to Couto applies, *mutatis mutandis*, to Erédia.

62. The king to the Archbishop of Goa – Lisbon, n.d. (1601?) – IAN/TT, *Corpo cronológico*, pt III, bundle 26, doc. 53. The work in question cannot be accurately identified. For Safavid chronicles, particularly those from the reign of Shah 'Abbas, see Sholeh A. Quinn, *Historical Writing during the Reign of Shah 'Abbas: Ideology, Imitation and Legitimacy in Safavid Chronicles*, Salt Lake City, 2000.

63. These three maps are reproduced in *PMC* (n. 40), IV, respectively pls. 413 B, 416 E and 416 F.

64. The first is in *Tratado Ophirico* (Paris, BNF, *Fonds portugais*, 44, f. 13), the other two are in *atlas-miscelânea* (*PMC* [n. 40], IV, pls. 415 A and 415 B).

65. Irfan Habib, 'Cartography in Mughal India', in *Medieval India – A Miscellany*, ed. I. Habib, New York, 1977, vol. IV, pp. 122–34; Joseph E. Schwartzberg, 'Geographical Mapping', in *The History of Cartography*, ed. J.B. Harley & David Woodward, vol. II, book 1: *Cartography in the Traditional Islamic and South Asian Societies*, Chicago/London, 1992, pp. 400–9, 507.

66. Habib 1977 (n. 65), p. 125.

67. See the pertinent comment made by Jos Gommans (*Mughal Warfare: Indian Frontiers and High Roads to Empire, 1500–1700*, London/New York, 2002, pp. 20–1), based on the existing bibliography on the cartography of the Mughal Empire.

68. The itineraries that Erédia shows can be compared to our knowledge of the routes in the Mughal empire in the sixteenth and seventeenth centuries (Abul Khair Muhammad Farooque, *Roads and Communications in Mughal India*, Delhi, 1977; Jean Deloche, *Recherches sur les routes de l'Inde au temps des Mogols. Étude critique des sources*, Paris, 1968).

69. See also the interesting study by Laura Hostetler, *Qing Colonial Enterprise: Ethnography and Cartography in Early Modern China*, Chicago/London, 2001, especially ch. 3, pp. 81 *et seq.* In early Qing

texts dealing with the empire's borders – the author works specifically on the encyclopaedia *Gujin tushu Jicheng*, which in turn uses information and illustrations from the Ming text *San cai tu hui* – there is no shortage of groups of weird and wonderful beings, shown with wings or absurdly long arms. For Japan see Ronald P. Toby, 'Imagining and imaging 'Anthropos' in early modern Japan', in *Visual Anthropology Review,* vol. 14, no. 1 (Spring–Summer 1998), pp. 19–44.

70. *Fonds portugais* (n. 64), 44, ff. 17 and 22 (drawing: 'Gente da Ilha Zanzi').

71. 'Mongolicae Legationis Commentarius' in *Memoirs of the Asiatic Society of Bengal*, vol. III, no. 9 (1914), pp. 513–704. On this, see J. Mcfarland, 'Monserrate's map of India', in *New Review*, vol. X (1939), pp. 473–86.

72. 'Descripção do Reyno de Guzarate' and 'Descripção do Reino de Bengalla'. These maps were included in João de Barros, *Década IV*, which Erédia completed and prepared for publication (Madrid, 1615). They are reproduced in *PMC* (n. 40), IV, pls 424 B and D.

73. *PMC*, IV, pp. 59–60. Jean Deloche (see n. 68) mentions Monserrate's map, but makes no reference to those of Erédia and Lavanha. In similar fashion, Susan Gole ignores Portuguese cartography of the Mughal Empire (*Indian Maps and Plans: From Earliest Times to the Advent of European Surveys*, New Delhi, 1989). Moreover, to the best of my knowledge, Baffin's map has not been the subject of any recent study (I would like to thank Tony Campbell and Andrew Cook for this information).

74. 'Asian Despotism? Mughal Government as seen from the Dutch East India Company Factory in Surat', in *Journal of Early Modern History*, vol. 3, no. 3 (August 1999), pp. 256–80.

THE PALACE OF THE VICEROYS IN GOA (PP. 68–97)

1. *Itinerário, viagem ou navegação de John Huyghen van Linschoten às Índias Orientais ou portuguesas* (1596), ed. Arie Pos & Rui Loureiro, Lisbon, 1997, p. 162, quotations translated by the author.

2. Catarina Madeira Santos, '*Goa é a chave de toda a Índia'. Perfil político da capital do Estado da Índia (1505–1570)*, Lisbon, 1999, pp. 211 *et seq.*; Catarina Madeira Santos, 'A corte dos vice-reis da Índia no século XVI. Algumas questões', in *Vértice* (1997), no. 77, pp. 39–48; Helder Carita, *Palácios de Goa. Modelos e tipologias da arquitectura civil indo-portuguesa*, Lisbon, 1995, pp. 22 *et seq.*

3. M.J. Gabriel de Saldanha, *História de Goa. Política e arqueológica*, New Goa, 1926 (2nd edition, New Delhi/Madras, 1990), p. 166.

4. *Roteiro de Goa a Diu*, in *Obras completas de Dom João de Castro*, ed. Armando Cortesão & Luís de Albuquerque, Coimbra, 1971, pp. 1–163; Armando Cortesão & Adelino Teixeira da Mota, *Portugaliae monumenta cartographica*, Lisbon, 1960, vol. I, pl. 60, a, b, c.

5. The court was initially itinerant, operating on the fleets and accompanying the governor or viceroy wherever he went. It later officially adopted Cochin as its base, although its itinerant nature continued to be a constant feature.

6. The most important study in terms of understanding the urban development of Goa and other Portuguese cities in Hindustan is by Walter Rossa, *Cidades indo-portuguesas. Contribuição para o estudo do urbanismo português no Hindustão Ocidental*, Lisbon, 1997.

7. *Documentação ultramarina portuguesa*, ed. António da Silva Rego, Lisbon, 1960, vol. I, p. 627.

8. Dom Pedro de Mascarenhas was an exceptional man. A member of one of Portugal's leading families and a courtier, he had been King João

III's ambassador to Rome, helping the first Jesuits, including St Francis Xavier, to travel first to Portugal and then to the Orient. His military and diplomatic service in Morocco was equally distinguished. He only governed India for nine months before dying.

9. Santos 1999 (n. 2), pp. 216 et seq., and pp. 242–3.

10. António Bocarro, Livro das plantas de todas as fortalezas, cidades e povoações do Estado da Índia Oriental, ed. Isabel Cid, Lisbon, 1992, vol. II, pp. 136–7.

11. Documentação para a história das missões do Padroado Português do Oriente, Índia, ed. António da Silva Rego, 2nd edition, Lisbon, 1994, vol. VII, p. 329.

12. Documentos remetidos da Índia ou Livro das Monções, ed. António da Silva Rego, Lisbon, 1974, vol. VI, pp. 246–7; Vida e acções de Mathias de Albuquerque capitão e viso-rei da Índia, ed. Antonella Vignati, Lisbon, 1998–9, p. 99.

13. Pedro Dias, História da arte portuguesa no mundo. O espaço do Índico, Lisbon, vol. I, 1998, pp. 40 et seq.

14. Diogo do Couto, Obras completas de ..., Lisbon, 1808, pp. 66–9.

15. Lisbon, IAN/TT, Documentos remetidos da Índia, book 38, f. 1.

16. Manuel de Faria e Sousa, Ásia portuguesa, Oporto, 1947, vol. VI, p. 437. Anthony Disney produced a biography of Dom Miguel de Noronha in 'The viceroy count of Linhares at Goa. 1629–1635' in II Seminário de história indo-portuguesa (proceedings of), Lisbon, 1985, pp. 301 et seq., confirming this on p. 315.

17. Helder Carita, 'Maqueta do Palácio Fortaleza dos vice-reis em Goa', in Os espaços de um império, ed. Artur Teodoro de Matos (exhib. cat., Oporto, Edifício da Alfândega), Lisbon, 1999, p. 92; idem, 'Evolução da arquitectura civil indo-portuguesa e eas suas estruturas espaço-sociais', in Vasco da Gama e a Índia (proceedings of), Paris/Lisbon, 1998–9, vol. III.

18. Rego 1994 (n. 11), vol. VII, p. 329.

19. Pos & Loureiro 1997 (n. 1), p. 161.

20. Viagem de Francisco Pyrard de Laval, ed. Joaquim Heliodoro da Cunha Rivara & Artur de Magalhães Basto, Oporto, 1944, vol. II, p. 40.

21. See Xavier de Castro, 'Goa la Vieille', in Goa. 1510–1685. L'Inde Portugaise, apostolique et commerciale, ed. Michel Chandeigne, Paris, 1996, p. 200.

22. Gaspar Correia, Lendas da Índia, ed. Manuel Lopes de Almeida, Oporto, 1975, vol. IV. p. 716.

23. Frei João dos Santos, Etiópia Oriental e vária história de cousas notáveis do Oriente (1st edition, 1609), ed. Manuel Lobato, Lisbon, 1999, pp. 597–8.

24. Cartas de Afonso de Albuquerque seguidas de documentos que as elucidam, ed. Raimundo António Bulhão Pato, vol. II, 1884, p. 431.

25. Frazão de Vasconcelos, As pinturas das armadas da Índia e outras representações artísticas de navios portugueses do século XVI, Lisbon, 1951, p. 16.

26. Dias 1998 (n. 13), p. 212; Dalila Rodrigues, 'A pintura na antiga Índia Portuguesa', in Vasco da Gama e a Índia (proceedings of), Paris/Lisbon, 1998–9, vol. III.

27. Relação das naos e armadas da Índia, com os sucessos delas que se puderam fazer, para notícia e instrucção dos curiosos, e amantes da história, ed. Maria Hermínia Maldonado, Coimbra, 1985.

28. Rivara & Basto 1944 (n. 20), pp. 40–1.

29. Correia 1975 (n. 22), vol. IV, pp. 596–7.

30. Pos & Loureiro 1997 (n. 1), p. 161.

31. Diogo do Couto, Década VIII da Ásia, ed. Maria Augusta Lima Cruz, Lisbon, 1993, vol. I, pp. 376 et seq.

32. Santos 1999 (n. 23), p. 597.

33. Rego 1994 (n. 11), vol. VII, p. 329.

34. Pos & Loureiro 1997 (n. 1), p. 162.

35. Bernardo Ferrão, Mobiliário português, Oporto, 1990; Maria Helena Mendes Pinto, Artes decorativas portuguesas no Museu Nacional de Arte Antiga, século XV a XVIII, Lisbon, 1979; idem, Os móveis e o seu tempo, Lisbon, 1985–7; idem, 'Sentando-se em Goa', in Oceanos, no. 19-20 (1994); idem, 'Escritórios, contadores e outros móveis indo-portugueses', in Vasco da Gama e a Índia, Paris/Lisbon, 1998–9, vol. III; José Jordão Felgueiras, 'A arca de Aleixo de Sousa Chichorro. Notas para o estudo da génese do mobiliário luso-oriental', in A arte na Península Ibérica ao tempo do Tratado de Tordesilhas, Coimbra, 1994–8; José Jordão Felgueiras, 'Arcas portuguesas de Cochim', in Oceanos, no. 19–20 (1994); Pedro Dias, O contador das cenas familiares. O quotidiano dos portugueses de Quinhentos na decoração de um móvel indo-português, Oporto, 2002.

36. Rivara & Basto 1944 (n. 20), vol. II, p. 185.

37. Rivara & Basto 1944 (n. 20), vol. II, p. 194.

38. Pos & Loureiro 1997 (n. 1), p. 165.

39. Chandeigne 1996 (n. 21), pp. 160 et seq.

40. Documenta indica, ed. Joseph Wicki, S.J., 18 vols, Rome, 1948–88, vol. XI, p. 364.

41. Rivara & Basto 1944 (n. 20), vol. II, pp. 183–5.

42. Pedro Dias, 'A descoberta do Oriente', in A herança de Rauluchatim (exhib. cat., Lisbon, Museu de São Roque), ed. Nuno Vassallo e Silva, Lisbon, 1996, pp. 30 et seq.

43. Pedro Dias, 'La tapisserie flamande au Portugal', in Flandre et Portugal, ed. J. Everaert & E. Stools, Antwerp, 1991, pp. 178 et seq. Flemish tapestries were given to the rulers of several Indian regions and even to those of areas further afield. One such case was the king of Cochin, who was given two Arras tapestries by Vasco da Gama on the latter's second voyage; another was the king of Cambay, who was given six tapestries depicting the story of Aeneas by Afonso de Albuquerque.

44. Maria José Mendonça, 'Alguns tipos de colchas indo-portuguesas na Colecção do Museu Nacional de Arte Antiga', in Boletim do Museu Nacional de Arte Antiga, vol. II (1949); Teresa Pacheco Pereira & Teresa Alarcão, Fábulas bordadas. Uma colcha indo-portuguesa do século XVII, Lisbon, 1988.

45. Dias 1998 (n. 13), p. 32.

46. Maria Helena Mendes Pinto, 'Colcha', in de Matos 1999 (n. 17), pp. 104–6.

47. Maria Helena Mendes Pinto, 'Aube', in De Goa a Lisboa (exhib. cat.), ed. Maria Helena Mendes Pinto, Brussels, 1991, p. 100; idem, 'Alva', in Vasco da Gama e a Índia (exhib. cat., Paris, Chapelle de la Sorbonne), ed. Maria Helena Mendes Pinto & José Manuel Garcia, Paris/Lisbon, 1998, p. 136.

48. I believe that this coverlet was first published in a photograph by M. M. de Cagigal e Silva (A arte indo-portuguesa, Lisbon, n.d., p. 81), although the arms are not identified.

49. I am grateful to José Jordão Felgueiras for this information.

50. Lisbon, BNL, Reservados, codex 1486, ff. 9 et seq.

51. Maria Helena Mendes Pinto, 'Capa', in Paris 1998 (n. 47), p. 136.

52. Pinto 1998–9 (n. 35), p. 320.

53. Francisco Hipólito Raposo, 'O encanto dos contadores indo-portugueses', in Oceanos, no. 19–20 (1994), pp. 16–7.

54. Bernardo Ferrão studied a large cabinet with a three-legged support from the collection of the Counts of Lavradio. The coat-of-arms it bears is

of the Almeida family – the Counts of Avintes and later Marquises of Lavradio – which suggests that its owner was someone other than Dom Luis de Mendonça Furtado e Albuquerque, although he was the viceroy of India between 1671 and 1677. He died in Brazil while returning to Portugal.

55. *Exotica: The Portuguese Discoveries and the Renaissance Kunstkammer* (exhib. cat., Lisbon, Calouste Gulbenkian Museum), ed. Helmut Trnek & Nuno Vassallo e Silva, Lisbon, 2001.

56. Annemarie Jordan Gschwend, 'Catarina de Áustria: Colecção e Kunstkammer de uma Princesa Renascentista', in *Oceanos*, no. 16 (1993), pp. 62–70; *idem*, 'As maravilhas do Oriente: Colecções de curiosidades renascentistas em Portugal', in Vassallo e Silva 1996 (n. 42).

57. Wicki 1948–88 (n. 40), vol. X, p. 1061.

58. Arthur da Motta Alves, 'O precioso arreio, feito em Goa, no século XVI, para D. Sebastião', in *O Oriente Português*, no. 18 (1937), pp. 299–304.

59. Nuno Vassallo e Silva, 'Cofre', in Vassallo e Silva 1996 (n. 42), p. 191.

60. Leonor d'Orey, 'Tesouros indianos do convento do Carmo da Vidigueira e da Graça de Lisboa', in Vassallo e Silva 1996 (n. 42), pp. 156 *et seq.*

61. Frei Agostinho de Santa Maria, *Santuário mariano*, vol. VIII, p. 167.

62. *Documentos para a história da arte em Portugal*, Lisbon, 1976, vol. XV, p. 47.

63. Frei António da Purificação, *Chronica da antiquíssima província de Portugal da Ordem dos Eremitas de Santo Agostinho*, Lisbon, 1656, book V, pp. 112 *et seq.*

64. Garcia de Orta, *Colóquios dos simples ou drogas da Índia* (1563), ed. Count of Ficalho, Lisbon (1891), 1987, vol. II, pp. 231–5.

65. Nuno Vassallo e Silva provides a more detailed analysis of this in: 'Subsídios para o estudo do comércio das pedras preciosas em Lisboa, no século XVI', in *Boletim Cultural da Assembleia Distrital de Lisboa*, 3rd series, no. 91, tome 2 (1989), pp. 3 *et seq.*; *idem*, 'The Portuguese Gem Trade in the Sixteenth Century', in *Jewellery Studies*, no. 6 (1993), London.

66. Nuno Vassallo e Silva, 'Ouro, marfim, cristal e jade. Objectos preciosos de Goa e do Ceilão', in Lisbon 1996 (n. 42), pp. 170 *et seq.*; *idem*, 'Bezoar', in Lisbon 2001 (n. 55), pp. 152–5.

67. Nuno de Castro, *A porcelana chinesa e os brasões do império*, Oporto, 1987, p. 23.

'RARITIES FROM GOA' AT THE COURTS OF HUMAYUN, AKBAR AND JAHANGIR (1530–1627) (PP. 98–115)

1. Abu'l Fazl, *The A'in-i-Akbari*, 3 vols, trans. H. Blochmann (1873), ed. D.C. Phillott, Calcutta, 1927 (reprint, New Delhi, 1989), vol. I, p. 73.

2. Jahangir, *The Tuzuk-i-Jahangiri or Memoirs of Jahangir*, 2 vols, trans. A. Rogers, ed. H. Beveridge, London, 1909–14 (reprint, New Delhi, 1978), vol. I, p. 5.

3. José Lico Collection, Lisbon. For an illustration and discussion of this piece, see *The World of Lacquer: 2000 Years of History* (exhib. cat., Lisbon, Calouste Gulbenkian Museum), ed. Pedro Moura Carvalho, Lisbon, 2001, cat. 71.

4. Jahangir himself (Jahangir 1909–14 [n. 2], vol. I, p. 215) states that Babur did not commission any paintings of animals.

5 St Petersburg, Institute of Oriental Studies. Illustrated in St Petersburg, *The St. Petersburg Muraqqa: Album of Indian and Persian miniatures from*

the 16th through the 18th century, F. Habsburg project, 2 vols, Milan, 1996, vol. II, fig. 147, f. 80r.

6. Jahangir 1909–14 (n. 2), vol. I, p. 215.

7. London, Victoria and Albert Museum, inv. no. IM 135-1921.

8. *The History of India, as Told by its own Historians: The Muhammadan Period. The Posthumous Papers of the Late Sir H.M. Elliot*, ed. H.M. Elliot & J. Dowson, vol. VI, Calcutta, 1875, p. 165. The arrival of tobacco in the court is also confirmed by Jesuit sources (E. Maclagan, *The Jesuits and the Great Mogul*, London 1932 [reprint, Haryana, 1990], p. 62). On Asad Beg's journey to Bijapur, see the essay in this volume by M. Alam and S. Subrahmanyam.

9. Maclagan 1932 (n. 8), p. 67, f. 35.

10. Jahangir 1909–14 (n. 2), vol. I, pp. 370–71.

11. The last Portuguese diplomatic mission was to the court of Emperor Aurangzeb (r. 1658–1707). Among other goods, it took large quantities of tobacco (Panduronga Pissurlencar, 'Antigualhas' part I: 'Últimas embaixadas portuguesas à corte Mogol', in *Boletim do Instituto Vasco da Gama*, no. 38 [1938], pp. 143–85).

12. See Pedro Moura Carvalho, 'Goa's pioneering role in transmitting European traditions to the Mughal and Safavid courts', in *Exotica: The Portuguese Discoveries and the Renaissance Kunstkammer*, ed. Helmut Trnek & Nuno Vassallo e Silva (exhib. cat., Lisbon, Calouste Gulbenkian Museum), Lisbon, 2001, pp. 68–79.

13. Two Mughal miniatures where two different types of organs are shown suggest in fact that more than one organ must have reached the court (see *ibid.* pp. 75–6).

14. Abu'l Fazl, *The Akbarnama of Abu'l-Fazl*, 3 vols, trans. H. Beveridge, London, 1902–39 (reprint, New Delhi, 1993), vol. III, p. 322–3.

15. *Ibid.*, p. 323.

16. A simple flute with no keys.

17. A circular drum covered in stretched skin and played using two sticks.

18. Cf. Luís Keil, *As tapeçarias de D. João de Castro*, Lisbon, 1928, p. 11.

19. Such instruments may be seen in several of the so-called 'tapestries of Dom João de Castro', particularly one of c.1555 depicting his entry into Goa, Kunsthistorisches Museum, Vienna. Illustrated in *Die Portugiesen in Indien: die Eroberungen Dom João de Castros auf Tapisserien 1538–1548* (exhib. cat., Vienna, Kunsthistorisches Museum), Vienna, 1992, cats 2, 3 and 5.

20. Pierre du Jarric, *Akbar and the Jesuits: An Account of the Jesuit missions to the Court of Akbar*, translation by C.H. Payne, London, 1926 (reprint, New Delhi, 1997), pp. 91–2.

21. Father Fernão Guerreiro, S.J., *Jahangir and the Jesuits, with an account of the travels of Benedict Goes and the mission to Pegu*, translation by C.H. Paine, London, 1930 (reprint, New Delhi, 1997), p. 33.

22. *Ibid.*, p. 45.

23. A wind instrument. For an illustration, see Abu'l Fazl 1927 (n. 1), I, pl. VIII, fig. 6.

24. *Ibid.*, vol. I, p. 53.

25. Bonnie C. Wade, *Imaging Sound: An Ethnomusicological Study of Music, Art, and Culture in Mughal India*, Chicago, 1998, p. 154.

26. See, for example, Milo Cleveland Beach, *The Grand Mogul: Imperial Painting in India 1600–1660* (exhib. cat., Williamstown, Sterling and Francine Clark Art Institute, etc.), Williamstown, Massachusetts, 1978, pp. 155–7.

27. On the influence that this Bible had on Mughal painting, see Ebba Koch, 'The influence of the Jesuit missions on symbolic representations of the Mughal emperors', in *Islam in India: Studies and Commentaries*, vol. I,

The Akbar Mission and Miscellaneous Studies, ed. C.W. Troll, New Delhi, 1982, pp. 14–29.

28. Houses apparently based on Portuguese models are also seen in other *Hamza Nama* miniatures; their identification is nevertheless more problematic since they are less detailed. See, for example, John Seyller *et al.*, *The Adventures of Hamza: Painting and Storytelling in Mughal India* (exhib. cat., London, Arthur M. Sackler Museum), London, 2002, cats 55 and 58.

29. 'The Spy Zambur takes Mahiya to Tawariq, where they Meet Ustad Khatun', The Metropolitan Museum of Art, Rogers Fund, 1923 (23.264.1), New York.

30. The 'cross' is formed by five holes corresponding to the absence of five bricks on the facade; these holes had a practical role, that of allowing air to circulate and light to enter.

31. 'The Capture of Port Hoogly', in a *Padshah Nama*, f. 117a, Royal Library, Windsor. Illustrated in M.C. Beach & E. Koch, *King of the World, the Padshahnama: An Imperial Mughal Manuscript from the Royal Library*, Windsor Castle, with a new translation by W. Thackston (exhib. cat., London, National Museum of India), London, 1997, cat. 20.

32. Leonardo Nunes, *Crónica de D. João de Castro*, ed. L. Albuquerque, Lisbon, 1989, p. 17.

33. *Ibid.*, p. 20.

34. 1531, according to Beveridge (Gulbadan Begam, *The History of Humayun (Humayun-nama)*, trans. Annette S. Beveridge, Delhi, n.d. [reprint, New Delhi, 2001], p. 114, no. 1).

35. *Ibid.*, p. 113.

36. Leão Crisóstomo Fernandes, 'O livro e o jornal em Goa', parte II: 'Introdução da imprensa em Goa – o primeiro livro impresso: "Conclusiones Philosophicas"', in *Boletim do Instituto Vasco da Gama*, no. 25 (1935), pp. 49–54, p. 50.

37. The first book printed in Índia was *Conclusiones philosophicas*, also printed in several other Paulist colleges around the world. St Francis Xavier's *Doutrina cristã* was published the following year (1557), followed by Garcia de Orta's *Colóquios* in 1563. For a more complete list of early publications, see Leão Crisóstomo Fernandes, 'O livro e o jornal em Goa', parte III, 'Algumas das primeiras tipografias na Índia', in *Boletim do Instituto Vasco da Gama*, no. 27 (1935a), pp. 82–6; part IV, 'Um século de actividade tipográfica: 1556 a 1660. Bibliografia', no. 27 (1935b), pp. 87–96; part IV (cont.), no. 30 (1936), pp. 66–77.

38. For illustrations of some imperial portraits with *putti* see Amina Okada, *Imperial Mughal Painters*, Paris, 1992, figs. 44, 48, 49 and 53.

39. Paris, Musée Guimet, MA 6768. The origin of these jewels is difficult to establish. Amina Okada attributes the piece in question, with some reservations, to a Mughal workshop (Amina Okada, *L'Inde des princes. La donation Jean et Krishna Riboud*, Paris, 2002, p. 147), while Untracht attributes it to Madurai, southern India (cf. *ibid.*, p. 149). Meanwhile, Keene suggests that the Deccan is the probable origin of a similar pendant (Manuel Keene, *Treasury of the World: Jewelled Arts of India in the Age of the Mughals* [exhib. cat., London, BM], London, 2001, cat. 8.38).

40. For example, at the church of São Francisco de Assis, Old Goa.

41. For example, one of the panels in polychrome carved wood decorating the main altar of the church of the Rachol seminary.

42. Including possibly Mughal India as well as territories under Portuguese rule, notably Macao. The central zone of the tympanum of the church of São Domingos in Praça do Leal Senado, for example, is still decorated with the dove of the Holy Spirit.

43. According to Untracht, *mangalsutram* (O. Untracht, *Traditional Jewellery of India*, London, 1997, p. 156). This author also confirms that this jewel consists of a string of small black beads, as stated by A.F. Propércia Figueiredo ('Símbolos zoomórficos', parte II, 'Animais simbólicos', in *Boletim do Instituto Vasco da Gama*, no. 21 [1934], pp. 36–89, p. 66).

44. *Ibid.*

45. For an illustration, see Koch 1982 (n. 27), fig. 1.1.

46. 'Shah Jahan receives his three eldest sons and Asaf Khan during his accession ceremonies', Beach & Koch 1997 (n. 31), cat. nos 10–11.

47. 'Jahangir's dream', *c*.1618, signed Abu'l Hasan. From the St Petersburg Album. Freer Gallery of Art, inv. no. 45.9, Washington D.C.

48. This is based on a sentence from the *Book of Revelation* (12:1): 'And there appeared a great wonder in heaven; a woman clothed with the sun, and the moon under her feet …' later becoming part of the Virgin's iconography (see George Ferguson, *Signs and Symbols in Christian Art*, New York, 1966, p. 45). An engraving by Master E.S. of St John at Patmos, *c*.1460, at the State Hermitage Museum (inv. no. 149673, St Petersburg) shows that such iconographic elements had already been adopted by then.

49. Some examples can still be found in Goan collections, including two images of Our Lady in the Museu do Xavier Centre of Historical Research. For illustrations, see Charles J. Borges, 'Questões em torno das formas de representação na arte religiosa indo-portuguesa' in *Oceanos*, nos 19–20 (September–December 1994), pp. 72–86 (p. 86).

50. Du Jarric 1926 (n. 20), p. 19.

51. *Ibid*, p. 19; Maclagan 1932 (n. 8), p. 226.

52. Cf. Vítor Serrão, 'A pintura na antiga Índia Portuguesa nos séculos XVI e XVII', in *Oceanos*, nos 19–20 (September–December 1994), pp. 102–112, p. 104.

53. *Ibid.*, p. 108.

54. Du Jarric 1926 (n. 20), p. 67. Maclagan (1932 [n. 8], p. 67) suggests 1594 as the date of their arrival in the court. See essay by Asok Kumar Das in this catalogue.

55. Du Jarric 1926 (n. 20), p. 82.

56. *Ibid.*, p. 111.

57. Maclagan 1932 (n. 8), p. 226.

58. Just as in Abu'l Fazl 1927 (n. 1), vol. I, p. 115.

59. See, for example, D. Barrett & B. Gray, *Indian Painting*, Geneva, 1963 (reprint New York, 1985), p. 87; J. Michael Rogers, *Mughal Miniatures*, London, 1993, pp. 71–3.

60. Rogers 1993 (n. 60), p. 73.

61. Begam 1902 (n. 34), p. 113. See also Khwandamir, *Qanun-i-Humayuni: also known as Humayun-nama of Khwandamir*, translated and edited by B. Prashad, Calcutta, 1940 (reprint, Calcutta, 1996), p. 37.

62. Jahangir 1909–14 (n. 2), vol. I, p. 140.

63. Jacques de Coutre, *Andanzas asiáticas*, ed. E. Stols, B. Teensma & J. Werberckmoes, Madrid, 1991, p. 89.

64. Heinrich Göbel, *Die Niederlande*, 2 vols, Leipzig, 1923, vol. I, pp. 320 and 326.

65. Abu'l Fazl 1902–39 (n. 14), vol. III, p. 207.

66. *Ibid.*, vol. III, p. 322.

67. De Coutre 1991 (n. 63), pp. 345–50.

68. See Mark Zebrowski, *Gold, Silver and Bronze from Mughal India*, London, 1997, figs 44 and 46–52, for illustrations of objects at the State Hermitage Museum.

69. See, for example, *The Topkapi Saray Museum, the Treasury*, ed. J.M. Rogers & C. Köseoglu, London, 1987, cats 6 and 8–12.

70. London, The Khalili Collection of Islamic Art, acc. no. JLY 1856.

71. Jean-Baptiste Tavernier, *Travels in India by Jean-Baptiste Tavernier, Baron of Aubonne*, 2 vols, trans. V. Ball, ed. W. Crooke, London, 1925 (reprint, New Delhi, 1995), vol. II, pp. 82–3.

72. Garcia de Orta, *Aromatum et simplicium aliquot medicamentorum apud Indos nascentium historia de Carlos Clúsio; versão portuguesa do epítome latino dos Colóquios dos simples de Garcia de Orta*, trans. J. Walter & M. Alves, Lisbon, 1964, p. 199.

73. Nuno Vassallo e Silva, 'Jewels and gems in Goa from the sixteenth to the eighteenth century', in *The Jewels of India*, ed. S. Stronge pp. 53–62, Bombay, 1995, pp. 53–62, p. 54.

74. Its whereabouts have been unknown since the invasion of Kuwait. Illustrated in Keene 2001 (n. 39), cat. 9.1.

75. As discussed in Pedro Moura Carvalho, 'What happened to the Mughal furniture? The role of the imperial workshops, the decorative motifs used and the influence of western models', in *Muqarnas*, vol. 21, forthcoming (2004).

76. *Portrait of Rustam Khan*, c.1550–58, Late Shah Jahan Album, Chester Beatty Library, lib. no. 7B. 35, Dublin.

77. Lisbon, Fundação Ricardo do Espírito Santo Silva, inv. no. 46.

78. London, Victoria and Albert Museum, inv. no. IM 16–1931.

79. The relationship between the two is analysed in Moura Carvalho 2004 (n. 75).

80. London, Victoria and Albert Museum, inv. no. 15-1882.

81. Oporto, Távora Sequeira Pinto Collection.

82. Sir Thomas Roe, *The embassy of Sir Thomas Roe to the court of the Great Mogul, 1615–1619, as narrated in his journal and correspondence*, ed. W. Foster, London, 1899 (reprint, Nendeln, 1967), vol. I, p. 134.

83. *Early travels in India, 1583–1619*, ed. William Foster, London, 1921 (reprint, New Delhi, 1968), pp. 101–03.

84. Tavernier 1925 (n. 71), I, pp. 303–6.

PRECIOUS STONES, JEWELS AND CAMEOS: JACQUES DE COUTRE'S JOURNEY TO GOA AND AGRA (PP. 116–33)

1. I would like to thank Jorge Flores, Susan Stronge and Stephen Markel for their help in preparing this article.

2. George Winius, 'Jewel trading in Portuguese India in the XVI and XVII Centuries', in *Indica*, vol. 25, no. 1 (March 1988), pp. 15–34; Nuno Vassallo e Silva, 'Jewels and gems in Goa from the sixteenth to the eighteenth century', in *The Jewels of India*, ed. Susan Stronge, Bombay, 1995, pp. 53–62; idem, 'Jewels for the Great Mughal: Goa as a centre of the gem trade in the Orient', in *Jewellery Studies*, no. 10 (forthcoming).

3. Cf. the essay by Milo C. Beach in this volume and Michael Brand & Glenn D. Lowry, *Akbar's India: Art from the Mughal City of Victory*, New York, 1985; Pedro Moura Carvalho, 'O papel pioneiro de Goa na difusão de tradições europeias nas Cortes Mogol e Safávida', in *Exotica: The Portuguese Discoveries and the Renaissance Kunstkammer* (exhib. cat., Lisbon, Calouste Gulbenkian Museum), ed. Helmut Trnek & Nuno Vassallo e Silva, Lisbon, 2001, pp. 69–79.

4. Diogo do Couto, *Asia, Década IX*, ch. XXVIII, Lisbon, 1974, p. 247.

5. *Ibid.*, ch. XIII, pp. 66–7.

6. IAN/TT, *Miscelâneas manuscritas do Convento da Graça*, book 4, ff. 361–3.

7. Couto 1974 (n. 4), p. 246.

8. *Documentação para a história das missões do padroado português do Oriente – Índia*, Lisbon, 1958, vol. XII, p. 452.

9. *Documenta indica*, ed. Joseph Wicki, S.J., Rome, 1948–98, vol. XVIII, p. 567.

10. Fernão Guerreiro, *Relação anual das coisas que fizeram os padres da Companhia de Jesus nas suas missões*, Coimbra, 1930, vol. I, p. 11; Jorge Flores & António Vasconcelos de Saldanha, *Os 'firangis' na chancelaria mogol: cópias portuguesas de documentos de Akbar (1572–1604)*, Lisbon/New Delhi, 2003, doc. 7, p. 77.

11. R.W. Lightbown, 'Oriental art and the Orient in late Renaissance and Baroque Italy', in *Journal of the Warburg and Courtauld Institutes*, no. 32 (1969), p. 240.

12. Guerreiro 1930 (n. 10), p. 11; Flores & Saldanha 2003 (n. 10), doc. 7, p. 77.

13. *Goa, 1510–1685: l'Inde portugaise, apostolique et commerciale*, ed. Michel Chandeigne, Paris, 1996, p. 162.

14. Susan Stronge, *Painting for the Mughal Emperor: The Art of the Book, 1560–1660*, London, 2002, figs 58–60.

15. Brand & Lowry 1985 (n. 3), p. 28, ill. 1.

16. Milo C. Beach, *The Imperial Image: Paintings for the Mughal Court*, exhib. cat., Washington, 1981, cats 16b and 16c.

17. Nuno Vassallo e Silva, 'Goa or Lisbon: Problems of attribution', in *Jahrbuch des Kunsthistorichen Museum Wien*, ed. Helmut Trnek & Sabine Haag, Mainz, 2001, vol. 3, pp. 135–8.

18. *A herança de Rauluchantim* (exhib. cat., Lisbon, Museu de São Roque), ed. Nuno Vassallo e Silva, Lisbon, 1996, cat. 5.

19. Xarco Cuevas, *Inventario de las alhogas, pinturas e objectos de valor y curiosidades donadas por Felipe II al Monasterio de El Escorial (1571–1598)*, Madrid, 1930.

20. *Exotica: Portugals Entdeckungen im Spiegel fürstlicher Kunst- und Wunderkammern der Renaissance*, Vienna, Kunsthistorisches Museum, 2000, cat. no. 84; Lisbon 2001a, cat. 36.

21. Lisbon 1996 (n. 18), cat. 7.

22. *The Indian Heritage: Court Life and Arts under Mughal Rule* (exhib. cat., Victoria & Albert Museum, London), ed. Robert Skelton, London, 1982, cat. 341.

23. Mark Zebrowski, *Gold, Silver and Bronze from Mughal India*, London, 1997, p. 40. fig. 9.

24. Nuno Vassallo e Silva, 'Apito', in Lisbon 2001a (n. 3), cat. 45, pp. 147–9.

25. Victoria & Albert Museum, inv. no. 173-1910.

26. Zebrowski 1997 (n. 23), pp. 67–70.

27. Lisbon 2001a (n. 3), cat. 57, pp. 164–5.

28. Winius 1988 (n. 2), p. 47.

29. BNL *Reservados*, Mss. 219, doc. 83.

30. Winius 1988 (n. 2), p. 26.

31. João Teles e Cunha, 'Hunting Riches: Goa's gem trade in the early modern age' in *Portuguese, Indian Ocean and European Bridgeheads 1500–1800: Festschrift in Honour of Prof. K.S. Mathew*, ed. Pius Malekandathil and Jamal Mohammed, Tellicherry, 2001, p. 287.

32. Ruby Maloni, *European Merchant Capital and the Indian Economy: A Historical Reconstruction Based on Surat Factory Records, 1630–1668*, New Delhi, 1992.

33. Jacques de Coutre, *Andanzas asiáticas*, ed. Eddy Stols, B. Teensma & J. Werberckmoes, Madrid, 1991, p. 293.

34. AHU, *Índia*, box 4, doc. 135.

35. Stephen Markel, 'Jades, jewels and objects of art', in *Romance of the Taj Mahal*, ed. Pratapaditya Pal, London/Los Angeles, 1989, p. 131. Curiously, Shahjahan's liking for precious objects seems to have escaped the attention of some merchants. Regarding the lack of interest shown by the Mughal court, in a letter dated 18 December 1628 the factors of Surat

mention that all the jewels and rarities should be sent back to England, as the gifts did not even cover ¼ of its cost (in William Foster, *English Factories in India 1624–1629*, Oxford, 1909, p. 303).

36. Coutre 1991 (n. 33), p. 303.

37. *Ibid.*, p. 304.

38. Paul Guth, 'Le bestiaire fabuleaux des orfèvres de la renaissance allemande', in *Connaissance des Arts*, 27 (May 1954), pp. 20–5; J.F. Hayward, *Virtuoso Goldsmiths and the Triumph of Mannerism, 1540–1620*, New York/London, 1976, illus. 508 and 517; *Silber und Gold: Augsburger Goldschmiedekunst für die Höfe Europas*, ed. Lorenz Seelig, exhib. cat., Munich, 1994, cat. 9–10.

39. Beach 1981 (n. 16), cat. 17c, pp. 170–71.

40. *Documentação ultramarina portuguesa*, ed. António Silva Rego, Lisbon, 1963, vol. III, p. 168.

41. London 1982 (n. 22), cat. 323.

42. Lisbon, Museu Nacional de Arte Antiga, inv. no. 1301.

43. *Die Pracht der Medici. Florenz und Europa* (exhib. cat.), Vienna, Kunsthistorisches Museum, 1999, I, cats 48–52; Alvar Gonzalez-Palacios, *Las colecciones reales españolas de mosaicos y piedras duras*, Madrid, 2001, pp. 22–4; Rudolf Distelberger, *Die Kunst des Steinschmitts*, Vienna, 2003, pp. 331–8, cats 206–9. See also the plaque showing Christ in the Garden, from the Spanish royal collections, Museo del Prado inv. no. O – 588 (see also Gonzalez-Palacios 2001, cat. 8).

44. Ebba Koch, *Mughal Art and Imperial Ideology: Collected Essays*, New Delhi, 2001, pp. 64–91. I would like to thank Susan Stronge for pointing out this important essay to me.

45. There are Mughal works from later periods that have jade inlays with gold settings. See *Catalogue of a Special Exhibition of Hindustan Jade in the National Palace Museum*, Taipei, 1983, pl. 47, pp. 218–19.

46. For the art of glyptics in the Mughal Empire, see London 1982 (n. 22), cat. 377 *et seq*; Markl 1989 (n. 35), pp. 143–5; Shanti Swarup, *Mughal Art: A Study in Handicrafts*, Delhi, 1996, p. 72; Oppi Untracht, *Traditional Jewelry of India*, New York, 1997, pp. 375–7.

47. Robert Skelton, 'Cameo', in London 1982 (n. 22), cat. 377.

48. *Ibid.*, cat. 378.

49. Markl 1989 (n. 35), p. 145. A fine example in sardonyx bearing an imperial portrait – in this case of Shahjahan – appeared recently on the art market. It is dated to 1630–40. Cf. Bonhams, *Islamic & Indian Art* (1 May 2003), lot 380.

50. Amina Okada, 'Les Jésuites à la cour du Grand Moghol: Modèles et influences artistiques XVIe–XVIIe siécle', in *La route des Indes* (exhib. cat.), ed. Thierry-Nicolas Tchakaloff, Bordeaux, 1998, p. 37.

51. Coutre 1991 (n. 33), p. 308.

52. *Ibid.*

53. Okada 1998 (n. 50), p. 36.

54. Coutre 1991 (n. 33), pp. 306–7.

55. Susan Stronge, 'Gold and silver in 16th and 17th century Mughal India', in Lisbon 1996 (n. 18), p. 70; Manuel Keene, 'Developments in enamels', in *Treasury of the World: Jeweled Arts of India in the Age of the Mughals*, ed. Manuel Keene, New York, 2001, p. 62.

56. Coutre 1991 (n. 33), p. 309.

57. *Ibid.*, p. 310.

58. Chandeigne 1996 (n. 13), p. 161.

59. Coutre 1991 (n. 33), p. 312.

60. *Itinerário de Sebastião Manrique*, ed. Luís Silveira, Lisbon, 1956, vol. II, pp. 331–4.

THE LAND OF 'MOGOR' (PP. 134–47)

1. Wheeler M. Thackston, *The Baburnama: Memoirs of Babur, Prince and Emperor*, Washington, 1996, p. 35. The book includes a concise introduction to Babur's life and Timurid background.

2. Abu'l Fazl, *The Akbar Nama*, trans. H. Beveridge, reprint, New Delhi, vol. III, 1972–3, p. 37.

3. António Cabral and his companions were sent by the Portuguese viceroy in 1573 and 1578. See Pierre du Jarric, *Akbar and the Jesuits: An Account of the Jesuit Missions to the Court of Akbar …* trans. and ed. C.H. Payne, London, 1926, p. 14, and note 2, pp. 217–18. Another Portuguese traveller, Pêro Tavares, also apparently lived for some years at the Mughal court after his arrival in 1578 (*ibid.*, note 4, p. 218).

4. Catherine Asher, *Architecture of Mughal India*, vol. I-4, *The New Cambridge History of India*, 1992, p. 41.

5. Abu'l Fazl, *The Ain-i Akbari*, ed. H.S. Jarrett and Sir Jadunath Sarkar, New Delhi, 1978 (3rd edn), vol. II, pp. 190–91.

6. See *Fatehpur-Sikri: A Sourcebook*, ed. Michael Brand & Glenn D. Lowry, Cambridge, Mass., 1985, for a useful outline of the history of the city, detailed plans, translations of Persian inscriptions on its monuments and an extensive compilation of sources, translated into English where necessary.

7. Akbar's unofficial historian, Badauni, notes that the emperor gave an order for Miyan Mustafa of Gujarat to stay in the house of Abdu's Samad. The holy man was in fragile condition, and died soon afterwards on his return to Gujarat: 'This event took place in the year 938 AH [AD 1575–6]'. See Sir Wolseley Haig & Brahmadeva Prasad Ambashthya, *Muntakhabu-t-Tawarikh by 'Abdu-l-Qadir ibn-i-Muluk Shah known as al-Badaoni* (reprint edition), Delhi, 1986, p. 85.

8. Shaikh Salim Chishti's tomb is inscribed with the completion date of 1580–81. See Asher 1992 (n. 4), p. 56.

9. The detailed account of Father Monserrate has provided crucial information for identifying the surviving monuments: see latterly S. Ali Nadeem Rezavi, 'Revisiting Fatehpur Sikri. An interpretation of certain buildings', in *Akbar and his India*, ed. Irfan Habib, Delhi, 1997, pp. 173–87, including references to all the monographs on the city.

10. See Asher 1992 (n. 4), p. 52, referring to Father Monserrate's *Commentary*.

11. Gauvin Alexander Bailey, *Art on the Jesuit Missions in Asia and Latin America 1542–1773*, University of Toronto Press, Toronto, 1999, p. 116.

12. Edmund W. Smith, *The Moghul Architecture of Fathpur-Sikri*, part III, Allahabad, vols I–IV, 1894–8, *passim*, for details of plain tiles and painted decoration of various kinds. Persian couplets are reproduced in vol. I, pls V–VI, and translated p. 3; paintings of men in boats relating to the *Hamza Nama* are to be seen in vol. I, pls XII–XIII, described in detail pp. 4–5; other pictorial decoration is illustrated in vol. I, pl. XI (a, b and c) and described pp. 5–6.

13. Bailey 1999 (n. 11), p. 121.

14. *Ibid*, pp. 114–30.

15. For a comprehensive survey of Mughal carpet production, see Daniel Walker, *Flowers Underfoot: Indian Carpets of the Mughal Era* (exhib. cat., Metropolitan Museum of Art, New York), 1997–8, New York, 1997. For weavers see Abu'l Fazl 1978 (n. 5), vol. II, p. 191.

16. Abu'l Fazl 1978 (n. 5), vol. II, p. 353. The first monograph on this subject was John Irwin's *The Kashmir Shawl*, London, 1969. Since then Frank Ames has written the more comprehensive *The Kashmir Shawl: A Study in Indo-French Influences* (3rd revised edition), 1997.

17. Abu'l Fazl 1978 (n. 5), vol. II, p. 136, for a reference to the production

of Gangajal ('Ganges water') meaning 'muslin'; for Golconda painted cottons, the definitive study is still John Irwin, 'Golconda cotton paintings of the early seventeenth century', in *Lalit Kala*, no. 5 (April 1959), pp. 11–48.

18. Abu'l Fazl 1978 (n. 5), vol. II, p. 207; see also pp. 213 and 217.

19. *Ibid.*, p. 247.

20. The fire destroyed much of the store for tents and their furnishings. Arif Qandahari's contemporary reference quoted in Michael Brand & Glenn D. Lowry, *Akbar's India: Art from the Mughal City of Victory* (exhib. cat., The Asia Society Galleries, New York, 1985–6), New York, 1985, p. 114, mentions the loss of European velvets and cloth.

21. See Richard Ettinghausen, *Paintings of the Sultans and Emperors of India in American Collections*, Delhi, 1961, pl. 13. The author notes the presence in an allegorical picture of Jahangir and Shah 'Abbas of a gilt bronze Diana riding on a stag of a kind made in Augsburg in the late 16th and early 17th centuries (also an Italian ewer and square table, a Venetian wine glass, and a Chinese cup).

22. A comprehensive study of base metalwork from the Mughal period remains to be written. For a very fine metal vessel of purely Hindustani form with Safavid-style decoration, see A.S. Melikian-Chirvani, *Islamic Metalwork from the Iranian World*, London, 1982, cat. 164, pp. 348–50; other Mughal-period metalwares are cats 158, 165, 166, 167, and 167 a and b. For preliminary surveys see the same author's 'Islamic metalwork as a source on cultural history' in *Arts & the Islamic World*, vol. 1, no. 1, Winter 1982/3, The Islamic Art Foundation, London, pp. 36–44, 14 figs, and 'The Iranian style in North Hindustan Metalwork' in *Confluence of Cultures: French Contributions to Indo-Persian Studies*, ed. Françoise 'Nalini' Delvoye, New Delhi, 1994, pp. 54–81 inc. 22 pls.

23. Abu'l Fazl, *The Ain-i Akbari*, trans. H. Blochmann and ed. D.C. Phillott, reprint, New Delhi 1977, vol. I, pp. 162–70. For the organization of the news department, see *ibid.* pp. 268–9. See also Abu'l Fazl 1989 (n. 2), pp. 372–3.

24. Abu'l Fazl 1977 (n. 23), vol. I, pp. 292–320.

25. Akbar's enjoyment of music is noted when Tansen arrived at court in 1563. The musician remained in royal service until his death in 1589 (Abu'l Fazl 1989 [n. 2], vol. II, pp. 279–80, and vol. III, p. 816). His portrait is illustrated in Stuart Cary Welch, *India: Art and Culture 1300–1900* (exhib. cat., Metropolitan Museum of Art, New York), New York, 1985, pl. 106, p. 172.

26. Abu'l Fazl 1977 (n. 23), vol. I, p. 110.

27. For a survey of the role of Fathpur in book production, the location of the various parts of the royal library and a survey of illustrated manuscripts known to have been produced there, see Brand & Lowry 1985 (n. 20), chs III and IV, pp. 57–105.

28. Abu'l Fazl 1977 (n. 23), vol. I, pp. 276–277.

29. Shahjahan modified the ceremony in his first regnal year (see W.E. Begley & Z.A. Desai, *The Shah Jahan Nama of 'Inayat Khan: An Abridged History of the Mughal Emperor Shah Jahan, Compiled by his Royal Librarian*, Delhi, 1990, p. 28). The event was occasionally illustrated: Jahangir is shown weighing his son, Khurram, in a painting now in the British Museum (reproduced, for example, in Michael Rogers, *Mughal Miniatures*, London, 1993, cover and fig. 58, p. 92), and the adult Khurram (Shahjahan) is shown in an illustration to the *Padshah Nama* now in the Royal Library at Windsor Castle (reproduced in Milo Cleveland Beach, *King of the World: The Padshahnama, an Imperial Mughal Manuscript from the Royal Library, Windsor Castle* (exhib. cat., Arthur M. Sackler Gallery in conjunction with the Royal Library, Windsor), London,

1997, cats 12–13, illus. pp. 44–5. For Aurangzeb's abolition of the ceremony, see *Maasir-i-'Alamgiri. A history of the emperor Aurangzib-'Alamgir (reign 1658–1707 A.D) of Saqi Must'ad Khan*, translation by Sir Jadu-Nath Sarkar, Lahore, 1981, p. 6.

30. See Abu'l Fazl 1978 (n. 5), vol. II, pp. 29–30.

31. Abu'l Fazl 1977 (n. 23), vol. I, pp. 286–7.

32. See *The History and Culture of the Indian People: The Mughul Empire*, ed. R.C. Majumdar, Bombay, 1974, pp. 83–6.

33. Abu'l Fazl 1977 (n. 23), vol. I , pp. 12–16.

34. For the contents of the treasury, see the account of William Hawkins, who lived at Agra between 1609 and 1611, in *Early Travels in India 1583–1619*, ed. William Foster, New Delhi, 1985, pp. 101–3; for the contents of the library, see Bailey 1999 (n. 11), pp. 116–17.

35. *Ibid.*, p. 14.

36. Brand & Lowry 1985 (n. 6), p. 2, and pp. 3–4 for subsequent royal sojourns; see Begley & Desai 1990 (n. 29), p. 28, for the Fathpur birthday weighing.

37. Abu'l Fazl 1977 (n. 23), vol. I, pp. 47–50.

38. Du Jarric 1926 (n.3), p.67.

39. See Ilay Cooper, 'Sikhs, saints and shadows of angels: Some Mughal Murals in buildings along the north wall of Lahore Fort', in *South Asian Studies*, vol. 9 (1993), pp. 11–28; Pope Gregory is illustrated in colour on plate 11, between pp. 10 and 11.

40. Bailey 1999 (n. 11), p. 123.

41. Frederike Weis, 'The impact of Nadal's *Evangelicae Historiae Imagines* on Three Illustrations of the Akbarnama in the Victoria and Albert Museum', in *Indo-Asiatische Zeitschrift*, 2002–3 (in press). For the dating of the V&A illustrations see Stronge, *Painting for the Mughal Emperor: The Art of the Book 1560–1660*, London, 2002, pp. 42–5.

42. Alexander Rogers & Henry Beveridge, *The Tuzuk-i-Jahangiri or Memoirs of Jahangir*, New Delhi, 1978, vol. I, p. 215, refers to the arrival of these birds and animals at court; Mansur's painting is illustrated in Stronge 2002 (n. 41), pl. 100, p. 135.

43. One of the earliest representations of Europeans in Mughal painting is in Akbar's *Hamza Nama* manuscript. No colophon has been found among the small proportion of surviving folios from the multiple volumes of this first major project of the new Mughal studio, and opinions concerning its date have varied considerably. It is known to have taken fifteen years to complete and most scholars have agreed with the dates, *c.*1562–77, put forward by Pramod Chandra (Pramod Chandra, *The Tuti-nama of the Cleveland Museum of Art and the Origins of Mughal Painting*, Graz, 1976, p. 67). John Seyller has recently given an inception date of 1557–8 (John Seyller with contributions from Wheeler M. Thackston, Ebba Koch, Antoinette Owen & Rainald Franz, *The Adventures of Hamza* [exhib. cat., Arthur M. Sackler Gallery of Art and Freer Gallery of Art], Washington, 2002, pp. 37–41), proposing that the illustration depicting European soldiers came from volume 6, which he dates to 1564–5 (*ibid.*, p. 39; the heavily damaged painting now in the V&A is illustrated in black and white on p. 260, cat. R31, p. 261; colour illustration in the facsimile *Hamza-Nama*, Graz, 1982, vol. LII/2, V&A 26). This proposal is based on the contentious identification of numbers found on another page from the same volume as a date, and would mean contact between the Mughal court and Europeans was made considerably before the Gujarat campaign. Given Akbar's reaction to his first encounter with Europeans, and the fact that the figures wear black hats, white ruffs and slashed doublets, which seem plausibly to have come from direct observation rather than from copying printed or painted images, this early dating seems unlikely.

44. See Bill Frank, 'A European view of life in 16th-Century Goa. The images of Jan Huygen van Linschoten', in *India and Portugal: Cultural Interactions*, ed. José Pereira & Pratapaditya Pal, Bombay, 2001, p. 48 and pls 1, pp. 50–51, and 5, p. 57.

45. Father Botelho was born in Portugal in 1600 and was nominated Visitor and Superior and Rector of the College at Agra where he worked from 1648 to 1654 before being made Provincial of India at Goa in 1667 where he died (Sir Edward Maclagan, *The Jesuits and the Great Mogul*, London, 1932, p. 109). A Portuguese manuscript account of his Indian career in Portuguese with abbreviated Latin summary is in the British Library, Marsden Mss Add. 9855. The reference to the Tagus is on f. 5 recto (Latin) and to roses and medicinal herbs on f. 22 recto (Portuguese).

46. See, for example, the painting of c.1530 by the great Iranian artist Behzad copied first by Abdu's Samad during Akbar's reign, and later by the Hindu artist Nanha in 1608 for Jahangir. See Ebadollah Bahari, *Bihzad. Master of Persian painting*, London 1996, pp. 215–16 for Behzad's original and references to its copies; Behzad's work and Nanha's copy are illustrated in colour in Mohammad-Hasan Semsar (trs. Karim Emami), *Golestan Palace Library. A portfolio of miniature paintings and calligraphy*, Tehran, 2000, pls. 187–188.

47. Tripti Verma, *Karkhanas under the Mughals. From Akbar to Aurangzeb: A Study in Economic Development*, Delhi, 1994, p. 99, for a reference to Muhammad Suleh Beg, the Iranian in the household of Abdur Rahim, Akbar's leading noble, whose guns were said to be superior to those of Europe.

48. See Simon Digby, 'The Mother-of-Pearl Overlaid Furniture of Gujarat: The Holdings of the Victoria and Albert Museum', in *Facets of Indian art*, ed. Robert Skelton *et al.*, London, 1985, pp. 213–22, for the first monograph on the industry; see also José Jordão Felgueiras, 'A family of precious Gujurati objects', in *A herança de Rauluchantim/The Heritage of Rauluchantim* (exhib. cat., Lisbon, Museu de São Roque), ed. Nuno Vassallo e Silva, Lisbon 1996, pp. 128–55. Sigrid Sangel provides a fascinating insight into the markets, Mughal and European, for luxury inlaid game boards from Gujarat in the late 16th century in *Exotica: The Portuguese Discoveries and the Renaissance Kunstkammer* (exhib. cat., Lisbon, Calouste Gulbenkian Museum), ed. Helmut Trnek & Nuno Vassallo e Silva, Lisbon, 2001, cat. 21, pp. 114–16.

49. For Chinese porcelain at the Mughal court, see Brand & Lowry 1985 (n. 6), pp. 115–16; for porcelain in Goa, see for example *Voyage de Pyrard de Laval aux Indes orientales (1601–1611)*, ed. Xavier de Castro, Paris, 1998, vol. II, pp. 610 and 688.

50. Abu'l Fazl 1978 (n. 5), vol. II, pp. 164 and 192.

51. India has always produced glass of poor quality, though its applied decoration can be very refined (see Moreshwar G. Dikshit, *History of Indian Glass*, Bombay, 1969, for a flawed survey of the industry, which should be read in conjuction with Simon Digby's 'A corpus of "Mughal" glass', in *Bulletin of the School of Oriental and African Studies*, London, 1973, vol. XXXVI, part 1 (1973), pp. 80–96. See also Stephen Markel, 'Western imports and the nature of later Indian glassware', in *Asian Art* (Fall 1993), pp. 34–59. Glass flasks of Iranian form are visible in many paintings of the Akbar period (a point made by Digby, p. 84): see for example, Stronge 2002 (n. 41), pl. 23, p. 38, from the *Akbar Nama* of c.1590–95, and pl. 57, p. 88, from a *Babur Nama* of about the same date.

52. Archibald Constable, *Travels in the Mogul empire AD 1656–1668 by François Bernier*, London, 1891, pp. 228–9 and 254–6.

53. The earliest reference to enamelling in Mughal India seems to be in Abu'l Fazl's *A'in-i-Akbari*, where he lists the enameller among the 'workers

in decorative art' (Abu'l Fazl 1978 [n. 5], vol. III, p. 346). There is no clear evidence for the technique having been introduced from Europe, but craftsmen were included in the first embassy from the Mughal court to Goa, and had instructions to copy any new techniques they found (see Abu'l Fazl 1989, vol. III, p. 207). By Shahjahan's reign enamelling is frequently mentioned on artefacts made for the court, notably in the work commissioned by the emperor from Sa'ida-ye Gilani, and its superb quality may be seen in surviving examples, notably those in the al-Sabah Collection, Kuwait National Museum, published in Manuel Keene with Salam Kaoukji, *Treasury of the World: Jewelled Arts of India in the Age of the Mughals* (exhib. cat., Dar al-Athar al-Islamiyyah, Kuwait National Museum, 2001–2), London, 2001, *passim.*

54. A.S. Melikian-Chirvani, 'Sa'ida-ye Gilani and the Iranian Style Jades of Hindustan', *Bulletin of the Asia Institute*, Bloomfield Hills, New Series/Volume 13, 1999, pp. 83–140.

55. *Ibid.*, pp. 109–10, for the arguments in favour of Sa'ida having made the handle, with illustrations of the inscription and the careful positioning of the dragon's head in figs 23 and 24 on the same pages.

56. Augustin's four extant letters were first published by Sir E.D. Maclagan: 'Four letters by Austin of Bordeaux', in *Journal of the Punjab University Historical Society*, vol. IV, no. 1 (1916), pp. 3–17. His travels with von Poser were first highlighted by William Irvine, 'Austin of Bordeaux', in *Journal of the Royal Asiatic Society* (1910), pp. 1343–5; see also H. Beveridge, 'Von Poser's Diary in Persia and India', in *The Imperial and Asiatic Quarterly Review*, third series, vol. XXIX, no. 57 (January 1910), pp. 96–100.

57. I am greatly indebted to Nuno Vassallo e Silva for showing me this important passage from Jacques de Coutre (*Andanzas asiàticas*, ed. Eddy Stols, B. Teensma & J. Werverckmoes, Madrid, 1991, pp. 306–7) and for providing an English translation.

58. Begley & Desai 1990 (n. 29), p. 22.

59. *Ibid.*, pp. 146–7.

60. Revd H. Hosten, 'European art at the Moghul court', in *The Journal of the United Provinces Historical Society*, vol. III (May 1922), part I, pp. 123–4. The description of Shahjahan's departure begins on f. 8v (Latin) and f. 28r (Portuguese). Hosten translates the references to Mendes found on f. 10r (Latin), f. 33v (Portuguese).

61. Begley & Desai 1990 (n. 29), p. 9.

62. Sarkar 1981 (n. 29), pp. 49–50.

63. *Ibid*, p. 100.

64. *Ibid.* pp. 313 and 318.

65. *Ibid.* p. 322.

66. See Tripti Verma, *Karkhanas under the Mughals. From Akbar to Aurangzeb. A study in economic development*, Delhi, 1994, chapter 2 (State Karkhanas during the Mughal Period).

67. Sanjay Subrahmanyam, *The Portuguese Empire in Asia 1500–1700: A Political and Economic History*, London/New York, 1993, p. 188.

68. See Bailey 1999 (n. 11), p. 142.

Between Religions: Christianity in a Muslim Empire (pp. 148–61)

1. *See my Art on the Jesuit Missions in Asia and Latin America, 1542–1773*, Toronto/Buffalo, 1999, pp. 112–43; and *The Jesuits and the Grand Mogul: Renaissance Art at the Imperial Court of India, 1580–1630*, Washington, 1998. See also my 'The Catholic Shrines of Agra' in *Arts of Asia* (July–August 1993), pp. 131–7; 'A Portuguese doctor at the Maharaja

of Jaipur's court' in *South Asian Studies*, 11 (Summer 1995), pp. 51–62; 'The Lahore *Mirat al-Quds* and the impact of Jesuit theater on Mughal painting' in *South Asian Studies*, 13 (1997), pp. 95–108; 'The Indian conquest of Catholic art: The Mughals, the Jesuits, and imperial mural painting' in *Art Journal* (Spring 1998), pp. 24–30; 'The truth-showing mirror: Jesuit Catechism and the arts in Mughal India' in *The Jesuits: Cultures, Sciences, and the Arts, 1540–1773*, ed. John O'Malley, Gauvin Alexander Bailey, T. Frank Kennedy & Steven J. Harris, Toronto, 1999, pp. 380–401.

2. This anonymous painter is only mentioned in one published letter (Sir Edward Maclagan, 'Jesuit missions to the Emperor Akbar', in *Journal of the Asiatic Society of Bengal*, 65 [1896], p. 67) and in the history of du Jarric (Pierre du Jarric, *Akbar and the Jesuits*, trans. C. H. Payne, London, 1926, p. 67). I have found two additional letters that mention him (Rome, ARSI, Goa 14, f. 288r and f. 30v).

3. For example, John Correia-Afonso, *Letters from the Mughal Court*, Bombay, 1980, pp. 33–4; Antonio Monserrate, *The Commentary of Father Monserrate, S.J.*, trans. J. S. Hoyland, London, 1922, pp. 59–60.

4. Sir Edward Maclagan, *The Jesuits and the Grand Mogul*, London, 1932, p. 228; Monserrate 1922 (n. 3), p. 176. This tradition of displaying the picture on the feast of the Assumption was carried on in the years after the first mission left, when there were no longer any priests at the court.

5. See Bailey 1999 (n. 1a), pp. 137–41.

6. See Bailey 1999 (n. 1g). Original manuscript copies of this Catholic literature include Abd al-Sattar b. Qasim Lahori and Jerome Xavier, *Mirat al-Quds* (Lahore Museum, M-645/MSS-46), and *Ayine-ye Haqq Numa* (London, BL, Harley 5478). For a thorough study of the theological content of these treatises, see Arnulf Camps, *Jerome Xavier S.J. and the Muslims of the Mogul Empire*, Schoeneck-Beckenried, 1957.

7. Christopher Dawson, *Mission to Asia*, Toronto, 1980, pp. xiii–xiv.

8. J.J. Saunders, *The History of the Mongol Conquest*, London, 1971, p. 92; Janet Abu Lughod, *Before European Hegemony*, Oxford, 1989, p. 162; Dawson 1980 (n. 7), xv.

9. Dawson 1980 (n. 7), xix, pp. 162–80. The khans had also captured Western European artisans, for example the Parisian goldsmith family of Buchier and William of Paris, a furniture maker who carved a statue of the Virgin for the friars 'sculptured after the French fashion'.

10. A. van der Wyngaert, *Sinica Franciscana I*, Florence, 1929, pp. 289–97; Dawson 1980 (n. 7), pp. 188–94.

11. S.A.A. Rizvi, *The Wonder that Was India*, London, 1987, pp. 191–3.

12. Shaikh Nur al-Haqq, *Zubdat al-Tavarikh* (London, BL, MS Ethé 290), f. 157a. The translation from the Persian is my own.

13. Abd al-Sattar Ibn Qasim Lahori, *Thamrat al-Falasafah* (London, BL, Or. 5893), ff. 4–5. The translation from the Persian is my own.

14. Monserrate 1922 (n. 3), p. 37.

15. *Ibid.*, p. 127.

16. *Ibid.*, p. 138.

17. Annual letter of Jerome Xavier, Agra, 24 September, 1608 (London, BL, Add. MSS 9854, f. 66v); published in *Documentação ultramarina portuguesa*, Lisbon, 1963, vol. III, p. 116.

18. London, BL, Add. MSS 9854, f. 68r, published in *Documentação* 1963 (n. 17), vol. III, p. 119.

19. *Ibid.*, f. 67r, published in *Documentação* 1963 (n. 17), vol. III, p. 117.

20. *Ibid.*

21. *Ibid.*, f. 72 r–v, published in *Documentação* 1963 (n. 17), vol. III, pp. 126–7.

22. *Ayine-ye Haqq Numa* (London, BL, Harley 5478), f. 279r. The translation from the Persian is my own.

23. *Ibid.*, f. 280r. The translation from the Persian is my own.

24. As Milo Beach has indicated in the only article to deal with this enigmatic artist, Kesu Khurd held a secondary position within Akbar's atelier, since he was most often assigned to paint illustrations for manuscripts designed by more prominent artists. See Milo Cleveland Beach, 'The Mughal painter Kesu Das', in *Archives of Asian Art* 30 (1976–7), p. 46. See also Pratapaditya Pal, *Indian Painting*, Los Angeles, 1993, p. 237.

25. In 1573 a delegation from Portuguese Goa met with Akbar at the north-western port town of Surat and presented him with 'many of the curiosities and rarities of the skilled craftsmen of [Portugal]'. (Abu'l Fazl 'Allami, *Akbarnama*, trans. H. Beveridge, Calcutta, 1902–39, vol. III, pp. 37 and 207; J.F. Júdice Biker, *Colecção de tratados*, Lisbon, 1887, vol. XIV, pp. 25–6; du Jarric 1926 (n. 2), p. 219, note 12.) Akbar's appetite for curiosities was immediately whetted, and he responded by sending an embassy under Haji Habibullah to Goa in 1575, which returned two years later with lavish gifts, textiles, Portuguese costumes and musical instruments – as well as European musicians to play them – one of which was a fancy pipe organ whose panels were painted inside and out with devotional images of Jesus and the saints ('Allami, *Akbarnama* III, pp. 207 and 322; Al-Badaoni, *Muntakhab ut-Tawarikh* II, translation and ed. George S.A. Ranking, Calcutta, 1898, p. 299).

26. This was first suggested by Milo Beach, *The Grand Mogul*, Williamstown, 1978, p. 56.

27. For example, Beach 1976–7 (n. 24), pp. 38–9; Amina Okada, *Indian Miniatures of the Mughal Court*, New York, 1992, p. 97. Michelangelo's work was published in a 1515 engraving by Agostino Musi (Veneziano) which identified the figure as *Diogenes*, and another version was made in 1564 by Mario Cartaro as *St Jerome* (Alida Moltedo, *La Sistina reprodotta*, Rome, 1991, fig. 3).

28. Glenn Lowry, 'Manohar', in Beach 1978 (n. 26), pp. 130–31; Milo Cleveland Beach, The Imperial Image, Washington, 1980, p. 112; Terence McInerney, 'Manohar', in *Master Artists of the Imperial Mughal Courts*, ed. Pratapaditya Pal, Bombay, 1991, p. 54; Okada 1992 (n. 27), p. 136.

29. See Bailey 1997 (n. 1), pp. 31–44.

30. Amina Okada, *Miniatures de l'Inde impériale* (exhib. cat.), Paris, 1989, cat. 58; Sven Gahlin, *Indian Miniatures from the Collection of the Fondation Custodia*, Paris, 1991, p. 16.

31. Beach 1976–7 (n. 27), p. 46.

32. Many sculptures were free-standing and nearly life-sized. For example, two European visitors to the Perimahal Palace in Lahore in the early eighteenth century saw a group of alabaster or marble statues of Jesus, Mary, other saints and angels, which had been erected there in the previous century (J.J. Ketelaar, *Journaal*, Gravenhage, 1937, p. 155; Ippolito Desideri, *Viaggi*, ed. Luciano Petech, Rome, 1954, pp. 158–9). A single statue of this type survives at the Old Cathedral at Agra, which I have published elsewhere (Bailey 1993 [n. 1], pp. 133, 135). It was found during excavations at the Red Fort, Agra, in the mid-nineteenth century.

33. Michael Brand & Glenn D. Lowry, *Akbar's India: Art from the Mughal City of Victory*, New York, 1986, p. 97, cat. 60. The engraved model is published in Adam von Bartsch, *The Illustrated Bartsch*, ed. Walter L. Strauss, 20 I (9), no. 104 (365), New York, 1978– . The identification is my own.

34. Salim's obsession with copying not only the Christian art brought by the Jesuits but also his father's collection suggests that he was already anticipating his estrangement from Akbar and the foundation of his own

studio in Allahabad in 1599.

35. An example in the British Museum of an engraving that is only half painted by a Mughal hand shows the way in which these were executed (Michael Rogers, *Mughal Miniatures*, London, 1993, fig. 71).

36. J.V.S. Wilkinson and Basil Gray, 'Indian paintings in a Persian museum', in *Burlington Magazine*, 66 (1935), p. 174; Yedda Godard, 'Un album des princes timourides de l'Inde', in Athar-e Iran, II, 2 (1937), fig. 110; Asok Kumar Das, *Mughal Painting during Jahangir's Time*, Calcutta, 1978, p. 46; Jean Soustiel & David Soustiel, *Miniatures orientales de l'Inde*, Paris, 1986, p. 15.

37. Das 1978 (n. 36), p. 45, describes these differences. See also Yedda Godard, 'Les marges du Murakka' Gulshan', in *Athar-e Iran*, vol. I (1936), pp. 11–33; and Hermann Goetz, 'The early Muraqqas of the Mughal emperor Jahangir', in *East-West*, 8 (1957), pp. 157–85. Most of the European figures have already been identified by Goetz, and by Nancy Graves Cabot (Milo C. Beach, 'The Gulshan Album and its European Sources', in *Museum of Fine Arts, Boston, Bulletin*, 63 [1965], pp. 63–91). The published pages include: Godard 1936, fig. 1; Goetz 1957, pl. X; Aboulala Soudavar, *Art of the Persian Courts*, New York, 1992, cats 28a–d; Ernst Kühnel & Hermann Goetz, *Indian Book Painting from Jahangir's Album in the State Library*, Berlin, London, 1926, f. 1a, B.18, pl. 39; Milo C. Beach, *The Imperial Image*, Washington, 1981, pp. 157 and 163; Beach 1978 (n. 26), fig. 5, p. 76.

38. Beach is the only source to mention signed marginalia by Basawan, which he noted on f. 84b of the Gulshan Album in the Golestan Library, Tehran (Beach 1978 [n. 26], p. 183, note 6).

39. Beach 1965 (n. 37), p. 73.

40. See my 'The end of the "Catholic Era" in Mughal painting: Jahangir's dream pictures, English painting, and the Renaissance frontispiece', in *Marg*, 53, 2 (December 2001), pp. 46–59.

PRINCE SALIM AND CHRISTIAN ART (PP. 162–9)

1. E.D. Maclagan, 'Jesuit Missions to the Emperor Akbar', *Journal of the Asiatic Society of Bengal*, 1896, pp. 66–7.

2. Gauvin A. Bailey, *Art on the Jesuit Missions in Asia and Latin America 1542–1773*, Toronto, 2000, p. 116; E.D. Maclagan, 'Jesuit missions to the emperor Akbar', in *Journal of the Asiatic Society of Bengal* (1896), p. 50.

3. Andrew Topsfield, *Indian Paintings from Oxford Collections*, Oxford, 1994, pp. 22–3. The full inscription reads: [above] *Shah Salim*, [below] *mashqahu Abu'l Hasan ibn Riza murid dar sinni sizdah salagi sakhta ba tarikh yazdahum shahr-I rabi'al akhir sanna 1009 ruz-I jumi surat itimam raft*. I am grateful to Dr Andrew Topsfield for supplying me with the full transcript of the inscription.

4. See Asok Kumar Das, *Mughal Painting during Jahangir's Time*, Calcutta, 1978, p. 233, quoting original and secondary sources.

5. J. Correia-Afonso, *Letters from the Mughal Court*, Bombay, 1980, pp. 30–31, 33.

6. Bailey 2000 (n. 2), pp. 124 and 233, notes 96, 97 quoting ARSI *Goa*, vol. 14, f. 288, and *Goa*, vol. 461, f. 30v; Maclagan 1896 (n. 2), p. 67. Xavier describes the artist's dilemma in a 1596 letter, 'The Portuguese painter who came with us had no time for anything except painting images for [Salim] of Christ Our Lord, and of Our Lady. He makes him paint the ones his father owns.'

7. Gauvin A. Bailey, *The Jesuits and the Grand Mogul: Renaissance Art at the Imperial Court of India 1580–1630*, Washington D.C., 1998, pp. 27–30, figs 19–22 and note 32 on p. 44. First suggested by Milo Beach

while publishing the Harvard folio: Milo C Beach, *The Grand Mogul: Imperial Painting in India 1600–1660*, Williamstown, Mass. 1978, p. 56.

8. Beach 1978 (n. 7), nos. 10 and 10A. For the Beatty painting, see Linda Y. Leach, *Mughal and other Indian paintings from the Chester Beatty Library*, London, 1995, vol. I, pp. 135–37, no. 1.233.

9. Milo C. Beach, 'The Gulshan Album and its European sources', in *Bulletin of the Museum of Fine Arts, Boston*, vol. LXVIII (1965), p. 73, figs 3, 3a, 1a.

10. *Ibid.*, fig. 1.

11. *Ibid.*, fig. 4.

12. J.V.S. Wilkinson & B. Gray, 'Indian paintings in a Persian museum', in *The Burlington Magazine* (April 1935), p. 174; Beach 1965 (n. 9), figs 4, 4a.

13. Wilkinson & Gray 1935 (n. 12), p. 174, pl. II E.

14. See note 3. Incidentally, another page of the Gulshan Album containing marginalia details including European figures was completed in the same year and at the same place by Abu'l Hasan's father Aqa Reza: Yedda Godard, 'Les marges du Murakka'Gulshan', in *Athar-e Iran*, vol. I (1936), fig. 1.

15. E. Kuhnel & H. Goetz, *Indian Book Painting from Jahangir's Album in the State Library in Berlin*, London, 1926, pl. 30.

16. *Intercultural Encounter in Mughal Miniatures (Mughal-Christian Miniatures)*, ed. Khalid Anis Ansari, Lahore, 1995, back cover; Bailey 2000 (n. 2), fig. 77.

17. Beach 1965 (n. 9), fig. 2, second figure from top of right-hand side.

18. Wilkinson & Gray 1935 (n. 12), pl. I B; Beach 1965 (n. 9), p. 73, fig. 5. Among other figures in the folio there is a tiny, delightfully coloured copy of Dürer's *Friedrich the Wise, Elector of Saxony* (Bartsch no. 104).

19. Beach 1978 (n. 7), pp. 57, 59, no. 11; Bailey 1998 (n. 7), fig. 28.

20. Susan Stronge, *Painting from the Mughal Emperor: The Art of the Book 1560–1660*, New Delhi, 2002, pl. 85.

21. Sven Gahlin, *The Courts of India: Indian Miniatures from the Collection of the Fondation Custodia, Paris*, 1991, pl. 5, no. 6.

VISIONS OF THE WEST IN MUGHAL ART (PP. 170–89)

1. *A Journal of the First Voyage of Vasco da Gama 1497–1499*, ed. E.G. Ravenstein, reprint New Delhi-Madras, 1995, p. 52.

2. Frederick Charles Danvers, *The Portuguese in India*, London, 1966, vol. I, p. 44.

3. For example, see: Jorge Manuel Flores, 'A "Gift from a Divine Hand" – Portuguese Asia and the treasures of Ceylon', in Exotica: *The Portuguese Discoveries and the Renaissance Kunstkammer* (exhib. cat., Lisbon, Calouste Gulbenkian Museum), Lisbon, 2001, pp. 91–2.

4. Khwandamir, *Qanun-i-Humayuni*, trans. with explanatory notes Baini Prashad, Calcutta, 1940, p. 20.

5. Gulbadan Begam, *The History of Humayun (Humayun-nama)*, trans. Annette S. Beveridge, Delhi, n.d., p. 113.

6. Khwandamir 1940 (n. 4), p. 46.

7. *Ibid.*, p. 49.

8. Abu'l Fazl, *Akbarnama*, trans. H. Beveridge, Delhi, 1972–3, vol. I, p. 289.

9. *Ibid.*, p. 323.

10. On this subject, see Muzaffar Alam & Sanjay Subrahmanyam, 'Letters from a Sinking Sultan', in *Aquém e além da Taprobana. Estudos luso-orientais à memória de Jean Aubin e Denys Lombard*, ed. Luís Filipe Thomaz, Lisbon, 2002, pp. 239–69.

11. The dating of these manuscripts has been the subject of much controversy. For the most recent discussion (and a proposal that the fourteen-year project was begun in 1557–58), see John Seyller, *The Adventures of Hamza*, Washington, 2002, pp. 37–41.

12. It also reveals the logical and continuing association of the Portuguese in India with seafaring. For other examples, see BL Or 12988/66a, and fig. 3.

13. Ziya'u'd-din Nakshabi, *Tales of a Parrot*, trans. and ed. Muhammad A. Simsar, Graz, 1978, p. 204.

14. The *Hamza Nama* illustration, by contrast, shows accurately delineated European soldiers, but they too are placed at an event because of the artist's wish to include them and not because they are part of the narrative. The importance of this scene was recently recognized by Susan Stronge (see Susan Stronge, *Painting for the Mughal Emperor: The Art of the Book 1560–1660*, London, 2002, pp. 18–19 and pl. 5).

15. *The Baburnama: Memoirs of Babur, Prince and Emperor*, translated, edited and annotated by Wheeler M. Thackston, Washington/New York/Oxford, 1996.

16. See, for example, the cloth in the background archways in David Coll. 6/1981, Beatty Ms. 11A/11, and Bodleian Or.a.1/41v. In *Khorshid's Travels to Mecca* the trees in the background – seemingly executed with free and quick brushstrokes rather than by the meticulous filling in of carefully drawn and decoratively arranged vegetal patterns, as in early Indian and Islamic tradition – correspond to the visual effect of vegetation in European tapestry; and it may be textiles rather than prints or paintings that introduced this technique to Mughal painters. Documented evidence of tapestries at the Mughal court at an early date is absent, although they were known by the early 17th century. For comparative examples of vegetation types, see: Thomas P. Campbell, *Tapestry in the Renaissance: Art and Magnificence*, New Haven and London, 2002 (especially nos 30–4).

17. Abu'l Fazl 1972–3 (n. 8), vol. iii, p. 13.

18. *Ibid.*, p. 37.

19. *Ibid.*, p. 207.

20. 'Abdu-l-Qadir ibn-i-Muluk Shah al Badaoni, *Muntakhabu-t-Tawarikh*, trans. and ed. W.H. Lowe, Patna, 1973, vol. II, p. 299.

21. Abu'l Fazl 'Allami, *A'in-i-Akbari*, trans. H. Blochmann, Calcutta, 1927, vol. I, pp. 113–14.

22. The identity of the second man has been debated. For a summary of the arguments, see Linda York Leach, *Mughal and other Indian Paintings from the Chester Beatty Library*, London, 1995, pp. 291–2.

23. Abu'l Fazl 1927 (n. 21), vol. I, p. 115.

24. Earliest among these is a depiction of a Portuguese sailor with a woman (Sotheby's sale, 12 December 1972, lot 21). While generalized depictions of 'loving couples' abounded in Indian art, usually in a symbolic context, such a direct study of European behaviour is unprecedented and would have been intriguing to a society where the free, public association of men and women was unknown. As in the *Tuti Nama* page, the subject must have been based on figures the painter actually saw.

25. For further discussion, see Stronge 2002 (n. 14), pp. 138–9.

26. *The Jahangirnama – Memoirs of Jahangir, Emperor of India*, translated, edited and annotated by Wheeler M. Thackston, Washington/New York/Oxford, 1999, p. 133. The illustrated page of this episode is in the Raza Library, Rampur, and is unpublished.

27. See Stronge 2002 (n. 14), pl. 99.

28. See also Milo Cleveland Beach, *The Grand Mogul: Imperial Painting in India 1600–1660*, Williamstown, Mass., 1978, pp. 61–3. Depictions of Jesuit priests abound in Mughal painting of this period and will be separately discussed here by Amina Okada.

29. For further discussion of the event and a translation of the relevant text, see Milo Cleveland Beach, Ebba Koch & Wheeler Thackston, *King of the World: The Padshahnama, an Imperial Mughal Manuscript from the Royal Library, Windsor Castle*, Washington, D.C., 1997, pl. 20.

30. Abu'l Fazl 1972–3 (n. 8), vol. ii, p. 372.

31. See Beach *et al.* 1997 (n. 29), no. 19, for textual references and further discussion.

32. Pierre du Jarric, *Akbar and the Jesuits: An Account of the Jesuit Missions to the Court of Akbar*, trans. C.H. Payne, London, 1926, p. 69. On this subject see the essay by Asok Das in this volume.

33. See Beach 1978 (n. 28), pp. 43–59, for a brief discussion and bibliography.

34. For the role of wall-paintings at Akbar's court, see Gauvin Bailey, *Art on the Jesuit Missions in Asia and Latin America 1542–1773*, Toronto, 1991, pp. 121–2.

35. Such details are frequently found in ceremonial scenes set during Jahangir's reign; see, for example, Beach 1997 (n. 29), pls 38–9.

36. *Jahangir and the Jesuits, from the Relations of Father Fernão Guerreiro*, S.J., trans. C. H. Payne, London, 1930, p. 65.

37. See Milo Cleveland Beach, 'The Mughal painter Abu'l Hasan and some English sources for his style', in *Journal of the Walters Art Gallery*, vol. 38, pp. 6–33.

38. His colleague Manohar, on the other hand, was strictly reproducing the effect of an engraving in his drawing of *Arithmetica* (St Petersburg, f. 33r), a literal replication of a print by Georg Pencz. For discussions by Gauvin Bailey of all these works, see The *St. Petersburg Muraqqa'*, Lugano/Milan, 1996, entries for pls 33 and 60–61.

39. For example, see Milo Cleveland Beach, *The Imperial Image: Paintings for the Mughal Court*, Washington, 1981, nos 17a and 31.

40. At least three identical versions by the same painter, Manohar, are included in Jahangir's great album project alone. They are unpublished.

41. The composition expands and adapts a particularly popular composition, *Joseph Telling his Dream to his Father*, an engraving by the German artist Georg Pencz in which a standing man leans on a staff before a seated figure. Here the staff has been omitted, but the hand placement has not been changed. For further discussion of the role of this print, see Milo Cleveland Beach, 'A European source for early Mughal painting', in *Oriental Art*, vol. 22, no. 2 (1976), pp. 180–88.

42. For further discussion, see Leach 1995 (n. 22), no. 1.235.

THE REPRESENTATION OF JESUIT MISSIONARIES IN MUGHAL PAINTING (PP. 190–99)

1. Michael Brand & Glenn D. Lowry, *Akbar's India: Art from the Mughal City of Victory* (exhib. cat., New York, The Asia Galleries), New York, 1985, p. 98.

2. Ashok Kumar Das, *Mughal Painting during Jahangir's Time*, Calcutta, 1978, p. 232.

3. Sir Edward Maclagan, *The Jesuits and the Great Mogul*, reprint, Gurgaon, 1990, p. 300.

4. *Ibid.*, p. 301.

5. Linda York Leach, *Mughal and other Indian Paintings from the Chester Beatty Library*, Dublin, 1995, I, pp. 291–2, no. 2.152.

6. *Ibid.*, p. 291, and T.W. Arnold & J.V.S. Wilkinson, *The Library of A.*

Chester Beatty: A Catalogue of the Indian Miniatures, Oxford, 1936, I, p. 11, no. 60.

7. Pierre Du Jarric, *Akbar and the Jesuits* (trans. C. H. Payne), London, 1926, p. 222, note 17.

8. Arnold & Wilkinson 1936 (n. 6), I, p. ii, no. 60, note 1.

9. David James, *Islamic Masterpieces of The Chester Beatty Library*, London, 1981, p. 37.

10. At the request of the Provincial Father in Goa, Father Monserrate was charged with writing the history of the mission to the court of the Emperor Akbar led by Rudolf Aquaviva. He was the author of *Relaçam do Equebar Rei dos Mogores* and the celebrated *Mongolicae Legationis Commentarius*, a work of considerable historical interest and an inestimable source of information about the first Jesuit mission to the court of Akbar (see Maclagan 1990 [n. 3], pp. 148–56).

11. Leach 1995 (n. 5), p. 292.

12. The Emperor Akbar had ordered Abu'l Fazl to teach Persian to the Jesuit missionaries and also to translate the Bible into Persian (see Maclagan 1990 [n. 3], pp. 33 and 213).

13. Leach 1995 (n. 5). p. 292.

14. Abu'l Fazl states in *A'in-i-Akbari*: 'His Majesty himself sat for his likeness, and also ordered the likenesses taken of all the grandees of the realm. An immense volume was thus formed: those that have passed away have received a new life, and those who are still alive have immortality promised them' (*A'in-i-Akbari*, trans. H. Blochmann, Calcutta, 1938–9, I, p. 115).

15. Gauvin Alexander Bailey, 'The Lahore Mirat Al Quds and the impact of Jesuit theatre on Mughal painting', in *South Asian Studies* 13, 1997, p. 37.

16. Maclagan 1990 (n. 3), p. 26.

17. The first known work signed by Manohar dates from 1582; it is unlikely that the portrait in the Musée Guimet, said to be of Father Monserrate, dates from the time the Jesuit missionary was at the Mughal court, where he arrived in 1580 and left in 1582 to return to Goa. It is very possible that the two similar portraits of Monserrate by Manohar and Nar Singh were both after a contemporary portrait that has now disappeared. Moreover, there exists a faithful copy of the *Jesuit Missionary* by Manohar, though reversed and slightly later (c.1620; see Christie's, London, 19–21 October 1993, lot 9). On the career and work of Manohar, see Milo Cleveland Beach, *The Great Mogul: Imperial Painting in India 1600–1660* (exhib. cat., Williamstown, Sterling and Francine Clark Institute), Williamstown, 1978, pp. 130–37; Terence McInerney, 'Manohar', in *Master Artists of the Imperial Mughal Court*, ed. P. Pal, Bombay, 1991, pp. 53–68; Amina Okada, *Le Grand Moghol et ses peintres, Miniaturistes de l'Inde aux XVIème et XVIIème siècles*, Paris, 1992, pp. 136–47.

18. See Beach 1978 (n. 17), pp. 61–3, no. 14; and Vishakha N. Desai, *Life at Court: Art for India's rulers, 16th–19th Centuries* (exhib. cat., Boston,

Museum of Fine Arts), Boston, 1985, pp. 12–14, no. 11.

19. For the date of this durbar and Father Corsi at the court in Agra, see Beach 1978 (n. 17), p. 63.

20. See A.A. Ivanova, T.V. Grek, O.F. Akimushkina & L.T. Gyuzabyana, *Albom Indiyskikh y Persidskikh Miniatyur XVI–XVIII*, Moscow, 1962, pl. 7; and Das 1978 (n. 2), p. 139, for the identification of Father Jerome Xavier.

21. See Maclagan 1990 (n. 3), p. 258 and pl. p. 84; and Das 1978 (n. 2), p. 151. It should be noted that Corsi, if it is he who is depicted here, has a hooked nose, a physiognomic detail that is not so pronounced in other portraits of the missionary.

22. Bailey 1997 (n. 15), p. 33.

23. *Ibid.*, pp. 35–6, fig. 5.

24. See Isabel Soler, 'La ultima immensidad', in *Cuadernos Hispano-americanos*, 620, February 2002, pp. 55–6: the miniature from the National Museum of New Delhi is reproduced at the end of the work with the caption 'Antoni de Montserrat; Miniatura mogol del siglo XVI'. Sanjay Subrahmanyam kindly drew my attention to this recent study devoted to Father Antonio Monserrate.

25. See Bailey 1997 (n. 15).

26. *Ibid.*, p. 35, where G.A. Bailey, drawing on accounts in letters from the Jesuit missionaries, recalls that the Portuguese, Italian and British mercenaries and merchants attended the processions and plays organized by the Jesuits.

27. Edwin Binney, 3rd, *Indian Miniature Painting from the Collection of Edwin Binney, 3rd: The Mughal and Deccani Schools* (exhib. cat., Portland, The Portland Art Museum), Portland, 1973, p. 51, cat. 28b.

28. See T. Falk & M. Archer, *Indian Miniatures in the India Office Library*, London, 1981, p. 48, no. 5.

29. On the painting of Kesu Das, see M.C. Beach, 'The Mughal painter Kesu Das', in *Archives of Asian Art*, XXX (1976–7), pp. 35–52; and Okada 1992 (n. 17), pp. 95–103.

30. Leach 1995 (n. 5), p. 304, no. 2.165.

31. J. Michael Rogers, *Mughal Miniatures*, London, 1993, p. 68, no. 44.

32. Note that the cap, usually worn by the Portuguese, is also worn by the *Jesuit Priest* in the National Museum, New Delhi (fig. 5).

33. Rogers 1993 (n. 31), p. 68, no. 44.

34. Private collection; see A. Okada, *Miniatures de l'Inde imperiale, Les peintres de la cour d'Akbar (1556–1605)* (exhib. cat., Paris, Musée national des Arts asiatiques – Guimet), Paris, 1989, pp. 88–9, no. 11.

35. Early 17th century, Academy of Sciences (Institute for Asian Peoples), Leningrad (see Ivanova et al. 1962 [n. 20], pl. 22).

36. E. Maclagan mentions a hypothetical portrait of Jerome Xavier, with black robe and thin, white beard, in a miniature depicting the Emperor Jahangir at the *Jharokha*, with various members of his court and a Jesuit priest (see Maclagan 1990 [n. 3], pp. 257–8 and 267 note 185). Also see n. 20.

CATALOGUE

Catalogue items are listed in the order and under the section headings used in the exhibition. Page numbers after the titles refer to illustrations, and entries without any bibliographical references indicate items that are previously unpublished.

I. CONNECTING THE EMPIRES

1. Jar (p. 45)
Eastern Iran, Samarkand, c.1447–9
White jade (nephrite); H 14.5 cm, D 16 cm
Lisbon, Calouste Gulbenkian Museum,
inv. no. 328
Lit: Stephen Markel, 'Fit for an Emperor:
Inscribed works of decorative arts acquired
by the Great Mughals', in *Orientations*,
21, no. 8 (August), 1990, pp. 22–5; *'Only
the best': Masterpieces of the Calouste
Gulbenkian Museum, Lisbon* (exhib. cat.),
ed. Katharine Baetjer and James David,
New York, The Metropolitan Museum of
Art, 1999, cat. 3, pp. 20–21; Souren
Melikian-Chirvani, 'Saida-ye Gilani and the
Iranian Styles Jades of Hindustan', in
Bulletin of the Asia Institute, vol. 13, (1999),
pp. 105–14.

2. *Princes of the House of Timur* (p. 46)
Mir Sayyid Ali
Mughal India, c.1550–55 (repainted in
Jahangir's time)
Opaque watercolour on paper;
108.5 x 108 cm
London, British Museum,
inv. no. OA 1913.2-08.01
Lit: *India Art and Culture, 1300-1900*
(exhib. cat.), ed. Stuart Cary Welch, New
York, The Metropolitan Museum of Art,
1985, cat. no. 84, pp. 143–4; *Humayun's
Garden Party: Princes of the House of Timur
and Early Mughal Painting*, ed. Sheila
Canby, Bombay, 1994.

**3. *Mughal Emperors and Princes
Sitting with their Ancestor Amir Timur***
(p. 15)
Mughal India, c.1658
Gouache and gold on paper; 32 x 22.6 cm
(page: 45.7 x 32.4 cm)

Paris, Collection Frits Lugt, Institut
Néerlandais, inv. no. 1970-T.38
Lit: *The Courts of India*, ed. Sven Gahlin,
Zwolle/Paris, 1991, cat. 36, plate 34.

4. Tent hanging (p. 28)
Mughal India, mid-17th century or later
Cotton, silk and gilded silver thread;
181 x 162 cm
London, Victoria and Albert Museum,
inv. no. IM 48-1928
Lit: J.C. Irving, 'Textiles and the minor arts',
in *The Art of India and Pakistan* (exhib.
cat.), dir. L. Ashton, London, 1950, cat.
1006; *The Indian Heritage: Court Life and
Arts under Mughal Rule* (exhib. cat.),
London, 1982, cat. 207.

5. Powder-flask (p. 23)
Mughal India, 17th century
Ivory; L 26.5 cm
Oporto, private collection.

6. Dagger (p. 92)
Mughal India, 18th century
Rock crystal and steel; L 34.5 cm
Oporto, private collection.

7. Dagger (p. 55)
Mughal India, 17th century
Jade and steel; L 38.5 cm
Oporto, private collection.

8. Prayer rug
Mughal India, 1640
Silk; 152 x 98 cm
London, Nasser D. Khalili Collection of
Islamic Art, inv. no. TXT 93
Lit: *Earthly Beauty, Heavenly Art, Art of
Islam* (exhib. cat.), Amsterdam, De Nieuwe
Kerk, 1999, cat. no. 2.

**9. 'Ho estreito de Meca com has
fortalezas q[ue] são do Grã Turco' (The
Strait of Mecca and the Fortresses of the
Great Turk)**
From the atlas of Lázaro Luís, f. 8v, 1563
Parchment; 62.5 x 43.5 cm
Lisbon, Biblioteca da Academia das
Ciências, Res. – Ms Azul 14.1
Lit: *Portugaliae Monumenta Cartographica*,
ed. A. Teixeira da Mota e A. Cortesão,
IN-CM, Lisbon, 1987, vol. II, p. 116, plate
222; *Os construtores do Oriente Português*
(exhib. cat.), ed. Jorge Flores, Lisbon,
CNPCDP, 1998,
cat. 5.

10. The Construction of Fathpur Sikri
(p. 137)
Tulsi and Bhawani
Lahore or Agra, from an *Akbar Nama*,
1590–95
Opaque watercolour on paper;
32.7 x 19.5 cm
London, Victoria and Albert Museum, inv.
no. I.S. 2-1896, 86/117
Lit: *Akbar's India: Art from the Mughal City
of Victory* (exhib. cat.), ed. Michael Brand
& Glenn D. Lowry, New York, Asia Society
Galleries, 1985, cat. 16; *Indian Heritage*,
cat. 29; Susan Stronge, *Painting for the
Mughal Emperor, The Art of the Book,
1560–1660*, London, V&A Publications,
2002, p. 50.

**11. Akbar's Triumphal Entry into Surat in
1573** (p. 135)
Farrokh Beg
Lahore or Agra, from an *Akbar Nama*,
1590–95
Opaque watercolour on paper;
31.9 x 19.1 cm
London, Victoria and Albert Museum,
inv. no. I.S. 2-1896 (117/117)
Lit: Stronge, *Painting for the Mughal
Emperor*, p. 55, plate 37.

**12. Hosein Qulij Khan Presents Prisoners
of War from Gujarat** (p. 17)
Basawan, coloured by Mansur

Lahore or Agra, from an *Akbar Nama*,
1590–95
Opaque watercolour on paper;
32.8 x 19.2 cm
London, Victoria and Albert Museum,
inv. no. IS.2-1896-112/117
Lit: Amina Okada, *Imperial Mughal
Painters: Indian Miniatures from the
Sixteenth and Seventeenth Centuries*, New
York, 1992, p. 88, fig. 88.

13. The Drowning of Bahadur Shah
(p. 176)
La'l
Agra, c.1603–4
Opaque watercolour on paper;
24 x 12.5 cm (page: 32 x 20.5 cm)
London, British Library, inv. no. Or 12988,
f. 66
Lit: *A arte e a missionação na rota do
Oriente. XVII Exposição Europeia de Arte,
Ciência e Cultura* (exhib. cat., Mosteiro dos
Jerónimos), ed. Avelino Teixeira da Mota &
Maria Helena Mendes Pinto, Lisbon, 1983,
cat. 75.

14. 'Chronicle of Gujarat'
Diogo de Mesquita Pimentel (?)
1535–6
Manuscript on paper; 29.2 x 22 cm
Lisbon, Instituto dos Arquivos
Nacionais/Torre do Tombo, *Colecção de
São Vicente*, liv. XI, ff. 91–111 (f. 91)

Lit: *Os construtores do Oriente português*,
cat. 15: Sanjay Subrahmanyam, 'A crónica
dos reis de Bisnaga e a crónica do
Guzerate: Dois textos indo-portugueses do
século XVI', in *Os construtores do Oriente
português*, ed. Jorge Flores, Lisbon, 1998,
pp. 131–53.

**15. 'Descripção do Reino de Guzarate'
(Description of the Kingdom of Gujarat)**
(p. 67)
João Baptista Lavanha
From João de Barros, *Ásia, Década IV*,
Madrid, 1615
Printed on paper; 28 x 19 cm
Lisbon, Biblioteca Nacional de Lisboa,
Res. 1390 v
Lit: *Portugaliae Monumenta Cartographica*,
ed. A. Teixeira da Mota & A. Cortesão,
Lisbon, IN-CM, 1987, vol. IV, pp. 71–2,
plate 424B.

16. 'Tavoa de Dio' (Map of Diu) (p. 173)
From *Roteiro de Goa a Diu*, 1538–9
Attributed to Dom João de Castro
Watercolour on paper; 28.5 x 43 cm
Coimbra, Biblioteca Geral da
Universidade, inv. 'Cofre' 33
Lit: *Portugaliae Monumenta Cartographica*,
ed. A. Teixeira da Mota & A. Cortesão,
IN-CM, Lisbon, 1987, vol. I, p. 139,
plate 63 N.

CAT. 17

17. Model of the fortress at Diu
19th century
Stone; 42 x 95 x 85 cm
Lisbon, Sociedade de Geografia, inv. no.
AB-964
Lit: Jerónimo Quadros, *Catálogo do Museu
Archeologico de Diu*, Nova Goa, Imprensa
Nacional, 1907, cat. XLII, pp. 19–21;
Fernando Castelo Branco, 'Models of the
fortress of Diu', in *Boletim do Instituto
Menezes de Bragança*, 152 (1987);
Tapeçarias de D. João de Castro (exhib.
cat.), ed. Francisco Faria Paulino, Lisbon,
CNCDP/IPM., 1995, p. 156; *Os espaços de
um império* (exhib. cat.), ed. Artur Teodoro
de Matos, Lisbon, CNCDP, 1999, cat. 116.

18. 'The Conquest of Diu' (p. 107)
From *Sucesso do Segundo Cerco de Diu*
(The Success of the Second Siege of Diu),
Part XII
Jerónimo Corte-Real
Lisbon, 1574
Manuscript on paper; 31.5 x 22 cm
Lisbon, Instituto dos Arquivos
Nacionais/Torre do Tombo, col. Casa
Cadaval, book 31 (f. 114)
Lit: Jerónimo Corte-Real, *Sucesso do
Segundo Cerco de Diu: códice Cadaval 31
- ANTT* (facsimile), introd. Martim de
Albuquerque, Lisbon, INAPA, 1991; *Os
construtores do Oriente português*, cat. 54.

19. *Portrait of Diogo do Couto* (p. 21)
Portugal, 18th century (?)
Oil on canvas; 147 x 119 cm
Lisbon, Instituto dos Arquivos
Nacionais/Torre do Tombo, inv. 66
Lit: *Os Espaços de um Império*, cat. 42.

20. *Farman* of Akbar to the empire's officials (p. 136)
18 March 1573
From Diogo do Couto, *Ásia, Década IX*,
ch.13, pp. 82–4
Lisbon, Regia Officina Typografica, 1786
Printed on paper; 17.9 x 11.5 cm
Lisbon, Biblioteca Nacional, Res. VAR
2845.
Lit: Jorge Flores & António Vasconcelos de
Saldanha, *Os Firangis na Chancelaria
Mogol. Cópias portuguesas de documentos
de Akbar (1572–1604)*, New Delhi, 2003,
doc. 2, p. 65.

21. *Firman* (or *farman*) cases (p. 18)
Mughal India, 18th century
Leather, stamped, painted and gilt;
23 x 10.4 cm
London, Victoria and Albert Museum,
inv. IM 234, 235, 236-1923
Lit: *The Indian Heritage*, cat. no. 247.

22. *Ordenações Manuelinas* (Manueline Laws) (p. 140)
Published by Valentim Fernandes, Lisbon,
1512
Printed on paper; 29 x 21 cm
Lisbon, Biblioteca Nacional de Lisboa,
Res. 2342 A
Lit: Nuno J. Espinosa Gomes da Silva,
*Algumas notas sobre a edição das
Ordenações Manuelinas de 1512–1513*,
sep. *Scientia Iuridica*, tomo XXVI, 1977;
Mário Júlio de Almeida e Costa,
'Ordenações', in *Dicionário de História de
Portugal*, dir. Joel Serrão, vol. IV, Oporto,
pp. 441–6; idem (ed.), *Ordenações
Manuelinas*, 5 vols, Lisbon, FCG, 1984.

23. *Relacam annval das cousas que fizeram os Padres da Companhia de Iesus na India & Iapão nos annos de 600 & 601* (Annual report of the things that the Fathers of the Society of Jesus did in India and Japan in the years 1600 and 1601) (p. 198)
Fernão Guerreiro
Évora, 1603
Printed on paper; 19.5 x 14 cm
Lisbon, Biblioteca Nacional de Lisboa,
Res. 444 P
Lit: *Relação anual das coisas que fizeram
os Padres da Companhia de Jesus nas suas
missões …*, ed. Artur Viegas, 3 vols,
Coimbra/Lisbon, 1930–41.

24. *Comentários do Grande Afonso de Albuquerque* (Commentaries of the Great Afonso de Albuquerque) (p. 140)
Published by João de Barreira, Lisbon,
1576 (2nd edn)
Printed on paper; 27.5 x 17.5 cm
Lisbon, Biblioteca Nacional, Res. 430v
Lit: *Os construtores do Oriente português*,
cat. 53; *Comentários de Afonso de
Albuquerque*, ed. Joaquim Veríssimo
Serrão, 2 vols, Lisbon, 1973.

25. *Darbar of Jahangir* (p. 180)
Attributed to Manohar
Mughal India, c.1620
Opaque watercolour and gold on paper;
35 x 20 cm
Boston, Museum of Fine Arts, Francis
Bartlett Donation of 1912 and Picture
Fund, inv. 14.654
Lit: *The Grand Mogul: Imperial Painting in
India 1600–1660* (exhib. cat.), ed. Milo
Cleveland Beach, Williamstown, Sterling
and Francine Clark Art Institute, 1978,
cat. 14.

26. *Tratado da Corte e Caza de Iamguir Pachá Rey dos Mogores* (Treatise on the Court and Household of Iamguir Pachá King of the Mughals), f. 81 (p. 49)
Attributed to Jerónimo Xavier, 1610
Manuscript on paper; 31 x 22 cm
Lisbon, Instituto dos Arquivos
Nacionais/Torre do Tombo, Cartório
da Casa Real, bundle 49B, box 7420,
cap. 897
Lit: Jorge Flores, 'The Jahangir's Court
through Jesuit Spectacles: The *Tratado da
Corte e Casa de Iamguir Pachá Rey dos
Mogores* (1610), by Father Jerónimo Xavier'
in Rosa M. Perez & Stefan Halikowski
Smith, eds, *Portugal Indico*, Providence
(Rhode Island), Brown University, 2004.

27. 'Seal of Jahangir' (p. 59)
Manuel Godinho de Erédia
[Goa] 1611
Drawing on paper; 31 x 21 cm
Lisbon, Biblioteca Nacional de Lisboa,
cod. 11410, f. 51
Lit: Jorge Flores, 'Two Portuguese visions
of Jahangir's India: Jerónimo Xavier and
Manuel Godinho de Erédia', in this
volume.

28. Portuguese-Hindustani-Persian Vocabulary (not illustrated)
Attributed to Jerónimo Xavier
Mughal India, early 17th century
Manuscript on paper; 21.5 x 15.5 cm
London, School of Oriental and African Studies, Ms. 11952
Lit: E. Denison Ross, 'The manuscripts collected by William Marsden with special reference to two copies of Almeida's *History of Ethiopia*', in *Bulletin of the School of Oriental Studies*, vol. II (1923), pp. 513–38; Arnulf Camps, O.F.M., *Jerome Xavier S.J. and the Muslims of the Mogul Empire: Controversial Works and Missionary Activity*, Schöneck-Beckenried, 1957, pp. 38–9.

29. *Rudimenta Linguae Persicae* (not illustrated)
Attributed to Jerónimo Xavier
Mughal India, early 17th century
Manuscript on paper; 23.5 x 16 cm
London, School of Oriental and African Studies, Ms 12198
Lit: E. Denison Ross, 'The manuscripts collected by William Marsden with special reference to two copies of Almeida's History of Ethiopia', in Bulletin of the School of Oriental Studies, vol. II (1923), pp. 513–38; Arnulf Camps, O.F.M., *Jerome Xavier S.J. and the Muslims of the Mogul Empire: Controversial Works and Missionary Activity*, Schöneck-Beckenried, 1957, pp. 38–9.

30. *The Capture of Da'ud during the Conquest of Bengal*
Attributed to Sanwlah
Mughal India, *c*.1602–4
Gouache and gold on paper;
24.1 x 13.1 cm (page: 34.5 x 22.3 cm)
Paris, Collection Frits Lugt, Institut Néerlandais, inv. no. 1973-T.5
Lit: Robert Skelton, 'Facets of India Art', in *Apollo* (October 1976), pp. 269–70; *L'Inde des légends et des réalités*, Paris, Institut Néerlandais, 1986, cat. 18; *Miniatures de l'Inde impériale: les peintres de la cour d'Akbar, 1556–1605*, Paris, 1989, cat. 9; *The Courts of India*, cat. 21, pl. 20.

CAT. **30**

31. 'Descripção do Reino de Bengala'
(Description of the Kingdom of Bengal)
(p. 67)
João Baptista Lavanha
From João de Barros, *Ásia, Década IV*,
Madrid, 1615
Printed on paper; 28 x 19 cm
Lisbon, Biblioteca Nacional de Lisboa,
Res.1398 v
Lit: *Portugaliae Monumenta Cartographica*,
ed., A. Teixeira da Mota & A. Cortesão,
Lisbon, IN-CM, 1987, vol. IV,
pp. 71–2, pl. 424D.

32. 'Reino de Orixa. Reino de Bengala'
(Kingdom of Orixa. Kingdom of Bengal)
(p. 61)
From *Livro das plantas das fortalezas,
cidades e povoações do Estado da Índia
Oriental*
c.1633–41
Manuscript on paper; 42.5 x 27.5 cm
Vila Viçosa, Fundação da Casa de
Bragança (Biblioteca do Paço Ducal),
inv. no. Ms. Res. 21
Lit: *Livro das Plantas das Fortalezas,
cidades e povoações do Estado da India
Oriental … Contribuição para a história das
fortalezas dos Portugueses no Ultramar*, ed.
Luís Silveira, Lisbon, 1991; *Os construtores
do Oriente Português*, cat. 7.

33. *Breve Relatione de i Regni di Pegv,
Arracan, e Brama, e degl' Imperij del
Calaminan, Siamom, e gran Mogor …*
(Brief Report on the Kingdoms of Pegu,
Arrakan and Brama, and of the Empires of
Calaminan, Siam and the Great Mughal …)
(p. 65)
Sebastião Manrique
Published by Francesco Moneta, Rome,
1648
Printed on paper; 20.3 x 14.2 cm
Lisbon, Biblioteca da Ajuda,
inv. no. 55-IV-10.6
Lit: *Relação breve dos reinos de Pegu,
Arracão, Brama, e dos impérios Calaminhã,
Siammon e Grão Mogol*, ed. Maria Ana
Marques Guedes and trans. Raffaella
d'Intino, Lisbon, Cotovia, 1997.

34. *Itinerario de las Missiones del India
Oriental* (Itinerary of the Missions in East
India) (p. 62)
Sebastião Manrique
Published by Guillelmo Halle, Rome, 1653
Printed on paper; 26.4 x 20 cm
Lisbon, Biblioteca Nacional de Lisboa,
Res. 1947 V
Lit: *Travels of Fray Sebastien Manrique,
1629–1643*, ed. C.E. Luard & H. Hosten,
2 vols, The Hakluyt Society, London, 1927;
Itinerário, ed. Luís Silveira, 2 vols, Lisbon,
1946.

35. Coverlet (p. 63)
India (Bengal), 17th century
Cotton and silk; 326 x 280 cm
Lisbon, Fundação Medeiros e Almeida,
inv. no. 1363
Lit: *Vasco da Gama e a Índia* (exhib. cat.),
ed. Maria Helena Mendes Pinto and José
Manuel Garcia, Lisbon/Paris, Fundação
Calouste Gulbenkian, 1998, cat. 104.

II. THE COURT OF THE *FIRANGIS* AND THE COURT OF THE *MOGORS*

36. *View of Goa* (p. 121)
Manuel Furtado, Goa, 1716
Oil on linen canvas; 265 x 575 cm
Lisbon, private collection.

37. *Dom João de Castro,
4th Viceroy of India (1545–8)* (p. 78)
Flanders, 16th century
Wood with colour remains;
95 x 28 x 20 cm
Oporto, private collection
Lit: Anízio Franco & Rui A. Santos,
'Escultura de madeira de D. João de
Castro', in *Arte Ibérica*, no. 3, 1997,
p. 151; *Os construtores do Oriente
Português*, cat. 40.

38. *Portrait of Dom Francisco de
Mascarenhas*, 13th Viceroy of India
(1581–4) (p. 89)
Goa, 16th century
Mixed technique on wood; 188 x 98 cm
Lisbon, Museu Nacional de Arte Antiga,
inv. no. 2146
Lit: *A arte e a missionação na rota do
Oriente*, XVII Exposição Europeia de Arte,
Ciência e Cultura, Lisbon, Mosteiro
Jerónimos, 1983, dir. Avelino Teixeira da
Mota, Maria Helena Mendes Pinto, p. 199;
Vasco da Gama e a Índia, cat. 89.

39. *Portrait of Aires de Saldanha,
17th Viceroy of India (1600–1605)* (p. 109)
Follower of Juan Pantoja de la Cruz
Spain, c.1590
Oil on canvas; 200 x 130 cm
Lisbon, Museu Nacional do Traje,
inv. no. 14.399
Lit: Miguel Soromenho, 'Aires de Saldanha
(1542–1606): décimo-sétimo vice-rei da
Índia', in *Nossa Senhora dos Mártires.
A última viagem* (exhib. cat., EXPO' 98,
Portugal's Pavilion), Lisbon, 1998,
pp. 165–73.

40. *Portrait of António Pais de Sande*,
Governor of India (Council of 1678–81)
(p. 97)
Goa (?) 17th century
Oil on canvas; 210 x 120 cm
Lisbon, collection of José Lico
Lit: *A construção do Brasil: 1500–1825*
(exhib. cat., Galeria de Pintura do Rei
D. Luís), ed. Ana Maria Rodrigues, Lisbon,
CNCDP, 2000, cat. no. 92.

41. *Portrait of Dom Luís de Meneses
(5th Count of Ericeira)*, Viceroy of India
(1717–20) (p. 97)
Pompeu J. Batoni, 1781
Oil on canvas; 128 x 95 cm
Cascais, Câmara Municipal de
Cascais/Museu Condes de Castro
Guimarães, inv. no. 159
Lit: *Os construtores do Oriente Português*,
cat. 37.

42. Model of the Fortaleza Palace of the
viceroys in Goa (p. 76)
Lisbon, 1999
Project: Helder Carita; production:
Augusto Bolotinha
Wood and acrylic; 55 x 140 x 194 cm
Lisbon, Museu Militar, inv. no. MGO AO1
Lit: *Os Espaços de um Império*, cat. 52.

43. 'Plan of the Fortaleza Palace, Goa'
(p. 76)
João Baptista Vieira Godinho, Goa, 1779
Watercolour on paper; 121.8 x 47.2 cm
Lisbon, Sociedade de Geografia, inv.
Cartografia, 6-E-5
Lit: Helder Carita, *Palácios de Goa:
modelos e tipologias de arquitectura civil
Indo-Portuguesa*, Lisbon, Quetzal Editores,
1995, pp. 14, 23 and 25; Pedro Dias,
História da arte portuguesa no mundo,
1415–1822: *O espaço do Índico*, Lisbon,
Círculo de Leitores, 1998, pp. 102–4;
Os Espaços de um Império, cat. 45.

44. Bed (p. 83)
Goa (?), late 16th–early 17th century
Teak and lacquer; 198 x 211 x 140 cm
Azeitão, Quinta da Bacalhoa
Lit: Pedro Dias, *O contador das cenas
familiares: o quotidiano dos portugueses de
quinhentos na Índia na decoração de um
móvel indo-português*, Oporto, Pedro
Aguiar Branco, 2002, p. 55.

**45. Coverlet with the coat of arms of
Dom Vasco de Mascarenhas, 27th Viceroy
of India (1652–3)** (p. 91)
Goa, 1652–3
Cotton and linen; 267 x 220 cm
Lisbon, Museu Nacional do Traje,
inv. no. 14408
Lit: *Os Espaços de um Império*, cat. 66.

46. Sacristy armoire (p. 93)
Goa, c.1660–70
Teak, ebony and gilded copper;
211.5 x 133.5 x 37 cm
Oporto, private collection.

**47. Tiles at the Santa Mónica Convent,
Goa**
Multan (?)/Bijapur (?), 1625–50
Glazed terracotta; A: 22 x 19 cm;
B: 17.5 x 18.5 cm; C: 13.7 x 15.5 cm;
D: 10 x 20 cm
Lisbon, Museu Nacional do Azulejo, inv.
nos 476 and 480
Lit: *Azulejos* (exhib. cat., Porte de Hal,
Brussels), Brussels, 1991, cat. no. 53; João
Castel-Branco Pereira *et al., As Colecções
do Museu Nacional do Azulejo Lisboa*,
London, Zwemmer/Lisbon, IPM, 1995,
cat. nos 67 and 68.

**48. Mughal carpet from the Santa Clara
Convent, Évora** (p. 39)
Agra or Lahore, late 16th–early 17th
century
Wool; 200 x 133 cm
Lisbon, Museu Nacional de Arte Antiga,
inv. 10 tap
Lit: *De Goa Lisboa* (exhib. cat., Museu
Nacional de Arte Antiga), Lisbon, 1980;
*A arte e a missionação na rota do Oriente,
XVII Exposição Europeia de Arte, Ciência e
Cultura* (exhib. cat., Mosteiro Jerónimos),
ed. Avelino Teixeira da Mota & Maria
Helena Mendes Pinto, Lisbon, 1983, cat.
64; *Via Orientalis* (exhib. cat.), ed. Maria
Helena Mendes Pinto, Brussels, Galerie de
la CGER, 1991, cat. no. 119.

CAT. **47A**

CAT. **47B**

CAT. **47C**

CAT. **47D**

49. Casket of Matias de Albuquerque, 15th Viceroy of India (1591–7) (p. 94)
Portuguese India (Goa?), third quarter of the 16th century
Gold filigree with enamels;
14 x 19.5 x 9.6 cm
Lisbon, Museu Nacional de Arte Antiga, inv. no. 577
Lit: Sousa Viterbo, 'A Arte indo-portuguesa' in *A Exposição de Arte Ornamental*, Lisbon, 1883, p. 14; *Influências do oriente na arte portuguesa continental: a arte nas províncias portuguesas do ultramar* (exhib. cat., Museu Nacional de Arte Antiga), ed. João Couto, Lisbon, 1957, cat. no. 37; Nuno Vassallo e Silva, Tesouros da 'Terra de promissam': a ourivesaria entre Portugal e a Índia, in *Oceanos*, no. 19/20, 1994, p. 94; *A herança de Rauluchantim* (exhib. cat., Museu de S. Roque), ed. Nuno Vassallo e Silva, Lisbon, Museu de S. Roque/CNPCDP, 1996, cat. 3.

50. Plate with the coat of arms of Matias de Albuquerque, 15th Viceroy of India (1591–7) (p. 96)
China, Qing dynasty, Wanli period, last quarter of the 16th century
Blue-and-white porcelain; D 26 cm
Lisbon, Museu Nacional de Arte Antiga, inv. no. 5489
Lit: *A arte e a missionação na rota do Oriente*, at. 221; *Du Tage à la mer de Chine: une épopée portugaise* (exhib. cat.), Musée national des Arts asiatiques – Guimet, Paris, 1992, cat. 41.

51. Plate with the coat of arms of Dom Francisco da Gama, 16th Viceroy of India (1597–1600) (p. 96)
Portugal, *c.*1600
Gilded silver; D 33 cm
Lisbon, Santa Casa da Misericórdia de Lisboa/Museu de S. Roque, inv. no. 613
Lit: Nuno Vassallo e Silva e Julio Parra Martinez, *Ourivesaria e iluminura, século XIV ao século XX*, Lisbon, Museu de S. Roque, 1998, no. 6.

52. Shaving basin with the coat of arms of Dom Rodrigo da Costa, Viceroy of India (1686–90) (p. 88)
China, *c.*1690–1710
White porcelain with cobalt blue underglaze decoration; H 6.3 cm, D 42 cm
Lisbon, Fundação Oriente, inv. no. FO/374
Lit: *Caminhos da porcelana. Dinastias Ming e Qing* (exhib. cat.), Lisbon, Fundação Oriente, 1998, cat. no. 38.

53. *Akbar Greeting Rajput Rulers and Nobles* (p. 16)
Miskin, Sarwan and portraits by Madhav
Lahore or Agra, from an *Akbar Nama*, 1590–95
Gouache on paper; 32.9 x 19.8 cm
London, Victoria and Albert Museum, inv. no. IS 2 - 1896. 114/117
Lit: Stronge, *Painting for the Mughal Emperor*, p. 41, plate 25.

54. Relief portrait bust of Shahjahan (p. 146)
Mughal India, second quarter of the 17th century
Alabaster with remains of gilding and polychromy; 11.5 x 8.5 cm
Amsterdam, Rijksmuseum, inv. no. AK-NM-12249
Lit: *The Indian Heritage*, cat. no. 375; *Romance of the Taj Mahal*, ed. Pratapaditya Pal, London, 1989, pp. 145, fig. 145;

Pauline L. Scheurleer, *Hoofse Snuisterijen uit India* (*Asiatische Kunst*, no. 3), Amsterdam, 1991, cat. no. 15.

55. *Young Prince Miza Selim with his Tutor*
Mughal India (?), 17th century
Ink, colour and gold on paper;
37.6 x 22.5 cm
Lisbon, Calouste Gulbenkian Museum, inv. no. M. 32
Lit: *Culturas do Índico* (exhib. cat., Museu Nacional de Arte Antiga), Lisbon,1998, cat. 79.

56. Jar (p. 139)
India (Gujarat), 17th century
Mother-of-pearl; H 22 cm
Oporto, private collection.

57. Primer (?) (p. 139)
Mughal India/Deccan, 17th century
Steel and gold; L 13 cm
Oporto, private collection.

CAT. **55**

58. Cup
Mughal India, 17th century
Jade; H 6.7 cm, D 16.2 cm
Oporto, private collection.

59. Wine cup of Emperor Jahangir (p. 52)
Mughal India, 1612–13
Jade; H 8.1 cm, D 10.2 cm
Providence, Museum of Art, Rhode Island
School of Design, Helen M. Danforth
Acquisition Fund, inv. no. 84. 163
Lit: *India Art and Culture*, cat. no. 126;
Stephen Markel, 'Inception and Maturation
in Mughal Jades', in *The Art of Jade*, Marg,
vol. XLIV, no. 2, Bombay, 1992, p. 56, fig.
6; René Morales, 'Emperor Jahangir's wine
cup', in *Glimpses of Grandeur: Courtly
Arts of the later Islamic Empires (Exhibition
notes)*, The Rhode Island School of Design
Museum, no. 8 (Fall 1999), pp. 18–19.

60. *A Turkey* (p. 99)
Mughal India, *c*.1678–98
Ink and gold on paper; 20.8 x 13.6 cm
Cambridge, Fitzwilliam Museum,
inv. no. PD 83.1948
Lit: Milo Beach, *Mughal and Rajput
Painting*, Cambridge, 1992, pp. 90–91.

61. Archer ring (p. 145)
Mughal India, *c*.1630–40
White jade, gold, rubies and emeralds;
4.1 x 3.2 cm
London, Victoria and Albert Museum,
inv. 02522 (I.S.)
Lit: *The Indian Heritage*, cat. no. 304.

62. Mughal carpet (fragment) (p. 147)
Kashmir or Lahore, *c*.1620–25
Wool and silk; 570 x 125 cm
Lisbon, Calouste Gulbenkian Musem,
inv. no. T 72
Lit: Maria Fernanda Passos Leite, *Tapetes
Orientais*, Lisbon, Museu Calouste
Gulbenkian, 1985, fig. XVIII; *India Art
and Culture*, cat. 153; *Flowers Underfoot:
Indian Carpets of the Mughal Era* (exhib.
cat., Metropolitam Museum of Art), ed.
Daniel Walker, London/New York, 1997,
cat. 17, fig. 74–5; Maria Fernanda Passos
Leite, *Obra de arte em foco: um tapete
da Índia Mogol da Colecção Calouste
Gulbenkian*, Lisbon, Museu Calouste
Gulbenkian, 1999; Steven Cohen, 'Safavid
and Mughal Carpets in the Gulbenkian
Museum, Lisbon', in *Hali*, 114 (2001),
pp. 81, fig. 7.

63. 'Portuguese' carpet (p. 72)
Persia (?), Safavid period, 17th century
Wool and cotton; 447 x 200 cm
Lisbon, Calouste Gulbenkian Musem,
inv. no. T 99
Lit: *Portugal e a Pérsia*, Lisbon, Fundação
Calouste Gulbenkian, 1972, cat. 19; *A arte
e a missionação na rota do Oriente*, XVII.
Exposição Europeia de Arte, Ciência e
Cultura (exhib. cat., Mosteiro Jerónimos),
ed. Avelino Teixeira da Mota and Maria
Helena Mendes Pinto, Lisbon, 1983, cat.

60; Maria Fernanda Passos Leite, *Tapetes
Orientais*, fig. XII; *Museu Calouste
Gulbenkian*, Lisbon, 2001, cat. 46; Steven
Cohen, 'Safavid and Mughal Carpets in
the Gulbenkian Museum, Lisbon', pp. 76,
fig. 2.

64. Spoon
Mughal India, late 16th century (?)
Jade, ivory, gold and enamels; L 15 cm
Oporto, private collection
Lit: *Os Espaços de um Império*, cat. no.63.

CAT. **58**

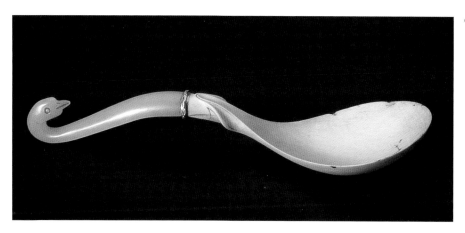

CAT. **64**

CAT. 66

65. Staff handle (p. 143)
Mughal India, 17th century
Jade, emeralds, rubies and gold; H 10 cm,
W 13.5 cm
Oporto, private collection.

66. Sheath for dagger
Mughal India, 17th century
Silver, enamel, diamonds and emeralds;
L 19 cm
Oporto, private collection.

III. Between Religions:
Christianity in a Muslim Empire

67. *Akbar Presiding over Discussions in
the* 'Ibadat Khana (p. 191)
Nar Singh
From an *Akbar Nama, c.*1604
Coloured pigments and gold on paper;
43.5 x 26.6 cm (page)
Dublin, The Chester Beatty Library,
inv. no. IN 03.263
Lit: *Akbar's India*, cat. 18; Linda York
Leach, *Mughal and other Indian Paintings
from the Chester Beatty Library*, I, London,
Scorpion Cavendish, 1995, no. 2.152,
pp. 291–2.

68. *Dastan-i-Masih* (**Life of Christ**) (p. 149)
Translated by Jerome Xavier, S.J., with
Abdu-s-Sattar ibn Qasim
Mughal India, *c.*1604
Coloured pigments and gold on paper;
25.3 x 16.6 cm
Lisbon, Biblioteca da Ajuda, BA 52-XIII-32
Lit: Roberto Gulbenkian, 'Os quatro
Evangelhos em persa da Biblioteca
Nacional de Lisboa, o Grão Mogol, os

Jesuítas e os Arménios' in *Estudos
Históricos*, 3 vols, 1995, vol. I: *Relações
entre Portugal, Arménia e o Médio Oriente*,
pp. 255–300.

69. *The Deposition from the Cross* (p. 168)
Mughal India, Lahore, *c.*1598
Gouache and gold on paper;
19.4 x 11.3 cm
London, Victoria and Albert Museum, IS
133-1964, f. 79b
Lit: *Arts of India, 1500–1900*, ed. John Guy
& Deborah Swallow, London, Victoria and
Albert Museum, 1990, p. 721; Stronge,
Painting for the Mughal Emperor, p. 111,
plate 77; Gauvin Alexander Bailey,
'Counter Reformation Symbolism and
Allegory in Mughal Painting', Ph.D. thesis,
Harvard University, 1996, plate 188.

70. Reliquary cross and pair of cruets
(p. 164)
Mughal India, 17th century
Jade, gold, silver gilt, quartz and glass;
28.1 x 12.5 cm (reliquary cross),
12 x 8.5 cm (cruets)
Oporto, Museu Nacional de Soares dos
Reis, inv. nos. 120 (1, 2 and 3)
Lit: Ramalho Ortigão, 'Catalogo da Sala de
Sua Magestade El-Rei', in *Obras completas
de Ramalho Ortigão – Arte Portuguesa*, II,
Oporto, n.d., p. 34, cat. no. 115; Nuno
Vassalo e Silva, 'Obras de arte mogol no
Mosteiro de Santa Maria de Alcobaça', in
*Arte e Arquitectura nas Abadias
Cistercienses nos séculos XVI, XVII e XVIII*,
proceedings, Lisbon, IPAAR, 2000, pp.
301–6; *A herança de Rauluchantim*, cat.
no. 33; *Os construtores do Oriente
Português*, cat. no. 98.

71. *Jesuit Missionary* (p. 193)
Manohar
Mughal India, *c.*1590
Ink on paper; 12.7 x 6.8 cm
Paris, Musée national des Arts asiatiques –
Guimet, inv. 3619, Gc
Lit: *Miniatures de l'Inde impériale*, cat. 59;
Bailey, 'Counter Reformation Symbolism
and Allegory', plate 126.

72. *The Virgin and Child* (p. 164)
Portuguese India, mid-17th century
Ivory; 17 x 12.7 cm
Braga, Universidade do Minho/Museu
Nogueira da Silva, inv. 689-ES-17.

73. *The Madonna* (p. 165)
Manohar
Mughal India, *c.*1600
Ink on paper; 7.5 x 5.3 cm (page:
25.4 x 15.4 cm)
Paris, Collection Frits Lugt, Institut
Néerlandais, inv. 1974-T.67
Lit: *L'Inde des légends et des réalités*, cat.
no. 14, plate 12; Gauvin Alexandre Bailey,
*Art on the Jesuit Missions in Asia and Latin
America (1542–1773)*, Toronto, 1999,
p. 120, fig. 68.

74. *Christ and the Woman of Samaria*
(p. 159)
Attributed to Manohar
Mughal India, *c.*1602
Gouache and gold on paper;
23.1 x 11.8 cm (page: 26.3 x 14.5 cm)
Paris, Collection Frits Lugt, Institut
Néerlandais, inv. 1988-T.12
Lit: *The Courts of India*, cat. no. 19A,
plate 23; Bailey, 'Counter Reformation
Symbolism and Allegory in Mughal
Painting', plate 151; Bailey, *Art on the
Jesuit Missions*, p. 128, ill. 72.

75. *The Nativity* (p. 160)
Attributed to Manohar
Mughal India, *c.*1600–2
Ink, gold and colours on paper;
18.7 x 10.3 cm
Paris, Collection Frits Lugt, Institut
Néerlandais, inv. 1972-T.42
Lit: Skelton, 'Facets of India Art', pp.
268–9, ill. 2; *L'Inde des légends et des
réalités*, cat. no. 15, plate 13; *Miniatures de
l'Inde impériale*, cat. no. 58; *The Courts
of India*, cat. no. 16, plate 12.

76. *St Jerome* (p. 157)
Signed by Kesu Das (after Michelangelo)
Mughal India, *c.*1580–85
Gouache on paper; 17 x 10 cm
Paris, Musée nationale des Arts asiatiques –
Guimet, inv. no. MA 2476
Lit: Milo Beach, 'The Mughal painter Kesu
Das', in *Archives of Asian Art*, vol. XXX,
1976–7, pp. 38–9, plate 7; *Miniatures de
l'Inde impériale*, cat. no. 66; *A la court du
grand Mogol*, Paris, Bibliothèque nationale
de France, 1986, cat. no. 98; Bailey, *Art on
the Jesuit Missions*, p. 119, plate 65.

77. *The Last Supper* (p. 157)
Attributed to Kesu Das
Mughal India, *c.*1580–85
Gouache on paper; 18.8 x 12.6 cm
Paris, Musée national des Arts asiatiques –
Guimet, MA 2475
Lit: Amina Okada, *Miniatures de l'Inde
impériale: les peintres de la cour d'Akbar,
1556–1605* (exhib. cat.), Paris, Musée
national des Arts asiatiques – Guimet,
1989, cat. no. 67; Bailey, 'Counter
Reformation Symbolism and Allegory in
Mughal Painting', cat. no. 51.

78. *St Luke* (p. 155)
Mughal India, *c.*1600–4
Opaque watercolour on paper;
10.6 x 5.7 cm
London, Victoria and Albert Museum,
inv. no. IS-218-1952
Lit: Stronge, *Painting for the Mughal
Emperor*, p.120, pl. 85.

79. *The Virgin and Child* (p. 161)
Kesu Khurd
Mughal India, *c.*1590–95
Slightly tinted drawing; 19.5 x 16.8 cm
(page)
Dublin, The Chester Beatty Library,
inv. no. 11 A.19
Lit: Leach, *Mughal and other Indian
Paintings*, no. 1.234, pp. 137–8.

80. *Joseph Telling his Dream to his Father*
(p. 167)
Kesu Das
Mughal India, *c.*1590
Coloured pigments on paper; 30.1 x 20 cm
(page)
Dublin, The Chester Beatty Library,
inv. no. IN 41.2
Lit: Leach, *Mughal and other Indian
Paintings*, no. 1.233, pp. 135–7.

81. *A Jesuit Priest* (p. 197)
Attributed to Kesu Das
Mughal India, *c.*1595–1600
Coloured pigments on paper;
22.5 x 15.7 cm (page)
Dublin, The Chester Beatty Library, inv. no.
IN 44.5
Lit: Leach, *Mughal and other Indian
Paintings*, no. 2.165, p. 304, plate 44.

82. *The Martyrdom of St Cecilia* (p. 168)
Nini, after an engraving by Hieronymus
Wierix
Mughal India, Salim School, *c.*1600
Watercolour and gold on paper;
13.5 x 10.4 cm (page: 38.3 x 25.8 cm)
London, Victoria and Albert Museum,
inv. IM.139a-192
Lit: Asok Kumar Das, *Mughal Painting
during Jahangir's Time*, The Asiatic Society,
Calcutta, 1978, p. 237, pl. 68; Bailey,
'Counter Reformation Symbolism and
Allegory in Mughal Painting', cat. no. 199;
Stronge, *Painting for the Mughal Emperor*,
pl. 70, p. 104.

83. *The Nativity* (p. 153)
Mughal India, *c.*1605–10
Opaque watercolour and gold on paper;
17.7 x 11.6 cm
London, Victoria and Albert Museum,
inv. no. D 402-1885
Lit: Stronge, *Painting for the Mughal
Emperor*, pp. 111–13, plates 78–9.

84. Altar front preserved as a table top
(p. 115)
Gujarat or Sind, 1600–10
Lignum vitae and ivory; 82 x 106 cm
London, Victoria and Albert Museum,
inv. no. 15-1882
Lit: *A arte e a missionação na rota do
Oriente*, cat. no. 95; *Arts of India:
1550–1900*, p. 53, fig. 38; Amin Jaffer,
*Luxury Goods from India: The Art of the
Indian Cabinet-Maker*, London, V&A, 2002,
no. 9, pp. 33–5.

85. Allegorical figure in Polyglot Bible
(*Biblia sacra Hebraice, Chaldaice, Graece
& Latine*, vol. I) (p. 154)
Published by Christopher Plantyn, Antwerp,
1569
Engraving on paper; 38 x 25 cm
Lisbon, Biblioteca Nacional de Lisboa,
Res. 1348 A
Lit: *Akbar's India*, cat. no. 61; Gauvin
Alexander Bailey, *The Jesuits and the
Grand Mogul: Renaissance Art at the

Imperial Court of India, 1580–1630*,
Washington, D.C., Freer Gallery of Art,
Arthur M. Sackler Gallery, 1998, p. 25, fig.16.

86. *Calvary* (p. 169)
Northern India (?), 17th century
Wood and ivory; 75 x 35.9 cm
Oporto, private collection.

87. *The Birth of Christ* (p. 163)
Attributed to Manohar, after a European
engraving
From the St Petersburg *Muraqqa*
Mughal India, early 17th century
Watercolour, silver and gold on paper;
21.3 x 13.5 cm
St Petersburg, The St Petersburg Branch of
the Institute of Oriental Studies/Russian
Academy of Sciences, Ms E-14, f. 62r
Lit: *The St. Petersburg Muraqqa: album of
Indian and Persian miniatures from the 16th
through the 18th century and specimens
of Persian calligraphy by `Imad al-Hasani*,
2 vols, Milan, Leonardo arte, 1996, p. 62,
plate 36 (illustrations vol.).

IV. EXCHANGING IMAGES: VISIONS OF THE WEST IN MUGHAL ART

88. *A European* (p. 171)
Mughal India, *c.*1610–20
Gouache and gold on paper;
29.5 x 18.3 cm
London, Victoria and Albert Museum,
inv. no. IM 386-1914
Lit: *Arts of India, 1500–1900*, p. 154,
fig. 131; Stronge, *Painting for the Mughal
Emperor*, p. 139, fig. 105.

89. *European Scene with Portuguese
Figures* (p. 186)
Agra or Lahore, *c.*1595
Opaque watercolour on paper;
26.4 x 17.5 cm (page: 33.5 x 21.6 cm)
London, British Library (India Office
Library), inv. J16.6
Lit: *Akbar's India*, cat. no. 65.

90. *A European Scene*
Sanwlah (p.187)
Mughal India, *c.*1590–95
Coloured pigments on paper;
30.6 x 20.8 cm (page)
Dublin, The Chester Beatty Library,
inv. no. IN 11A.11
Lit: Leach, *Mughal and other Indian
Paintings*, no. 1.235, pp. 138–40.

91. *Angel Receiving a Group of Europeans*
(p. 186)
Mughal India, c.1600
Gouache on paper
18 x 9.5 cm; 18.6 x 10.2 cm (page)
Copenhagen, The David Collection,
inv. no. 6/1981
Lit: *Sultan, Shah, and Great Mughal: The
History and Culture of the Islamic World*
(exhib. cat.), ed. Kjeld von Folsach,
National Museum, Copenhagen, 1996,
cat. no. 323.

92. *King David Playing the Harp* (p. 172)
Manohar
Mughal India, c.1610–20
Gouache on paper; 21.5 x 13.5 cm
(page: 38.5 x 26.3 cm)
Copenhagen, The David Collection,
inv. no. 31/2001
Lit: Joachim K. Bautze, *Interaction of
Cultures: Indian and Western Painting,
1780–1910: The Ehrenfeld Collection*,
Alexandria (VA), 1998, pp. 42–8.

93. *Majnun with a European Lady* (p. 185)
Manohar
Mughal India, c.1600
Coloured pigments on paper;
39 x 30.2 cm (page)
Dublin, The Chester Beatty Library,
inv. no. 11A.12
Lit: Leach, *Mughal and other Indian
Paintings*, no. 1.240, pp. 143–6.

94. *Akbar Receives Congratulations on
the Birth of his Son Murad* (p. 177)
Dharm Das
From an *Akbar Nama*, c.1603–5
Mughal India
Coloured pigments and gold on paper;
43.5 x 26.6 cm
Dublin, The Chester Beatty Library,
inv. no. IN 03.147
Lit: Leach, *Mughal and other Indian
Paintings*, no. 2.123, pp. 266–8.

95. *Portrait of a Portuguese Gentleman*
(p. 179)
Mughal India, c.1600
Ink, opaque watercolour and gold on paper
13.9 x 11.6 cm
Boston, Museum of Fine Arts, Francis
Bartlett Donation of 1912 and Picture
Fund, inv. 14. 661
Lit: Ananda K. Coomaraswamy, *Catalogue
of the Indian Collections in the Museum of
Fine Arts, Boston, Part IV – Mughal*

Paintings, Boston, Museum of Fine Arts,
1930, cat. no. LVII, p. 35, fig. XXVI.

96. *A Portuguese Man* (p. 178)
Mughal India, early 17th century
Gouache on paper; 28 x 17.7 cm
Lisbon, Museu Nacional de Arte Antiga,
inv. no. 15 Min
Lit: *A arte e a missionação na rota do
Oriente. XVII Exposição Europeia de Arte,
Ciência e Cultura* (exhib. cat., Mosteiro dos
Jerónimos), ed. Avelino Teixeira da Mota &
Maria Helena Mendes Pinto, Lisbon, 1983,
cat. no. 93, p.149; *Os construtores do
Oriente Português*, cat. no. 195.

97. *Festivities on the Occasion of the
Accession of Emperor Jahangir* (p. 195)
Abu'l Hasan
Mughal India, c.1605–15
Watercolour, silver and gold on paper;
37.8 x 22 cm
St Petersburg, The St Petersburg Branch of
the Institute of Oriental Studies/Russian
Academy of Sciences, Ms E-14, f. 21r
Lit: *The St. Petersburg Muraqqa*, p. 106,
plate 176.

98. *Darbar of Jahangir* (p. 53)
Attributed to Manohar
Mughal India, c.1607
Watercolour, ink, silver and gold on paper;
37.9 x 22.7 cm
St Petersburg, The St Petersburg Branch of
the Institute of Oriental Studies/Russian
Academy of Sciences, Ms E-14, f. 22r
Lit: *The St. Petersburg Muraqqa*, p. 106,
plate 177.

99. *Isabel of Bourbon, Queen of Spain*
(p. 175)
Gul Mohammad (copy of an engraving by
F. Bolognus, after Velázquez)
From the St Petersburg *Muraqqa*
Mughal India, mid-18th century
Watercolour, ink, silver and gold on paper;
19.2 x 16.8 cm
Also on the page, top left: *Madonna of
St Luke*, first half of the 18th century
(7.7. x 4.6 cm); top right: *Madonna of
St Luke*, first half of the 17th century
(7.7. x 5.1 cm); top middle: *Arithmetica*,
attr. Manohar Das, c.1590–95
(7.5. x 5.5 cm)
St Petersburg, The St Petersburg Branch
of the Institute of Oriental Studies/Russian
Academy of Sciences, Ms E-14, f. 88r

Lit: *The St. Petersburg Muraqqa*, p. 60,
plate 33.

100. *Timiditas* (p. 183)
Attributed to Abu'l-Hasan
From the St Petersburg *Muraqqa*
Mughal India, c.1602
Watercolour, ink and gold on paper;
12.4 x 16.8 cm
Also on the page, top left: Payak, *Ascetics
by the Fire*, c.1925 (12.4 x 16.8 cm); top
right: Govardhan, *Two Courtiers Visit a
Hermit*, c.1630 (7.3 x 4 cm)
St Petersburg, The St Petersburg Branch of
the Institute of Oriental Studies/Russian
Academy of Sciences, Ms E-14, f. 44r
Lit: *The St. Petersburg Muraqqa*, plate 60,
p. 69.

101. *Dialectics* (p. 183)
Attributed to Abu'l-Hasan
From the St Petersburg *Muraqqa*
Mughal India, c.1615
Watercolour, silver and gold on paper (over
an engraving by Jan Sadeler, 1550–1600,
after Martin de Voos, 1532–1603);
14.5 x 16.3 cm
Also on the page, top left: attr. Govardhan,
A Sanyasi, c.1630 (9.3 x 3.6 cm); top right:
Payak, *A Sanyasi*, c.1630; top middle:
Nanha, *Bayazid and Jalal al-Din*, c.1620
(9.7 x 9 cm)
St Petersburg, The St Petersburg Branch of
the Institute of Oriental Studies/Russian
Academy of Sciences, Ms E-14, f. 46r
Lit: *The St. Petersburg Muraqqa*, plate 61,
p. 71.

102. *A Distant Landscape* (p. 188)
Mughal India, c.1585–90
Ink and watercolour on paper;
12.1 x 7.3 cm
Providence, Museum of Art, Rhode Island
School of Design, Museum Appropriation
Fund, inv. no. 17.457
Lit: *Akbar's India*, cat. no. 44; Rhode Island
School of Design Museum, *Exhibition
Notes*, no. 8 (Fall 1999), p. 27.

103. *Shah Shuja Hunting* Nilgae (p. 184)
Attributed to Payag
Mughal India, c.1650
Watercolour on paper; 16.8 x 26 cm
Providence, Museum of Art, Rhode Island
School of Design, Museum Works of Art
Fund, inv. no. 58.068
Lit: *Romance of the Taj Mahal*, ed.

Pratapaditya Pal, London, 1989, p. 95, fig. 89; *Glimpses of Grandeur: Courtly Arts of the later Islamic Empires (Exhibition notes), The Rhode Island School of Design Museum*, no. 8 (Fall 1999), p. 28; *A Handbook of the Museum of Art, Rhode Island School of Design*, ed. Carla M. Woodward & Franklin W. Robinson, Providence (Rhode Island), 1985, no. 69, p. 156; E. Smart, 'A recently discovered Mughal painting picture by Payag', in *Art History* (December 1979), p. 396.

104. *The Private Pleasures of the Portuguese Commander-in-Chief* (p. 189)
Ruknuddin, School of Bikaner
Mughal India, Rajasthan, *c.*1678–98
Bodycolour and gold on paper
27 x 19.5 cm
Cambridge, Fitzwilliam Museum, inv. no. PD 205-1948-13
Lit: *The Raj: India and the British, 1600–1947* (exhib. cat.), ed. C.A. Bayly, London, National Portrait Gallery, 1990, cat. no. 75 (II).

V. Mughal Influence on Portuguese Art

105. Portable cabinet (p. 113)
Mughal India, 17th century
Teak, ebony, ivory and brass;
26 x 39 x 28 cm
Lisbon, Fundação Ricardo do Espírito Santo Silva, inv. no. 46
Lit: *Fundação Ricardo do Espírito Santo Silva*, dir. Alexandra Jardim Oliveira, Lisbon, FRESS, 1994, pp. 48–51.

106. Pyramidal cabinet (p. 114)
Mughal India (?), 17th century
Ebony, teak, ivory and gilded copper;
50 x 36.5 x 25 cm
Oporto, collection of Távora Sequeira Pinto
Lit: Francisco Hipólito Raposo, 'O Encanto dos Contadores Indo-portugueses' in *Oceanos*, 19/20 (September–December), 1994, p. 20; *Os Construtores do Oriente Português*, cat. no. 204.

107. Writing box (p. 84)
Mughal India, 16th century
Ebony, exotic wood, teak, ivory and iron;
35 x 55 x 38.8 cm
Oporto, private collection
Lit; *Os Construtores do Oriente Português*, cat. no. 207.

108. Cabinet (p. 84)
Mughal India, first half of the 17th century
Ebony, *sissó* wood, ivory and horn, iron and brass; 51.5 x 80.5 x 45.2 cm
Funchal, Museu da Quinta das Cruzes, inv. no. 1418
Lit: Manuel Castilho, 'Contador' in *Rota do Oriente*, Lisbon, 1999, p. 30.

109. Cabinet
Mughal India, 17th century
Teak, ebony and ivory; 60 x 93.5 x 51 cm
Lisbon, private collection
Lit: Francisco Hipólito Raposo, 'O Encanto dos Contadores Indo-portugueses', in *Oceanos*, 19–20 (September/December), 1994, p. 20.

CAT. **109**

110. Missal stand
Goa (?), 17th century
Gilt and polychrome teak; 31 x 27 x 32 cm
Portalegre, Museu Municipal, inv. no. 321
Lit: *De Goa a Lisboa*, Lisbon 1992,
cat. no. 49; *Vasco da Gama e a Índia*,
cat. no. 76; *Os Espaços do Império*,
cat. no. 80.

111. Chair (p. 71)
Goa, late 16th–early 17th century
Teak; 91.5 x 52 x 52 cm
Lisbon, Museu da Cidade, inv. no. MOB 8
Lit: *Via Orientalis*, cat. 85.

112. *European Lady Writing a Book*
(p. 103)
Mughal India, 1610
Drawing on paper; 26.2 x 16.5 cm
London, British Museum,
inv. OA 1956.10-13.02.

113. *Portrait of Rustam Khan* (p. 112)
Mughal India, *c.*1650–58
Coloured pigments on paper;
37.8 x 26.7 cm
Dublin, The Chester Beatty Library,
inv. no. IN 7B.35
Lit: Leach, *Mughal and other Indian
Paintings*, no. 3.44, pp. 435–8.

114. Casket (p. 119)
India, *c.*1570–80
Tortoiseshell and silver; 12 x 25 x 15 cm
Lisbon, private collection
Lit: Reynaldo dos Santos & Irene Quilhó,
*Ourivesaria portuguesa nas colecções
particulares*, 2nd edn, Lisbon, 1974,
p. 214, fig. 295; *A Herança de
Rauluchantim*, cat. 7; Nuno Vassallo e
Silva, 'Goa or Lisbon: Problems of
Attribution', in *Jahrbuch des
Kunsthistorichen Museum Wien*, **vol. 3, ed.**
Helmut Trnek & Sabine Haag,
Mainz/Vienna, 2001, p. 237.

115. Casket (p. 119)
India, *c.*1570–80
Tortoiseshell and silver;
11.5 x 28 x 20.5 cm
Montijo parish church.

116. Cabinet and table (p. 113)
Gujarat or Sind, late 16th–early 17th
century
Ebony and ivory; table: H 136.5 cm;
cabinet: 73.5 x 65 x 36.5 cm
London, V&A, inv. no. IM 16-1931
Lit: *The Arts of India, 1500–1900*, fig. 35;
Jaffer, *Luxury Goods from India*, no. 8,
pp. 30–32.

117. Cabinet (p. 111)
Goa, 17th century
Wood and ivory; 32.5 x 44 x 32 cm
Lisbon, Museu Nacional de Arte Antiga,
inv. no. 1550
Lit: Francisco Hipólito Raposo, 'O Encanto
dos Contadores Indo-portugueses', in
Oceanos, 19/20 (September–December
1994), p. 18.

118. Beaker and cover (p. 117)
Mughal India, second half of the
17th century
Silver; H 14.2 cm, D 8.3 cm
London, Victoria and Albert Museum,
inv. no. IS 31-1961
Lit: *The Art of Mughal India: Painting and
Precious Objects*, ed. Stuart C. Welch, New
York, Asia Society, 1963, cat. no. 61; *The
Arts of India, 1500–1900*, p. 91, plate 67;
The Indian Heritage, cat. no. 323; Mark
Zebrowski, *Gold, Silver and Bronze from
Mughal India*, London, Alexandria Press,
1997, p. 84, plate 78.

119. Sheath for a dagger (p. 133)
Goa (?), late 16th–early 17th century
Gold; L 24.2 cm
London, Nasser D. Khalili Collection of
Islamic Art, inv. no. MTW 862
Lit: David Alexander, *The Arts of War, Arms
and Armour of the 7th to 19th centuries*,
London, The Nasser D. Khalili Collection
of Islamic Art vol. XXI, 1992, cat. no. 49,
p. 100.

CAT. **110**

GLOSSARY OF SELECTED TERMS

Amir — Nobleman – high-ranking official within the Mughal administrative system.

Cáfila — Caravan – term used by the Portuguese in maritime Asia for a convoy of small ships.

Cartaz — Safe-conduct – sort of maritime passport that the Portuguese supplied, in return for payment, authorizing ships to sail and trade in the Indian Ocean. The word was incorporated into Portuguese in the early sixteenth century from the Arabic word *qirtas* ('paper', 'document').

Darbar/ durbar — Audience with the emperor; reception at the Mughal court.

Decanim — Portuguese corruption of the Arabic-Persian word 'dakani' – an inhabitant of the Deccan.

Doab — Territory between two rivers – normally used in northern India to define the territory between the Ganges and the Jumna.

Estado da Índia — Portuguese State of India, a string of settlements stretching from the east coast of Africa to the Far East that was only formally extinguished in 1961. Although it was created in 1505 and its capital was established in Goa in 1510, the term only became common in the second half of the sixteenth century.

Farman/ Firman — Persian term that derives from *farmudan*, 'to order' ('firmão' or 'formão' in Portuguese) – a written imperial order that had a range of categories and variations.

Feitor — Factor, or commercial agent in Portuguese Asia; head of a factory-house (*Feitoria*).

Firangis — Name that the Mughals gave to the Europeans, particularly the Portuguese and Catholics – Arabic-Persian word that literally means 'Frank' and has the same meaning in several Asian languages.

Hajj — Pilgrimage to Mecca.

Hun — Gold coin circulating in the Deccan.

Jagir — Administrative land-grant whereby the revenue is paid to the beneficiary (*jagirdar*).

Jharoka — Window where Mughal emperors would appear before their subjects.

Khanazad — Literally, 'son of the house' – specifically used for Mughal officials who were hereditary disciples of the emperor.

Kos/Karoh — Measurement of distance used in India, around 4 km.

Kundam — Indian jewellery technique using pure gold to set gemstones.

Man — Measurement of weight, approximately 38 kg.

Mansab — Rank on a numerical scale within the Mughal bureaucratic system that established the status, payment and military force of the empire's nobles (*mansabdar*).

Mutasaddi — General term for an official, specifically used for the head of the customs at the ports of Surat and Cambay.

Nawroz/ Nowruz — Persian New Year.

Ouvidor — Portuguese judge within the administrative structure of the *Estado da Índia*.

Padshah — Emperor.

Pargana — Small rural administrative unit in the Mughal Empire.

Peshkash — Gift – tribute that subordinates paid to their superiors.

Província do Norte — Portuguese fortresses and territories in northern India – Diu, Daman and Bassein, the so-called 'Strongholds of the North' (*Praças do Norte*).

Qazi — Judge who enforces Islamic law.

Saguate — Gift.

Sayyid — 'Lord' in Arabic – descendant of the Prophet Mohammed.

Shaikh — 'Elder' in Arabic – leader of a Sufi order; title given to a religious leader.

Sijda — Action of Sufi disciples in prostrating themselves before their leaders. Emperor Akbar introduced its use at his court.

Subadar — Governor of a Mughal province (*suba*).

Taswirkhana — Painting atelier.

Ulema — Scholar and expert in *Shar'ia*, the holy law of Islam.

Wakil — Prime minister.

Wazir — Minister responsible for the empire's finances (also called *Diwan*).

Xerafim — From the Persian *ashrafi* – silver coin worth 300 *reis*.

Zat — Personal numerical rank of a Mughal official (cf. *mansab*).

REIGNING DATES OF MUGHAL EMPERORS AND PORTUGUESE RULERS
IN THE SIXTEENTH AND SEVENTEENTH CENTURIES

Mughal emperors

Babur	1526–30
Humayun	1530–40 and 1555–56
Akbar	1556–1605
Jahangir	1605–27
Shahjahan	1628–58
Aurangzeb	1658–1707
Bahadur Shah	1707–12

Kings of Portugal

Manuel I	1495–1521
João III	1521–27
Sebastião	1557–78
Queen Catarina, regent	1557–62
Cardinal Henrique, regent	1562–68
Henrique	1578–80
Philip II (I of Portugal)	1580–98
Philip III (II of Portugal)	1598–1621
Philip IV (III of Portugal)	1621–40
João IV	1640–56
Afonso VI	1656–83
Luisa de Gusmão, regent	1656–62
Pedro, regent	1667–83
Pedro II	1683–1706

Viceroys and governors of the State of India

Dom Francisco de Almeida*	1505–9
Afonso de Albuquerque	1509–15
Lopo Soares de Albergaria	1515–18
Diogo Lopes de Sequeira	1518–21
Dom Duarte de Menezes	1521–24
Dom Vasco da Gama*	1524
Dom Henrique de Meneses	1524–26
Lopo Vaz de Sampaio	1526–29
Nuno da Cunha	1529–38
Dom Garcia de Noronha*	1538–40
Dom Estevão da Gama	1540–42
Martim Afonso de Sousa	1542–45
Dom João de Castro*	1545–48
Garcia de Sá	1548–49
Jorge Cabral	1549–50
Dom Afonso de Noronha*	1550–54
Dom Pedro de Mascarenhas*	1554–55
Francisco Barreto	1555–58
Dom Constantino de Bragança*	1558–61
Dom Francisco Coutinho*	1561–64
João de Mendonça	1564
Dom Antão de Noronha*	1564–68
Dom Luís de Ataíde (Count of Atouguia)*	1568–71
Dom António de Noronha*	1571–73
António Moniz Barreto	1573–76
Dom Diogo de Meneses	1576–78
Dom Luís de Ataíde (Count of Atouguia)*	1578–81
Fernão Teles de Meneses	1581
Dom Francisco de Mascarenhas (Count of Santa Cruz)*	1581–84
Dom Duarte de Meneses*	1584–88
Manuel de Sousa Coutinho	1588–91
Matias de Albuquerque*	1591–97
Dom Francisco da Gama (Count of Vidigueira)*	1597–1600
Aires de Saldanha*	1600–1605
Dom Martim Afonso de Castro*	1605–7
Dom Fr. Aleixo de Meneses	1607–9
André Furtado de Mendonça	1609
Rui Lourenço de Távora*	1609–12
Dom Jerónimo de Azevedo*	1612–17
Dom João Coutinho (Count of Redondo)*	1617–19
Fernão de Albuquerque	1619–22
Dom Francisco da Gama (Count of Vidigueira)*	1622–28
Council	1629
Dom Miguel de Noronha (Count of Linhares)*	1629–35
Pedro da Silva*	1635–39
António Teles da Silva e Meneses	1639–40
Dom João da Silva Telo de Meneses (Count of Aveiras)	1640–45
Dom Filipe de Mascarenhas	1645–51
Council	1651–52
Dom Vasco de Mascarenhas (Count of Óbidos)	1652–53
Dom Brás de Castro (usurper)	1653–55
Dom Rodrigo da Silveira (Count of Sarzedas)*	1655–56
Manuel Mascarenhas Homem	1656
Council	1656–61
Council	1661–62
António de Melo e Castro*	1662–66
João Nunes da Cunha*	1666–68
Council	1668–71
Luís de Mendonça Furtado e Albuquerque (Count of Lavradio)*	1671–77
Dom Pedro de Almeida Portugal (Count of Assumar)*	1677–78
Council	1678–81
Francisco de Távora (Count of Alvor)*	1681–86
Dom Rodrigo da Costa	1686–90
Dom Miguel de Almeida	1690–91
Council	1691–93
Dom Pedro António de Noronha (Count of Vila Verde)*	1693–98
António Luís Gonçalves da Câmara Coutinho*	1698–1701

*asterisk indicates viceroy

BIBLIOGRAPHY

Abbreviations

AHU   Arquivo Histórico Ultramarino (Lisbon)

ARSI   Archivum Romanum Societatis Iesu (Rome)

BL   The British Library

BNF   Bibliothèque nationale de France

BNL   Biblioteca Nacional, Lisbon

BNM   Biblioteca Nacional, Madrid

IAN/TT   Instituto dos Arquivos Nacionais/Torre do Tombo (Lisbon)

Note: The Mughal chronicles translated into English and the main texts written by western travellers inside the Mughal empire have been republished and reprinted several times since the late nineteenth century. Since the authors have consulted different reprints of the same text (such as the works of Abu'l Fazl, for example), the publication dates given in the notes do not always match those in this bibliography.

Primary Sources

Abu'l Fazl 1993
Abu'l Fazl, *The Akbar-Nama*, trans. H. Beveridge, 3 vols, reprinted (bound in 2), New Delhi, 1993.

Abu'l Fazl Allami 2001
Abu'l Fazl Allami, *The Ain-i Akbari*, trans. H. Blochmann, 3 vols, reprinted (bound in 2), New Delhi, 2001.

Anonymous 1998–9
Vida e acções de Mathias de Albuquerque, capitão e viso-rei da Índia, ed. Antonella Vignatti, in *Mare Liberum*, no. 15 (June 1998) and no. 17 (June 1999).

Anonymous 1991
Livro das plantas das fortalezas, cidades e povoações do Estado da Índia Oriental [...]. Contribuição para a história das fortalezas dos portugueses no Ultramar, ed. Luís Silveira, Lisbon, 1991.

Arshad 1973
A.D. Arshad, ed., *Insha'-i Faizi*, Lahore, 1973.

Babur 1996
The Baburnama. Memoirs of Babur, prince and emperor, ed. Wheeler M. Thackston, Washington, 1996.

Badayuni 1986
'Abdul-Qadir Ibn-i Muluk Shah al-

Badaoni, *Muntakahb al-Tawarikh*, trans. & ed. George S.A. Ranking, 3 vols, reprinted, New Delhi, 1986.

Beach *et al.* 1997
King of the World: The Padshahnama: An Imperial Mughal Manuscript from the Royal Library, Windsor Castle, ed. Milo C. Beach & Ebba Koch, trans. W. Thackston, London/Washington, 1997.

Bernier 1994
François Bernier, *Travels in the Mogul Empire, AD 1656–1668*, ed. Vincent A. Smith, reprinted, New Delhi, 1994.

Bocarro 1992
António Bocarro, *Livro das plantas de todas as fortalezas, cidades e povoações do Estado da Índia Oriental*, ed. Isabel Cid, 3 vols, Lisbon, 1992.

Briggs 1997
History of the Rise of Mahomedan Power in India, ed. John Briggs, 4 vols, reprinted (bound in 2), New Delhi, 1997.

Correia 1975
Gaspar Correia, *Lendas da Índia*, ed. M. Lopes de Almeida, 4 vols, Oporto, 1975.

Correia-Afonso 1980
John Correia-Afonso, *Letters from the Mughal Court*, Bombay, 1980.

Corte-Real 1991
Jerónimo Corte-Real, *Sucesso do segundo cerco de Diu: Códice cadaval 31 – ANTT*, facsimile, introduction by Martim de Albuquerque, Lisbon, 1991.

Cortesão & Albuquerque 1968–81
Obras completas de D. João de Castro, ed. Armando Cortesão & Luís de Albuquerque, 4 vols, Coimbra, 1968–1981.

Cortesão & Mota 1960
Armando Cortesão & Avelino Teixeira da Mota, *Portugaliae monumenta cartographica*, 5 vols. (+ 1 of index), Lisbon, 1960 (2nd ed., 1987).

Couto 1999
Diogo do Couto, *Década Quarta da Ásia*, ed. Maria Augusta Lima Cruz, 2 vols, Lisbon, 1999.

Couto 1994
Diogo do Couto e a Década 8.ª da Ásia, ed. Maria Augusta Lima Cruz, 2 vols, Lisbon, 1994.

Couto 1973–5
Diogo do Couto, *Da Ásia. Dos feitos que os portuguezes fizeram na conquista e descubrimento das terras e mares do Oriente*, Décadas IV–XII, Lisbon, 1973–75 (facsimile 1778–88 edition).

Coutre 1991
Jacques de Coutre, *Andanzas asiáticas*, ed. Eddy Stols, B. Teensma & J. Werberckmoes, Madrid, 1991.

De Laet 1974
J. de Laet, *The Empire of the Great Mogol: De Laet's Description of India and Fragment of Indian History*, trans. J.S. Hoyland, ed. S.N. Banerjee, republished, New Delhi, 1974.

Elliot & Dowson 1996
The History of India, as Told by its own Historians: The Muhammadan Period, ed. H.M. Elliot & J. Dowson, 8 vols, reprinted, New Delhi, 1996.

Firishta: see Briggs 1997.

Foster 1985
Early Travels in India, 1583–1619, ed. William Foster, reprinted, New Delhi, 1985.

Guerreiro 1997
Fernão Guerreiro, S.J., *Jahangir and the Jesuits, with an Account of the Travels of Benedict Goes and the Mission to Pegu*, trans. C.H. Payne, reprinted, New Delhi, 1997 (Portuguese edition: *Relação anual das coisas que fizeram os padres da Companhia de Jesus nas suas missões ...*, ed. Artur Viegas, Coimbra/Lisbon, 1930–41).

Gulbadan Begam 2001
Gulbadan Begam, *Humayun-nama: The History of Humayun*, trans. A.S. Beveridge, reprinted, New Delhi, 2001.

Habsburg 1996
Francesca von Habsburg, ed., *The St. Petersburg Muraqqa': Album of Indian and Persian Miniatures from the 16th through the 18th Century and Specimens of Persian Calligraphy by 'Imad al-Hasani*, Lugano/Milan, 1996.

Haig 1923
The History of the Nizam Shahi Kings of Ahmadnagar, ed. & trans. Wolseley Haig, Bombay, 1923.

Humayun Nama: see Gulbadan Begam 2001.

'Inayat Khan 1990
The Shah Jahan Nama of 'Inayat Khan: An Abridged History of the Mughal Emperor Shah Jahan, Compiled by his Royal Librarian, ed. W.E. Begley & Z.A. Desai, trans. A.R. Fuller, New Delhi/Oxford/New York, 1990.

Jahangir 1978
The Tuzuk-i- Jahangiri or Memoirs of Jahangir, 2 vols, trans. A. Rogers, ed. H. Beveridge, reprinted, New

Delhi, 1978 (more recently trans. & ed. Wheeler M. Thackston, *The Jahangirnama. Memoirs of Jahangir, Emperor of India*, New York/Oxford, 1999).

Jarric 1997
Pierre du Jarric, *Akbar and the Jesuits: An Encounter of the Jesuit Missions to the Court of Akbar*, trans. C.H. Payne, New Delhi, 1997.

Khwandamir 1996
Khwandamir, *Qanun-i-Humayuni: Also Known as Humayun-nama of Khwandamir*, trans. & ed. B. Prashad, reprinted, Calcutta, 1996.

Laval 1944
François Pyrard de Laval, *Viagem de Francisco Pyrard de Laval*, ed. Joaquim Heliodoro Cunha Rivara & Artur Magalhães Basto, Oporto, 1944.

Linschoten 1997
John Huygen van Linschoten, *Itinerário, viagem ou navegação de John Huygen van Linschoten às Índias orientais ou portuguesas*, trans. Arie Pos, ed. Rui Manuel Loureiro, Lisbon, 1997.

Maldonado 1985
Relação das naos e armadas da Índia, com os sucessos delas que se puderam fazer, para notícia e instrucção dos curiozos, e amantes da história, ed. Maria Hermínia Maldonado, Coimbra, 1985.

Manrique 1927
Sebastião Manrique, *Travels of Fray Sebastien Manrique, 1629–1643*, ed. C.E. Luard & H. Hosten, 2 vols, London, 1927 (Portuguese edition: *Itinerário de Sebastião Manrique*, ed. Luís Silveira, 2 vols, Lisbon, 1946).

Monserrate 1922
Antonio Monserrate, S.J., *The Commentary of Father Monserrate S.J.*, trans. J.S. Hoyland & S. Banerjee, London, 1922 (Latin edition: 'Mongolicae legationis commentarius', in *Memoirs of the Asiatic Society of Bengal*, ed. H. Hosten, vol. III (1914), pp. 513–704).

Nunes 1989
Leonardo Nunes, *Crónica de D. João de Castro*, ed. Luís de Albuquerque, Lisbon, 1989.

Orta 1964
Garcia de Orta, *Aromatum et simplicium aliquot medicamentorum apud Indos nascentium historia de Carlos Clúsio. Versão portuguesa do epítome latino dos Colóquios dos simples de Garcia de Orta*, trans.

J. Walter & M. Alves, Lisbon, 1964 (see also the Conde de Ficalho edition, Lisbon, 1819, reprinted, 2 vols, 1987).

Padshahnama: see Beach *et al.* 1997.

Pelsaert 2001
Francisco Pelsaert, *Jahangir's India: The Remonstrantie of Francisco Pelsaert*, ed. & trans. W.H. Moreland & P. Geyl, republished, New Delhi, 2001.

Purificação 1656
Fr. António da Purificação, *Chronica da antiquíssima província de Portugal da Ordem dos Eremitas de Santo Agostinho*, Lisbon, 1656.

Rego 1991–6
Documentação para a história das missões do Padroado Português do Oriente, Índia, ed. António da Silva Rego, 2nd edn, 12 vols (+ 1 index), Lisbon, 1991–6.

Rego 1960–7
Documentação ultramarina portuguesa, ed. António da Silva Rego, 5 vols, Lisbon, 1960–7.

Rego & Pato 1880–1982
Documentos remetidos da Índia ou livros das monções, ed. António da Silva Rego & R.A. de Bulhão Pato, 10 vols, Lisbon, 1880–1982.

Roe 1990
Sir Thomas Roe, *The Embassy of Sir Thomas Roe to the Court of the Great Mogul, 1615-1619, as Narrated in his Journal and Correspondence*, ed. W. Foster, reprinted, New Delhi, 1990.

St Petersburg Muraqqa: see Habsburg 1996.

Santos 1999
Frei João dos Santos, *Etiópia oriental e vária história de cousas notáveis do Oriente*, ed. Manuel Lobato, Lisbon, 1999.

Shahjahan Nama: see 'Inayat Khan 1990.

Shahnawaz Khan 1999
Shanawaz Khan, *Ma'asir-ul Umara, Being Biographies of the Muhammadan and Hindu Officers of the Timurid Sovereigns of India from 1500 to 1780 AD*, trans. H. Beveridge, 2 vols, reprinted, New Delhi, 1999.

Sousa 1945–7
Manuel de Faria e Sousa, *Ásia portuguesa*, 6 vols, Oporto, 1945–7.

Tavernier 1995
Jean-Baptiste Tavernier, *Travels in India*, ed. V. Ball & W. Crooke, 2 vols, reprinted, New Delhi, 1995.

Vida e acções de Matias de Albuquerque: see Anonymous 1998–9.

Wicki 1948–88
Documenta Indica, ed. J. Wicki, S.J., 18 vols, Rome, 1948–88.

Secondary Sources

Ahmed 1995
Khalid Anis Ahmed, *Intercultural Influences in Mughal Painting*, Lahore, 1995.

Alam & Subrahmanyam 2000a
Muzaffar Alam & Sanjay Subrahmanyam, 'A place in the Sun: Travels with Faizi in the Deccan, 1591–93', in *Les sources et le temps/Sources and Time: A Colloquium*, ed. François Grimal, Pondicherry, 2000.

Alam & Subrahmanyam 2000b
Muzaffar Alam & Sanjay Subrahmanyam, 'Witnessing transition: Views on the end of the Akbari dispensation', in *The Making of History: Essays Presented to Irfan Habib*, ed. K.N. Panikkar *et al.*, New Delhi, 2000.

Alam & Subrahmanyam 1998
Muzaffar Alam & Sanjay Subrahmanyam, eds, *The Mughal State, 1526–1750*, New Delhi, 1998.

Ali 1985
M. Athar Ali, *The Apparatus of Empire: Awards of Ranks, Offices and Titles to the Mughal Nobility (1574–1658)*, New Delhi, 1985.

Ali 1970
M. Athar Ali, *The Mughal Nobility under Aurangzeb*, reprinted, Bombay, 1970.

Ansari 1995
Khalid Anis Ansari, *Intercultural Encounter in Mughal Miniatures (Mughal-Christian Miniatures)*, Lahore, 1995.

Anwar 2001
Firdos Anwar, *Nobility under the Mughals (1628–1658)*, New Delhi, 2001.

Asher 1992
Catherine Asher, *Architecture of Mughal India*, vol. I: 4, *The New Cambridge History of India*, Cambridge, 1992.

Bailey 2001
Gauvin Alexander Bailey, 'The end of the "Catholic Era" in Mughal painting: Jahangir's dream pictures, English painting, and the Renaissance frontispiece', in *Marg*, vol. 53, no. 2 (December 2001).

Bailey 1999a
Gauvin Alexander Bailey, *Art on the Jesuit missions in Asia and Latin America 1542–1773*, Toronto, 1999.

Bailey 1999b
Gauvin Alexander Bailey, 'The Truth-Showing Mirror: Jesuit Catechism and the arts in Mughal India', in *The Jesuits: Cultures, Sciences, and the Arts, 1540–1773*, ed. John O'Malley *et al.*, Toronto, 1999.

Bailey 1998a
Gauvin Alexander Bailey, *The Jesuits and the Grand Mogul: Renaissance Art at the Imperial Court of India, 1580–1630*, Washington DC, 1998.

Bailey 1998b
Gauvin Alexander Bailey, 'The Indian conquest of Catholic art: The Mughals, the Jesuits, and imperial mural painting', in *Art Journal* (Spring 1998).

Bailey 1997
Gauvin Alexander Bailey, 'The Lahore *Mirat al-Quds* and the impact of Jesuit theatre on Mughal painting', in *South Asian Studies*, 13 (1997).

Bailey 1996
Gauvin Alexander Bailey, 'Counter Reformation Symbolism and Allegory in Mughal Painting', unpublished doctoral thesis, Harvard University, 1996.

Barrett & Gray 1985
D. Barrett & B. Gray, *Indian Painting*, republished, New York, 1985.

Beach 1992
Milo Cleveland Beach, *Mughal and Rajput Painting*, vol. I: 3, *The New Cambridge History of India*, Cambridge, 1992.

Beach 1987
Milo Cleveland Beach, *Early Mughal Painting*, Cambridge (Mass.)/London, 1987.

Beach 1981
Milo Cleveland Beach, *The Imperial Image: Paintings for the Mughal Court*, Washington DC, 1981.

Beach 1980
Milo Cleveland Beach, 'The Mughal painter Abu'l Hasan and some English sources for his style', in *Journal of the Walters Art Gallery*, 38 (1980).

Beach 1976–7
Milo Cleveland Beach, 'The Mughal painter Kesu Das', in *Archives of Asian Art*, 30 (1976–7).

Beach 1976
Milo Cleveland Beach, 'A European source for early Mughal painting', in *Oriental Art*, vol. 22, no. 2 (1976).

Beach 1965
Milo Cleveland Beach, 'The Gulshan Album and its European sources', in *Museum of Fine Arts, Boston, Bulletin*, 63 (1965), pp. 63–91.

Beveridge 1910
H. Beveridge, 'Von Poser's diary in Persia and India', in *The Imperial and Asiatic Quarterly Society*, 3rd series, vol. XXIX, no. 57 (January 1910).

Borges 1994
Charles J. Borges, 'Questões em torno das formas de representação na arte religiosa indo-portuguesa', in *Oceanos*, nos. 19–29 (September–December 1994).

Brand & Lowry 1985
Michael Brand & Glenn Lowry, *Fathpur-Sikri: A Sourcebook*, Cambridge (Mass.), 1985.

Bresson 1994
Luigi Bresson, ed., *Intercultural Influences on Mughal Miniatures*, Lahore, 1994.

Camps 1957
Arnulf Camps, O.F.M., *Jerome Xavier S.J. and the Muslims of the Mogul Empire: Controversial Works and Missionary Activity*, Schöneck-Beckenried, 1957.

Carita 1995
Helder Carita, *Palácios de Goa. Modelos e tipologias da arquitectura civil indo-portuguesa*, Lisbon, 1995 (*Palaces of Goa: Models and Types of Indo-Portuguese Civil Architecture*, London, 1999)

Carvalho 2004
Pedro Moura Carvalho, 'What happened to the Mughal furniture? The role of the imperial workshops, the decorative motifs used and the influence of western models', in *Muqarnas*, 21 (2004), forthcoming.

Carvalho 2001
Pedro Moura Carvalho, 'Goa's pioneering role in transmitting European traditions to the Mughal and Safavid courts', in *Exotica: The Portuguese Discoveries and the Renaissance Kunstkammer* (exhib. cat.), ed. Helmut Trnek & Nuno Vassallo e Silva, Lisbon, 2001.

Castro 1987
Nuno de Castro, *A porcelana chinesa e os brasões do império*, Oporto, 1987.

Chandeigne 1996
Michel Chandeigne, ed., *Goa, 1510–1685, L'Inde portugaise, apostolique et commerciale*, Paris, 1996.

Chandra 1976
Pramod Chandra, *The Tuti-nama of the Cleveland Museum of Art and the Origins of Mughal Painting*, Graz, 1976.

Cohen 2001
Steven Cohen, 'Safavid and Mughal carpets in the Gulbenkian Museum, Lisbon', in *Hali*, 114 (2001).

Cooper 1993
Ilay Cooper, 'Sikhs, saints and shadows of angels: Some Mughal murals in buildings along the north wall of Lahore fort', in *South Asian Studies*, vol. 9 (1993).

Das 1978
Asok Kumar Das, *Mughal Painting during Jahangir's Time*, Calcutta, 1978.

Deloche 1968
Jean Deloche, *Recherches sur les routes de l'Inde au temps des Mogols. Étude critique des sources*, Paris, 1968.

Dias 2002
Pedro Dias, *O contador das cenas familiares. O quotidiano dos portugueses de Quinhentos na decoração de um móvel indo-português*, Oporto, 2002.

Dias 1998
Pedro Dias, *História da arte portuguesa no mundo. O espaço do Índico*, Lisbon, 1998.

Digby 1973
Simon Digby, 'A corpus of "Mughal" Glass', in *Bulletin of the School of Oriental and African Studies*, vol. XXXVI, pt I (1973).

Eaton 1978
Richard M. Eaton, *Sufis of Bijapur, 1300–1700: Social Roles of Sufis in Medieval India*, Princeton, 1978.

Ethinghausen 1961
Richard Ethinghausen, *Paintings of the Sultans and Emperors of India in American Collections*, Delhi, 1961.

Falk & Archer 1981
Toby Falk & Mildred Archer, *Indian Miniatures in the India Office Library*, London, 1981.

Farooque 1977
Muhammad Farooque, *Roads and Communications in Mughal India*, Delhi, 1977.

Felix 1916a
Pe. Felix, O.C., 'Mughal farmans, Parwanahs and Sanads issued in favour of the Jesuit missionaries', in *Journal of the Punjab Historical Society*, vol. V, no. 1 (1916).

Felix 1916b
Pe. Felix, O.C., 'The Mughal seals', in *Journal of the Panjab Historical Society*, vol. V, no. 2 (1916).

Ferguson 1966
George Ferguson, *Signs and Symbols in Christian Art*, New York 1966.

Ferrão 1990
Bernardo Ferrão, *Mobiliário português*, 4 vols, Oporto, 1990.

Flores & Saldanha 2003
Jorge Flores & António Vasconcelos de Saldanha, *Os firangis na chancelaria mogol. Cópias portuguesas de documentos de Akbar (1572–1604)*, New Delhi, 2003.

Foltz 1998
Richard Foltz, *Mughal India and Central Asia*, Karachi, 1998.

Galop 1999
Annabel Teh Galop, 'The genealogical seal of the Mughal emperors of India', in *Journal of the Royal Asiatic Society*, 3rd series, vol. 9, no. 1 (April 1999).

Ghani 1972
M.A. Ghani, *A History of Persian Language and Literature at the Mughal Court*, 2 vols, Westmead, 1972 (reprinted, Mashhad, 1990).

Godard 1937
Yedda Godard, 'Un album des princes timourides de l'Inde', in *Athar-e Iran*, vol. II (1937).

Godard 1936
Yedda Godard, 'Les marges du Murakkka' Gulshan', in *Athar-e Iran*, vol. I (1936).

Goetz 1957
Hermann Goetz, 'The early Muraqqas of the Mughal Emperor Jahangir', in *East-West*, 8 (1957).

Gole 1989
Susan Gole, *Indian Maps and Plans: From Earliest Times to the Advent of European Surveys*, New Delhi, 1989.

Gommans 2002
Jos Gommans, *Mughal Warfare: Indian Frontiers and Highroads to Empire, 1500–1700*, London/New York, 2002.

Guy & Swallow 1999
John Guy & Deborah Swallow, *Arts of India: 1550–1900*, London, 1999.

Habib 1997
Irfan Habib, ed., *Akbar and his India*, New Delhi, 1997.

Habib 1982
Irfan Habib, *An Atlas of the Mughal Empire: Political and Economic Maps*, New Delhi, 1982.

Habib 1977
'Cartography in Mughal India', in *Medieval India – A Miscellany*, ed. I. Habib, New York, 1977, vol. IV.

Hasan 1980
Ibn Hasan, *The Central Structure of the Mughal Empire and its Practical Working up to the Year 1657*, New Delhi, 1980.

Hosten 1922
H. Hosten, 'European art in the Moghul court', in *The Journal of the United Provinces Historical Society*, vol. III (May 1922), part I.

Keil 1928
Luís Keil, *As tapeçarias de D. João de Castro*, Lisbon, 1928.

Khan 1999
Iqtidar Alam Khan, ed., *Akbar and his Age*, New Delhi, 1999.

Koch 2001
Ebba Koch, *Mughal Art and Imperial Ideology Collected: Essays*, New Delhi, 2001.

Kühnel & Goetz 1926
Ernst Kühnel & Hermann Goetz, *Indian Book Painting from Jahangir's Album in the State Library in Berlin*, London, 1926.

Lal 1988
K.S. Lal, *The Mughal Harem*, New Delhi, 1988.

Leach 1995
Linda York Leach, *Mughal and other Indian paintings from the Chester Beatty Library*, 2 vols, London, 1995.

Mcfarland 1939
J. Mcfarland, 'Monserrate's map of India', in *New Review*, vol. X (1939).

Maclagan 1990
Sir Edward Maclagan, *The Jesuits and the Great Mogul*, republished (1st edn, London, 1932), Gargaon, 1990 (Portuguese translation: *Os Jesuítas e o Grão Mogol*, Oporto, 1940).

Maclagan 1916
Sir Edward Maclagan, 'Four letters by Austin of Bordeaux', in *Journal of the Punjab University Historical Society*, vol. IV, no. 1 (1916), pp. 3–17.

Maclagan 1896
Sir Edward Maclagan, 'Jesuit Missions to the emperor Akbar', in *Journal of the Asiatic Society of Bengal*, 1896).

Mendonça 1949
Maria José Mendonça, 'Alguns tipos de colchas indo-portuguesas na colecção do Museu Nacional de Arte Antiga', in *Boletim do Museu Nacional de Arte Antiga*, vol. II (1949).

Mitchell 2000
Colin Paul Mitchell, *Sir Thomas Roe and the Mughal Empire*, Karachi, 2000.

Mohiuddin 1971
Momin Mohiuddin, *The Chancellery and Persian Epistolography under the Mughals*, Calcutta, 1971.

Naik 1966
C.R. Naik, *'Abdu'r Rahim Khan-i Khanan and his Literary Circle*, Ahmadabad, 1966.

Nayeem 1974
M.A. Nayeem, *External Relations of the Bijapur Kingdom (1489-1686 AD): A Study in Diplomatic History*, Hyderabad, 1974.

Okada 2002
Amina Okada, *L'Inde des princes, La Donation Jean et Krishnâ Riboud*, Paris, 2002.

Okada 1992a
Amina Okada, *Indian miniatures of the Mughal Court*, New York, 1992.

Okada 1992b
Amina Okada, *Imperial Mughal Painters: Indian Miniatures from the Sixteenth and Seventeenth Centuries*, Paris, 1992.

Okada 1992c
Amina Okada, *Le Grand Mogol et ses peintres. Miniatures de l'Inde au XVIème et XVIIème siècles*, Paris, 1992.

O'Malley 1999
John W. O'Malley, S.J., et al., ed., *The Jesuits: Cultures, Sciences and the Arts 1540–1773*, Toronto/Buffalo/London, 1999.

Pal 1993
Pratapaditya Pal, *Indian Painting*, Los Angeles, 1993.

Pal 1991
Pratapaditya Pal, *Master Artists of the Imperial Mughal Court*, Bombay, 1991.

Pal 1989
Pratapaditya Pal, ed., *The Romance of the Taj Mahal*, London/Los Angeles, 1989.

Pearson 1989
M.N. Pearson, 'The Estado da Índia and the hajj', in *Indica*, vol. XXVI, nos. 1–2 (1989).

Pereira & Alarcão 1988
Teresa Pacheco Pereira & Teresa

Alarcão, *Fábulas bordadas. Uma colcha indo-portuguesa do século XVII*, Lisbon, 1988.

Pereira & Pal 2001
José Pereira & Pratapaditya Pal, eds, *India and Portugal: Cultural Interactions*, Bombay, 2001.

Pinto 1985–7
Maria Helena Mendes Pinto, *Os móveis e o seu tempo*, Lisbon, 1985–7.

Pinto 1979
Maria Helena Mendes Pinto, *Artes decorativas portuguesas no Museu Nacional de Arte Antiga, século XV a XVIII*, Lisbon, 1979.

Pissurlencar 1938
Panduronga Pissurlencar, 'Antigualhas', part I: 'Últimas embaixadas portuguesas à corte mogol', in *Boletim do Instituto Vasco da Gama*, 38 (1938).

Raposo 1994
Francisco Hipólito Raposo, 'O encanto dos contadores indo-portugueses', in *Oceanos*, nos 19–20 (September–December 1994).

Richards 1998
John F. Richards, 'The formulation of imperial authority under Akbar and Jahangir', in *The Mughal State, 1526–1750*, ed. M. Alam & S. Subrahmanyam, New Delhi, 1998.

Richards 1995
John F. Richards, *The Mughal Empire*, vol. I: 5, *The New Cambridge History of India*, republished, New Delhi, 1995.

Rizvi 1987
S.A.A. Rizvi, *The Wonder that Was India*, London, 1987, vol. II.

Rogers 1993
J.M. Rogers, *Mughal Miniatures*, London, 1993.

Rogers & Köseoglu 1987
J.M. Rogers & C. Köseoglu, eds, *The Topkapi Saray Museum: The Treasury*, London, 1987.

Rossa 1997
Walter Rossa, *Cidades indo-portuguesas. Contribuição para o estudo do urbanismo português no Hindustão ocidental*, Lisbon, 1997.

Santos 1999
Catarina Madeira Santos, 'Goa é a chave de toda a Índia'. Perfil político da capital do Estado da Índia (1505-1570), Lisbon, 1999.

Serrão 1994
Vitor Serrão, 'A pintura na antiga Índia Portuguesa nos séculos XVI e XVII', in *Oceanos*, nos. 19–20 (September–December 1994).

Sherwani 1974
H.K. Sherwani, *History of the Qutb Shahi Dynasty*, New Delhi, 1974.

Silva n.d.
M.M. de Cagigal e Silva, *A arte indo-portuguesa*, Lisbon, n.d.

Silva 2004a
Nuno Vassallo e Silva, 'Jewels for the Great Mughals: Goa as a centre of the gem trade in the Orient', in *Jewellery Studies*, no. 10 (2004), forthcoming.

Silva 2004b
Nuno Vassallo e Silva, 'The treasury of Sultan Bahadur of Gujarat: Notes for the study of Northern Indian jewellery in the sixteenth century', in *The Art of Mughal India: Studies in Honour of Robert Skelton*, London, 2004, forthcoming.

Silva 1995
Nuno Vassallo e Silva, 'Jewels and gems in Goa from the sixteenth to the eighteenth century', in *Jewels of India*, ed. Susan Stronge, Bombay, 1995.

Silva 1993
Nuno Vassallo e Silva, 'The Portuguese gem trade in the sixteenth century', in *Jewellery Studies*, no. 6 (1993).

Silva 1989
Nuno Vassallo e Silva, 'Subsídios para o estudo do comércio das pedras preciosas em Lisboa no século XVI', in *Boletim Cultural da Assembleia Distrital de Lisboa*, 3rd series, no. 91, tomo 2 (1989).

Soustiel & Soustiel 1986
Jean Soustiel & David Soustiel, *Miniatures orientales de l'Inde*, Paris, 1986.

Souza & Garcia 1999
Teotónio R. de Souza & José Manuel Garcia, eds, *Vasco da Gama e a Índia* (proceedings), 3 vols, Lisbon, 1999.

Streusand 1989
Douglas E. Streusand, *The Formation of the Mughal Empire*, New Delhi, 1989.

Stronge 2002
Susan Stronge, *Painting for the Mughal Emperor: The Art of the Book, 1560-1660*, London, 2002.

Subrahmanyam 2002
Sanjay Subrahmanyam, 'Frank submissions: The Company and the Mughals between Sir Thomas Roe and Sir William Norris', in *The Worlds of the East India Company*, ed. H.V. Bowen *et al.*, Suffolk, 2002.

Subrahmanyam 1995a
Sanjay Subrahmanyam, 'A matter of alignment: Mughal Gujarat and the Iberian world in the transition of 1580–81', in *Mare Liberum*, no. 9 (1995).

Subrahmanyam 1995b
Sanjay Subrahmanyam, 'The viceroy as assassin: The Mughals, the Portuguese and Deccan politics, c.1600', in *Santa Barbara Portuguese Studies*, special edition (1995).

Subrahmanyam 1993
Sanjay Subrahmanyam, *The Portuguese Empire in Asia, 1500–1700: A Political and Economic History*, London/New York, 1993.

Swarup 1996
Shanti Swarup, *Mughal Art: A Study in Handicrafts*, Delhi, 1996.

Teltscher 1995
Kate Teltscher, *India Inscribed: European and British Writing on India, 1600–1800*, New Delhi, 1995.

Topsfield 1994
Andrew Topsfield, *Indian Paintings from Oxford Collections*, Oxford, 1994.

Tracy 1999
James Tracy, 'Asian despotism? Mughal government as seen from the Dutch East India Company factory in Surat', in *Journal of Early Modern History*, vol. 3, no. 3 (August 1999).

Untracht 1997
Oppi Untracht, *Traditional Jewellery of India*, London, 1997.

Verma 1994
Tripti Verma, *Karkhanas under the Mughals, from Akbar to Aurangzeb: A Study in Economic Development*, New Delhi, 1994.

Wade 1998
Bonnie C. Wade, *Imaging Sound: An Ethnomusicological Study of Music, Art, and Culture in Mughal India*, Chicago, 1998.

Welch 1978
Stuart Cary Welch, *Imperial Mughal Painting*, New York, 1978.

Winius 1988
George Winius, 'Jewel trading in Portuguese India in the XVI and XVII centuries', in *Indica*, vol. 25, no. 1 (March 1988).

Zebrowski 1997
Mark Zebrowski, *Gold, Silver and Bronze from Mughal India*, London, 1997.

Zebrowski 1983
Mark Zebrowski, *Deccani Painting*, London, 1983.

Exhibition Catalogues

Amsterdam 1991
Sven Gahlin, ed., *The Courts of India: Indian Miniatures from the Collection of the Foundation Custodia, Paris*, Zwolle/Paris, 1991.

Boston 1985
Vishakha N. Desai, ed., Life at Court: *Art for India's Rulers, 16th–19th Centuries* (Museum of Fine Arts), Boston, 1985.

Brussels 1991
Maria Helena Mendes Pinto, ed., *Via orientalis* (CGER Gallery), Brussels, 1991.

Coimbra 1992
Maria Helena Mendes Pinto, ed., *De Goa a Lisboa. A arte indo-portuguesa dos séculos XVI a XVIII* (Museu Nacional de Machado de Castro), Coimbra, 1992.

Copenhagen 1996
Kjeld von Folsach *et al.*, eds, *Sultan, Shah, and Great Mughal: The History and Culture of the Islamic World* (The National Museum), Copenhagen, 1996.

Lisbon 2001a
Helmut Trnek & Nuno Vassallo e Silva, eds, *Exotica: The Portuguese Discoveries and the Renaissance Kunstkammer* (Calouste Gulbenkian Museum), Lisbon, 2001.

Lisbon 2001b
Pedro Moura Carvalho, ed., *The World of Lacquer: 2000 Years of History* (Calouste Gulbenkian Museum), Lisbon, 2001.

Lisbon 1998
Rosa Maria Perez, ed., *Culturas do Índico* (Museu Nacional de Arte Antiga), Lisbon, 1998.

Lisbon 1996
Nuno Vassallo e Silva, ed., *A herança de Rauluchantim* (Museu de São Roque), Lisbon, 1996.

Lisbon 1983
Avelino Teixeira da Mota & Maria Helena Mendes Pinto, eds, *A arte e a missionação na rota do Oriente. XVII exposição de arte, ciência e cultura* (Mosteiro dos Jerónimos), Lisbon, 1983.

London 2001
Manuel Keene, ed., *Treasury of the World: Jewelled Arts of India in the Age of the Mughals* (The British Museum), London, 2001.

London 1990
C.A. Bayly, ed., *The Raj: India and the British* (National Portrait Gallery), London, 1990.

London 1982
Robert Skelton, ed., *The Indian

Heritage: Court Life and Arts under Mughal Rule (Victoria & Albert Museum), London, 1982.

New York 1999
Katharine Baetjer & James David Draper, eds, *Only the Best: Masterpieces of the Calouste Gulbenkian Museum, Lisbon* (The Metropolitan Museum of Art), New York, 1999.

New York 1997
Daniel Walker, ed., *Flowers Underfoot: Indian Carpets of the Mughal Era* (The Metropolitan Museum of Art), New York, 1997.

New York 1985a
Michael Brand & Glenn D. Lowry, eds, *Akbar's India: Art from the Mughal City of Victory* (The Asia Galleries), New York, 1985.

New York 1985b
Stuart Cary Welch, ed., *India: Art and Culture, 1300–1900* (The Metropolitan Museum of Art), New York, 1985.

Paris 1998
Maria Helena Mendes Pinto & José Manuel Garcia, eds, *Vasco da Gama et l'Inde* (Chapelle de la Sorbonne), Paris, 1998.

Paris 1989
Amina Okada, ed., *Miniatures de l'Inde impériale. Les peintres de la cour d'Akbar, 1556–1605* (Musée national des Arts asiatiques – Guimet), Paris, 1989.

Paris 1986
L'Inde des légendes et des realités. Miniatures indiennes et persanes de la Fondation Custodia, Collection Frits Lugt, Paris, 1986.

Portland 1973
Binney (Edwin), *Indian Miniature Painting from the Collection of Edwin Binney 3rd: The Mughal and Deccani Schools* (The Portland Art Museum), Portland, 1973.

Oporto 1999
Artur Teodoro de Matos, ed., *Os espaços do Império* (Edifício da Alfândega, Oporto), 2 vols, Lisbon, 1999.

Oporto 1998
Jorge Flores, ed., *Os construtores do Oriente português* (Edifício da Alfândega, Oporto), Lisbon, 1998.

Washington 2002
John Seyller, ed., *The Adventures of Hamza; Painting and Storytelling in Mughal India* (Arthur M. Sackler Gallery, The Smithsonian Institution), London, 2002.

Williamstown 1978
Milo Cleveland Beach, ed., *The Grand Mogul: Imperial Painting in India 1600–1660* (Sterling and Francine Clark Art Institute), Williamstown (Mass.), 1978.

Vienna 1992
Die Portugiesen in Indien: die Eroberungen Dom João de Castros auf Tapisserien 1538–1548, (Kunsthistorisches Museum), Vienna, 1992.

LENDERS TO THE EXHIBITION

Denmark
The David Collection, Copenhagen

France
Collection Frits Lugt, Institut Néerlandais, Paris
Musée national des Arts asiatiques – Guimet, Paris

Holland
Rijksmuseum, Amsterdam

Ireland
The Chester Beatty Library, Dublin

Portugal
Biblioteca da Academia das Ciências, Lisbon
Biblioteca da Ajuda, Lisbon
Biblioteca Geral da Universidade, Coimbra
Biblioteca Nacional, Lisbon
Câmara Municipal de Cascais/Museu Condes de Castro Guimarães, Cascais
Collection of José Lico, Lisbon

Collection of the Roboredo Madeira family, Vilar de Amargo
Collection of Távora Sequeira Pinto, Lisbon
Fundação da Casa de Bragança (Biblioteca do Paço Ducal), Vila Viçosa
Fundação Medeiros e Almeida, Lisbon
Fundação Oriente, Lisbon
Fundação Ricardo do Espírito Santo Silva, Lisbon
Igreja Paroquial, Montijo
Instituto dos Arquivos Nacionais/Torre do Tombo, Lisbon
Museu da Cidade, Lisbon
Museu da Quinta das Cruzes, Funchal
Museu Militar, Lisbon
Museu Municipal, Portalegre
Museu Nacional de Arte Antiga, Lisbon
Museu Nacional de Soares dos Reis, Oporto
Museu Nacional do Azulejo, Lisbon
Museu Nacional do Traje, Lisbon
Quinta da Bacalhoa, Azeitão
Santa Casa da Misericórdia de Lisboa/Museu de S. Roque, Lisbon

Sociedade de Geografia de Lisboa
Universidade do Minho/Museu Nogueira da Silva, Braga

Russia
The St Petersburg Branch of the Institute of Oriental Studies/Russian Academy of Sciences, St Petersburg

United Kingdom
British Library, London
British Museum, London
Fitzwilliam Museum, Cambridge
Nasser D. Khalili Collection of Islamic Art, London
School of Oriental and African Studies, London
Victoria and Albert Museum, London

United States of America
Museum of Fine Arts, Boston
Providence Museum of Art, Rhode Island School of Design

PHOTOGRAPHIC CREDITS

References are to page numbers

Albertina, Vienna: 156
Arquivo Nacional de Fotografia (ANF): 227, 228 (Photos José Pessoa)
Arthur M. Sackler Museum, Harvard University Art Museums: 151 (Photo Junius Beebe)
Biblioteca da Academia das Ciências, Lisbon: 217L (Photo Reinaldo Carvalho)
Biblioteca da Ajuda, Lisbon: 65, 149, 194 (Photos Francisco Ruas)
Biblioteca Geral da Universidade, Coimbra: 173
Biblioteca Nacional, Lisbon: 19, 59, 62, 67, 136, 140, 154, 198
British Library, London: 176, 186R
© The British Museum: 14, 35, 46, 100, 103
Calouste Gulbenkian Museum, Lisbon: 5R, 72, 138 (Photos Carlos Azevedo); 26, 45 (Photos Catarina Gomes Ferreira); 222 (Photo Margarida Ramalho); back cover, 134, 147 (Photo Reinaldo Viegas); other collections: 63, 71, 74, 76B, 83, 97T, 119B, 119T, 121 (Photos Carlos Azevedo)
© The Trustees of the Chester Beatty Library, Dublin: 112, 161, 162, 167, 177, 185, 187, 191, 197
Collection Frits Lugt, Institut Néerlandais, Paris: 15, 152, 159, 160, 165, 219
The David Collection, Copenhagen: 170, 172, 186L

Deutscher Orden, Vienna: 4, 125L
Divisão de Documentação Fotográfica – IPM: 7, 39, 69, 79, 86 (Photos Luís Pavão); 89, 91, 94, 95, 96T, 111, 122, 123, 178 (Photos José Pessoa); 109 (Photo Arnaldo Soares); 164R (Photo Carlos Monteiro); 221 (Photo Francisco Matias)
Fitzwilliam Museum, Cambridge: 99, 189
Freer Gallery of Art, Smithsonian Institution, Washington DC: Purchase, F1942.16a: 129
Fundação da Casa de Bragança (Biblioteca do Paço Ducal), Vila Viçosa: 61
Fundação Oriente, Lisbon: 88
Fundação Ricardo do Espírito Santo Silva, Lisbon: 113T
Gabinete de Estudos Arqueológicos de Engenharia Militar, Lisboa: 75
© President and Fellows of Harvard College: p.11 (Photo David Mathews)
Instituto dos Arquivos Nacionais/Torre do Tombo, Lisbon: 21, 49, 107, 217R
Photos Luís Seixas Ferreira Alves: 23, 55, 74, 78, 84T, 86, 92B, 93, 139, 143, 169, 223, 224
The Metropolitan Museum of Art, New York: 104
Musée national des Arts asiatiques – Guimet, Paris: 98, 106, 157 (© Photo RMN – Ravaux), 193 (© Photo RMN – Thierry Ollivier)

Photos © Museum of Fine Arts, Boston: 179, 180
Museu da Quinta das Cruzes, Funchal: 84B (Photo Rui Carvalho)
Museu de Arte Sacra, Goa: 125R (Photo Rui Ochôa, courtesy International Dept., Calouste Gulbenkian Foundation, Lisbon)
Museu Municipal, Portalegre: 228
The Nasser D. Khalili Collection of Islamic Art, London: 110, 133, 216
Rhode Island School of Design, Helen M. Danforth Fund: 5L, 52, 184, 188
Rijksmuseum, Amsterdam: cover, 146
The Royal Collection © 2004, Her Majesty Queen Elizabeth II: 105, 181
Saint Petersburg Branch of the Institute of Oriental Studies, Russian Academy of Sciences: 2, 53, 163, 175, 183, 190, 195
Santa Casa da Misericórdia de Lisboa/Museu de S. Roque: 96B
Sociedade de Geografia de Lisboa: 76T, 218 (Photos Carlos Ladeira)
Staatliche Kunstsammlungen, Dresden: 8
Universidade do Minho/Museu Nogueira da Silva, Braga: 164L
V&A Picture Library: 16, 17, 18, 28, 30, 113B, 115, 117, 135, 137, 145, 153, 155, 168, 171

INDEX

Page references in *italics* indicate captions